HOW FAST THE WIND?

Southern Africa, 1975–2000

Coordinated by

Sergio Vieira,
William G. Martin,
and Immanuel Wallerstein

Africa World Press, Inc.

P.O. Box 1892
Trenton, New Jersey 08607

Africa World Press, Inc.

P.O. Box 1892
Trenton, New Jersey 08607

Copyright © 1992 by Africa World Press
First Printing 1992

Book design and typesetting by Malcolm Litchfield
This book is composed in Sabon

0-86543-306-2 *Cloth*
0-86543-307-0 *Paper*

To the memory of

Aquino de Bragança

Contents

The wind of change is blowing through [Africa], and whether we like it or not this growth of national consciousness is a political fact. We must accept it as a fact, and our national policies must take account of it.

Prime Minister Harold Macmillan
Speech to Houses of Parliament
of the Union of South Africa
February 3, 1960

This book was born out of the strong desire of Aquino de Bragança for a prospective analysis of southern Africa that went beyond the headlines of current newspapers and beyond the slogans of political parties to enable all of us (but most of all, the peoples of southern Africa) to make more intelligent choices.

He saw two essential elements in making such an analysis. The first was that it should cover southern Africa as a "region" of the world-system, and not merely as a collection of neighboring states. The second was that the analysis should be done collaboratively by scholars of the region and scholars from outside the region, on the grounds that each might be likely to have insights the other might not, and the combined work might therefore be more sensitive to the integral truth.

That is why he conceived of this work as a joint effort of the institute he founded, the Centro de Estudos Africanos of the Universidade Eduardo Mondlane in Maputo, and the Fernand Braudel Center for the Study of Economies, Historical Systems, and Civilizations in Binghamton.

Aquino de Bragança could not bring this project to completion. He died, a victim of the political struggle he was analyzing. But the two Centers have persisted in this work, and we dedicate it to Aquino de Bragança for his vision and his commitment to a democratic, egalitarian world.

The structure of the book is simple and straightforward. The period under analysis is 1975–2000. It is being completed in 1991. The year 1975 was chosen to symbolize two phenomena crucial to our analysis. 1974–75 represented a political turning-point in the history of the region. The collapse of Portuguese colonialism and its sequel for southern Africa—the independence of Mozambique and Angola—transformed the *rapport de forces* of the political struggle in the region. But 1975 also represented the beginning of the movement (some say more exactly 1967, some say 1973) of the downturn or stagnation of the capitalist world-economy in which we still, as of 1991, find ourselves. The year 2000 represents, by contrast, the moment just ahead, a moment by which we project that the final liquidation of the colonial regime in southern Africa will have occurred. We presume, as do most people, that by the year 2000, we shall have seen the installation of a democratic regime, a post-apartheid regime, in South Africa, the colossus of the region, and the last country in the zone to "decolonize."

Our question for the years 1975–2000 is not merely what has happened (and why) in the various states, but what has happened in the region as a region. We know that, as of 1975, the region was internally hierarchical, and an integral part of a hierarchical world-system. What has changed in this regard between 1975 and 2000? How fast the wind, that wind of change of which Macmillan spoke to the South African all-White Parliament already in 1960? Or if nothing much has changed yet, what is likely to change in the twenty-first century as a result of the political struggle of 1975–2000?

We have tried to treat the question holistically—seeing the region as a whole, and analyzing its political economy integrally. Each chapter has been written by different persons, but the entire group has planned the work together, has discussed together each chapter, and assumes collective responsibility for the work. We intend this book as a contribution to intelligent choice.

We acknowledge gratefully the assistance of the Ford Foundation in making this collaborative research possible.

Southern Africa as of 1975

_____ *Immanuel Wallerstein and Sergio Vieira*

A. Historical Development of the Region in the Context of the Evolving World-System

Africa has a social history that goes back as far as hominids inhabited the earth. But "southern Africa" is a comparatively recent phenomenon. It is a construct of the twentieth century, with a pre-history that may be usefully traced back at most to 1873. The year 1873 marked no particular event in southern Africa. It marked rather the beginning of the so-called Great Depression of the capitalist world-economy which is conventionally thought to have lasted until 1897. It marked also the end of unquestionable British hegemony in the world-system, and consequently the beginning of the long struggle for succession, which ultimately pitted the United States against Germany in two world wars, and which was only definitively decided in 1945.

One consequence of the relative decline of British power combined with the world economic stagnation was the so-called "scramble for Africa." This scramble represented an attempt of preemptive economic enclosure by various European states of African land areas (as well as land areas elsewhere in the world), in the hope that, by colonizing these areas, their economic activities would be conducted exclusively by agents or nationals of the colonial power, thereby denying access to agents or nationals of

3

rival states. Great Britain did not start this scramble. But once the scramble was launched, Great Britain, which was still the most powerful state in the world (even if less powerful than previously), was able to acquire more territory than any other state.

In this situation, the area we have come to call southern Africa was different from other parts of Africa (and Asia) in that it joined together two features, whose combination has shaped its destiny from then to now. Its lands were the site of incredible mineral wealth (whose very existence was a social discovery only of that era). And it already had a White settler population of some size and cultural cohesion, who were determined to maintain and enhance their group power and status. Hence from the beginning of the mineral production era, the list of actors included not merely the various African peoples resident in the area, the capitalist entrepreneurs, and the various European governments with colonial pretensions—in this area, primarily Great Britain; its historic ally, Portugal; and Germany—but also a vigorous Afrikaner community composed largely at that time of small farmers, who had created two autonomous state structures, the Orange Free State and Transvaal.

There was, as we know, a struggle for political control in the region. As everywhere else in Africa at this time, African kingdoms and other political units were defeated in battles, ravaged by disease, and forced into signing disadvantageous treaties. They saw part or all of their lands confiscated, and found themselves included in new political units established by colonial authorities. In the process, the British also made war on the Boer settlers and defeated them as well. By 1910, the current political boundaries of southern Africa were very largely in place. Because Germany lost the First World War, she was divested of her control over Southwest Africa (now Namibia), which was given as a League of Nations Mandate to the Union of South Africa (at the time a quasi-independent British Dominion under White settler rule). In 1923, the British designated Southern Rhodesia (now Zimbabwe) as a self-governing Crown Colony, thus effectively turning over political power to a second White settler group, this one largely of British extraction. The White settlers in Southern Rhodesia were even smaller as a percentage of the total population than the Whites (Afrikaners plus English-speaking "British") in the Union of South Africa.

If we are to understand how the social construct "southern Africa" came into existence, we must place it in the context of the cyclical rhythms of capitalist world-economy. It is useful to tell the story in terms of successive Kondratieff cycles: the downturn from 1873–1897; the upturn from 1897–1913/20; the downturn from 1913/20–1945; the upturn from 1945–1967/1973; the downturn since then. These dates, drawn from worldwide economic rhythms, in fact correlate very well with the political (as well as economic) history of the southern African region as a whole, and of the individual states of the region. The processes within the region—political struggles, economic transformations, and social restructuring—occurred within the framework of the larger world-system of which they were now a part, and local actors had to take account of far-away actors, but conversely far-away actors now were being directly affected by developments in southern Africa.

The first period (1873–1897), as we have already noted, marked the beginning of British decline in the world-system, and the acute competition between the core powers for maintaining their economic strength relative to each other. The rise of protectionist legislation is a standard feature of such periods, and this one was no exception. The "scramble for Africa"—its invasion by imperialist outsiders—was viewed as a "protectionist" mechanism from the perspective of the imperialist powers. Each imperialist power was seeking primarily to close off a particular part of the periphery of the world-system to economic access by other imperialist powers. The impact as the lives of those in the region was to them a very secondary concern.

It is, as part of this imperialist struggle, that Cecil Rhodes conceived his dream of continuous British colonial authority "from the Cape to Cairo," a dream which was never in fact truly realized, except technically (and not in real economic terms) when after 1918 Tanganyika (German East Africa) became a British Mandate. In a very real sense, the 1873–1897 period was primarily a period in which the contemporary chess pieces were being set into place. New political boundaries—the ones we know today—were being drawn, and more or less officially recognized internationally. The new political entities were thus now part of the interstate system. Prior to that time, only the Cape Colony and Natal, two British colonies, could be said to have been really incorporated into the world-system, and they were marginal at best.

This period was that of the so-called "mining revolution." Diamonds had already been discovered in Griqualand in 1867, which had led quickly to British annexation. But even more important, gold was now discovered, and in 1886, the Witwatersrand was proclaimed to be a gold-mining area. The immediate economic consequences were to be several. Since the mineral zones were in the interior, railroad lines to the coast were needed as infrastructure. And since miners were needed, wage-laborers would have to be recruited at two levels of skill: non-Whites—initially Africans, Indians and Chinese, but eventually only Africans from "southern Africa"—who were employed in the more menial work; and Europeans (primarily Britons) who were employed in supervisory roles or in tasks requiring specialized technical skills.

The upturn in the world-economy at the beginning of the twentieth century marked in fact a political crisis in the region. It was now crucial who would politically control an area that had become economically significant in world terms, and which generated so much potential surplus-value. In this largely rural region of the world-economy, mineral speculation had added to already acute competition over land, and suddenly the region was faced with the phenomenon of rural cultivators being pushed off the land, and therefore moving into and creating urban areas. Blacks were being forced off the land, under both economic and legislative pressures. But so were many White Afrikaner (Boer) farmers, whose legal system of equally-shared division among heirs in families that were for the most part large was certainly an additional factor of considerable importance in this regard.

The two Boer republics were not always very cooperative with British plans, and they sat on the gold mine lands. Their diplomatic links with Germany were troublesome. Great Britain had now crushed Ndebele and Shona resistance in what would become Southern Rhodesia. Great Britain wanted the political (or at the very least the customs) unification of the region. In 1899, Great Britain, having assured itself the subsequent neutrality of Germany, France, and Portugal, precipitated the Boer War. Three years later, she had won. The Boer states were no more. Having won and therefore having ensured the eventual creation of a coherent, strong political entity under British control on the southern tip of Africa (and one that would include the mining areas), the British did the sensible thing. They came to a political compromise with the new White-dominated state created in 1910, the Union of South Africa. This political arrangement was of course made at the expense of the Black majority, but these were the political realities of the time.

The whole period from the turn of the century to the First World War was one in which the British sought to create (or encourage the creation of) the infrastructure of a southern African region, of which the Rand would be the economic focal point and South Africa the central political entity in the region. 5,500 miles of railways were added to the 4,000 that had already been in existence in the earlier period. A road network was put into place. A formal labor-recruitment structure was instituted. And all of this began to link systematically the juridically-separated zones of (at least) Basutoland, Mozambique, Southern Rhodesia, and Nyasaland to South Africa, which as a direct result enjoyed a rise in wealth and living standards, at least of the growing White population. But while mining (diamonds, gold, and coal) was rapidly displacing agriculture in South Africa's exports figures, South Africa remained an exporter of primary products and very much a peripheral zone of the capitalist world-economy. Furthermore, it had become clear by 1910 that the actual political incorporation of neighboring areas into South Africa was not likely. If South Africa were to dominate the region, the prime weapons would have to be economic.

If the Kondratieff B-phase of 1873–1897 saw the creation of the very concept of southern Africa, and the subsequent upturn saw the creation and consolidation of the necessary political and material infrastructure for the operation of such a region, the interwar B-phase saw a radical revision of the political economy of the region. The negative economic impact of stagnation in the world-economy was felt throughout the region, as well as, of course, in the now only two metropoles, Great Britain and Portugal. In hard times, states tend to draw inward, as protection and out of necessity. The Portuguese colonies, in particular Mozambique, weakened their economic links with South Africa. The objective of closer links of Southern Rhodesia with the Union of South Africa lost support, in Southern Rhodesia at least. The local White population pushed for and obtained the creation of a self-governing White settler state in Southern Rhodesia, which was proclaimed in 1923. One of its express objectives was to circumvent any South African mediation in its economic links to Great Britain.

South Africa was pushed to turn inwards as well as a result. The world agricultural depression exacerbated the plight of rural areas including the plight of White Afrikaner farmers. There was now considered to be a "poor-White" problem. To be sure, gold production is historically countercyclical and this helped some, but not enough. Tight conditions led precisely at this time to Black labor unrest and political and trade-union organization, which further threatened the relatively privileged position of White industrial workers, who became very militant in defending their position.

The organization of White workers turned out to be more effective in the short run than the organization of Black workers. The South African state responded to the pressures by three significant decisions: the strengthening of the color bar, which lessened economic pressure on White workers; the reduction of migrant labor recruitment from zones outside of South Africa itself, which lessened economic pressure on Black workers inside South Africa; and the establishment of state industrial monopolies, in order to create jobs as well as to substitute for imports the state could no longer afford.

The results were very straightforward. On the one hand, South Africa would become a country with a significant industrial sector. Mining would continue to be important, but there was now a sectoral balance of a sort. But at the same time the "region-ness" of southern Africa suffered significantly. The geographic zone of southern Africa now appeared somewhat segmented: a peripheral Portuguese colonial zone; a peripheral British colonial zone; and an economically somewhat more autonomous Union of South Africa, but one that was also structurally stronger than previously in its relation to the world-economy.

Thus when the post–1945 upturn in the world-economy occurred, South Africa was in a good position to try to create the "region" of southern Africa with itself as a now clearly semi-peripheral power, one that would dominate the region economically, and even politically and militarily.

South Africa emerged from the Second World War in a strong political position. Prime Minister Jan Christiaan Smuts was a respected world political figure. The mineral production of southern Africa seemed even more crucial to the world-economy than before. In the new geopolitical alignments, South Africa laid claim to be a strategic location for fleet movements. In 1948, however, the Anglo-Boer political compromise of 1910 was undone by the coming to power of the Afrikaner-led Nationalist Party, which soon set about implementing a program of apartheid, which they saw as the social basis of the intensified industrial growth they projected. The Nationalists sought actively to project South Africa as a country with its own hinterland, the neighboring states of southern Africa. They came eventually to talk of a "Constellation of Southern African States."

There was a lot of resistance to South Africa's attempts at regional dominance. African nationalism was now emerging as a force throughout the continent, and South Africa apartheid was a nemesis. Within South Africa itself, the democratic movements showed renewed energy. Portugal sought to pursue an intensified White-settler colonialism of its own, and was suspicious of the South African Whites. And the White settlers of Southern Rhodesia had their own mini-regional dreams of dominance, in the creation of the Federation of the Rhodesias and Nyasaland, designed to keep at bay both African nationalists in the three colonies and the South African Whites.

Still, Portuguese and Rhodesian resistance to a South Africa-centered "region," which had been so intense in the interwar period, began to be vitiated by the changing political situation in Africa and the world-system as a whole. The post–1945 world-system was one based on United States hegemony. It included as a basic element in its program the so-called decolonization of the colonial world. The emerging national liberation movements sought to take advantage of the changed *rapport de forces* in the world-system. They began to demand "independence," by which they expected to resume political control of their own immediate countries and to be in a position to struggle more effectively against the increasing economic polarization of the capitalist world-economy. They pursued this objective in each country, but also collectively (Bandung Conference, non-aligned powers, Group of 77, etc.).

Seen from the perspective of the U.S. as the hegemonic power, these nationalist movements could be beneficial to the stability of the world-system insofar as it could be arranged that any "decolonization" took place with relative smoothness, with a minimum of popular mobilization and violence, and under the aegis of so-called moderate movements. Moderation was defined as not intending to interfere unduly with the existing world division of labor. The United States also saw special advantage to itself in such a decolonization, to the extent that the period 1945–67/73 was one of unprecedented expansion in the world-economy, from which they sought to profit commercially. The prospective economic advantages could only be hindered by excessive political disequilibrium; a continuous, relatively peaceful decolonization would best serve such an objective.

There were nonetheless those in the world-system who felt they were likely to lose from even a "moderate" decolonization. The old colonial powers feared they might be ceding economic advantages to the United States, all the more likely for those among them who had the weakest economic structures (such as Portugal). And White settlers in Africa believed that the inevitable political changes implied by decolonization would end their positions of special privilege. This was acutely felt in South Africa itself, but it was also felt in Southern Rhodesia, and in Angola and Mozambique, all of whose settler communities were in fact growing after 1945 precisely because of the world economic boom.

When the process of political decolonization began to make spectacular advances on the (northern half of the) African continent between 1954 and 1965, the three settler-dominated zones of southern Africa began to put aside their previous quarrels and to draw closer politically. By 1965, wars of liberation were in progress in all of Portuguese-speaking Africa. The White regime in Southern Rhodesia proclaimed a Unilateral Declaration of Independence, which resulted in U.N. sanctions. However weak the U.N. embargo on Southern Rhodesia, the Rhodesian Whites felt beleaguered. A de facto tripartite alliance between South Africa, Rhodesia, and Portugal thus came into existence. Furthermore, the U.N. boycott against Rhodesia forced it not only into industrial development but into much closer economic linkage with South Africa, its agent in circumventing the boycott. Similarly, the Portuguese in Angola and Mozambique intensified their economic cooperation (including infrastructural links) with South Africa. In the fifteen years between 1960 and 1975, the "region" of southern Africa had become an economic reality in a way that it had never been before. Looked at as a whole from say 1920–1973, the southern Africa "region" had come to be restructured as one dominated by South Africa as a semiperipheral state. The process of restructuring South Africa had occurred during the interwar B-phase; but the process of restructuring the region occurred during the postwar A-phase. Then, in 1974–75, the politics of the region were once more transformed. The collapse of the Portuguese dictatorship, and the independence of Angola and Mozambique focused the political struggle on the three remaining White-dominated zones: Rhodesia, Namibia, and South Africa. But this was the very same moment in time that the world-economy entered once again into a period of worldwide stagnation. The combination of intense political struggle (including warfare) plus worldwide economic difficulties would in fact lead to still another restructuring of the political economy of the region.

At the beginning of the 1970's, Angola, Mozambique, Namibia and Zimbabwe were all, to varying degrees, fighting wars of liberation. The governments in Lisbon, Salisbury, and Pretoria collaborated more or less openly in repressing the forces of liberation.

Their goals were, however, different. Lisbon was trying to uphold its "Luso-African" myth, and the unity of its empire.

Salisbury wanted to preserve White independence. The basic aim of Pretoria was Afrikaner national hegemony, safeguarding South African domination of the region, and containing Black independence north of the Zambezi.

In reality, the varying goals reflected the emerging contradictions between the differing positions of the three regimes in the context of the world-economy. South Africa behaved in the region as though it were a country of the core, though globally it was part of the semiperiphery of the developed North. Zimbabwe, Namibia, Mozambique, and to some extent Angola were considered to be within Pretoria's sphere of influence, and to remain its satellites. The presence of Portugal was only justified in terms of the defence of the White *cordon sanitaire*. Rhodesian independence, without its controversial unilateral character, would have satisfied fully Pretoria's concerns about Angola and Mozambique.

Though unhappy about the excessively suffocating embrace of its southern neighbor, Rhodesia became, due to sanctions, more dependent on it. The composition of the White sector of the population changed too, with the increase of Afrikaner emigration north of the Limpopo. The proportion of Afrikaners in the White Rhodesian population began to approach 50 percent. In relation to Mozambique in particular, Salisbury wanted in the end a development along the same lines as Pretoria had designed.

But for Portugal, still in transition to modern forms of economy, the independence of the colonies was something not to be tolerated. The sale of Mozambican labor, cotton, and sugar, and the export of Angolan oil, diamonds, and other minerals were indispensable to the Portuguese economy.

The final objectives of Lisbon's White allies in the region were thus totally opposed to Portuguese interests. Nonetheless, Portuguese manpower in the metropolis and in the colonies was the only pool from which could be drawn the large number of troops needed to hold back the liberation struggles in the vast territories of Angola and Mozambique, even though an important financial and military contribution was made by Pretoria and Salisbury to the Portuguese war effort.

In 1970 the new Portuguese high command launched "Operation Gordian Knot" in northern Mozambique, which became the most important operation in Lisbon's colonial war fought on three fronts. The operation failed: Frelimo, taking the opportunity offered by the concentration of Portuguese forces in the north, managed to establish itself south of the Zambezi, thus opening the way for Zimbabwean guerrillas to reach the entire northern and eastern area of Rhodesia. The goal of the White bastions of restricting the guerrillas to north of the Zambezi was thus threatened. The settler population in Mozambique began to leave, and between 1970 and the eve of the coup d'état in Lisbon, about 40,000 Whites, almost a quarter of the community, left the country for good. This was the turning-point that determined a sharpening of the contradictions and recriminations among the allies. Ian Smith publicly denounced the incapacity and incompetence of the Portuguese military, while South Africa began to organize its plan for a "Constellation of States."

At the end of the 1960's, the U.S. administration began its opening towards China, as part of a global strategy to oppose Soviet designs. The subsequent period bore witness to the collapse of the military option in Indochina, and the rebirth of the fighting capacity of the Egyptian army. Concern with major global objectives, and with regional crises in the Middle East and in Southeast Asia, relegated the prevailing tensions in southern Africa to a position much lower down on the agenda. The 1973 Kissinger report concluded that the White bastion remained solid, and that the liberation movements would be unable to impose significant changes until the end of the millennium. Since the end of the Kennedy administration, Washington and Lisbon had been moving closer together, and this process was accelerated by the 1973 Arab-Israeli war, when Portugal made logistic facilities on the Azores available to the United States in the airlift of supplies to Israel. The new cycle of worldwide recession affected not only the developed countries of the core, but still more seriously the countries of the periphery.

In January 1974, after a visit to the Mozambican theater of operations, the Chief of Staff of the Portuguese Armed Forces warned Prime Minister Marcello Caetano that it was impossible for the army to avoid defeat much longer. A similar situation prevailed in Guinea-Bissau, worsened by the fact that PAIGC had begun to possess mobile armored forces. It had also started a growing and irreversible process of international de jure recognition of the state of Guinea-Bissau declared in 1973.

Though Guinea-Bissau is not in the southern African region, the immobilization of about 40,000 Portuguese troops there prevented military reinforcements for the Angolan and Mozambican fronts. The Portuguese General Staff found itself obliged to fight on three fronts. Although these fronts were separate, they became interdependent. Caetano's reply to the Armed Forces' concerns was that they might surrender, but the government would not. The Portuguese political class had already been traumatized by the army's surrender of Goa in December 1961, a capitulation imposed by the government when it demanded that its soldiers carry out a mission without supplying them with the means to do so.

On April 15, 1974, the Armed Forces Movement overthrew the Lisbon government and took power. The first phrase in its manifesto declared that, after 13 years of war, the government was once more preparing to turn the army into a scapegoat for its policies. It declared categorically that the solution to the conflict was political and not military.

The new Portuguese government began negotiating with the various independence movements. On September 7, 1974, in Lusaka, the process of negotiations with Frelimo came to an end. Lisbon recognized Mozambique's right to immediate and complete independence, accepting the transfer of the powers that it still held to Frelimo as the sole representative of the Mozambican people, and fixing the date of independence. Weeks earlier, Portugal had recognized the independence and the government of Guinea-Bissau. In December, at Alvor in Portugal, the end of Portuguese rule in Angola was agreed upon between Lisbon and the Angolan nationalist movement, represented jointly by the MPLA, FNLA, and UNITA. On June 25, 1975, in Lourenço Marques, and on November 11 in Luanda, Frelimo and the MPLA respectively proclaimed the national independence of Mozambique and of Angola.

The flanks of the White bastion had fallen. The frontier of

Namibia with militant and anti-colonial Africa now extended from the Caprivi Strip to the Atlantic. South of the Limpopo and as far as the Maputo river and the Indian Ocean, South Africa now shared a border with liberation movements that had won power through armed struggle. With the exception of its southern border, Rhodesia was surrounded by a hostile Africa.

The Angolan situation became more complex with the presence of Cuban forces and the substantial Soviet support in equipment and advisers. Exploiting the splits in the Angolan nationalist movement, various interests tried to impose their own programs and ambitions on the Angolan scenario. To the north, Zaire, after the FNLA's failure to take Luanda, invaded the country. To the south, in August 1974, even before Portugal had withdrawn, South Africa occupied the Calueque strip, and began destabilizing actions. Allied with the forces of the then dissident Daniel Chipenda, the South African army invaded the country after independence and advanced towards Luanda. Resorting to its traditional allies, the MPLA organized the defence and a counter-offensive. The governments of Nigeria, Guinea-Bissau, Guinea-Conakry, Congo, Mozambique, and Tanzania sent troops or equipment and supplies. The first Cuban contingent arrived, and the Soviet Union organized a gigantic airlift.

The Soviet and Cuban presence, at a time when the United States had been forced, under far from prestigious conditions, to evacuate Vietnam, introduced a new perception and dimension to the rivalry between the two super-powers. The Washington government felt humiliated, and believed that the U.S.S.R. was exploiting its internal difficulties and its Asian retreat to win positions in an area of previously uncontested Western influence.

On the other hand, African opinion and that of the non-aligned countries as a whole believed that the South African invasion legitimized the Soviet and Cuban presence, however suspect or disagreeable this might be. Through the polarization of the conflict, southern Africa became, albeit unwillingly, a crucial point on the East-West agenda. The end of the Rhodesian rebellion, the independence of Namibia and the disappearance of apartheid became major questions in the international arena.

B. 1974–1975, The Great Turning-Point: The Consequences of Angolan and Mozambican Independence

The year 1975 marks an important shift in the history of southern Africa, the winning of independence by Mozambique and Angola.[1] These were two former Portuguese colonies that, after a decade of armed struggle, proved the Portuguese colonial system could be beaten. With independence, they proclaimed the first states of people's democracy in the southern part of the continent.

They brought to the region a new kind of concept of the state, and a new definition of the enemy, based on class attitudes and positions, as against the traditional definition of opponents on the basis of race, tribe, and region. They rejected, and were committed to fighting against colonialism, neocolonialism, and imperialism. They refused to be anyone's satellites, and rejected economic, political and social subordination. They fought against domination and hegemony. They brought a new economic system, based on a planned and centralized economy, resting on a "strong" state sector, on cooperatives, and on the limitation of private property. They introduced the primacy of the political over the technical.

These concepts were stated in the ideology of the regimes as from the declaration of independence, and in their constitutional texts.[2] The regimes were characterized by more than just a practice conditioned by the economic balance of forces and by the international system. They were characterized by a radical affirmation of their principles and their options. The ideological discourse was rigorous, and in the Mozambican case it was served by the charisma and the communication abilities of Samora Machel.

It is here that the importance of the winning of political power in Angola and Mozambique can be seen. Their political and ideological choices came as a shock to the racist regimes of Rhodesia and of South Africa, which was colonizing Namibia. Angola would be a base for the struggle against South African colonial rule in Namibia, while Mozambique would serve as a rearguard for the liberation of Zimbabwe and for the struggle against apartheid in South Africa. The two regimes proposed a new architecture of regional integration, based on cooperation, mutual security of the Front Line States, and opposition to racist and to western hegemony. The socialist bloc, which was supporting the liberation cause, was regarded as a "natural ally."

But the content of the main struggle waged in the subcontinent was determined by the domination of racist and colonial minority regimes. In 1974–75, southern Africa as a whole was still under the historic domination of the apartheid state. The interests of this state were:

1. to maintain the structures of apartheid's economic and political domination in the region;
2. to divide and eliminate the liberation movements;
3. to preserve the region's status as a supplier of cheap labor, and as an importer of South African manufactured goods;
4. to consolidate Pretoria's political and military supremacy.

In this context, Pretoria's main ally was Ian Smith's Rhodesia, while Malawi was a useful satellite for the purposes of domination. Internationally, Pretoria tried to present itself to the West as the champion of the interests of the free world and of democracy facing the "onslaught from Moscow" against the region and the invasion of Marxism. It was against this alleged danger, and the pressing need to resolve the crisis of the apartheid system and its state, that Botha began the "Total Strategy" that would lead him to take power in September 1978, imposing new stresses and a new class alliance inside the ruling social sector, that is an alliance between Afrikaner monopoly capital and the top command of the South African Defence Force (SADF) (Davies, 1986: 175–76; Ohlson, 1990).

From South Africa's geostrategic point of view, it had to confront Mozambique on its eastern and Angola on its western fronts. These states became Pretoria's main enemies. Apart from this, it had to cope with SWAPO in Namibia, with the Front Line States, and with the challenge to the Constellation of Southern African States (CONSAS) posed by the nine countries who formed SADCC in 1980.

We find two camps demarcated in the regional confrontation. South Africa felt itself subverted by the opposition of the Black, Coloured, and Indian populations for whom the victories in Mozambique and Angola demonstrated the possibility of insurrectionary triumph, and put on the agenda the immediate end of apartheid. Demonstrations in Soweto occurred in solidarity with the Mozambican declaration of independence.

The Portuguese defeat, though predictable, had not been expected so soon. The famous Kissinger Report of 1973 did not envisage substantial changes until the year 2000. Only Rhodesian military and intelligence circles, who were closer to the Mozambican war zones, felt that collapse was imminent (Flower, 1987: 300–02). They were denounced as "alarmist" by Marcello Caetano (1974) in his "family talks" on television. Faced with a fait accompli, the Vorster government in South Africa opted for a policy of external detente and a hard line internally, in the framework of the so-called Constellation of States.

Pretoria did not have sufficient White manpower to support an occupation of Mozambique and Angola, while simultaneously defending Rhodesia and South African soil itself. Since Mozambique, along with Rhodesia, was South Africa's main weak point, in terms of its borders, the Vorster government took the initiative of accepting the status quo. It declared it would not interfere in

Mozambican affairs, and decided to sacrifice its Rhodesian ally. Thus Pretoria, through President Kaunda, told the Front Line States that it was prepared to withdraw its forces from Rhodesia, and put pressure on the Smith regime in Rhodesia to release political prisoners and to start negotiations with the liberation movement.

However, the situation in Angola opened the possibility of other scenarios. The MPLA was being harried by invasions of Zairean forces and the FNLA in the north, while internal dissent, led by Daniel Chipenda, was threatening its presence in the south. As early as August 1975, before independence but after the Alvor accord, South African forces occupied the Calueque dam. This occurred without any reaction from the Portuguese army and from the Lisbon authorities, who were, according to the terms of the Alvor agreement, still responsible for Angola's territorial integrity. Following this, and at the instigation of the neighboring states, South Africa unleashed its first major invasion, driving towards Luanda. This invasion internationalized the Angolan conflict. The South Africans had however underestimated the Soviet and Cuban reaction, at a time when the U.S. administration had been doubly weakened by the withdrawal from Vietnam and the Watergate scandal (Stockwell, 1978).

On the Eastern Front: The Role of Mozambique

"You don't ask a slave if he wants to be free, particularly when he is already in revolt, and much less if you happen to be a slave-owner" Samora Machel (1974a).

The process following the Portuguese coup d'état of April 25, 1974, which led to the confirmation of Guinea-Bissau's independence, and to the possibility and necessity of the other African states ruled by Portugal achieving their independence, has sometimes been interpreted in such a way as to assume that all five countries were the objects of a decolonization undertaken by Portugal. The appearance of the word "decolonization" in the speeches and writings of the time might lead us into mistakes in interpreting each of the struggles for national independence in the countries previously ruled by Portugal. The cases of Guinea-Bissau and Mozambique are clear examples of this.

Guinea-Bissau declared its independence in 1973, and its government received de facto recognition from all O.A.U. members and from 82 member states of the United Nations. Even before this, Portuguese strategists had raised the hypothesis of a military withdrawal from Guinea-Bissau in order to concentrate all efforts on the main fronts which were in Angola and Mozambique. Portugal's head of state, Marcello Caetano was opposed to this. He feared the effects that such a political precedent would have on the defence of the remaining territories, notably Angola and Mozambique. The essence of the negotiations with Guinea-Bissau was Portuguese recognition of the State of Guinea-Bissau, which had been proclaimed at Medina de Boe on September 24, 1973.

In fact, General Antonio de Spinola, who had taken power in Portugal after the coup d'état, confirmed that it was impossible to refuse to transfer power in Guinea-Bissau, when he stated:

> [I]n mid-August, the Portuguese delegation went once more to Algiers, already empowered to accept the conditions demanded by PAIGC, since the unequal positions imposed this. With its signature of August 16, 1974, the Portuguese state undertook to recognize de jure the Republic of Guinea-Bissau as a sovereign state, and after the ratification, the two sides were obliged to respect a mutual cease-fire (1978: 283).

A situation that was identical in several respects arose in Mozambique. In the Lusaka negotiations of June 1974, Portugal presented as its priorities the building of democracy in Portugal, the restructuring of its economy, and (in last place) decolonization. Statements by President Spinola, and the Portuguese position at Lusaka, let it be understood that independence would only be desirable over a period of five years or so, and only within the framework of a Luso-African federation. In the Portuguese conception, the goal of the negotiations should be to obtain a cease-fire. But in Frelimo's conception, a cease-fire was the corollary of a political agreement. Frelimo refused to allow the colonizing power, ten years after the war had started, to come and ask the people about the principle of independence. Regarding the plebiscite among the colonized population which Spinola claimed was necessary, Samora Machel declared:

> Independence is not negotiable. It is an inalienable right of the Mozambican people. However, we are prepared to discuss the modalities of the transfer of sovereignty to the Mozambican people, of whom Frelimo is the sole legitimate representative (1974a: 3).

Angola and Mozambique were not important merely because they had won independence after a prolonged struggle against the colonizing power, nor because they were the bearers of socio-economic systems based on popular mobilization and participation, with philosophies inspired by Marxism-Leninism. They were important because of their geostrategic significance, as rearguards committed to the liberation of the region and of the continent against the remaining backward regimes, and for the alternative rail and port facilities they put at the disposal of landlocked countries. This opened the possibility of struggling against the dependence on and subordination to the transport routes and modalities offered by South Africa.

Mozambican independence freed Tanzania from the pressure it had borne up until then. Its territory could now benefit from a buffer zone thousands of miles deep, putting it beyond the reach of Rhodesian or South African aircraft. With vulnerability now extended to Mozambican and Angolan soil, Zambia could believe to some extent that the pressure to which it was subject had lessened. This was also true for Malawi, Swaziland, and Botswana.

In 1974–75 Rhodesia and South Africa considered the disapperance of the buffer states of the Portuguese colonies to be a threat to their own historical and institutional survival. In Rhodesia, the liberation of Mozambique opened access for ZANU not only to Tete province, but also allowed new guerrilla bases to be established in the other provinces bordering Rhodesia, namely Manica and Gaza. ZANU could thus operate against the Ian Smith regime over a much wider space. The ANC of South Africa would enjoy a rearguard closer to the object of its struggle, namely access to the Transvaal and Natal borders, while in southern Angola, SWAPO would have the possibility of fighting South African colonialism in Namibia over a much wider area than the tiny Caprivi Strip to which it had been confined up to then.

The specific form whereby each country was integrated into the region and its political and material gains were to determine the role and conduct of each state in the struggle for the transformation of the region at each stage of the regional struggle.

After the coup d'etat of April 25, some of the Mozambican soldiers serving in the Portuguese Special Groups (GEs) and Special Paratroop Groups (GEP), as well as in other military units deserted to the ranks of Frelimo. This was the case with the 5,000 soldiers who handed themselves over in Zambezia to the People's Forces for the Liberation of Mozambique. 2,000 Portuguese soldiers from the Lourenço Marques engineering barracks and others stationed at Boane demonstrated their support for Frelimo, and bluntly refused to go to the theater of operations, recognizing Frelimo as the only force that represented the Mozambican people. Meanwhile, the armed struggle was continuing, and had already extended from the Rovuma to south of the Zambezi and was heading towards the other extreme of the country, namely the Maputo river. This fact disturbed Ian Smith's Rhodesia, and alerted Pretoria to the inevitability that the liberation movement would advance south of the Zambezi and Limpopo rivers.

General Antonio de Spinola recalled the general demoralization of the Portuguese Armed Forces and the inevitability of submitting to Frelimo's demands in these terms:

> Units from the Cabo Delgado, Niassa and Tete sectors held "plenary meetings" of officers, sergeants and privates which, to cries of "no more operations," "no more shooting," and similar phrases, decided to suspend operational activities. This decision was immediately transmitted to other units in the theater of operations through a leaflet campaign. At the same time, the commander of the air force, in perfect timing

with the revolutionary military left, took the arbitrary decision to suspend technical support to the ground forces. This was the first step towards totally paralysing them. It should be noted, however, that only after the visit to the Nampula Military Headquarters of a group of representatives of the central MFA [Armed Force Movement], consisting of Lt.-Colonel Franco Charais, Major Otelo Saraiva de Carvalho and Captain Vasco Lourenço, did the process of degradation in the armed forces speed up. In this respect, it is worth stressing that, although affected, activity in the Cabo Delgado sector continued for some time, despite the fact that the General Staff there was already contaminated with the revolutionary virus. But soon operational activity throughout the theater of operations was to be really suspended, although the special African and metropolitan forces—Special Groups, Special Paratroop Groups, Commandos and Paratroopers—were disciplined and strongly in favor of fighting for a dignified and just decolonization.

It was in this perspective of degradation that the first official contacts with Frelimo took place in Lusaka on June 5–6. In this meeting there took part, on the Portuguese side, Dr. Mario Soares; the Minister of Foreign Affairs, Dr. Manuel Sa Machado from the same ministry; Major Otelo Saraiva de Carvalho, representing the central MFA; and Lt.-Colonel Nuno Lusada, representing the local MFA. At this first meeting, Major Saraiva de Carvalho, placing himself above the Foreign Minister, called for the solution of handing Mozambique over unconditionally to Frelimo, in an act of irresponsible subordination to the will of that movement (1978: 295–97).

Despite these accusations against the leadership of the Portuguese Armed Forces, the process of the national liberation war had become irreversible, and a political solution for the colonies could no longer be delayed. The General's drama was the prospect of an independence to promote the domination of one race or another, while Frelimo, MPLA, and PAIGC declared their opposition to the dichotomy of ruling and ruled races, and proposed to avoid the domination of one class or nation by another. Spinola saw the war in Mozambique in these terms:

> The next goal, naturally, would be Mozambique where the situation was explosive. Its economy had been deteriorating dangerously. Financially, it was on the verge of bankruptcy. From the socio-political point of view it was threatened by antagonistic choices—White independence or Black independence—in a possibly dramatic perspective, while on the terrain of armed struggle, terrorism was advancing systematically southwards, in a climate of growing concern. This somber panorama of a physical and human space where the forces of collapse were going from strength to strength had its effects (1978: 289).

As a result of the conjuncture the country was going through, Frelimo could, in absolute security, claim and demand from the representatives of the Portuguese state three points in order to reach an agreement leading to peace:

1. the recognition of Mozambique's right to total and complete independence;
2. the recognition of Frelimo as the legitimate representative of the Mozambican people in accordance with O.A.U. and United Nations decisions;
3. the acceptance of the principle of transferring the powers that Portugal was exercising to the institution representing the Mozambican people, Frelimo.

As a result of the politico-military victory, the Lusaka Agreement signed on September 7, 1974 between the Portuguese government and Frelimo, basically involved not a process of decolonization but mechanisms for the transfer of power. In this agreement, the Portuguese state recognized the basic demands of the Mozambique Liberation Front, of which we stress the following points:

a) the right of the Mozambican people to independence;
b) the transfer of power to Frelimo over a nine-month transition period;
c) the solemn proclamation of Mozambican independence on June 25, 1975, the anniversary of the foundation of Frelimo;
d) the creation of a transitional period for the transfer of powers during which there would exist a High Commissioner appointed by the Portuguese state on Frelimo's proposal, a Prime Minister of the Transitional Government appointed by Frelimo, and an executive where 9 of the 12 members were appointed by Frelimo from among its own members, with the other 3 appointed by the Portuguese state;[3]
e) the formation of a Joint Military Commission by common consent between the Portuguese state and Frelimo to supervise the ceasefire and the handover of military equipment and installations to Frelimo;
f) a ceasefire to come into force as from zero hour on September 8, 1974;
g) the establishment of a completely Mozambican police force;
h) the establishment of a central bank that would function as an issuing bank.

During the transition process there were only a few upsets that disturbed public order. The main event of the transitional period was a settler uprising on September 7, 1974, which was part of a broader project to sabotage the process of transferring power. But it failed due to popular opposition and lack of support from the Portuguese army. The great majority of the colonized took part in smashing this settler mutiny.

During the transitional period, Frelimo set up Dynamising Groups in all sectors of economic and social activity, so that the people might be able to exercise power. These structures were important in the struggle against the effects of economic sabotage and the acts of vandalism practiced by the enemies of independence and of the class power instituted in Mozambique.

The independence of Mozambique was finally declared on June 25, under the emblem of the power of the worker-peasant alliance, and in the presence of the then chairman of the O.A.U., Siad Barre, of high-ranking officials of the United Nations and of the non-aligned movement, and of representatives of the Portuguese state. Samora Moises Machel was appointed the first head of state of independent Mozambique.

Nine months after the declaration of independence, Mozambique closed its borders with Southern Rhodesia. This allowed the Zimbabwean armed struggle to be stepped up. Due to increased aggression by Smith's forces, Frelimo sent a contingent of its own troops to support ZANU's armed struggle. In 1980 Zimbabwe became independent. South Africa was now the main obstacle on the eastern front.

On the Western Front: The Role of Angola

In Angola, the existence of three principal movements competing in the struggle to win state power made the transition to independence more difficult. This struggle became still more complex because of divergent concepts of liberation, the lack of internal unity among the parties and the pressure from external regional or international forces on the political practice of each political formation. This lack of unity meant that independence was proclaimed on November 11, 1975 to the sound of gunfire.

On April 25, 1974, the struggle against colonialism was being led principally by the MPLA, which was acting on the Northern Front and in the east. As for the other two movements, once the Kinkusu revolt by FNLA officers against the movement's leader, Holden Roberto, had failed, the FNLA went on to fight against, not the army of colonial occupation, but the MPLA on the Northern Front. And the Southern Front was at the mercy of Jonas Savimbi, the leader of UNITA, who had collaborated with the Portuguese army against the MPLA. UNITA was in fact the first organization to lay down its arms after the MFA's coup d'état, and it presented itself to the settler community as the organization that defended peace.

To make matters worse, not only was there the factional division between the three movements, but the MPLA had to confront internal dissent in the form of the "Active Revolt" of Mario Pinto de Andrade, and the "Eastern Revolt" of Daniel Chipenda. In November 1974, the FNLA and UNITA came to an agreement to fight against the MPLA, the only Angolan political organization that had managed to win significant support from all sections of the population.

General Spinola made use of the lack of unity among the Angolan fighting forces to try to implement his own decolonization project and to transfer power in his own way. General Spinola believed that Portugal could not live without its colonies. Thus it was urgent to hang on in Angola to what had already been lost in Guinea-Bissau and Mozambique. For Angola, he argued that the decolonization process had to pass through a phase of democracy, which meant political pluralism, direct suffrage, citizens' participation in making and altering the laws, citizens' participation in political life, and responsibility of elected officials before their electorate.[4]

To ensure the success of his plan, the General relied on support from the FNLA, from Pres. Mobutu of Zaire, from the U.S. and from the apartheid state. The first step Spinola took to maintain the balance of forces in his favor was to appoint as Governor of Angola a conservative officer, General Silverio Marques. The term of office of Silverio Marques was characterized by well thought-out passivity, which allowed the political forces playing on the Angolan stage to organize themselves. Massacres carried out by settler groups in the suburbs forced the mass of the colonized people to organize against the killings. The masses, including the lumpen-proletariat, took part in people's defence units, organized into fighting brigades named after fictional adventure heroes such as "Sandokam," "Sabata," and "Bandeira Rasgada" against the "Dragons" and "Death Squads" of the settlers.

In January 1975, the three movements signed an agreement in Portugal known as the Alvor Accords. In this agreement Portugal recognized the MPLA, the FNLA, and UNITA as "the sole legitimate representatives of the Angolan people." It recognized the right of the Angolan people to independence, which was to be solemnly declared on November 11, 1975 by the President of the Portuguese

Republic or his representative (this was a new clause in the history of Portuguese colonialism, because in Guinea-Bissau and Mozambique independence had been proclaimed by the leaders of the liberation movements). Under the agreement, Cabinda was described as an integral part of the territorial unity of Angola; powers were to be gradually transferred to Angola; patriots of the liberation struggle were to be amnestied for acts formerly punishable under the law then in force (another new clause). A High Commissioner was appointed to defend Portuguese interests and a Presidential College was set up to lead the transitional government, which included three members from each organization. A National Defence Commission was to be formed by the High Commissioner, the Presidential College, and the Unified General Staff. General elections were to be held within nine months of January 31, 1975. The agreement also defined Angolan citizenship (another new clause for this kind of process).

Although the Transitional Government was sworn into office, in practice this agreement was unable to succeed due to the frictions between the parties involved. The "Second War of Liberation" was begun by Daniel Chipenda who demanded important positions in the Transitional Government and called himself President of Angola. The FNLA attacked Luanda suburbs with mortars and rockets, and the Portuguese Armed Forces took no action. The MPLA closed its offices in the north due to the Zairean invasion. Savimbi's UNITA reappeared with a racist and tribalist discourse, defending the south and the Umbundus against invaders from the north. South Africa began its invasion, and the MPLA requested aid from Cuba. The Cubans responded first by sending instructors, and later combat troops to Angola, particularly for the defence of Luanda. Angolan decolonization became a new war of liberation. The conflict took on an international dimension, because of which many lost sight of the central problem of decolonization.

With Cuban assistance, the MPLA managed to defeat the Zairean and South African troops, and it declared independence while at war.[5] This opened the possibility for SWAPO in Namibia to organize better its armed struggle against South Africa and its colonial rule of Namibia. This country was to become independent in 1990.

While still at war, independent Angola became a base of support for the liberation of southern Africa from colonialism and racism. The example of the struggles waged by Frelimo and MPLA was to serve as a source of inspiration for the liberation of southern Africa from colonialism and from rule by racist and illegal regimes.

Notes

1. Mozambican independence was declared by Frelimo in Lourenço Marques on June 25, 1975. Angolan independence was declared by MPLA in Luanda on November 11, 1975. This declaration was recognized internationally. On the same date, the FNLA and UNITA declared Angolan independence in Huambo, but this regime was not recognized.

2. For Mozambique see Reis (1976); for Angola, see Queiroz (1978).

3. The Portuguese state appointed the Health Minister, a Portuguese citizen, and two Frelimo sympathisers, Engineer Alcantara Santos, who died in the Mbuzini disaster when he was Transport Minister in the People's Republic of Mozambique, and Air Force Lt.-Colonel Eugenio Picolo, who is currently teaching at Eduardo Mondlane University. The Transitional Government took office in Lourenço Marques on September 20, 1974, and its mission ended on June 25, 1975. The Transitional Government was led on the Mozambican side by Joaquim Alberto Chissano, and on the Portuguese side by Rear-Admiral Vitor Crespo.

4. For further clarification of Spinola's concept of democracy, see Spinola (1976).

5. The MPLA declared Angola's national independence on November 11, 1975. This was the only declaration recognized by the concert of nations, that is by the U.N. and by the O.A.U.

The Political Crisis and Its Impact on the Region's Basic Economic Structure

William G. Martin

A. Southern Africa and the World-Economy: Regionality and Trade Regimes

Southern Africa is fragmented, grossly exploited and subject to economic manipulation by outsiders. Future development must aim at the reduction of economic dependence not only on the Republic of South Africa, but also on any single external state or groups of states. (SADCC, Lusaka Declaration, 1980)

Introduction

As we move into the 1990's the prospect of a peaceful reconstruction of southern Africa is once again being heralded across the region. The stimulus for such hopes is quite evident: the movement towards a majority-ruled South Africa and, accordingly, the possibility of interstate cooperation replacing interstate conflict across region.

Such hopes express neither simple optimism nor triumphalism, but the high costs of the struggles of the 1970's and, especially, the 1980's. If the future promises much, it does so in large part upon reflection upon the very recent past. This is however hardly a new phenomenon. Indeed as the 1980's began, expectations for advancing regional development ran similarly high across the region only to be shattered over the course of the next decade. Is there anything to be learned, one might well ask, in the expectations and disillusions of the last decade?

The basis for optimism in the early 1980's was surely well-founded. Building upon the independence of Mozambique and Angola five years earlier, the independence of Zimbabwe brought to an end almost two decades of armed struggle for national liberation. Freed from the ravages of colonial war, the frontline states moved forward to tackle an intractable problem: the continuing chains of underdevelopment that left their peoples dependent upon the export of primary products and the importation of manufactured goods.

The creation of the Southern African Development Coordination Conference (SADCC) in 1980 signalled, furthermore, the widespread recognition that no single state could achieve these ends alone. It marked as well a recognition of the dual faces of unequal exchange that operate across the economic landscape of southern Africa. As SADCC's opening declaration noted, the search for economic liberation would confront both overseas core areas and apartheid South Africa. At the same time the South African state, facing the loss of compliant partners in dominating the region, sought to reassert its regional economic and political primacy by promoting a "Constellation of States" revolving around itself. The 1980's saw ever-escalating military attacks from the heartland of apartheid upon neighboring states. As other essays in this volume document, the costs of destabilization short-circuited any prospects for cooperative regional development.

The very basis of South African destabilization indicated, however, the extensive degree to which the peoples and states of the region were bound together. While the military form of destabilization was clearly dominant, it was equally evident that the power of the apartheid regime rested not simply upon disparities in economic resources and capabilities, but upon the high degree of regional economic interdependence which had existed for decades.

In this respect past studies of regional conflict, focused as they have been upon the contesting agendas of SADCC and the apartheid regime, have left us ill-prepared to evaluate the center-hinter-land relationships of the southern African "region" upon which rest both conflict and cooperation. If we are not to repeat the disap-pointments of the 1980's it would be well to recognize this. As a result, it is exceedingly difficult to distinguish which facets of this region are undergirded by deeply entrenched networks, and which facets are more subject to alteration in the present conjuncture. Studies of the means to increase cooperation amongst SADCC members, for example, have rarely included an examination of the structure and trends of the SADCC-South African network. This is especially striking given that SADCC has made relatively little advance in increasing its cohesiveness (at least in commodity trade) at the expense of older regional patterns. Even fewer studies have attempted to discern regional patterns within the changing structure of the world-economy, a rather striking omission.[1] For if SADCC members and South Africa remain bound together, so too are they inextricably part of the capitalist world-economy—a fact particular-ly important in the present conjuncture. As SADCC itself has argued (SADCC, 1986a), and as we will stress for South Africa itself, the transition to global depression and the decline of U.S. hegemony has had an immediate and direct impact on prices, production, and investment trends—not to mention the prospects and possibilities for cooperative regional planning.

It follows that to act concretely under contemporary conditions requires an analysis not simply of regional political or even eco-nomic relationships, but also of the region as part of the global division of labor. The need for such a perspective has only in-creased, moreover, as a majority-ruled South Africa looms on the horizon.

As a partial contribution to such an analysis, we shall focus upon an examination of the structure of commodity trade flows within and across the boundaries of southern Africa. Our primary concern is with the years from 1975 to the present, a period marked by substantial political and economic crisis within and across both southern Africa and the world-economy. The distinc-tiveness of this period is revealed, however, only by demarcating it against both preceding patterns of regional and global trade, and the possibilities offered by regional cooperation, including the prospect of a majority-ruled South Africa.

In so proceeding our analysis falls into four parts, each with its own task in the untangling of intraregional relationships as well as those between the region and the world-economy. We seek first to uncover the trajectory of southern Africa's position within the global division of labor: has the gap between core states and the region (and the states that compose it) been growing or shrinking over the course of recent global cycles? Secondly, to what extent has southern Africa become less or more dependent upon commodity trade relationships with other areas of the world-economy? How has the composition of, and gains and losses from, these relationships changed over time? Thirdly, what differences may be discerned among the states of the region and their dependence upon regional trade? How does this reveal changing levels of regional cohesion and regional relationships of a center-hinterland nature? Finally, in the light of these overall patterns, how might one assess the contribution of current and prospective strategies to alter, on a regional basis, the economic prospects of southern Africa through changing commodity flows? This analysis includes a discussion of the efforts of SADCC, the PTA (Preferential Tariff Area), and other African regional associations during the 1980's, as well as the implications of majority rule in South Africa for southern Africa as a region.

Southern Africa and the Global Division of Labor

To examine contemporary patterns of economic activity and foreign trade in southern Africa is to encounter the enduring legacy of the area's colonial incorporation into the world division of labor. All of the states of southern Africa remain dependent upon the export of primary products in order to earn the funds to pay for consumer and capital goods imports and, increasingly in the last ten years, debt servicing. This is true even of Zimbabwe and South Africa, where substantial manufacturing sectors remain largely uncompetitive on the world market, particularly by comparison to other semiperipheral countries such as Brazil or South Korea. While

inter-industry and inter-territorial relationships among the states of
southern Africa have clearly grown over time, the region as a whole
nevertheless remains highly dependent upon overseas core areas.

One would expect that the rewards accruing to producers in
southern Africa would reflect this prevailing mode of participation
in the world division of labor. Yet we know of no study that has
investigated either the character and degree of integration between
core areas and southern Africa or the gap between them, much less
the changes in these relationships over time. In large part this
reflects the assumption that development is a national process,
whose outcomes—and who bears responsibility for them—reflect
little relationship to the processes of unequal exchange that define
core-periphery relationships. For economists the standard procedure
is thus to measure and compare—but not relate—individual states'
level of "national" economic growth. Using such a method it is
impossible to ascertain an area's trajectory as part of changing
global economic processes and relationships. Did South Africa—or
indeed southern Africa—actually improve its relative position in the
global division of labor over this time period? We are hard pressed
to know.

Such questions cannot be analyzed within the developmentalist
unit of analysis, the nation-state, not even if one tacks on a state's
relations to world markets. We start from a different perspective,
assuming that the global division of labor and interstate system
systematically operate to ensure a highly unequal distribution of
wealth across the world-economy. It follows that one's procedures
must at least attempt to capture states' (or a region's) position
within such core-peripheral relationships. Analyses of individual
state's growth records cannot answer such questions as: Is southern
Africa today becoming more or less peripheral, more or less
dependent on overseas core areas? Have there been moments of
advance and regression for the region since the Second World War,
related to changes in the interstate system and global cycles and
trends? In short, the lack of any long-term analysis of southern
Africa position within the world-economy make its almost impossible to analyse the degree to which integrating mechanisms such as
trade relationships have sustained—or can be altered to break—the

chains that bind southern Africa into the world-economy as a peripheral zone.

In order to approach an answer to these questions we have attempted to chart the region's position within the world-economy in the post-Second World War period, assuming that the outcomes of processes of unequal exchange should be reflected in the comparative levels of wealth (i.e., long-term income) which residents of core and peripheral areas receive through participation in the global division of labor. Even a crude empirical indicator, such as share of global GNP/capita, should reveal the proportion of world aggregate income which residents of an area command.[2] As Arrighi and Drangel have shown for the world-economy as a whole (Arrighi & Drangel, 1986), such a procedure indicates that very little change in either the global distribution of income or the membership of core, semiperipheral, and peripheral zones has occurred in the post-Second World War period.

Our focus is narrower, seeking to estimate over time southern Africa's distance from core areas. We thus begin by calculating average regional GNP per capita (i.e., summing national GNP's of the region and dividing by population) and presenting this as a *percentage* of average GNP per capita for four organic members of the core zone (United States, United Kingdom, F.R. Germany, and France).[3] The results for South Africa, the region as a whole and the region minus South Africa are indicated in Graph 1, while Table 2-A-1 indicates trends for states in the region.

Graph 1 indicates quite sharply that southern Africa, when its GNP is calculated as a percentage of core trends, retained but did not advance its position vis-à-vis core areas during the post-1945 boom period. This stability broke, however, with the onset of the current global stagnation. Even when measured against indices of stagnation in core areas, the region has quite clearly reaped lower and lower returns from its position in the global division of labor over the 1970's and 1980's. This trend has been halted but not reversed at two points when, as noted below, commodity prices for several of the region's central exports momentarily rose (ca. 1973–74 and, largely for South Africa, 1980–81). The 1980's have in fact been disastrous: each country in 1987 (the most recent data

Graph One
Distance from Core:
South Africa, Region, Region minus S. Africa

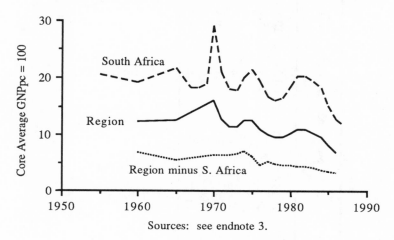

Sources: see endnote 3.

presented here) stands lower than in 1980, often sharply so. Contrary to some expectations derived from dependency theory, which assert on the basis of interwar patterns that peripheral areas advance rapidly in periods marked by world-economic crisis, the data strongly suggest that stagnation and hegemonic rivalry in the current great depression have not resulted in expanded economic growth along this segment of the periphery.

One cannot presume that all the component parts of southern Africa have followed similar trajectories. As the strongest economic power in the region, and one marked by a high degree of inter-industry linkages serving its home market, one might have expected South Africa to diverge from the pattern of peripheral countries so closely tied to the exigencies of the world market. And indeed South Africa's semiperipheral position in the world-economy stands out sharply in Graph 1, contrasting sharply with the much more peripheral rankings of the other states of the region. It alone stands above the regional average, and outranks markedly even Zimbabwe.[4]

Yet South Africa shows above all the impact of falling returns

Table 2-A-1
Regional States' Distance from Core
(Percentage of "Organic Core" GNP per Capita)

Year	Angola	Botswana	Lesotho	Malawi	Mozam-bique	S. Africa	Swaziland	Zambia	Zimbabwe
1960	7.0	1.6	2.1	2.4	7.3	19.2	3.5	8.9	10.5
1965	7.8	1.7	2.5	2.5	6.2	21.7	5.5	10.5	9.3
1970	6.7	3.5	2.6	1.9	6.4	20.9	7.5	10.1	7.5
1975	6.1	5.3	3.5	1.8	5.4	21.4	9.0	8.4	8.7
1980	7.3	6.8	3.6	1.6	2.8	18.6	7.1	5.2	6.1
1985	7.2	6.3	3.0	1.2	1.3	15.0	5.3	3.0	4.6
1988	—	6.3	2.3	1.1	.6	14.2	5.0	1.8	4.0

Sources:

1960–65: World Bank, 1984.
1967–87: World Bank, 1989a.
1988: World Bank, 1990a.

Exceptions:

Angola 1977–1986: OECD, 1984, 1989.
Mozambique 1977–81: OECD, 1984, 1989.

Table 2-A-2
Distance from South Africa
South Africa GNPpc = 100

	S.A. GNPpc US $	Angola	Botswana	Lesotho	Malawi	Mozam-bique	Swaziland	Zambia	Zimbabwe
1955	358							48	
1960	410	36	8	11	13	38	18	47	55
1965	551	36	8	11	11	29	25	49	43
1970	1150	24	11	9	5	20	23	39	24
1985	2080	48	42	20	8	9	36	20	31
1986	1840	55	49	20	9	12	38	15	32
1987	1870		56	20	9	9	37	13	32
1988	2290		44	18	7	4	35	13	28

Sources: as for Table 2-A-1.

from its participation in the international division of labor after the early 1970's. Only a few countries have escaped this trend as indicated in Table 2-A-1, most notably Botswana after the opening of new mines (esp. diamonds). Possessing the most advanced industrial base on the continent, and dominating other territories in the region, has not, however, allowed South Africa to escape the chilly winds blowing across the world-economy. As chapter 3 indicates at greater length, South Africa's decline, by comparison to a wide range of states similarly positioned in the global division of labor, has been faster and farther (see chapter 3 and Martin, 1990a).

It is further apparent that several of the other countries in the region (Botswana, Lesotho, Swaziland) closed the gap between themselves and South Africa up to the outbreak of the current great depression, while most have maintained or closed the gap with South Africa since 1970 (see Table 2-A-2 which charts individual countries GNP per capita as a percentage of South Africa's GNP per capita). Mozambique and Zambia stand out, falling sharply vis-à-vis South Africa since 1970.

In summary, southern Africa's position in the world-economy has not improved over the course of the postwar period as a whole. A steady relationship vis-à-vis core areas turned, moreover, sharply downwards after the outbreak of the current great depression in the early 1970's, and then plunged in the 1980's. In relation to other similarly situated areas, it is further apparent that the region performed poorly even during the period of global expansion, and shares a common situation of an ever-growing gap between itself and core areas of the world-economy. As noted at the outset, these are only indicators of the region and its component parts' position in the world-economy, and southern Africa's susceptibility to the forces of unequal exchange. It remains to be determined how the latter have operated over time.

Regional Trading Patterns with the World-Economy

Import and export dependence
Trade is but one of the many economic flows that bind together

different zones of the world-economy. However, for the countries of southern Africa, it is an exceedingly important one. The degree of openness towards the world market and dependence on trade is conventionally indicated by the degree to which exports and imports form a percentage of GDP. Graph 2 and Table 2-A-3 show this for exports while Graph 3 and Table 2-A-4 indicate this relationship for imports.[5]

As the data indicate, export dependence for the region and most countries rose through the 1960's and accelerated through the 1970's, only to fall sharply in the early 1980's. Clearly during the post-war boom southern Africa's integration into and dependence upon world markets deepened. This increasing export orientation paralleled, as indicated in the previous section, the rather steady distance from core areas of both South Africa and southern Africa as a whole.

Given the weight and structure of its GDP, it is striking that South Africa showed one of the sharpest rises from 1970 onward in the importance of exports, indicated by statistics for the South African Customs Union (SACU), an entity that included not only South Africa and Namibia but Botswana, Swaziland, and Lesotho as well. This largely reflected the high degree of openness towards the world-economy that emerged after the Second World War, a process cemented by membership in GATT under rules applicable to developed countries. In the most recent period, export growth has taken place, moreover, through the continued expansion of primary product exports. As Table 2-A-3 shows, most countries of the region have followed South Africa's trajectory. In general, mineral exporting countries have exhibited a higher degree of export dependence than agricultural exporters.[6] Decreasing export reliance in the early 1980's has however been sharply reversed in the last several years, and in a deleterious manner: In general GDP has fallen while exports have decreased at a lower rate.[7] With few exceptions economic crisis has not made the region less dependent; even where GDP has grown, as in the case of Botswana, such growth has rested upon rising levels of export production. These observations might be set against, for example, the World Bank's argument that economic decline for Sub-Saharan Africa has been

Graph Two
Exports as a Percentage of GDP

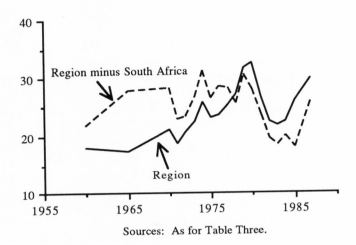

Sources: As for Table Three.

Graph Three
Imports as a Percentage of GDP

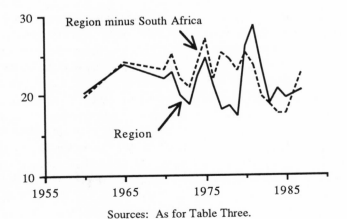

Sources: As for Table Three.

Table 2-A-3
Regional Export/GDP Ratios

Year	Angola	Malawi	Mozam- bique	SACU	Zambia	Zimba- bwe	Region	Region minus SACU
1965	19	16	9	13	50	41	17	28
1975	34	21	11	22	33	26	23	27
1980	30	24	20	34	33	27	33	28
1985	22	19	4	30	18	20	26	18
1987	29	21	15	31	43	19	30	26

Definitions:

Regional GDP=sum of Angola, Botswana, Lesotho, Malawi, Mozambique, South Africa, Swaziland, Zambia, Zimbabwe;

Regional Trade=sum of SACU, Angola, Malawi, Mozambique, Zambia, Zimbabwe.

Sources:

GDP: 1960-1979: Calculated from World Bank, 1984.

1980-87: UNDP and World Bank, 1989, except for South Africa from World Bank, 1980-83, 1984b, 1985-88, 1989c, 1990a; Angola 1987 figure from World Bank, 1989b.

Exports/Imports: IMF, Computer tape, 1986, 1989a; except for Zimbabwe 1967-79 from World Bank, 1989a.

Table 2-A-4
Regional Import/GDP Ratios

Year	Angola	Malawi	Mozam- bique	SACU	Zambia	Zimba- bwe	Region	Region minus SACU
1965	18	25	14	24	31	35	24	24
1975	17	38	22	24	46	23	25	27
1980	22	35	28	26	17	23	26	25
1985	14	24	12	20	29	22	20	18
1987	15	23	48	20	40	21	21	23

Sources: As for Table 2-A-3.

due to the withdrawal from, or intervention upon, commodity markets (World Bank, 1989b: 19–20).

For countries such as those composing southern Africa export earnings are critical in order to finance consumer and capital goods imports, and, increasingly, to finance debt repayments (see chapter 2c below). In the most recent period, falling export prices and subsequent shortages of foreign exchange have exerted strong pressures against the importation of even those goods most essential to daily life and continued agricultural and industrial production. Falling capacity utilization ratios in existing factories due to a shortage of spare parts is, for example, a common experience under these conditions. Such realities are reflected in Graph 3 and Table 2-A-4, where momentary rises in import levels (ca. 1975, 1980) match rising import capabilities and/or oil price increases. Imports as a percentage of GDP have however fallen in the 1980's for the region as a whole and, with few exceptions, for all its component parts; even Zimbabwe and South Africa, with their large GDP's, have been seriously affected.

In summary, southern Africa over the whole of the post–1945 period has exhibited a steadily increasing dependence on trade with other areas of the world-economy. This conclusion stands in particularly sharp relief given the region's heavy reliance on primary product exports. In this respect falling import indices have not prefigured more inter-sectoral linkages and self-reliance, but rather the inability to finance needed consumer and capital goods imports.

Commodity concentration and terms of trade

Given the critical role played by export earnings, it is important to note not only that exports are primarily composed of primary products, but that for most countries of the region a few commodities account for the majority of export earnings. These commodities differ however between the states of the region and, to a lesser extent, have varied for each state over the post–1945 period. Commodity concentration in recent years shows Angola dependent upon oil and coffee; Namibia on diamonds, uranium, and copper/lead/zinc; Botswana on diamonds and meat; Lesotho on wool and sugar; Zambia on copper to a very high degree; Mozambique on cashews and seafood; Swaziland on sugar and wood pulp; and Malawi on tea and tobacco. Zimbabwe has a greater degree of diversification in its export profile, but even here tobacco, asbestos, and gold dominate export earnings.[8] For its part, even South Africa's exports remain dominated by gold and raw materials (e.g., wool, coal, and metal ores). By comparison regional imports remain concentrated upon fuels/energy (excluding Angola) and manufactured goods (varying from consumer goods to machinery, transport equipment, and capital goods).

Commodity concentration and dependence on imports for consumer and capital goods makes southern Africa highly sensitive to price changes in the global market. Table 2-A-5 presents approximate terms of trade trends for those countries where data is available.

With the possible exception of oil-exporting Angola, the terms of trade have decisively moved against these countries since the early 1970's, with South Africa suffering one of the sharpest falls. Nothing illustrates better the disaster befalling the region from its structural role in global commodity production during the current great depression. Recent global shortages in some minerals, specifically copper but not gold, may improve the situation for selected exporters.[9] In large part these trends reflect those for developing countries as a whole, where the 1980's ushered in an unremitting decline in export prices and terms of trade while terms of trade for core countries improved (World Bank, 1987: 176).[10]

Losses from declining terms of trade may be smaller than expected if measured in terms of percentage of GDP. Yet losses of foreign exchange—with their impact on import capacities—loom large. For any explanation of the region's economic decline, the decisive decline in terms of trade and the high dependence on primary product exports are surely critical. One can hardly thus either explain faltering economies, or place hopes for future expansion, on the capacity of southern Africa to expand exports from only its current group of export commodities. This assessment stands in stark contrast to recent World Bank conclusions for Sub-Saharan Africa, namely that export earnings and other external factors are insignificant factors in explaining economic decline.[11]

Table 2-A-5
Terms of Trade, 1967-1987
1980 = 100

	Angola	Bots-wana	Lesotho	Malawi	Mozam-bique	SACU	Zambia	Zim-babwe
1967		177	112	128		127	264	161
1970		180	137	126		122	314	178
1973		163	139	124		122	240	147
1975		116	100	118		115	101	111
1980	100	100	100	100	100	100	100	100
1981	110	98	97	94	90	95	80	
1982	106	98	96	93	84	86	71	
1983	99	98	96	95	85	83	78	95
1984	102	97	90	97	104	82	70	
1985		98	101	73		75	72	84
1986		105	91	76		71	71	78
1987		106	88	67		71	79	84
1988				72		73	107	83

Sources:
    1967–1987: Figures for Botswana, Lesotho, Malawi, South Africa, Zambia, and Zimbabwe from World Bank, 1989a; figures for Angola and Mozambique from World Bank, 1985, 1986.
    1988: Figures from World Bank, 1990a.

In summary, while the previous section had merely charted southern Africa's growing interdependence on world trade, this section has indicated that such interdependence worked seriously to the region's disadvantage.

Cycles and trends reconsidered

In an recent report SADCC noted that "since it was founded in 1980, SADCC has operated in an unfavorable world economic environment. This global economic environment has played a significant role in worsening the economic performance of the SADCC member countries" (SADCC, 1986a: 16). Examination of trading patterns serves to confirm and elaborate this statement. Locked into a role as primary product exporters, the countries of southern Africa have been severely affected by the transition from global expansion to depression. Weakening demand for primary commodities, falling terms of trade, and even growing protectionism in core countries have all served to constrict severely gains reaped from international trade. Subsequent foreign exchange shortages and reliance upon foreign loans have only further rebounded against the possibilities of enhanced economic growth. This holds true, as noted above, even for South Africa. Current world scenarios by such institutions as the International Monetary Fund and the World Bank, as instrumental as these agencies have been in solidifying southern Africa's role in the capitalist world-economy, do not proffer any significant reversal of present trends in the medium term.

If a radical transition to rapid expansion in core countries took place, and if this resulted in a growing demand and higher prices for the products of southern Africa, one might expect significantly higher levels of production and revenues across southern Africa—a development that would require the admittedly large assumption of low or absent levels of interstate and intrastate conflict across the region. This would not alter, however, the region's role in the global division of labor. And as many assessments have indicated, production of primary products is becoming less and less rewarding as highly competitive forms of manufacturing are being spun out of core areas towards semiperipheral and peripheral areas of the world-economy. In large part the growing gap in the current period between the region and core areas suggests that this process is already at work.

Such trends and assessments only render more important the prospects and possibilities of utilizing regional relationships in order to limit the debilitating effects of the region's current location within, and unfettered openness to, the global division of labor. As we have argued elsewhere, the South African state, spurred by a rising tide of class struggle and taking advantage of global conditions, embarked on this path during the interwar great depression. By the end of the Second World War the country had become a rising industrial power (Martin: 1990b, 1990c). Yet neither the global conditions nor single-state strategies of such a movement are applicable in the current conjuncture.[12] This in turn makes the consideration of regional cooperation ever more critical. It is to this dimension, with particular emphasis again on trading patterns and trade strategies, that we now turn.

Intraregional Trade Patterns

The region export and import reliance

None of the previous discussions indicate the degree to which trade flows take place *within* the region as opposed to with partners outside southern Africa. Over the course of the last ten years, approximately 4–6% of the region's global imports and exports have been traded within the region. Beneath such general figures, however, stand large and changing divergences between the countries of the region in the role that the regional market plays in meeting import requirements and an export market. In order to measure this, we have charted trends in the proportion of total world exports and imports that are captured within the region. Graphs 4 through 9 show this for each country where long-term and comparable data is available—Angola, Malawi, Mozambique, South Africa (SACU),[13] Zambia, and Zimbabwe.[14]

Regional Shares of Exports and Imports. We first ask: what have been long-term trends in the orientation of imports and exports across and within southern Africa? Here one needs to compare the six countries' data in Graphs 4 through 9 to each other.

Research on the period prior to the post–1945 boom suggests that exports directed towards the regional market rose through the First World War I, fell during the 1920's and early 1930's, and then rose sharply under the conditions of the Second World War.[15] In the post–1945 period intraregional export levels were sustained through the 1960's. It is clear from Graphs 4–9 that exports from southern African states to southern African states fell during the 1970's. In the 1980's this decline has either been halted or reversed, although at a lower level than obtained previously.

Trends in the reliance upon the region for imported goods follow analogous lines. Relatively strong percentages of regional imports were sustained for most countries through the 1950's and 1960's. As in the case of exports, however, the 1970's witnessed a

GRAPHS FOUR-NINE
Regional Percentage of Total Exports/Imports
(Note: Vertical Scales are Equal)

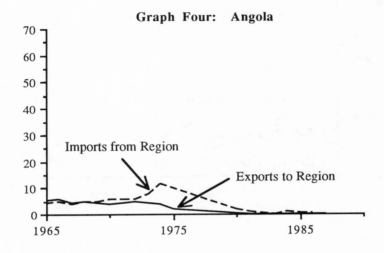

Graph Four: Angola

Imports from Region

Exports to Region

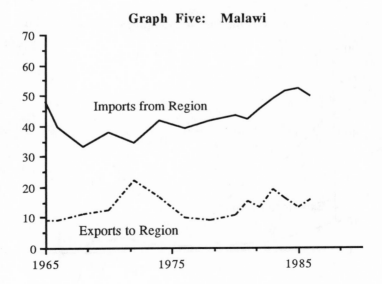

Graph Five: Malawi

Imports from Region

Exports to Region

Graph Six: Mozambique

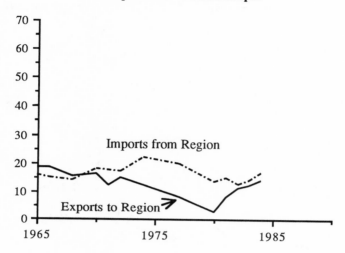

Graph Seven: Zambia

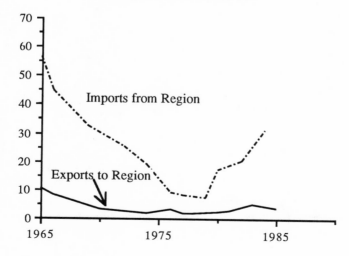

Graph Eight: Zimbabwe

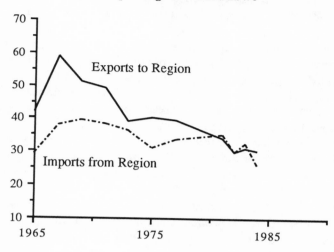

Graph Nine: South Africa

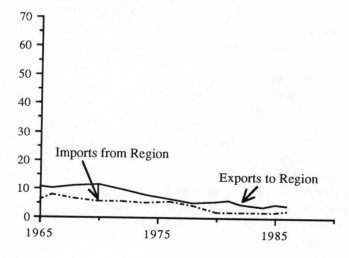

marked decline for most countries (Angola, South Africa, Mozambique, Zambia, Zimbabwe), a trend halted or reversed in the 1980's.

Summarizing the export/import picture, it would be accurate to state that regional trade linkages rose until the 1930's and 1940's, expanded in the post–1945 global boom, and then fell under the dual impacts of the struggle for national liberation and the vicissitudes of the outbreak of another great depression. While the ending of colonial wars assisted in contracting the downwards spiral of the 1970's, revival has been moderate at best as war and depression still operates across the region. Measuring the region strictly by trade flows would thus indicate that interdependence among the countries of southern Africa fell during the 1970's, a trend that has not been decisively reversed. Alternatively, the outward, extraregion orientation of production appears to have significantly accelerated in the 1970's, a pattern halted but not reversed in the present conjuncture.

A Closer Look: Individual Country Patterns in Regional Export and Import Shares. Within these broad trends the importance of the regional market has varied greatly among the countries of southern Africa as is shown in Graphs 4 through 9. Examining exports and SADCC countries first, at the low end currently stand Angola and Zambia: by the 1980's, Zambia (exporting almost exclusively copper and bearing the legacy of its rupture with the Zimbabwean market during UDI) and Angola (exporting primarily oil and with disrupted rail connections to the region) exported very little to the region (see Graphs 4 and 7).

At the other end of the export spectrum stand Zimbabwe and South Africa for very different reasons (see Graphs 8 and 9). Zimbabwe has consistently been far more reliant upon regional markets for both exports and imports than any other country in southern Africa, including South Africa. Indeed, on pure percentages of its total merchandise, world trade, South Africa ranks among the lowest of all states in regional trade orientation. The percentage of South Africa's total exports going to the region has, moreover, fallen significantly throughout the post–1970 period. What sets South Africa apart, however, is the large absolute volume of total

South African exports which dwarf the trade volumes of any other country. Even a small share of this trade thus looms large in its neighbors' eyes. This observation raises further questions as to the kind and direction of commodity exports from these countries.

Comparing each country's reliance on intraregional imports as opposed to intra-regional exports begins to provide part of the answer to these latter questions, as opposed to the previous presentation of export and import levels across countries. If one examines for example the relation between South Africa's import and export dependence on the region, its distinctiveness emerges quite sharply: its regional percentage of imports has consistently been below that of its export share to the region, particularly in the post–1945 period. By comparison to South Africa, Zambia and Malawi in the postwar period reveal a much higher reliance upon regional partners for imports than for exports. Mozambique had maintained historically a more balanced trade with the region until the 1970's.

As already suggested above, Zimbabwe presents a curious case. Its trade figures show high percentages of both exports and imports being directed towards the region. During the 1970's only South Africa (leaving aside Angola's low and falling trade with the region) has maintained a higher export share to the region than its import share. Zimbabwe and South Africa would thus appear, for very different reasons, to figure prominently in regional trade patterns.

Nodal points of regional trade: South African and Zimbabwean nodes

These latter points suggest that countries of southern Africa diverge into groups of regional exporters and regional importers. According to the usual assertions, South Africa should appear as the central pivot for regional commodity flows. In order to examine this concretely, we have charted for each country the percentage of total regional exports and imports going to the region and to South Africa. Separate graphs for both imports and exports are presented by country in Graphs 10–19. This allows us to determine the proportion of regional trade captured by South Africa.

As the graphs indicate, South Africa has indeed historically emerged as the central pole for regional trade, orienting over the

ANGOLA

Graph Ten: Import Trade

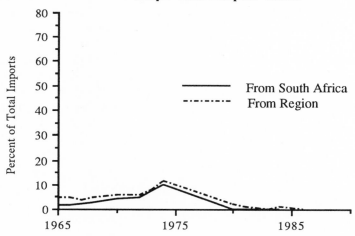

Graph Eleven: Export Trade

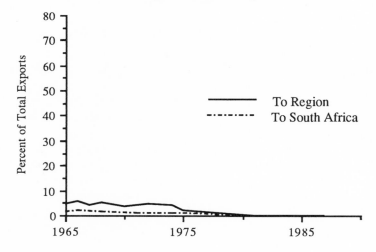

MALAWI

Graph Twelve: Import Trade

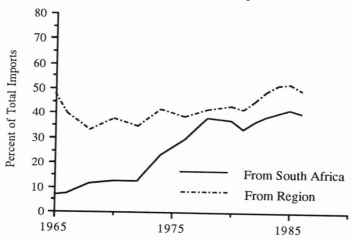

Graph Thirteen: Export Trade

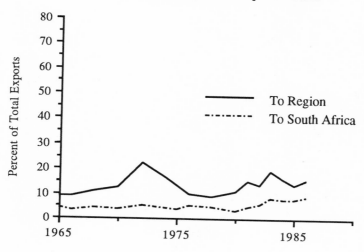

MOZAMBIQUE

Graph Fourteen: Import Trade

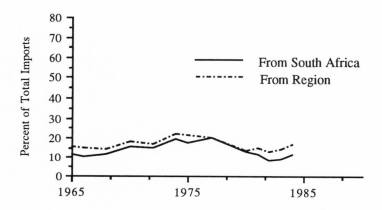

Graph Fifteen: Import Trade

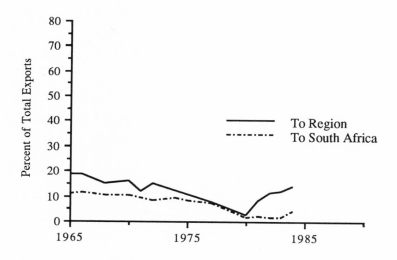

ZAMBIA

Graph Sixteen: Import trade

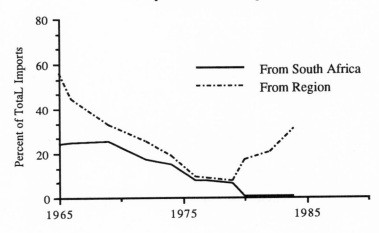

Graph Seventeen: Export Trade

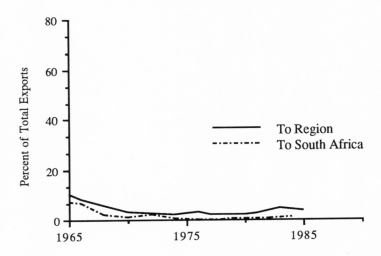

ZIMBABWE

Graph Eighteen: Import Trade

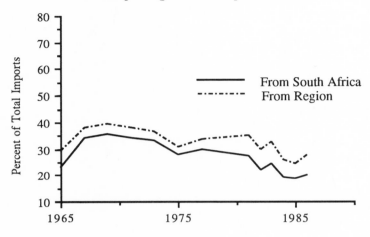

Graph Nineteen: Export Trade

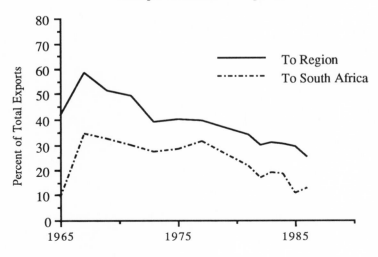

decades surrounding countries towards her more advanced industrial production processes. Over the course of this century South Africa has primarily imported primary products from surrounding territories, although for a few select Zimbabwean industries South Africa emerged and remains an important outlet. The actual commodity composition of South Africa's exports to the region have however changed over time, reflecting changes in the country's and the region's industrial base. While in the interwar period such goods as processed foodstuffs, textiles, and clothing were significant South African exports, by the present one finds more advanced consumer and capital goods. Seen from the South African side of the region, total trade engagement remains low, as indicated in previous sections.

For select industries however, the region remains a critical export market. As Table 6 indicates, the region has formed the only assured and successful market for many industrial goods; approximately 10% of South African exports were of manufacturing origin by the late 1980's.[16] This is particularly the case for many of the more capital intensive and technologically-advanced sectors (e.g., machinery, chemicals, vehicles, etc.) One must note, however, that the regional market for South African manufactured goods has apparently fallen from the early 1970's through the mid–1980's. This would be consistent with the finding above of a decline in regional cohesion as measured by trade flows over this period.

In this respect it is significant to note that Graphs 10–19 also show that South Africa's domination of regional trade has been neither unchanging nor uncontested. One might first note the hidden history of competition between producers based in Zimbabwe and South Africa over the market to Zimbabwe's north. During the interwar period and again in the post–1945 period up through UDI in 1965, Zimbabwe exported both to the region to a considerable degree *and* to countries other than South Africa. This sets Zimbabwe apart from other countries in the region, whose exports to the region have largely been low and to South Africa. Here one begins to perceive the historical struggle of settlers and capital in Zimbabwe to capture markets to its north, primarily Malawi and especially Zambia. Zambia in particular represents the

Table 2-A-6
South African Exports to Africa as a Percentage of Total Exports*

Brussels Section Description	1973	1977	1980	1981	1982	1984	World Exports Each Section 1984 (Rand)
01 Live animals, animal products	9.6	13.9	30.5	20.5	19.1	12.9	242,181,345
02 Vegetable products	12.5	7.5	31.2	16.1	8.7	10.2	635,320,019
03 Animal & vegetable fats, oils & by-products	7.3	9.8	3.0	27.3	35.4	37.6	39,661,646
04 Prepared foodstuffs, beverages, spirits, tobacco	6.1	5.3	4.9	7.4	6.4	7.9	556,009,264
05 Mineral products	2.8	2.9	6.9	4.2	1.6	1.3	3,037,858,486
06 Chemical & allied industrial products	55.6	35.4	32.2	41.2	36.0	33.3	672,557,296
07 Artificial resins, plastic products, rubber, etc.	91.1	85.6	58.1	64.8	53.5	45.1	96,118,076
08 Raw hides & skins, associated products	1.1	1.9	0.8	1.5	2.5	0.8	193,180,497
09 Wood, wood products, & wooden articles	38.0	23.2	17.3	25.2	18.9	13.4	60,232,583
10 Paper-making material	17.0	13.7	19.0	16.3	11.9	6.6	383,656,685
11 Textile & textile articles	5.6	6.3	9.0	8.0	8.6	4.7	766,168,108
12 Footwear, headware, etc.	73.8	30.4	20.7	32.7	41.9	40.8	7,395,358
13 Articles of stone, glass, etc.	76.3	63.4	42.1	50.3	44.1	44.0	44,443,686
14 Precious stones & metals	0.1	0.1	0.1	0.1	0.0	0.0	2,386,911,541
15 Base materials & articles	18.4	8.1	9.5	9.1	9.4	6.1	2,419,030,044
16 Machinery & equipment, etc.	73.4	49.7	63.6	60.3	51.4	40.7	309,849,804
17 Vehicles, aircraft, etc.	78.0	52.1	65.9	44.1	25.9	24.3	169,228,116
18 Instruments & apparatus, etc.	40.6	31.3	41.3	47.1	24.8	21.8	41,204,930
19 Misc. manufactured articles	55.1	42.9	13.8	15.9	19.2	17.7	18,298,208
20 Works of art, antiques, etc.	55.2	1.1	0.6	0.7	0.6	1.0	17,371,684
21 Other unclassified goods	5.1	1.5	0.1	0.1	0.1	0.6	13,487,825,928

*Figures are for SACU, i.e., include Botswana, Lesotho, Swaziland, South Africa, Namibia as one reporting territory.

Sources: South Africa, Commissioner for Customs and Excise. 1973 et seq. Figures by SITC sections would be preferable (especially for manufactures, SITC sections 5-8, less 67 & 68), but are unavailable for this purpose.

key case, and the extent of this trend is charted in Graphs 20 and 21, which show the proportion of Zambia's trade with Zimbabwe and South Africa. When political conditions permitted, Zimbabwe became a strong competitor with South Africa as an exporter to Zambia.

Graph Twenty
Zambian Imports: Regional Partners

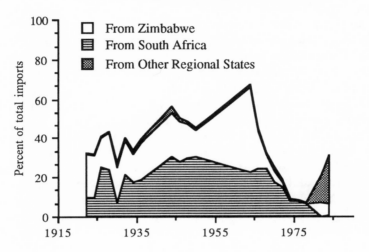

□ From Zimbabwe
☰ From South Africa
▨ From Other Regional States

Graph Twenty-One
Zambian Exports: Regional Partners

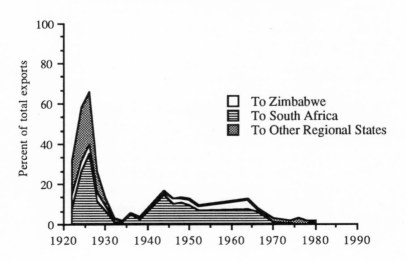

□ To Zimbabwe
☰ To South Africa
▨ To Other Regional States

Against this contest for northern markets, however, it neverthe-less remains the case that South Africa's far more advanced indus-trial sector has historically meant a tendency to rely upon South Africa as a regional supplier. Yet again, this has not been a un-changing relationship. The sharpest dependencies upon South Africa are indicated by both high levels of imports from South Africa and the disparity between the share of exports a country sends to South Africa and the level of imports it receives from South Africa. Here one needs to compare directly export and import shares with South Africa. This is presented in Table 7, which shows post–1945 percentage of each country's exports going to South Africa and the percentage of each country's imports derived from South Africa. Up to the early 1970's almost all territories exhibit strong disparities between imports drawn from South Africa and exports send to the South African market. As noted in our opening section, however, the subsequent fall in this relationship relates more to a fall in intraregional trade overall rather than to increasing non-South African, regional trade in the current conjuncture.

Taken together these data suggest that by the Second World War South Africa had become a center for the provisioning of the region but not an export market. This pattern continued to hold until the 1970's, when the weight of successive political defeats and the global depression put severe strains on the South African-centered trading network.

Regional Trade Strategies and Prospects

It is apparent from the above discussion that any changes in the intraregional and global pattern of southern Africa's trade can only take place over relatively long periods of time. In the postwar period we have witnessed at least one major transformation: the transition from a period of enhanced South African trade domina-tion to a significant fall in intra-regional trade during the current period of world-economic crisis. The latter has meant, however, neither a decline in dependence upon core areas nor increasing inter-industry linkages within and across the majority-ruled states

Table 2-A-7
South Africa Percentage of Regional States' Merchandise Exports (EXP) and Imports (IMP)

	Angola		Malawi		Mozam-bique		Zambia		Zimbabwe		Federation	
	Exp	Imp	Exp	Imp	Exp	Imp	Exp	Imp	Exp	Imp	Exp	Imp
1948	1.4	0.6			9.9	11.7	11.0	29.9	5.4	27.1		
1950	3.2	0.9			6.0	8.2	9.4	30.3	11.7	30.2		
1952	0.8	1.0			5.4	7.0	6.8		15.0	29.9		
1954	1.5	1.3			13.4	11.3					11.2	38.2
1956	1.2	0.9			5.5	9.2					10.4	37.3
1958	1.5	0.9			10.6	13.3					10.3	34.7
1960	0.5	1.5			2.5	12.1					8.2	
1962	0.6	1.6			8.9	12.4					8.2	33.1
1964	0.6	2.1	5.2	6.7	10.7	12.8	7.9	23.0	7.3	27.1		
1966	1.9	1.6	3.4	7.2	11.2	10.5	6.6	24.6				
1967									34.3			34.2
1968	1.8	2.5	4.3	11.1	10.4	11.8	2.2	24.9				
1969									32.4			35.5
1970	1.2	4.0	3.5	12.6	10.3	15.3	1.2	17.3				
1972	1.2	4.6	5.4	12.6	8.1	14.7	2.0	14.9				
1973									27.1			33.3
1974	1.0	9.9		23.2	9.3	19.6	0.4	7.6				
1975			3.7		8.1	17.5						
1976			5.0	29.5			0.2	7.6				
1977					7.0	19.8			32.5	29.7		
1978			4.4	38.2			0.1	6.6				
1979							0.4	10.8				
1980	0	0	3.1	37.3	1.5	12.9	0.6	15.6				
1981	0	0	4.9	33.3	2.1	11.6			21.4	24.7		
1982	0	0	5.8	36.4	1.3	8.4	0.3	14.5	17.7	23.2		
1983	0	0	8.0	38.5	1.8	9.1			18.5	24.2		
1984	0	0	7.5	40.4	4.3	11.9	0.8	22.8	18.3	19.3		
1985	0		7.7	41.8					10.8	18.9		
1986	0		8.6	40.0					13.0	20.0		

Sources: See note 14.

of southern Africa.

If trade networks reveal the enduring if faltering strengths of regional center-hinterland relationships, and demarcate even more clearly the region's subordinate position in the global division of labor, it remains uncertain whether and to what extent political forces can, by diverting trade flows, attack the continuing chains of uneven development. The history of the South African Customs

Union; the political struggles between Northern and Southern Rhodesia and South Africa in the interwar period; the politics of and benefits accruing to the different partners to Federation; and the shared defense of settler and colonial rule in the 1960's and early 1970's—all these indicate too well that strong shifts in the level and orientation of intraregional trade have only developed through such interventions. In the absence of politically-imposed regulations on trade, intraregional trade has and most likely will remain low as countries freely feel the effects of the global division of labor.

Conjunctural factors

Any analysis of the current potential for regional restructuring must begin by noting that present trade relationships have been cast in a minor key in relation to more major conjunctural problems and long-term determinants of regionality. Among the former stand the overwhelming effects of ten years of destabilization. Reviving and maintaining trade channels and levels of even the near past has properly consumed the attention of all the Front Line states. Even the South African state, facing international sanctions, has had to focus its attention upon retaining access to the global market. In this atmosphere there has been little room for innovative attempts to refashion trade relationships.

Compounding the effects of war has been the international environment. Here the effects of the current world depression are critical. Declining terms of trade and growing obstacles to penetration of core markets have made returns from export trade less and less capable of sustaining basic investment and foreign exchange requirements. These structural obstacles have turned attention towards securing needed funds from overseas areas. Yet by comparison to the heady days of the post–1945 period (or even the expansion of the early 1980's), investment and loan funds have proven increasingly difficult to solicit—and this even given the most favorable state investment codes, acceptance of structural adjustment conditions, or pro-Western diplomatic stances. Rising levels of foreign aid for a few select countries (see Table 8) have largely, moreover, been used to stave off the costs of long-term decline coupled with the ravages of destabilization. Aid has moreover generally been tied to the design, staffing, and import sourcing from donor countries (although no comprehensive study of this is known).[17] Contraction of significant debt burdens in the 1980's in order to ease the immediate effects of economic crisis and war, as international interest rates were rising, has resulted moreover in significant debt repayments (see chapter 2c). Given the lack of private investment flows, southern Africa states will in the short-term remain highly dependent upon loans and aid. Even these sources, which have served to reinforce the longer-term trend of orientation upon overseas areas, may dry up as Western aid, loans, and investment funds are oriented away from Africa and towards Eastern Europe, the Soviet Union, and the Pacific Basin.[18]

Programs of regional integration
Against these conjunctural and long-term constraints it is hardly be surprising that new life has been infused into the search for forms of regional cooperation, particularly in relation to the attempt to counter ongoing deindustrialization. Regional collaboration may of course take many forms, from the common management of lakes and rivers to full-fledged economic unions allowing the free flow of labor, commodities and capital with a common currency. Common wisdom now rejects any attempt to replicate the failed attempts of early post-independence regional organizations, which largely sought to create larger common markets. Lacking any formulation by which political forces could counteract uneven development, such regional organizations collapsed when one or another partner began to emerge as the dominant and most rewarded member.

Indeed it is precisely to avoid such developments that SADCC from its inception explicitly shunted trade issues aside. SADCC has not moved towards any common trade policies such as the elimination of tariffs and quotas on intra-SADCC trade, much less the creation of a common external tariff, a common foreign investment code, or a shared stance towards foreign debt. In light of these realities intra-SADCC trade levels and inter-industry linkages remain low.[19]

Attention has been focused instead upon immediate reconstruc-

Table 2-A-8
Net Disbursement of Overseas Development Assistance from All Sources 1977–87
(current million U.S. $)

	Angola	Botswana	Lesotho	Malawi	Mozam-bique	Swaziland	Zambia	Zimbabwe	Total
1977	48	48	39	79	80	29	109	7	410
1978	48	69	50	99	105	45	185	9	610
1979	47	100	64	142	146	50	277	13	839
1980	53	106	91	143	169	50	295	164	1071
1981	61	97	104	138	144	37	232	212	1025
1982	60	102	93	121	208	28	317	216	1145
1983	75	104	108	117	211	34	217	209	1075
1984	95	103	101	159	259	30	240	298	1285
1985	92	97	94	113	300	25	329	237	128
1986	131	102	88	198	421	35	465	225	2665
1987	135	154	108	280	649	45	429	295	2095

Sources: OECD: 1984, 1989.

tion of transport and communication links, the primacy of individual development projects, and collective bargaining for overseas funds. The logic adopted by SADCC has accordingly stressed the facilitation, by a very small administrative staff, of national projects and an united stance towards overseas funders. Programmatically this strategy is justified by the priority due to real and immediate achievements in the field of production. Trade policy and correlated financial arrangements are thus subordinated to, and to follow upon, cooperation in the productive field. In SADCC's own words:

> Regional trade and the development of financial institutions are seen to be important. However, they are perceived to be consequential on prior transport and production coordination and as a means to facilitate such coordination, not as *a priori* requirements or ends in themselves (1983: 19).

This analysis was confirmed by a 1986 study conducted for SADCC on intraregional trade, which concluded that SADCC should eschew any attempt to move beyond the simplest bilateral trading arrangements; emphasis should rather continue to be placed upon reviving production capabilities of SADCC member states. Lacking an industrial base, it was argued, precluded any immediate effort by SADCC states to replace imports from either South Africa or overseas core areas (SADCC, 1986b: xvi).

Such conclusions reflect SADCC's rejection of any attempt to construct a regional association along the lines of failed attempts in the region (e.g., the Federation of Rhodesia and Nyasaland), elsewhere on the continent (e.g., the East African Community), and elsewhere (e.g., various Latin American schemes). A decade of SADCC endeavors, however, indicates that hardly any cooperation has emerged in the planning of industrial capacity on a regional basis. Thus while considerable assistance has been achieved in infrastructural developments (which facilitate flows out of and into the region as much as within it), the initiation of new sites of industrial or energy production have almost always operated on a national basis. The result is multiple national capacities and little if any gains from an enhanced regional market.[20]

Such developments have turned attention once again to larger regional structures and the causes of failure in the region in the past. As noted above, almost all early regional associations' initial step was the facilitation of a free trade zone or customs union, which inexorably led towards growing inequalities between more advanced and peripheral areas within the regional association. Why this should be the outcome remains a subject of debate. For some critics such outcomes reflect the inapplicability of regionalism in the current ordering of the world-economy. Indeed regionalism in this view operates as a direct strategy of domination by core states and multinational capital.[21]

Even if one is not prepared to move towards such conclusions, many argue that SADCC has been captured by the West, or, in the words of Ibbo Mandaza,

> There has been little disengagement from South Africa and hardly any evidence of increased economic cooperation among the member states. . . . Dependence on foreign aid has been almost total in its operations: SADCC has tended to reinforce rather than challenge the historical relations of dependence, exploitation and domination (1987: 221–22).[22]

Many who espouse such views have nevertheless asserted that more, not less, regional cooperation is now necessary; that SADCC needs to transform limited political collaboration into a full-fledged regional economic alliance which would require a much stronger institutional base.

It is here perhaps, outside official SADCC circles, that the issue of trade reemerges in a most intriguing manner. For many the counter-example to SADCC programs and strategies has been the Preferential Trade Area (PTA) that aims to develop an economic community for eastern and southern Africa (see for example the essays by Wagao, Ng'andwe, and Mandaza in Amin et al., 1987). Unlike SADCC, the PTA has created extensive protocols and institutions (including financial and clearing house arrangements) to facilitate regional trading relationships. Its attempt, moreover, to restrict gains from lower regional tariffs to products produced by

PTA nationals (versus foreign-owned firms) has led many to applaud the PTA as "more openly nationalist, and therefore more anti-imperialist, in its aspiration than the SADCC" (Yash Tandon, as cited by Mandaza, 1987: 218).

There can indeed be little doubt that the PTA has attempted to address the bitter lessons of early post-independence regional schemes. In this respect, the PTA's efforts have matched and carried forward SADCC's expressed aim of countering polarizing forces emanating from without the region and from within. Its institutional base, discussion of regulating gains from higher levels of regional trade, and attention to the limited obstacle that free trade zones pose in a world marked by the transnational flow of capital, sets the PTA apart from SADCC's much more modest structures. Defusing the PTA vs. SADCC debate, however, is the movement towards full membership in the PTA by all SADCC members.

Assuming full participation within PTA structures, it is not difficult to envision SADCC as a sub-PTA region. What remains to be seen and assessed, however, is the degree and character of political will exercised to ensure a coherent program that seeks to both advance southern Africa's role in the world-economy and the equitable distribution of gains that accrue from such a position. One cannot assume that a regional market or the formal institutions of a regional association will necessarily lead to stronger regional alliances, the establishment of core-like production processes, or a balanced distribution of the rewards reaped from the regionalization of industrial production. The PTA has yet to move beyond the stage of discussion towards constructing compensatory mechanisms for those who suffer from trade liberalization or the concentration of industry in one or more member states. It is quite evident, for example, that given current PTA structures states such as Kenya and Zimbabwe will overwhelmingly benefit from trade liberalization. The addition of a majority-ruled South Africa to such an organization only serves to highlight such processes of uneven development.

State, class and the region after majority-rule in South Africa
To even pose the question of southern Africa after majority-rule in

South Africa indicates the highly political determinants of regional cooperation. No study to our knowledge substantively examines southern Africa economic relationships with a majority-ruled South Africa (see chapter six for an exploration of this issue). To date views have fluctuated between two poles: one, an assertion that a majority-ruled South Africa would dominate the region (and even perhaps be excluded from SADCC), and two, a rather unquestioning assertion that majority rule in South Africa will automatically unleash economic liberation across southern Africa if not across the continent.[23]

To move from such speculations to a more rigorous analysis of future regional prospects requires far more than simply calculating the macroeconomic gains from the end of war and the prospects of enlarged regional markets and institutions—even if one assumes, as we would, that South Africa will be a member of SADCC. Nor is it adequate, as is commonly the case, to pin the future solely upon the degree to which regional states ally and oppose overseas imperialism; to do so avoids confronting dominant class forces within the region, as well as the entrenched political and accumulation networks that sustain them. As the arguments of previous sections indicate, any regional agenda must address both the set of economic and political relationships that bind southern Africa together as a (declining) region within the capitalist world, and the cross-cutting local political and class forces that might forge regional unity as counterweight to this process—and be more successful than such attempts elsewhere on the continent.

For some it is precisely Africa's lack of a strong capitalist class that has inhibited economic growth and industrialization across the continent, and thus allowed the state (and the petit-bourgeoisie allied to it) a leading role. Thandika Mkandawire concludes, for example, that African industrialization "was strictly speaking not a class project. It was essentially a nationalist programme and as such it lacked the sharpness and purposefulness of a class-determined project" (Mkandawire, 1988: 18). The contemporary situation is thus marked by eroded state legitimacy and capacity, local capital without the means to foster industrialization, and international capital without any incentive to invest to any significant degree. The result is stagnation, deindustrialization, and a future which "will once again leave Africa unprepared to capture whatever new opportunities an upturn in the world-economy may have" (Mkandawire, 1988: 31). Indeed, in a world-economy where other semiperipheral areas are industrializing in order to only maintain their position in the changing global division of labor, Africa's future appears bleak.

Such conclusions cannot be straightforwardly applied to southern Africa. South Africa, Zimbabwe, and to a lesser extent perhaps Botswana and Zambia, all possess significant industrial sectors with defined class actors. Transnational capital, including most notably South African private and public firms, is moreover active and still interested in a region marked by significant resources, a strong infrastructural base, and a proven ability to generate investment returns given political stability. Presuming a transition to global expansion (including further relocation of industry outside core areas) and the absence of war (again, admittedly large assumptions), southern Africa may well be placed in a considerably different situation than the rest of the continent.

The question at this juncture becomes whether and to what extent political forces can shape accumulation patterns. If it is clear that no single SADCC state can expect to foster industrialization on its own, and South Africa's prospects without a regional market are significantly diminished, can one foresee a set of political forces that would utilize regional associations for more autonomous, self-reliant, and equitable advance? This topic requires a broader analysis than of simply trade patterns, and is tackled in more concrete and detailed terms in chapter 6. Consideration of trade flows alone illustrates, however, both the possibilities of regional cooperation and the array of forces poised for and against substantive regional cooperation.

One may begin by repeating that there is no reason to presume that a regional association in and of itself is a class-based project or either pro- or anti-imperialist. A free and open trade (and investment, labor, etc.) economic arena can quite obviously benefit multinational capital, while arrangements such as article 15 of the PTA treaty immediately provoke resistance from the same sources (and often by default states whose industry is based on foreign capital). It is for such reasons that core states and the World Bank do not necessarily stand against trade liberalization on a regional basis; indeed the most recent World Bank report calls for strengthening regional associations. The limits of such initiatives are however clear: to facilitate trade liberalization, the operation of "free markets" and competitiveness, and thus an enhanced openness to international forces and a diminished capacity for local political control by even the most democratic of states (World Bank, 1989b: 148–62).

If movement beyond either trade liberalization (or SADCC-type consultation) does occur, one may thus expect considerable opposition from international capital and international financial agencies. Nor would local forces be absent from this opposition front. What if one posits, for example, the privileging of regional manufactures by regional tariff agreements, matched to compensatory mechanisms for non-industrial states? The reaction of regionally-based capital to such measures would most likely diverge along the axes of orientation towards core areas of the world-economy. Those engaged in producing primary products for the export market will naturally feel driven to resist any agreement which places in jeopardy access to overseas markets and at the same time raises internal costs due to the initial effects of infant industry protection. Such a grouping may include for example mining capital, and cotton, coffee, tea—but not maize—farmers.

If one turns to regionally-based industrial capital, direct class interests are less evident. The essential point to grasp here is that accelerated accumulation and industrial growth would build upon and exacerbate existing center-hinterland relationships. South African firms would derive considerable advantages, to the detriment of other regional, especially Zimbabwean, firms. The pattern of past South African investment in the region, concentrated as it is in extractive production and commerce, only lends further emphasis to this observation. One need not elaborate to perceive that even if one holds international forces constant (or at bay), fissiparous tendencies among local dominant classes push toward the protection of national markets and thus diminish the prospects for regional development at the expense of overseas core areas. This would effectively in our view close the door to enhanced levels of industrialization and wealth within the region.

In light of this one returns yet once again to the political terrain: what class and political forces might forge the boundaries of a more cooperative, and possibly antisystemic, regional project?

The prospects here are at first sight little better. It is not difficult to discern local states (and the petit-bourgeoisie integrated by and within them) protecting national and state revenues. This has of course been the predominant tendency across Africa and the periphery, as the comments of Mkandawire suggest. It is equally feasible to expect local states to align—where the possibility exists—with local capitalist classes in the protection of shared national benefits. The limitations of SADCC to date reflect both these tendencies.

Future prospects must however include the decisive shift posed by the emergence of a progressive majority-ruled South African government. This will dramatically shift the political balance within any future regional negotiations or association, opening up the possibility of a regional alliance that taps widespread anti-imperialist and democratic tendencies. The force of conservative ideological and class forces tied to East-West conflicts or the apartheid state, for example, will hardly obtain. To this one may add the weight of popular, antisystemic revolts pitted against the accelerating costs of debt and stabilization programs. Even further shaping an antisystemic agenda will be the demands for democracy and socialist development flowing forth from South Africa's mobilized working class. Under the pressure of hostile core powers and multilateral institutions, there is a strong basis for a continuing struggle by the majority of the people and movements of the region against underdevelopment—including its local expressions, agents, and allies.

Even if this constellation of actual and potential forces distinguishes southern Africa on the continent, one may question why it should coalesce on a regional, versus national, basis. As chapter six will argue, one possible future path lies along the road of the breakup of the region and the intensification of more typical

North-South, core-peripheral linkages. Building upon incipient trends laid forth above, this might be most rapidly and dramatically achieved in the arena of trade relationships. Even in South Africa considerable debate is taking place within leading economic and political circles over whether South Africa's future lies with southern Africa versus engaging in a more specialized relationship with core areas.

Counterposed to such tendencies are the legacy and constraints of colonialism and apartheid. Here the distinctive faces of unequal exchange as they have developed in southern Africa are critical. On the one hand the defense of colonial and settler rule—unlike in the rest of Africa—have entrenched over past decades strong center-hinterland relationships across southern Africa, binding the daily existence and fate of the peoples of southern Africa together. On the other hand the struggles for independence, democracy, and prosperity have necessarily been cooperative ones—as so well illustrated in the wars for national liberation, majority rule, and even SADCC. As we move into the political and ideological uncertainties of the 1990's, these central features remain. Neither the deep structures of regional accumulation constructed during the apartheid period, nor the associated and shared fate of the peoples of southern Africa, are easily overturned.

The possibility of a more cooperative regional project thus exists. To be successful it would have to move well beyond coalescing state elites and constructing regional institutions. Indeed the technical details on the construction of regional institutions and the necessity of compensatory mechanisms among industrial and non-industrial producers and states are evident. The obstacles are clearly class and political ones: can a regional agenda and coalition—versus *both* regional and especially global forces—be fashioned and propelled by the class and political forces necessary for such a project? Or is the future of southern Africa to be limited to survival of individual states in an increasingly hostile capitalist world? The winds of change may have now blown across all of the political landscape of southern Africa. The question remains: can the landscape itself be altered by those who populate it?

Notes

1. A notable exception is SADCC (1986a). On SADCC trade arrangements and trends, which we will not cover here, see SADCC (1986b). This last study does not however analyse SADCC trade in relation to global trading patterns.

2. The methodology of this measure is elaborated in Arrighi & Drangel (1986). An extension of the argument, with particular emphasis on long-term trends and the periphery in the current conjuncture, is contained in Arrighi, Korzeniewicz & Martin (1985). Such a procedure will obviously *not* tell us anything of the distribution of wealth and income within any particular zone or state, or the modes by which the global division of labor systematically privileges agents in core areas and underdevelops peripheral areas. It shows us only outcomes of the processes through which the global division of labor operates. Hence the importance of companion studies on the various modes of interdependence (trade, investment, labor) and the political struggles which serve to shape and direct the possibilities of regional under/development. The level of inequality under apartheid gave South Africa one of the worst records in the world. Measured by the Gini coefficient, the level may be comparable to Brazil and Mexico (ca. 1970); measured by the share of the poorest 40%, South Africa stands alone. See for example Knight (1988).

3. As noted at the end of Table 2-A-3, we consider for these purposes southern Africa to be composed of Angola, Botswana, Lesotho, Malawi, Mozambique, South Africa, Swaziland, Zambia, Zimbabwe, and Namibia; unfortunately long-term statistics for Namibia are as yet unavailable for these and subsequent calculations. As noted the United Kingdom, France, F.R. Germany, and the United States are considered emblematic of core areas. For each of the groups (region and core), total GNP was divided by total population, with core figures then considered to be equal to 100. For 1950–1966 all GNP and population data are from the World Bank (1984), and for 1967–87 from World Bank (1989a). Exchange rates for the 1955–1966 period, in order to convert GNP in national currencies into GNP in U.S. dollars, are also from World Bank (1984). Additional estimates for Angola and Mozambique for the period 1977–87 are derived from OECD (1984, 1989). One must note that estimates for Angola and Mozambique (particularly for the period 1975-present) as reported by both international

agencies (OECD, IMF, World Bank) and national sources diverge quite significantly; these cases should be treated with great caution.

4. It should be noted that the size of South Africa's GNP and population obviously means that any regional GNP per capita calculation—obtained by summing all countries' GNP and dividing by all countries' population, and using generally the "World Atlas" three year moving average for exchange rate conversions into U.S. dollars, is sharply defined by trends for South Africa. Hence the importance of showing the region with and without South Africa, and examining the other countries' trajectories.

5. Sources and definitions as noted at the bottom of Table 2-A-3. Regional GDP calculations the GDP of the nine countries has been summed; export and imports calculations presume SACU figures cover Botswana, Lesotho, and Swaziland (BLS), no separate long-term accounting available in this latter case; see SADCC (1986b) for an indication of BLS trade patterns in the most recent period.

6. Figures for this period for Angola and Mozambique are suspect. The effects of destabilization in curtailing GDP and especially exports in Mozambique would however indicate a downward trend; for Angola sustained oil exports and a declining GDP support a rising ratio.

7. This is a somewhat unexpected trend. On the basis of early 1980's data, SADCC (1986a: 40) had concluded that both export and import ratios were on a downward trend, indicating less integration and dependence upon overseas areas.

8. One must be careful here in interpreting trade figure aggregates. Statistics for Zimbabwe in recent years, for example, pinpoint the manufacturing sector as contributing the highest proportion of exports (40% in 1980 and 41% in 1984). Yet as Zimbabwean officials stress, "it must be noted that a substantial proportion of manufacturing exports are processed products originating from agriculture, for example meat, cotton lint, refined sugar, tobacco manufactures, dairy products, and grain milling products" (Zimbabwe, 1986a: 41). While indicating the possibilities of inter-sectoral linkages and export performance, these types of exports are of a decidedly lower-stage than those of South Africa (steel, heavy chemicals, etc.)—not to mention the "newly-industrializing countries" of Latin America and the Pacific Basin. South Africa's inability to make the transition to becoming a manufacturing exporter to core markets worries

policymakers as well. See for example van Zyl (1984); at the time the article was published van Zyl was Executive Director of the South African Federated Chamber of Industries.

9. As the *Economist* (7/2/1988: 55–56) notes, overall the future for the sub-group of industrial raw materials, including minerals, exported by peripheral areas remains bleak. Of gold, one may note the recent statement by the South African banking house, Volkskas: "the entire world scenario is . . . unfavorable for a significantly higher price" (Volkskas, 1988: 3). The Economist Intelligence Unit in its *Gold to 1992* (1989c: 137) assumes a price range in the next five years of between $300-$500, roughly the same as during the 1980's. As for the strategic material question, particularly in the light of sanctions, it would appear that non-African—versus say SADCC—sources are being aggressively developed. See for example the *Wall Street Journal* (9/6/1988: 42).

10. Terms of trade for developing countries as a group were barely positive from 1965 to 1980 and then turned markedly downward. For Sub-Saharan Africa terms of trade were negative between 1965 and 1973, rose between 1973 and 1980 and then turned markedly negative.

11. Thus for example: "Falling per capita incomes for Africa as a whole since the late 1970s are explained largely by the declining level and efficiency of investment, compounded by accelerating population growth—and not primarily by external factors" (World Bank, 1989b: 3); against one must note a later argument, namely that "If Sub-Saharan countries had maintained their 1970 market share of non-oil primary exports from developing countries and prices had remained the same, their export earnings would have been $9 billion to $10 billion a year higher in 1986–87. The difference is approximately equal to the region's total debt service payments in this period" (pp.19–20). One hardly knows what to make of the assumption of stable world prices and a vastly expanded flow from Africa.

12. This is too long a subject to purse here. It might be noted briefly that the transition after the Second World War to direct investment as a mode of organizing the global division of labor under U.S. hegemony removed the possibility of altering trade regimes such as those pursued by South Africa in the interwar period. See also Martin (1990b).

13. As part of the South African Customs Union, the exports and imports of Botswana, Lesotho and Swaziland are included with South

African figures, precluding any separate, long-term time series for these countries. For more recent years, however, separate figures for Botswana, Lesotho, and Swaziland are available; on these see SADCC (1986b).

14. In order to retain as consistent a coverage as possible the same source was used as far as possible. For the period, 1948 to the present, base statistics were drawn from the International Monetary Fund (computer tape and 1984, 1986, 1989a printed versions). For Zimbabwe during the UDI period the recently released Zimbabwe Rhodesia (1979) study was used. For several countries over the last five years some supplemental estimates drawn from national statistical sources, SADCC, and the Economist Intelligence Unit.

Data relating to the last five years is less consistent and comprehensive. Undoubtedly appreciable irregularities remain, particularly for the interior countries of the region; reexports and clandestine trade are probably running at appreciable levels. No known estimates of such flows exist. Finally, since 1965 South Africa has refused to divulge a trade breakdown with African countries, while the standard DOT strategy of utilizing reports from trading partners fails to work in this instance. We have thus resorted to using South African reports for "Africa" as if all trade with Africa was trade with the region,which may be presumed to be valid only up to a point. If such a procedure were used for the years prior to 1965, it would yield results corresponding to known levels and trends in regional trade (i.e., trade with the rest of Africa was negligible by comparison to southern Africa). While one cannot presume that pre–1965 patterns extend twenty years forward, we know of no alternative to this admittedly undesirable assumption. As part of the attempt to break sanctions, South Africa has reported only the most cursory trade aggregates since 1987.

15. The following statements on pre–1945 trends rest on Martin (1990a, 1990b); the author's contribution (including comparable, time series data) to the forthcoming and accompanying study of historical, regional flows from 1870–1975; see also Phimister (1988: esp.239–57); and Kanduza (1986).

16. As reported by Ted Adlard, Chairman of the Federated Chamber of Industries Technology Development Committee (_Cape Times,_ 11/15/1989). No official figures are available for the latter part of the 1980's.

17. To pursue this would require another study focused on aid and

trade. One might note that the aid-trade relationship is not as straightforward as it seems. Thus, while bilateral aid arrangements are usually pinpointed as tying purchases and trade to the donor most tightly, USAID boasts that for every dollar the U.S. contributes to multilateral development banks (World Bank, IMF, UNDP, etc.) "the U.S. economy gets back $9 in procurements" (USAID, 1989: 3).

18. Thus, for example, while Western European states applauded themselves on agreeing under Lomé IV to $10 per capita in African aid over five years, offers to Poland and Hungary as of only late 1989 amounted to $60 per capita over three years (*Christian Science Monitor*, 12/6/1989).

19. As a SADCC study has argued, "In brief, recorded intra-SADCC trade represents 4–5% of the SADCC countries' total imports and exports . . . which is comparable with other groups of developing countries in Africa, but lower than similar groups in Asia and Latin America. It can be noted that the SADCC countries' trade with the Republic of South Africa is considerably higher, representing 7% of their total exports and 30% of their imports." (1986b: xv-xvi). This is less, one might note, than in other African economic organizations; 10% of the total trade in 1981 of La Communauté Economique de l'Afrique de l'Ouest (CEAO) was for example between member states (see Robson, 1985: 608).

20. See for example Østergaard (1989: 102), which charts such developments in detail for tractor production, and argues that simple industry-by-industry, bilateral agreements, have and will continue to fail in the industrial field.

21. See for example Nabudere (1985: 120ff). Other analysts would draw contrary conclusions. Thus for example Kanduza (1986: ch.5) argues that political demands during the latter phases of the Federation were able to attenuate, if not reverse, the unequal flows between Northern and Southern Rhodesia.

22. Or in the (unattributed) introduction to the same volume: "from the very beginning the SADCC idea has been dependent upon the blessings of imperialism in general" (Amin et al., 1987: 8).

23. As Joseph Hanlon (1987: 441) argues, "it is highly unlikely that South Africa will be asked to join SADCC. Precisely because of its size and economic power, it would dominate SADCC. Rather neighboring states are more likely to see SADCC as a vehicle which gives them equal bargaining power with a more sympathetic South Africa." For a countervailing view

see Browne (1987). Or in even more apocalyptic terms, the "sudden collapse of white rule in South Africa would lead to a catastrophe similar to that of the Russian revolution itself" (Michael Howard, as cited by Mandaza, 1987: 210.)

B. Regional Labor Flows[*]

ith the creation of the mining industry, the colonial powers turned South Africa, and later also Southern Rhodesia, into the major economic growth points in southern Africa. Mining capital and, to a lesser degree in terms of organization and volume, capitalist agriculture in these two countries created a regional labor market for its demand of a cheap, unskilled, and expandable labor force. After the Second World War the rise of manufacturing industry, the modernization processes linked to the investments of transnational capital, and the mechanization of capitalist agriculture had a major impact on the regional labor market. In terms of the regional labor market, the first signal of the new trend was given by Rhodesia which, from the early 1960's onwards, ceased to be a labor-importing economy and even became in the 1970's a labor-exporting economy.

While the changes in Southern Rhodesia did have a major impact on Malawi and Central Mozambique, it's major regional labor recruitment grounds, the impact on the regional labor market was limited. But a similar process took place in South Africa, the major regional importer of foreign labor. The capitalist expansion

---

[*] The main argument of this essay is taken from Centro de Estudos Africanos (1987), which contains an extensive bibliography.

Table 2-B-1
Share of Foreign African Labor in Southern
Rhodesia, 1946–1976

Year	In Thousands	% All African Labor
1946	202.4	55.7
1951	246.8	50.5
1956	297.7	52.7
1961	na	51.0
1969	na	34.0
1975	na	24.0

Source: Schaedel, 1984: Tables 15 & 51.

of the postwar years had been characterized in South Africa by production methods that rationalized the use of human labor. The leader of the industrialization process was no longer mining, but the manufacturing industry; but the modernization process also affected sharply employment patterns in commercial agriculture. At the same time, the apartheid regime increasingly deprived the South African peasantry of the means of agricultural production. Outside of the increasingly impoverished Bantustans, a substantial number of African farmers, who up to that point had been able to defend their position, were now "endorsed out" of their landholdings by a general government policy aiming at "consolidating" the Bantustans, and the "White" areas. In the 1960's some 340,000 labor tenants, 656,000 other tenants, and about 97,000 small farmers were being driven out of the so-called "Black spots"; some 400,000 followed them in the early 1970's. Since the Bantustans did not offer an economically viable base, those who were dispossessed turned towards wage labor, in a controlled labor market already glutted by cheap unskilled foreign migrant laborers.

The result was that the capitalist sectors of Southern Rhodesia and of South Africa started to diminish the share of foreign labor in their respective national labor markets, because capitalist development of agriculture and industrialization had caused huge unemployment in their own countries. The process implied that not all of the unemployed African labor force could be absorbed by the capitalist sectors.

From the 1960's onward, the migrant labor force from various regional states, which for decades had been sought-after producers of surplus and the pillars of capital accumulation in Southern Rhodesia and South Africa, were now re-imported by their countries of origin, thus constituting surplus labor in their underdeveloped home areas which, on a more limited scale, were undergoing the same modernization processes.

Whereas the South African population census of 1960 had estimated the total number of foreign workers in South Africa to be about 586,000 (the Froneman Committee even suggested for 1960 the number of 836,000) the census for 1970 registered "only" 486,000 foreign workers in South Africa. Even if foreign workers tended to hide their country of origin from the authorities, the administrative apparatus of control had also improved so that probably the census of 1970 came nearer to the facts than that of 1960. The reduction of foreign labor was most important in commercial agriculture; even though data were unreliable, one can estimate that the employment of foreigners in this sector declined from 144,000 in 1964 to about 45,000 in 1970.[1] However, in the mining industry, the share of foreigners in the workforce nonetheless increased from about 63% to 75% during the 1960's.

The trend to drastic reduction of the share of foreign labor in the mining industry and changes in the composition of the labor force was to start only in the 1970's. According to official statistics, the number of registered foreign African workers in South Africa dropped by 26% from 485,100 in 1975 to 358,035 in 1983; if Namibian workers are excluded from the latter figure, the drop is 40 percent.

Table 2 indicates a major change in the composition of the foreign African labor force in South Africa. In 1973, before the abrupt Malawian pull-out and before Mozambican independence in 1975, these two countries had supplied 55% of the total foreign labor force; in 1983, their proportion had dwindled to 25.4 percent. Lesotho and Swaziland on the other hand were able to

Table 2-B-2
Origin of Foreign African Workers in South Africa

Country of Origin	1973	1975	1977	1979	1981	1983
Angola	42	623	805	275	69	689
Botswana	46,192	37,016	43,527	32,463	29,169	25,967
Lesotho	148,856	152,188	173,867	152,023	150,422	145,797
Malawi	139,714	39,308	12,412	35,803	30,602	29,622
Mozambique	127,198	150,738	68,232	61,550	59,391	61,218
Swaziland	10,032	16,390	18,195	13,005	13,417	16,773
Zambia	684	914	682	809	727	743
Zimbabwe	3,258	8,890	37,919	21,547	16,965	7,742
Other	9,132	8,512	1,030	9,224	996	70,105*
Total	485,100	414,586	357,356	326,709	301,758	358,035

Source: South Africa. Department of Foreign Affairs and Information (1973–1984).

* Includes Namibia.

Note: Because of the repeal of the Black Labor Act of 1964 with effect from July 1, 1986, official statistics on the number of migrants in South Africa are no longer available.

maintain and even to increase slightly their proportion of the foreign labor force. But evidently the share of migrant labor from South Africa's Bantustans grew mostly at the cost of that of foreign labor.

Mechanization in agriculture and the modernization processes in industry tended to be incapable of absorbing the regional and national labor force, especially since they coincided in the period after the mid–1970's with a global downswing in the world-economy, with the result that underemployment and unemployment were growing rapidly.

Table 2-B-3
Employment Structure in South Africa
Absolute Figures in Thousands; Percentages of Total

Year	Skilled (%)	Unskilled (%)	Unemployed* (%)	Total Econom. Active Pop.
1960	1,655 (26.4)	3,027 (48.4)	1,576 (25.2)	6,258 (100)
1970	2,233 (26.4)	3,935 (46.6)	2,278 (27.0)	8,446 (100)
1980	2,807 (26.0)	4,687 (43.4)	3,299 (30.6)	10,793 (100)
1985	2,879 (23.5)	4,842 (39.5)	4,547 (37.0)	12,268 (100)

Source: Bethelhem, 1988: 118.

* The category "unemployed" includes both subsistence agriculture and the informal sector, which says something about the income level of these sectors.

Structural Changes in the Pattern of Labor Demand and Recruitment in the South African Mining Industry

This trend can be seen even more clearly in the employment pattern developing in the mines affiliated to the Chamber of Mines. Until 1970, gold production was an activity with limited profit rates and future perspectives. On the one hand, the income per production unit was limited because of the international fixing of the gold price in the framework of the international exchange rate system established at Bretton Woods. On the other hand, prices for the elements of constant capital increased while the percentage of ore content per ton of rock decreased and the costs of opening up viable ore deposits increased. The strict maintenance of low wage levels was therefore seen as a decisive factor of the continued profitability of the mines. Capital intensive mechanization measures could not be implemented as long as the economic future of gold mining remained uncertain.

With the end of the Bretton Wood System and the liberalization of the price of gold, the situation of the gold mining industry was changed completely. An ounce of gold was valued at $35 from 1938–1970, $125 in 1975–76, $150 in 1977, $175 in 1978 and $400 in 1979. These are only very rough approximations, whose sole aim is to indicate the trend after 1971. Gold mining capital achieved sensational profits, the expected life of existent mines was extended, new shafts were being sunk, and, especially, new technology was finally being introduced. All of this had consequences for the pattern of labor demand and recruitment of the mines. Until the 1970's, almost 70% of Black underground mine workers were recruited for unskilled manual work; they could easily be replaced after their contract ended. It meant that the migrant system remained economic, provided that the wages paid to workers were low enough to compensate for recruiting costs and the costs associated with a high labor turnover. Real wages hardly increased until the 1970's; they remained at levels first established in the early years of the century. If one takes the real earnings of African workers in the South African mines paid in 1936 as equal to 100, the index value of 1911 wages stood at 111 and of the 1969 wages at 108% (Wilson, 1972: 66). Before 1970, mining capital's labor policy revolved around having adequate quantities of unskilled labor available, when it needed it. Although it did encourage miners to return to the mines after their contracts had expired by offering bonuses to those who did so, capital was not interested in Black "career" miners. Thus, it was not until the mid 1970's when recruitment of foreign miners starts to be curtailed, that the Chamber of Mines distinguished between experienced men with valid re-engagement guarantee certificates and novices.

As far as labor catchment areas were concerned, most of the countries of southern Africa formed part of mining capital's industrial reserve army of labor. Tanzania and Zambia withdrew from the migrant labor system soon after their independence. Rhodesia turned into a labor-exporting country only during the 1970's, but independent Zimbabwe soon stopped the export of mine labor to South Africa. However, other countries of the region were to a varying degree locked into the system. Continued revenue from migrant labor was vital for their balance of payments, especially in the case of Lesotho and Mozambique. In the mid 1970's, fundamental changes occurred within the structure of production in the mining industry accompanied by a number of conjunctural changes within South Africa and the southern African region. Together, this led to the emergence of a new pattern of employment on the mines, a new recruitment strategy, and the reorganization of internal and regional labor markets.

Technical Changes within the Mining Industry

High gold prices on the world market throughout the 1970's and early 1980's stimulated production and the mining of marginal, low grade ore seams.[2] In 1970, 75 million tons of ore milled produced about 1,000 tons of pure gold. In 1989, 106 million tons of ore milled resulted in 610 tons of pure gold. Also the coal mining

Table 2-B-4
Origin of Migrant Labor Employed by Affiliates of the Chamber of Mines at End of Year, 1970 to 1988, in Thousands

Origin	1970	1975	1980	1983	1986	1988
South Africa	96.9	121.8	279.1	289.5	313.5	348.7
Botswana	16.3	16.6	19.3	17.6	19.1	18.9
Lesotho	71.1	85.5	109.0	102.8	112.6	111.8
Malawi	98.2	8.5	14.3	15.9	18.1	15.5
Mozambique	113.3	118.0	45.8	44.8	57.9	47.7
Swaziland	5.4	7.2	9.4	11.8	14.9	17.7
Zimbabwe	0	7.0	5.0	0	0	0
Foreign	304.2	242.9	204.3	193.8	222.6	211.7
as % of Total	75.8	66.6	42.3	40.1	41.5	37.8

Source: Witwatersrand Native Labour Association (WNLA) (various), The Employement Bureau of Africa (TEBA) (various); SAIRR, 1989: 420.

industry expanded rapidly, stimulated by rising oil prices and the reduction in unit transport costs by the development of very large maritime coal carriers (*Mining Survey,* No. 72, 1973: 9–14).

The massive capital expenditure involved in the sinking of new shafts for the deep level gold mines (over 3000 m. is not unusual) under difficult technical conditions, since gold reefs average about 10 cm. in width (*Mining Survey,* No. 94, 1979: frontpiece), promoted research into more productive and profitable technologies. New methods of shaft sinking and excavating, of the marking off of drilling areas, of cleaning stopes and transporting rock have all contributed to that end, and thus reduced labor needs (*Mining Survey,* No. 77, 1975: 24–26; also Salaman, 1975: 26–27). The ratio of capital to labor increased.[3] These developments also meant that workers have had to acquire new skills.

There is extensive training of team leaders. It includes every aspect of underground team work, literacy and numeracy, if necessary, as well as management skills and "industrial education." Apart from the training of higher grades of the Black labor force, all production workers needed more training because of the shift away from unskilled to a semiskilled and skilled labor force. With the concomitant increased investment in the labor force, the former high labor turnover of manual labor, characteristic of the past migrant system, had ceased to be economic. Now there was an increased demand for more educated, English-speaking workers, who would return regularly to the mines after short periods of leave at home.

Changes in the Regional Labor Markets

During the period that gold mining was undergoing technical changes which altered the character of the labor process, the southern African region was undergoing fundamental political changes which also influenced mine labor recruitment policies. Mozambique's independence came shortly after the sudden withdrawal of the apparently secure supply of Malawian labor in April 1974. These two events, together with the end of the Bretton Woods agreement, the expansion of now highly-profitable mining, and the technological changes in the industry, which demanded a higher trained and more stable labor force, led the Chamber of Mines to rethink the question of labor supply. To meet the need for secure long-term reserves of skilled and unskilled workers, it increasingly began to turn to the industrial reserve army within South Africa itself, the Bantustans. It therefore embarked on a deliberate policy of reducing the numbers of foreign workers. To guarantee the heterogeneity of supply, it started to reduce the numbers and proportions of workers drawn from the main foreign supplier states. (There was never a threat of the mines becoming dependent on any one supplier state, because the regional labor market was glutted with surplus labor.) By the mid 1970's, "stabilization" and "internalization" of the Black work force had become the new watchwords of the Chamber of Mines. The number of foreign novices was reduced in favor of first time workers from within the borders of South Africa. Stabilization did not mean settling a permanent labor force around the mines. Rather it meant offering financial incentives to encourage experienced workers to return regularly, and within an agreed time period, to the mines. Those who failed to return in time either lost their bonuses and were considered novices or they found they were not being reemployed (MacArthur, 1980; Murray, 1980b).

Changes in South Africa Itself

The early 1970's were also years of heightened mass struggle in South Africa itself, which coincided with the economic boom in the mining industry. Following a wave of strikes in Durban 1973, which spilt over into the mines in the same year, the Chamber of Mines increased money wages substantially and embarked on a program to improve the working conditions of (skilled and semi-skilled) workers. As a result of the increasing real wages of Black miners, the gap between their wages and those in manufacturing closed.[4] At the same time the advancing proletarianization of Blacks and the decline in industrial production led to more South African Black workers signing on with the mines.

As popular struggles began to gather momentum, massive

unemployment in South Africa, both structural and cyclical, began to be seen as a serious threat to the stability of apartheid society. Thus at the time when the mines traditional sources of labor appeared "unreliable," the reserve army of labor located in the Bantustans began to appear as an attractive alternative.

From the 1980's onwards, the growth of militant Black workers unions (the National Union of Mineworkers of SA was founded in 1982) and their successful bargaining was pushing up labor costs and expenses in lost labor time.[5]

Since the late 1980's the price of gold has been falling. The average London price in 1982 had been about $376 per fine ounce; in 1984 it fell to about $361, in 1985 to $317. It then recovered to $447 in 1987 to fall again to $371 in May 1989 and $350 in June 1990. Gold's continuing weakness is putting the future of several marginal gold mines in doubt, like the East Rand Proprietary Mines and a number of GENCOR mines. The prolongation of the life of the South African gold mining industry necessitates sinking ever deeper shafts. The technical problems associated with

Figure One
South African Union Membership & Strike Action

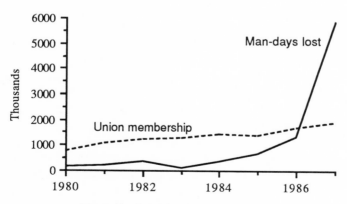

Note: Registered unions only.
Source: South Africa (1989a), Tables 5.1.1 & 5.4.1.

this endeavor (heat, humidity, seismicity, length of stopes, rock removal logistics, etc.) cause massive capital expenditure in research and capital investment.[6] In terms of profit performance, the Chamber of Mines reckons that the first quarter of 1990 was the worst since 1970. Working costs swallowed 75% of revenues; a mere 6% was left for shareholders. The prospects were painted dim (*Financial Mail*, May 11, 1990: 28).

These last three mentioned factors cause the gold mining industry to drive hard for an continuous increase in labor productivity. This was one of the main reasons for the industry to free itself or modify of apartheid legislation that tended to impede the upward mobility of skilled Black workers in the industry. Industry needed to reduce the shortage of skilled (White) workers. It therefore continued to increase its demand for educated Black workers. Progress, however, was slow. In June 1988 the president of the Chamber of Mines stated that over 5,000 non-Whites were employed on mines in jobs previously reserved for Whites only, which equalled about 12% of the skilled work force and 17% of all apprentices in training. As the slow process of the "reform" of apartheid began to unfold, the mining industry began to expand its labor stabilization program to a small proportion of the Black labor force, by exploring ways and means of financing housing development for the Black work force. Flexible housing arrangements including a mix of municipality, private enterprise, self help and company investment were elaborated.

Conclusion

A new type of labor force is emerging on the mines and with it a new hierarchy of labor supply states, divided by function. At the top of the new pyramid stands South Africa itself. It provides the small stream of permanent, skilled Black workers. The bulk of the labor force, i.e., the semiskilled "commuters," are also drawn from South Africa. However, some foreign states, notably Lesotho, will probably continue to supply significant numbers of workers, also mainly located in the "commuter" category. Lesotho will also be called on for the third and lowest category, the "supplementary labor," because it is close to the mines and workers can be engaged very quickly. Demand for Mozambican labor is likely to be limited and declining and most likely to be confined to the category of "supplementary labor." The emerging new division of supplier states into suppliers of particular categories of mine labor will have important implications for the region, i.e., in terms of building up relationships between regional trade unions and South African trade unions. It also has implications for the internal planning and employment creation program of the labor supplying states. Their programs of economic readjustment and development will have to include considerations of how to reintegrate former migrant labor into their national development programs. This, of course, cannot but be a long term perspective. Even in a post-apartheid situation, the contract labor system can only slowly be phased out. Not only will the mining industry be hesitant to dismiss suddenly great numbers of experienced semiskilled Black foreign miners, but regional supplier states have to create alternative employment and income opportunities. In a region whose economy has been severely distorted by colonialism and South Africa's traditional economic dominance, not to speak of massive destruction of economic infrastructure caused by the destabilization period (no one will compensate the affected states for these losses), the development of diversified economies no longer condemned to be the exporters of unprocessed raw materials for ever-decreasing prices will need a huge collective effort in terms of finance, technology transfers, and training. However, one long term objective could remain to create a free regional labor market that allows for the free movement of labor across national boundaries in the region of southern Africa, including a liberated South Africa, thereby eliminating the migrant labor system once and for all.

Notes

1. The percentage of the economically active population working in South Africa's agriculture stood at 31% in 1970, at 15.9% in 1980, and at 13.9% in 1985. Of economically active Blacks 36.8% had worked in agriculture in 1970; in 1980 this was reduced to 19% and in 1985 to

18.8%, a reflection of the mechanization process in agriculture.

2. Since 1975,the volume of rock treated has steadily risen from 75.1 million tons to 110.7 million tons in 1984. The production of gold, on the other hand, has declined. The paradox is explained by the fact that in periods of rising gold prices it is worthwhile to mine low grade ore which in times of low gold prices would not be profitable to mine.

3. One indication of this change is the growing consumption of electrical power. Whereas in 1967, 25.09 megawatt hours of electric power were consumed per worker on the gold mines, this ratio had risen by 1984 to 39.83 megawatt hours per worker (see Chamber of Mines of South Africa, 1967: 99 & 1984: 122). The National Union of Mineworkers estimates that 8% of the total number of jobs have been lost on the coal mines in the past 8 years because of mechanization. The smaller workforce has, however, increased production by 48% (see *New Nation,* 7/17/1986: 15).

4. Black mining wages as a percentage of Black manufacturing wages rose from 29.% in 1971, to 70% in 1976, to 79.4% in 1984 (South Africa. Central Statistical Services, 1986: Tables 4.1.1.2 & 4.1.1.3.)

5.

Strikes in South Africa

Year	Number of strikes & work-stoppages	Number of employees	Number of man days lost (all workers)
1974	384	59,244	98,583
1978	106	14,160	10,558
1982	394	141,571	365,337
1983	336	64,469	124,596
1984	469	181,942	379,712
1985	389	239,816	678,273
1986	793	424,340	1,308,958
1987	1,148	591,421	5,825,231
1988	1,025	161,679	914,388

Source: South Africa. National Manpower Commission, 1986; SAIRR, 1989.

Average Earnings Per Black Worker in the South African Mining Industry Related to the Consumer Price Index for Lower Income Groups

Year	Average Monthly Black Wages South African Mining Constant 1980 Prices (1980=100)	Consumer Price Index Lower Income Groups (1980=100)
1970	29.1	na
1971	19.1	na
1972	32.3	na
1973	37.8	na
1974	52.3	na
1975	75.0	57.2
1976	81.9	62.6
1977	83.7	69.3
1978	88.3	77.5
1979	92.4	87.0
1980	100.0	100.0
1981	104.6	117.2
1982	109.8	133.1
1983	111.0	149.6
1984	116.9	165.0

Source: South Africa. Central Statistical Services, 1986: Tables 4.1.1.2 & 4.3.2.1 (averages).

6. As the table on the following page shows, the capital-to-labor ratio in South African Mining grew signficantly from the mid–1970's onward.

Year	Rand per Worker (Constant 1980 Prices)	1980=100
1973	9 976	65.9
1974	10 808	71.4
1975	12 863	85.0
1976	13 420	88.6
1977	13 290	87.8
1978	13 634	90.1
1979	14 061	92.9
1980	15 139	100.0
1981	16 522	109.1
1982	18 245	120.5
1983	19 308	127.5
1984	19 326	127.7

Source: South Africa. Central Statistical Services, 1986: Table 7.1.5

C. Corporate Capital in Southern Africa

Introduction

S ince the 1970's there has been an increasing shift of capital investment from material production into more speculative ventures throughout the world-economy. This in itself is not a new phenomenon. Such recurrent "financial rebirths," the periodic shift of capital from commodity capital into money capital, are a basic aspect of the historical development of capitalism, occurring when processes of material expansion, constituted at a given time, are approaching their limits (Arrighi, forthcoming; Hicks, 1969; Braudel, 1984: 604).

Yet from the point of view of the southern African regional economy whose "organic" character has been consolidated on the basis of the current regime of the multinational corporation in the post–1945 period, this withdrawal of productive capital resulting from the decline of direct investment to the region cannot but raise basic questions regarding the regionality of southern Africa in the 1990's and beyond. However, the impact of global changes on southern Africa can at best only present a partial explanation without the simultaneous consideration of the long-term implications of the current crisis in the apartheid system. For, as is well known, the joint exploitation of southern African resources by the nationally diverse cohort of multinational corporations, including those of South African origin, has been based on the industrial dominance of South Africa in the region.

Put in historical context, the evolution of these patterns is clear. Since the late 1940's foreign investment has come to play a significant role in the regional character of southern Africa. The hegemony of the United States in the 1950's and 1960's and the consequent central role of the transnational corporation, along with other new types of supranational financial institutions (such as the IMF), as the chief agents of foreign capital investment have had significant implications for the regional economy of southern Africa. Not only did U.S. capital come to challenge the traditional economic dominance of Great Britain in the region, but it also helped to consolidate the industrial dominance of South Africa in the region. South Africa now, even more than before, became the central node around which regional integration was constructed, revitalizing old networks as well as forging new linkages.

These patterns were further restructured and enhanced by the rise of capital investment from western Europe and Japan in the late 1960's and early 1970's, which in turn came to challenge the dominance of both the U.S. and Great Britain in the region. As in the past the bulk of these new investments went into the economy of South Africa, often using the latter as a base for region-wide undertakings, and thus enhancing the position of South Africa as the center of vertical and horizontal regional networks. It was also during the late 1960's and particularly the 1970's that local South African capital started making significant and further inroads in the region, alongside out-of-region capital.

The integration of the regional economy around the industrial base of South Africa has remained one of the most influential and persistent continuities in the socio-economic character of southern Africa into the 1990's, and has been a major constraint on the autonomous development of national policies in the region. To put it differently, the political changes of the 1960's, 1970's, and 1980's, which resulted in majority rule for most of these countries, and which in turn facilitated the intensification of the struggle against apartheid in South Africa, were counterposed to the more rigid constraints embedded in the character of the regional economy. Hence development policy at the level of the nation-states has been progressively forced to address itself not only to the traditional constraints of neo-colonialism but also to the limitations imposed by the "organic" character of an integrated regional economy. The emergence of the SADCC program in the early 1980's is the most visible expression of such policy concerns.

The activities of corporate capital in southern Africa have parallelled the overall global patterns of corporate investment in reproducing a hierarchical division of labor between geographical areas, with the most beneficial aspects of the production processes based in the more advanced centers of the world-economy, in this case both in core countries and in South Africa. In line with the law of uneven development—the tendency to produce poverty alongside wealth, underdevelopment as the other side of development—income, status, authority and consumption patterns radiate from the center along a declining curve (Hymer, 1976: 38).

The 1970's and the 1980's have seen marked changes in the nature of investment patterns and their consequent impact on the economic character of the region. These changes have been concentrated in three main arenas. First, as already pointed out, the restructuring of the world-economy has, among other things, resulted in decreased capital flows to the region. Secondly, SADCC was formed in 1980 with the aim among others of addressing the economic imbalance between South Africa and the rest of the countries in the region. And thirdly, there was a general increase in strength and diversity of the anti-apartheid movement, including the divestment drive, whose focus on the apartheid economies of South Africa and Namibia has had far-reaching implications on its continued industrial development. The degree to which the economic character of southern Africa is likely to change in the 1990's and beyond is difficult to predict. However the combined impact of these factors on current patterns of regional investments is likely to be at the center of such a process of restructuring.

Saul Among the Prophets: South African Capital in the Region—The Late 1960's and 1970's

With respect to the key overseas investors in the region there have been marked changes since at least the late 1960's as already pointed out. Of particular importance have been (F.R.) Germany and Japan.[1] The changing positions of the different out-of-region investors relative to each other will be dealt with in subsequent sections. Here emphasis is put on the often theoretically unconceptualized role of intraregional investors.

Regional investors are mainly of South African origin. Zimbabwe is the other possible source, though to a much smaller extent. In the latter case, available data cannot support a detailed elaboration of the role of capital from this source in the region at large, though in a limited way this role has been acknowledged (Hamer, 1964: 28). The future role of Zimbabwean investment regionwide will depend on the degree of the continued expansion of its manufacturing industry which will serve not only as an original source of investment but also as an attractive base and a springboard into the region for overseas corporations, as is the case with South Africa at present. Should this develop to a substantial degree in the 1990's and beyond it could spell some changes in current investment patterns which are dominated by the South African industrial base. At this stage it is difficult to predict the degree to which Zimbabwe will increase its stakes within the SADCC countries at the expense of South Africa.

The regional involvement of South African capital, from the 1960's on, cannot be attributed to single cause. Nor can this role be assumed to be a linear process which, once started, merely continues to expand without regard to periodic changes in the world-economy or in the contending forces within the apartheid system. While the initial waves can be explained by the emergence of monopoly capital in this country (Innes, 1984; Kaplan, 1983), subsequent outflows are better understood in terms of the crisis of the apartheid system. There is also the need to distinguish private monopolies from state monopolies, since both the dimensions of regional involvement as well as future trajectories of these forms of capital are quite distinct. This distinction could not be better illustrated than by the initial conflict of interest between Anglo American and ESCOM (Electricity Supply Commission), the parastatal concerned with the energy supply needs of South Africa, in the construction of the Cahora Bassa dam. ESCOM, fearing an increased dependency of South Africa on foreign energy sources, was initially opposed to participation in the project, while Anglo American, mindful of gain from infrastructural development, was in favor (Middlemas, 1975). As shall become clear, such differences in the rationality of regional involvement between state-centric and capital-centric enterprises, though not necessarily mutually exclusive, seem quite distinct.

According to David Kaplan, the growing centralization of South African capital has been the primary factor behind the growth of direct foreign investment from this country. By the 1960's and 1970's, the "large profitable opportunities [were] all locked up" (Kaplan, 1983: 482), and an outward movement of capital became the only means of ensuring continued accumulation. By the 1970's these outflows had become pronounced. In the primary sector this expansion also meant an increasing horizontal and vertical integration of production processes at the regional level, reinforcing well established regional patterns of private capital. De Beers, for example, was already in control of almost all the significant diamond mines in the region involving not less than seven countries. In the four countries of South Africa, Namibia, Lesotho, and Botswana alone, this dominance involves at least sixteen mines (United Nations, 1985: 128). Diamond products from these and other mines are sold through the Central Selling Organization, a highly centralized and vertically-integrated marketing structure which itself consists of numerous subsidiary corporations.

The Anglo American group of companies in general have also significantly diversified their investment in the region from the traditional concentration in mining into other aspects of primary production, as well as into manufacturing and finance. The dominance of foreign investment in the agricultural sector across the region prior to the 1960's was quite limited, agriculture being the domain of national or local capital for the most part in the region.

However, Anglo American and other corporations had by the 1970's assumed a dominant role in this sector as well (Pangeti, 1986: 331). This increased role of corporate capital was also reflected in the regional finance sector, such as in the establishment of Rhobank in Zimbabwe as an affiliate of South Africa Nedbank. South African banking capital came to play a more forceful role alongside the regionally well-established Western banks, particularly Barclays and Standard Bank, both British banks, which have numerous branches in the region some of which date from the turn of the century.

With respect to manufacturing, South African capital featured prominently in the marked expansion of Zimbabwean manufacturing sector following UDI (1965) when South Africa became a most trusted ally in a period of international sanctions against the settler regime of Ian Smith (Stoneman, 1978; Clarke, 1980). In general, Zimbabwe, is the only country in the region other than South Africa where foreign investment played an important role in manufacturing.

The 1970's were also marked by a significant increase in exploration activities of Anglo American and other South African companies in the whole region. Such a burst of economic activities during this period, especially from the mid–1970's onwards, is not accidental. The outflow of South African private capital, particularly direct investment, rose significantly around this time. This was mainly due to a new willingness on the part of the South African Reserve Bank to permit capital export as result of massive surplus on the balance of payments from 1978 to 1980 (Kaplan, 1983: 475, 480). Even though most of these flows were outward directed beyond southern Africa, a sizeable amount still went into the region, and constituted a significant factor of economic integration in the region.

In my view, the most important development in the pattern of South African investment in the region since the late 1960's and 1970's is the role of state capital which added a new dimension to the regional character of foreign investment. Both the timing of increased regional involvement and the sectoral preference of South African state capital marked a significant historical development in the economy of southern Africa. Such developments reflected the particular needs and objectives of this form of capital which, while overlapping with those of private capital, remained distinct.

During the 1970's, South African state corporations stepped up their use of the region both as a market for locally-produced goods and as an arena of capital investment (United Nations, 1985: 160). This situation was an outcome of political and economic developments both within and outside South Africa. Notable among the latter was the oil crisis of 1973, which led to the expansion of SASOL (South African Coal, Oil and Gas Corporation) production. This expansion was further intensified as a result of the fall of the Shah of Iran and the subsequent cutoff of Iranian oil supplies to South Africa, which in previous years accounted for at least 90% of total South African oil imports. Growing international opposition to apartheid and the threat of economic boycotts also increased the need for the South African regime to become self-sufficient in all matters of strategic importance. This was especially the case in the face of the increasing political changes in southern Africa from the mid–1970's onwards, resulting from the collapse of the Portuguese empire in the region and the mounting drive for independence in Zimbabwe and Namibia. The unprecedented increase in the South African military budget since the mid–1970's was itself a reflection of these developments, which propelled the increased role of state corporations in the region. In the six years following 1975, the regional customers of ESCOM energy products grew to include Namibia, Botswana, Mozambique, Lesotho, and Swaziland (United Nations, 1985: 132). Likewise these countries, plus Zambia and Zimbabwe had since 1973 become important markets for SASOL products (United Nations, 1985: 160).

However, it is more in investment rather than trade that South African state capital in the region has expressed its overall "calling." In general, these corporations have been geared towards production of materials which are of immediate industrial and strategic needs to the South African state, unlike the products of private capital in the region which are generally geared towards overseas markets even after being processed in South Africa. State corporations predominate in the production of the so-called strategic raw materials—primarily, uranium, gas, the search for oil deposits, etc. However, their role in the search for other vital items, such as tin, zinc, and lead, which though not necessarily of comparable strategic importance as the former are still demanded by South African industry, is also quite pronounced. The latter are items either not produced at all or not produced in sufficient quantities within South Africa itself (CIIR, 1983: 28, 38).

Among the specifically strategic raw materials, the investment of state corporations outside South Africa in uranium has been the most important.[2] The importance to South Africa of uranium products from the region at large is not necessarily due to internal demand, as South Africa itself is a major producer and exporter of uranium, but rather to the strategic importance of uranium to the world nuclear industry. South Africa's share of the international markets gives her international leverage beyond the direct economic benefits for the corporations concerned.

The Industrial Development Corporation has had a significant stake in the Rossing uranium mine in Namibia since the commencement of production in the late 1970's (see Table 1). IDC and GENCOR, a private South African company, had a combined share of 20% equity in 1980.[3] Of greater significance however is the decisive voting right with veto powers of the IDC in the mine, which "means that all policy decisions at Rossing are likely to be heavily influenced by the IDC and the South African government."[4]

The more regionally inclusive involvement of South African state capital in terms of strategic investment is in the area of energy production in which state capital has been allegedly attempting to create a South African dominated regional grid (Ndlela et al., 1986: 37). In the late 1960's South African state corporations[5] were involved in the development of hydro-electric plants across the region in addition to projects such as the Kariba dam built in the 1950's. The Cahora Bassa dam in Mozambique and the Kunene project on the Angolan-Namibian border, were both undertaken in conjunction with the Portuguese authorities.

It is clear from the above that South African capital, both private and public, acted in concert with its out-of-region counter part to perpetuate and enhance the status quo. The underlying

Table 2-C-1
Ownership of the Rossing Mine (1980)

Corporation	Equity Holding %
Rio Tinto-Zinc, RTZ (U.K.)	46.5
Industrial Development Corporation, IDC (S.A.)	13.2
(100% owned by South Africa government)	
Rio Algom Mines Ltd. (Canada)	10.0
(51.3% owned by RTZ)	
Total (France)	10.0
(100% owned by Compagnie Française des Petroles)	
General Mining and Finance Corporation of South Africa	6.8
(62.5% owned by Federale Mynbou of South Africa)	
Others combined	13.0
TOTAL	100.0

Source: Roberts, 1980: 45.

implications of these regional patterns of uneven development are quite clear. In the first case, the underlying factors which make an industrially-advanced South Africa more attractive to foreign capital of the industrializing type, or conversely which make the rest of the regional economies less attractive to this type of capital, have been readily recognized in the literature on foreign investment in Africa. Giovanni Arrighi, expressing skepticism regarding both the speed and the degree of potential change in such investment patterns (which according to him are due partly to technological and partly to political reasons), argues that the dynamic sectors in question (such as heavy engineering and chemical industries) are those where there are the greatest economies of scale and the advantages of operating in an industrial environment—the low-cost buying, erecting, maintaining, and operating of machinery. Hence the very underdevelopment of Africa itself hinders the development of an organic capital goods industry. "The oligopolistic structure of advanced capitalist countries plays a more direct role in favoring the bias of investment in the periphery against the capital-goods industry" (Arrighi, 1977: 170). With specific reference to southern

Africa, Makgetla and Seidman captured the essence of the uneven development involved when they stated that:

> The transnational corporations' participation in South Africa's industrial expansion was integrally tied in with—in fact, in part built upon—that nation's domination of the neighboring countries (Makgetla & Seidman, 1980: 87–88).

Many of the big corporations investing in South Africa operate in the region at large without having to establish a significant direct presence in the form of a subsidiary in the latter. And even when they do, their headquarters remain in South Africa, where their investment is not limited to the primary sector, as is mostly the case in the rest of the region.

With respect to the second issue, the interpenetration of capital in the regional economy, this has been the rule rather than the exception in the case of the big companies. Once again this has been more prevalent in the last three decades with the increased involvement of different forms of capital from diverse national bases, and their increasing diversification beyond the sectors of their main concentration. This brings together not only capital of different national origins and units of different sizes, but also capital of different forms, i.e., private and public or state-related, as in the case of the Rossing uranium mine already discussed. All this has resulted in "cobweb-like" nodes constructed around the key production processes or industrial activities across the region based on joint ventures, shareholdings, joint board of directorships, and in some cases common participation in research and development, etc. In the more industrialized economies of South Africa and Zimbabwe, joint ventures often involved foreign and local as well as state capital in the same business undertakings. Elsewhere in the region, such ventures are not as common. The spectacular diamond deal between the government of Botswana and De Beers in 1987 must be seen against the particular economic background of that country, namely the future prospect of continued high profitability of the key diamond mines. It is such future prognosis which in some sense increased the bargaining power of the state vis-à-vis De

Beers, and not a change of heart on the part of the latter.

The integration of regional economic activities around the dominance of the South African industrial base, and the interlocking operations of companies at the regional level dominated by South African and overseas capital, together have provided a legacy which has thus far significantly constrained development policy at the level of nation-states in the periphery of southern Africa. What possible changes will take place in the regional character of southern Africa in the future will be dealt with in the succeeding sections.

The 1970's and 1980's

The tight integration of southern Africa into the world-economy is clearly evident in the character of capital flows into the region which reflect the impact of qualitative changes in global investment patterns. Most significant here are periodical shifts in the flows due to the constant restructuring of the global conditions of capital accumulation and the relative changes in the composition of investment with regard to forms of capital. In the latter case, the increase in financial and speculative investment has been particularly evident since the mid–1970's, when direct investment tended to give way to less risky forms of investment such as subcontracting and licensing (Arrighi, 1982: 89; IMF, 1985: 3ff.). The 1980's saw in turn the decline of flows of private capital, particularly commercial bank lending. The sharp rise in interest rates during the early 1980's dramatically raised the cost both of servicing old loans and of contracting new ones, when they were available. The decline of oil profits since the fabulous surpluses of the early to mid–1970's and the increased risk consciousness of moneylenders following the debt default of Mexico are some of the explanations given to reduced bank lending to non-core areas. To these must be added the general instability of primary commodity prices on the world market as a result of the current world recession. This scenario is not unrelated to the "securitization" of capital or the general increase in speculative ventures (as opposed to goods-producing investment) which has been observable even at the center of the world-system since the 1970's.

Taking a broad interpretation in terms of the dating of the major shifts in the flows of long-term capital[6] into the region, it is clear that the main turning-points for most of the countries converge around certain dates which can be stated as follows: 1973/74–1976/77, moderate increases to stable flows for some countries; 1976/77–1981/82, general massive increases (see Graphs A1–6). From 1982/83 to 1987, there has been a significant downward spiral across the board.

The case of South Africa presents special problems of interpretation. With respect to the flows we note a deep and prolonged fall from the mid- to late–1970's, a period which falls well within our general dates of massive increases. And the data used do not specify whether the outflow of investment of South African origin is included in this accounting or not. As we have seen elsewhere the period from 1976 to at least 1980 was marked by significant outflows of South African direct investment. It would seem that a satisfactory explanation must take into account more than the mere political developments of this period, the Soweto uprising of 1976, the 1984 political crisis, etc. It must start to approach the general crisis of the conditions of capital accumulation under the apartheid system.

In terms of changes in the composition of capital, the flows into the region also reflect global patterns of a relative decline of direct investment compared to loan capital up to 1981 followed by an absolute decline in all forms of capital.[7] These changes are clearest in the South African figures. According to IMF data (1985), the five years from 1976 to 1980 were marked by negative flows compared to the five years previous. These patterns are also reflected elsewhere in the region. In the case of Malawi for example, total direct investment for the period 1971–1975 was 51 million SDR's against 168m. SDR's for loans and other forms of financing, giving a difference of 117m SDR's. The difference increased to 265m. in the period 1976–1980. In the case of Zambia the corresponding difference rose from 245m. to 265m. SDR's for the respective periods. In the 1980's, direct investment remains much lower than the other forms of financing for all the countries,

Graph A1
Malawi: Foreign Long-term Investment

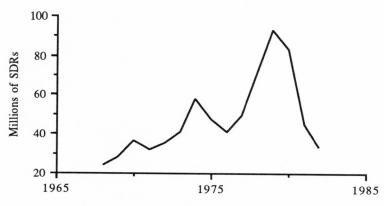

Source: IMF: 1984, 10, 110.

Graph A2
Zambia: Foreign Long-term Investment

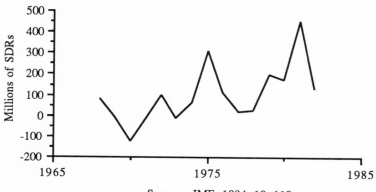

Source: IMF: 1984, 10, 110.

Graph A3
South Africa: Foreign Long-term Investment

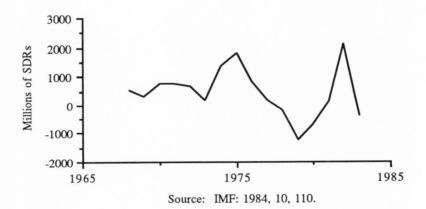

Source: IMF: 1984, 10, 110.

Graph A4
Swaziland: Foreign Long-term Investment

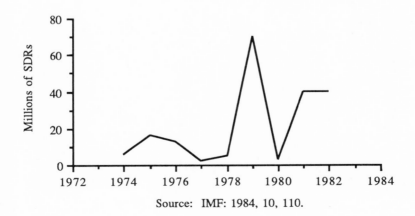

Source: IMF: 1984, 10, 110.

Graph A5
Botswana: Foreign Long-term Investment

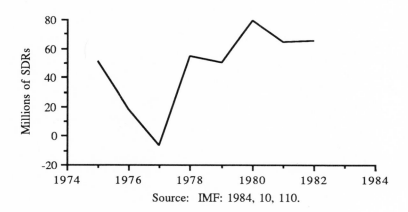

Source: IMF: 1984, 10, 110.

Graph A6
Zimbabwe: Foreign Long-term Investment

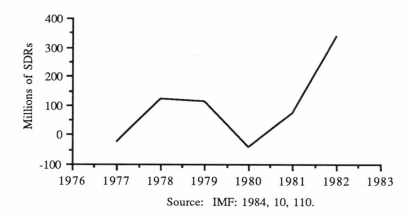

Source: IMF: 1984, 10, 110.

with the exception of Botswana whose total direct investment is higher than loan capital for the period, 1981–1986. It is clear that global patterns of capital flows are reflected in these changes in the composition of investment. Direct investment from the industrialized to non-oil developing countries as a group had increased significantly in the late 1960's. From this period to the mid–1970's net direct investment accounted for well over half of all private capital flows from the industrialized countries, reaching a peak of about $13 billion in 1981 compared to the average of $2 billion a year during the early 1960's. However by the late 1970's, it represented barely one-quarter of a greatly increased volume of total flows. This was the result of massive increase in commercial bank lending and other forms of financing. The absolute decline in all forms of capital that followed the 1981 peak slightly reversed the relative dominance of finance capital over direct investment. Direct investment fell by 27% between 1981 and 1983 as a result of recession during this period while borrowing fell by 72% (IMF, 1985:3).

The implication of this decline in capital investment in the 1980's for national or regional economic development was difficult to ignore. Such declines in the flows of private capital both reflected and contributed to a contraction in the private sector of the recipient countries. Attempts to reverse the situation from the point of view of policymakers in the region took many forms, from self-reliance to reliance on foreign official loans and grants, be they bilateral or multilateral. There seems to be a corresponding emphasis placed on this form of financing in the face of declining private investment (i.e., direct, portfolio, commercial bank loans, etc.). Official flows to most countries in the region showed a steady and continuous rise throughout the period from the early 1970's to the late 1980's, contrasting sharply with private investment in the 1980's (see Graphs B1–4). However the increased reliance on official flows raises important questions regarding the goal of the SADCC program for regional self reliance, given the fact that bilateral rather than multilateral flows dominate for all the countries, although in the cases of Malawi, Lesotho, and Swaziland the gap is quite narrow (see Graphs C1–5). To what degree will this increase in bilateral links to core countries impinge upon the regional integrity of SADCC? It must be noted however that, on the whole, there were no major differences in the trajectories of bilateral and multilateral flows during this period.

Apart from shifts in the volume and composition of foreign investment in the 1970's–1980's period, the relative position of sources of capital has also undergone significant changes throughout the region during this period. Some of these have been pointed out only with reference to South Africa as dimensions of the current economic crisis in that country. Alan Hirsch for example points out that:

> South Africa's major creditor nations have shifted relative positions since the debt crisis of 1985. U.S. and U.K. banks have been repaid the soonest and the most, increasing the relative importance of continental European banks as South Africa's creditors, rather than the traditional U.K. and U.S. banks (1989: 36).

He further points out that this trend towards greater reliance on continental Europe, especially Germany and Switzerland, appears to have begun before the credit crisis (i.e., before 1984). This observation no doubt applies more fully to the South African situation than to other countries in the region. Yet its undercurrents have strong resonance elsewhere in the region, where continental Europe headed by Germany has increasingly challenged the traditional investment sources, the U.K. and the U.S. for most of the period under discussion.

The breakdown of total investment of the three dominant investors U.K., U.S., and (F.R.) Germany for the period 1980–1985 shows Germany to have increased its relative share markedly during the period 1980–1985, and Great Britain to have declined the most (see Table 2 below). Viewed at the level of individual countries this process of restructuring becomes much clearer (see Graphs D2–4). In the cases of both Zambia and Zimbabwe for the ten-year period from 1977 to 1987, Great Britain (the more regionally-involved of the "traditional" sources) starts from a very

Graph B1
Mozambique
Total Official and Private Flows (Net) Direct Investment

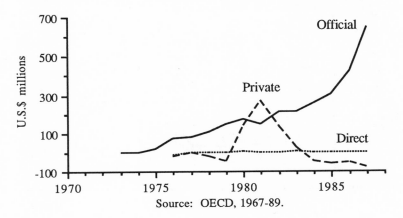

Source: OECD, 1967-89.

Graph B2
Malawi
Total Official and Private Flows (Net) Direct Investment

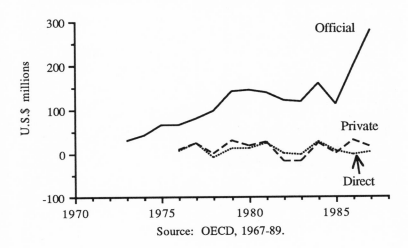

Source: OECD, 1967-89.

Graph B3
Angola
Total Official and Private Flows (Net) Direct Investment

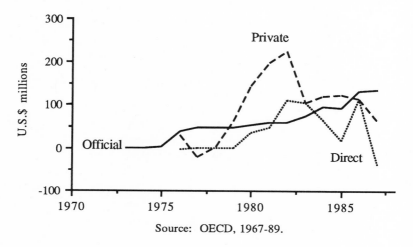

Source: OECD, 1967-89.

Graph B4
Zambia
Total Official and Private Flows (Net) Direct Investment

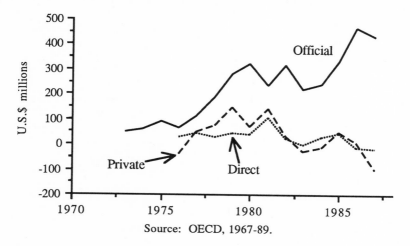

Source: OECD, 1967-89.

Graph C1
Zambia
Bilateral and Multilateral Financing (Commitments)

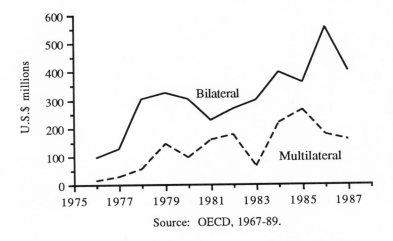

Source: OECD, 1967-89.

Graph C2
Zimbabwe
Bilateral and Multilateral Financing (Commitments)

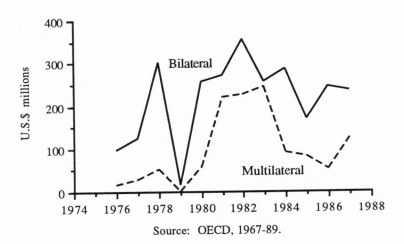

Source: OECD, 1967-89.

Graph C3
Angola
Bilateral and Multilateral Financing (Commitments)

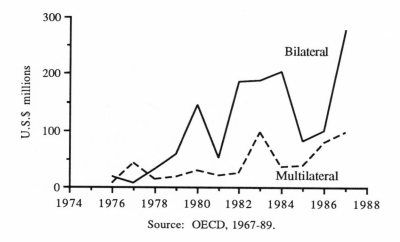

Source: OECD, 1967-89.

Graph C4
Lesotho
Bilateral and Multilateral Financing (Commitments)

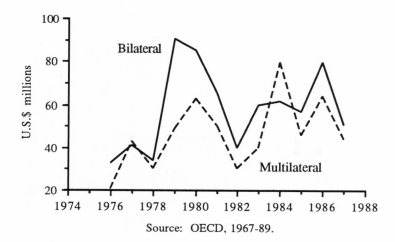

Source: OECD, 1967-89.

Graph C5
Malawi
Bilateral and Multilateral Financing (Commitments)

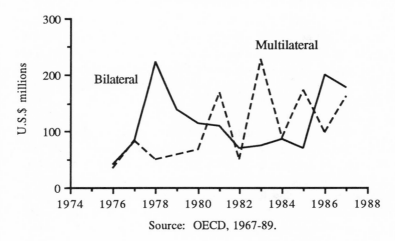

Source: OECD, 1967-89.

strong position relative to Germany at the beginning of the decade but declines the most towards the end of the decade, while Germany moves in the opposite direction. Similar trends of Germany's

Table 2-C-2
Investment Share of U.K., U.S., Germany, Japan as Percentage of Total of these Countries

Country	1980	1981	1982	1983	1984	1985	1980–1985
Germany	8	13	18	34	34	22	37
Japan	9	15	12	6	3	13	8
U.K.	60	49	47	27	28	23	32
U.S.	23	23	23	33	35	42	23

Source: Calculated from the OECD tables for recipient countries. OECD, 1984, 1987. Figures have been rounded. (OECD data does not include South Africa.)

upward mobility have been generally true for South Africa for forms of capital other than the commercial bank loans, as discussed by Hirsch. With specific reference to direct investment the percentage increase in German capital stock in South Africa rose from 5% in 1980 to 8% in 1981, while data for the first half of 1982 are reported to indicate "further substantial increases" (United Nations, Center on Transnational Corporations, 1984: 3). By contrast the percentage increase of U.S. direct investment fell from 16.8% in 1980 to 12% in 1981. It is also true that the ascendance of Germany started earlier in South Africa, where it goes back to the 1960's, than in the rest of the region.

Other European countries which have increased their presence in the region at large since the 1970's include France, Italy, Sweden, and the Netherlands. While none of these has a central role overall in the region, some of them have been very important for individual countries in the region. In the case of Angola, for example, during the 1970's–1980's period, the single most important investment was of French origin (see Graph D–1). Likewise Italy was the single most important investor in Mozambique during this period.

With respect to Japanese investment for this period, other than in South Africa, most of it has been concentrated in Zambia and perhaps also in Zimbabwe where it has been involved in joint-venture car assembly since 1989. In Africa in general Japanese capital has been quite minimal, being mostly concentrated in the shipping industry of Liberia. Liberia has consistently absorbed more than half of direct investment from Japan for the 1982–1986 period (U.S. Department of Commerce, 1988: 7).

In the light of this, and with particular reference to South Africa, it would seem clear that we are faced with converging dynamics. One is rooted in the global restructuring of the world-economy and is reflected at the level of the region as a whole (including South Africa), while the other is rooted in the declining conditions of capital accumulation or profitability brought about by the crisis of the apartheid system. Certainly the latter does not necessarily preclude the former.

It is important to note in general that all these foreign investors

Graph D1
Angola
Key Sources of Financial Resources (Net Receipts)

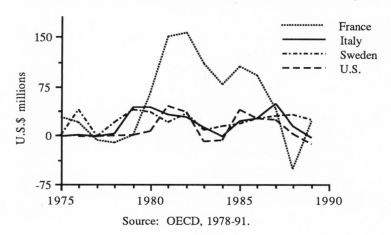

Source: OECD, 1978-91.

Graph D2
Mozambique
Key Sources of Financial Resources (Net Receipts)

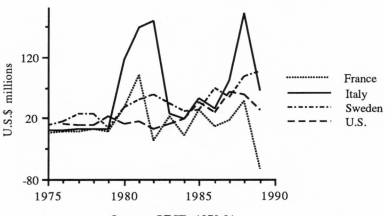

Source: OECD, 1978-91.

Graph D3
Zambia
Key Sources of Financial Resources (Net Receipts)

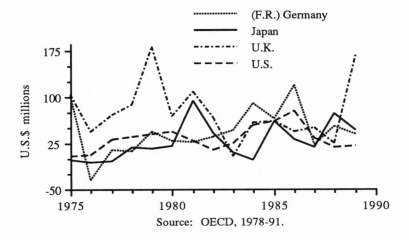

Graph D4
Zimbabwe
Key Sources of Financial Resources (Net Receipts)

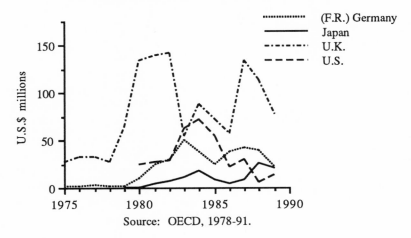

have shown a significant decrease in the late 1980's and future trajectories are not as yet clear. In conjunction with this, the transformation of central-east Europe looms as a significant factor in the redefinition of Western investment patterns. The unification of Germany in particular could have a significant impact upon the current position of German investment in southern Africa.

As far as the role of South African capital in the region is concerned it is likely to increase in the 1990's rather than decrease. Two basic developments seem to support this view. One is the well-noted crisis of the apartheid system which has not only affected Western investment in South Africa but has also resulted in the outflow of South African capital. Although the bulk of such capital may go beyond southern Africa, some of it will be invested in the region.

The second concerns the policy of a comprehensive and diversified response to the crisis of apartheid commonly known as the "Total Strategy" which involves the restructuring of economic relationships both at the national and international levels (Pickles & Woods, 1988, 1989; Pickles, 1988). At the national level (which is called by Pickles the "regional" level) it can be traced more directly to the 1979 Riekert Commission Report which impressed upon the state the need for a more coordinated economic development comprising, among other things, the urban/industrial nodes with some form of economic development in the homelands as a way of stemming the influx tide of unwanted rural migrants into the "White" areas. This is a process in which investors from the Pacific Rim are increasingly playing a major role.

This increase in the role of South African capital could be more substantial in the 1990's than during any other period before. Major policy decisions of the mid–1980's resulting from the economic crisis and international sanctions, which makes recovery at best a slow and uncertain process, seem to have set South African business on a course of concerted drive outward, seeking both markets for its products and sites for new investment. Available data show substantial growth in South African trade and investment with the rest of Africa and with some of the new industrializing countries of the Pacific Rim. According to Reserve

Bank figures, direct South African investment in Africa in 1988 was R2,2 billion, up from R2 billion in the previous year, constituting 12.6 and 12% respectively of total direct investment from South Africa overseas. Specific undertakings include joint ventures with local/state capital such as the Highland Water Project in Lesotho and the Sua Pan Soda Ash Project in Botswana (*Weekly Mail*, 2/23–3/1, 1990:14).

Perhaps the more interesting of the new sources of capital, though still small in size of current investment is that from the Pacific Rim, whose role is increasing in southern Africa, particularly in South Africa. While Western sources have shown a great deal of sensitivity toward apartheid despite their continued involvement and now generally shy away from more blatant and controversial aspects of involvement such as open dealing with homelands, as a result of the anti-apartheid pressures in their own countries, Pacific Rim investors in general seem unaffected by such political considerations. Japan, among other involvements, operates borderline industries employing migrant labor from the homelands. In addition, Taiwan, South Korea, and Hong Kong have stepped up their involvement in South Africa. Taiwanese investment has been of paticular importance in the new approach to homeland development, in which Taiwanese investors have established approximately 120 factories (Pickles & Woods, 1988: 50–53).

There is no question that this new drive outward of South African business, together with a new political stance on the part of South Africa necessary for its success, poses a significant challenge for SADCC as a program for reduced dependence on South Africa. Indeed the South Africans are not without new ideas of their own regarding a new regional structure. Henri de Villiers, chairman of Standard Bank, referring to a "Southern African Economic Community," pointed out that SADCC itself can be used in the formation of this new structure together with SACU (Southern African Customs Union) (*Weekly Mail*, 2/23–3/1, 1990:14). The success of such a regional structure depends on number of factors most importantly the dismantling of apartheid which precludes the existence of stable political relationships between South Africa and its neighbors, and the degree of resistance of

SADCC members against the continuation of South Africa's economic domination. In the case of the latter issue only a few countries could pose real resistance, perhaps only Zimbabwe.

Zimbabwe is the only country in the region where South African economic involvement seems to have decreased in the 1980's as a result of the independence government's policy. While vis-à-vis overseas capital the policy has been one of encouraging local participation and joint ventures, with respect to South African capital it has been one of consistent buying out of subsidiaries by local state capital. However, such takeovers must be viewed with caution. They are likely to involve continued indirect participation on the part of former parent companies, and some of them may be deliberate attempts to increase profitability under the new PTA regulations, which give preferential tariffs on manufactures of local business within the PTA region. As South African owned manufactures they could not take advantage of this, since South Africa is outside the PTA.

The Anti-Apartheid Drive and Capital Flows

The overall impact of the disinvestment drive on capital flows up to the early 1980's had been minimal in terms of reducing the level of investment in the economies of Namibia and South Africa. And in the light of the above discussion on both the crisis of apartheid and changes in the world-economy it will be misleading to approach "divestments" purely in terms of the anti-apartheid movement in general or the divestment drive in particular. We need nonetheless to take into account the declining prospect of future business profitability in the context of apartheid which started setting in since the middle of the 1980's, and which was partly the outcome of the anti-apartheid mobilization.

The attitude of foreign capital in the later years of the 1980's showed a marked deviation from trends of the past, and has been called "the great trek of the multinationals" (*Southern African Economist*, 1988: 14–15). Of more significance than the implied exodus of capital is the political "drifting apart" of Western investors and their respective national governments with respect to their continued involvement in the apartheid economies. Western governments had become more resistant to divestment, while capital had become more responsive, a situation that is parallelled by the increased role of bilateral financing in the region pointed out earlier.

The insensitivity of Western governments was not difficult to understand. What needs to be explained is why Western investors became more sensitive than their respective governments. If such sensitivity is induced by the deterioration of the conditions of capital accumulation within the apartheid system, then it is understandable. However as is well known, sporadic political unrest does not necessarily affect direct investment in the short run, even though it can result in the outflow of small scale or short-term capital. "The great trek of the multinationals" implies massive outflows of capital. In this respect, it is in line with numerous reportings concerning the increases in the number of "divested" corporations. Such developments can only be ascribed to a crisis of the apartheid system as whole, brought about by the interplay of many factors.

However, as is well known, most of these "divested" companies retain links with the now locally-owned subsidiaries in a number of ways such as licensing, distribution, franchising agreements, etc. Sometimes transnational corporations will sell off a small subsidiary, on condition that the new owner signs a long-term contract to distribute their product. None of this changes the basic relationship between the former parent company and the local partner as the critical outside technical support is still supplied, and profits are generated. Such activities of "discredited" divestment are numerous. Such business practices have been the basic form of operation by Japanese companies in South Africa as already pointed out. This seems to be the trend for most of the newly "divested" Western companies, at least in the short term.

There are a number of other factors that operated to reduce the level of direct pullouts by companies. Restrictive measures taken by the South African authority in the wake of the political and debt crises of 1984 allowed capital, for example, to be taken out only at the "financial rand" rate—which was about half the "commercial rand" rate at which profits could be taken out. This made real divestment costlier than even reduced profits for some corporations (depending on the size of their assets).

Complicating such decisions was the political calculation involved on the part of the corporations. Some corporations may have counted on a quicker and relatively more peaceful resolution of the apartheid problem, something akin to the Lancaster House settlement in Zimbabwe. In that settlement, foreign corporations were protected from nationalization by the new constitution, while in due time the new government also came to depend upon the skill potential of the old corporate managers to keep the wheels of the economic turning (Hanlon, 1986c).

SADCC

The potential role of the SADCC program in the restructuring of the economic character of southern Africa revolves around two central issues which are inextricably related. One is the reorganization of the economic/market space away from the constraining industrial dominance of South Africa, i.e., the breaking down or at least a reduction in capacity of the South African economy as the central node through which the SADCC countries relate both to the outside world and to each other. This as we have seen involves the forging of much denser economic (and other) linkages among these countries themselves, such as the opening up of new trade routes outside the region as an alternative to the heavily-skewed South African customs union, which hitherto had a negative impact on the terms of trade of these countries. By virtue of this of course, it also involves the development of coordinating measures regarding the best way possible of relating to the outside world other than through South Africa.

The second issue concerns the aim of making South Africa less relevant as the regional base of corporate capital, i.e., the spring-board from which corporations extend their activities into the region at large. This requires finding alternative sources for South African capital in the region as a means of reducing the economic role of South Africa.

Both these issues are related to the industrialization potential of SADCC in the foreseeable future. For not only is South Africa at the center of the economic network of the region, but it is itself one of the main suppliers of manufactured goods to the SADCC countries in competition with the core countries of the world-economy. Thus a reduction in the economic centrality of South Africa would also imply a correspondingly higher industrial capacity on the part of these countries that would allow them to attract a diversity of investment capital. Prospects for such a high level of economic development in a relatively short time are quite dim for most of the countries concerned, given the current rigidity of sectoral preference of corporate capital in these countries, which tends to shy away from the development of heavy industry and tends to be concentrated in the primary sector as already discussed, and the downward trend of loan capital in the current conjuncture of the world-economy. This situation renders the impact of SADCC on current regional investment patterns less important than the effects of the conjuncture of the world-economy and the current crisis of the apartheid system. The significance of these three arenas of action cannot be assessed in isolation since they make up an integral whole.

Conclusion

Assuming the continuation of both the current contraction of the world market for capital investment, and a crisis-ridden apartheid system into the late 1990's and beyond, what is the possible impact of such a situation on the current regional investment patterns? In my view, this scenario by itself will not necessarily spell a dramatic change in the position of South Africa as dominant center in the region during this period, given the fact that the flow of new capital has been significantly reduced as we have seen to the region as a whole and not only to South Africa. Even though the crisis of apartheid may have aggravated the situation for South Africa, the rest of the region may not necessarily benefit markedly at the expense of South Africa.

A continuing crisis of the apartheid system in a world-economy that once more begins to expand (a new A-phase) could however have a more dramatic impact on regional investment patterns, as the SADCC countries might attract capital at a relatively higher rate than South Africa. This could result in the industrial expansion of Zimbabwe and its transformation into a significant alternative capital base to South Africa in the region. Such a trend could be boosted by the cooperation of the SADCC countries in a relatively more integrated and expanded market.

Turning to South Africa itself, a decline in the flow of new capital from overseas in the current conjuncture does not necessarily mean a corresponding absolute decline in the position of South Africa as a source of capital investment into the region. We have seen for example that precisely during the crises of the 1970's and the current one since the mid–1980's there was an expanded role of South African capital in the region. This particular aspect of South African dominance is likely to continue. An increased deterioration of the economic situation in South Africa will more likely force Anglo American and other giants of the South African economy to continue to expand their activities beyond South Africa as shown earlier. Even though the bulk of such capital is likely to go out of the region, as we have noted earlier, some of it will continue to flow into the region. Given the current world-economic conjuncture, most SADCC countries facing reduced outside flows could well continue to be as receptive to South African capital as they have been to the present. Thus what South Africa is losing in terms of being the springboard of core capital to the region at large, it could gain by increased direct involvement. A qualification must be made here regarding the future role of South African parastatals. As in the case of private capital, which in time transcended its original areas of concentration in the mining industry and went into other sectors of the economy, state corporations have also broadened their role beyond the more political and ideological boundaries. Thus, they have come to resemble private capital in many respects. However, while the future role of private capital in the region appears to be more predictable, that of public corporations whose historic role has hitherto been mainly defined by current imperatives of the apartheid regime is difficult to predict. The present privatization drive of the South African government will certainly affect significantly the future role of these corporations. On the one hand, by virtue of the reduction in the magnitude of public capital, it suggests reduced South African state economic involvement in the region. On the other hand, more of a business rationale could now determine the regional operations of the newly privatized units. But this must be viewed in the light of current race-class struggles involving particularly the privatization of state monopolies. The perception that privatization will potentially weaken the post-apartheid state thereby limiting its redistributive capacity in terms of shifting economic resources towards the excluded majority, as South Africa did in Namibia just before independence where civil service pension funds amounting to R700 million were ceded to the private sector (*International Labor Reports,* No. 40, 1990), has lately been more forcefully and explicitly stated. Both the Black trade unions and the ANC leadership have taken up this issue. The March 1990 protests organized by the trade unions, for example, are said to have achieved a measure of success in this regard (*New York Times,* 11/13/90, p.9).

On the whole the post-apartheid economic viability of South Africa will be significantly influenced both by the duration of apartheid and by the manner of its resolution. A prolonged crisis of apartheid with an increase in the divestment of capital could significantly weaken the South African economy in the region. And if this were coupled with an intense military/violent conflict, it might as well partly destroy basic infrastructure such that an upturn in the world-economy and/or an eventual resolution of apartheid would benefit South Africa even less than when apartheid is dismantled relatively earlier and more peacefully. The regional role of a post-apartheid South Africa may be marked, however, by significant qualitative differences from the present in the manner of its domination. While a majority government in South Africa will almost certainly not prefer to reduce its economic profile in the region, the non-economic, i.e., the military and political aspects of such a domination, could change. The destabilization maneuvers such as achieved through the sponsoring of such movements as RENAMO in Mozambique, UNITA in Angola, and, if present developments persist, the emerging role of Koevoet or a similar group in Namibia, which has enhanced the dominance of South Africa, can hardly be a preferred policy of a post-apartheid state, especially in the immediate post-independence period. Of course other forms of non-economic domination can be established that are not necessarily violent in nature but still equally or more effective under the rubric of "normalization" of relations with neighbors.

Notes

1. The exact magnitude of Japanese capital in the region has been hard to determine. Nevertheless there is little doubt that Japanese corporations have increased their activities in the region. In the case of South Africa Japan by the 1970's had replaced the U.S. as South Africa's second largest trading partner after Great Britain (*Financial Mail,* 1971), and Japanese corporations have since increased licensing and other contracts through local trading companies in South Africa (Makgetla & Seidman, 1980: 99, 162, 171). Furthermore, Japanese corporations have established numerous purchasing contracts for raw materials in the region at large as in the case of Namibian uranium (CIIR, 1983: 38–39) and numerous other financial dealings as in the case of Zimbabwe (Stoneman, 1978: 69).

2. Oil and gas exploration has not however been been neglected.

3. In another strategic product, the IDC holds a 50% share in the Sortuem Oil Exploration Company (United Nations, 1985: 144).

4. United Nations (1985: 45). Also through legislation the South African government can demand as much of the Rossing uranium as it wishes to buy (CIIR: 1983: 37).

5. In conjunction with private capital of South African origin, as well as with private and non-private forms of capital of other origins. The latter, as in the case of the Cahora Bassa dam, range from international consortia to government guaranteed loans (Middlemas, 1975).

6. From 1968 to 1983 using IMF data for direct investment *plus* portfolio investment *plus* other long-term capital.

7. Caution must be used in the interpretation of the decline of direct investment in the world-economy at this stage. Such a decline seems to affect U.S. and British multinationals more than others. The latter including

direct investment from Third World countries could show different trends for given regions or countries.

D. The Creation of SADCC and the Problem of Transport

Introduction

On April 1, 1980, with Zimbabwean independence practically guaranteed, nine southern African states, namely Angola, Botswana, Lesotho, Malawi, Mozambique, Swaziland, Tanzania, Zambia, and Zimbabwe, united by economic, political, and geographical interests and links, met in Lusaka in order to set up the Southern African Development Coordination Conference, SADCC.

The strategic goals of SADCC were defined as:

· the reduction of economic dependence, particularly, but not exclusively, on South Africa;
· the establishment of linkages for the creation of genuine and balanced regional integration;
· the mobilization of resources to promote the implementation of national, interstate, and regional policies;
· concerted action to guarantee international cooperation in the context of a strategy for economic liberation.

To achieve these goals, SADCC defined areas for cooperation, among which transport and communication received the top priority, since it is particularly by means of transport and communications links that South Africa has maintained the region's dependency.

The economic structure of southern Africa, characterized by an asymmetric relationship between South Africa and the other countries of the region, was a further influential political and economic factor in the formation of SADCC. This dependence on South Africa was most marked in trade, transport, and labor, and it was in the BLS countries (Botswana, Lesotho, and Swaziland) and in Namibia that the level of dependence was at its highest. Although one can speak of some interdependence, relations were sharply asymmetrical in favor of South Africa. Any development strategy drawn up by the countries of southern Africa had to take this reality into consideration.

The Structure of SADCC

The need to reduce economic dependence and to make joint efforts to achieve future regional and national development can be regarded as the principal content of the Lusaka declaration, published by the heads of state of SADCC when the organization was founded.

Economic liberation was seen as a vital condition for political liberation, since the economic dependence to which the SADCC members were subjected made them extremely vulnerable to the means of economic coercion developed by South Africa.

Thus two concepts emerge from the SADCC goals: development and unity. But both development and unity are not abstract principles. They only exist in concrete actions, and in accordance with the particular context of the region. The strategy of SADCC had to take into account the existence of a neighbor that was not only a regional power, but also one that has been hostile and aggressive; hence the importance of considering the end of apartheid in South Africa as a vital condition for the development of the SADCC project. But, despite this context, SADCC has considered that it was not created as a form of unity against apartheid, but as unity for development.

Regional development would not be possible without establishing an adequate regional transport and communications system capable of replacing the current one, through which South Africa has tried to strengthen its domination over the region. Thus at Lusaka the transport and communications sector was given priority. This priority can be easily understood, given that six SADCC countries are landlocked. For them, transport has of necessity a vital importance in multistate cooperation.

At the time of its creation SADCC identified around 500 projects with a total value of $6.5 billion. About 40% of this value was pledged by donors from outside the region, particularly by the European Community, the Nordic countries, Canada, the United States, and the World Bank.

SADCC's struggle for self-sufficiency and for a reduction in dependence did not mean any desire for isolation or any rejection of interdependence. SADCC intended to be a project based on the principles governing the cooperation desired within Africa, between Third World countries, and between all countries of the world. It is also important to bear in mind that at the time of its creation SADCC made clear its willingness to cooperate with all countries and community and institutional organizations, starting from the principle that it would be the governments of the SADCC countries who would have the right and the duty to determine priorities.

The decision on the form of regional cooperation that SADCC should undertake was rather difficult. Certain considerations underlay the cautious conception that characterized the formation of SADCC:

1. the political and ideological diversity in the region;
2. the varying characteristics of underdevelopment and unequal development inherited at the time of the independence of the countries of the region, resulting from the different forms of colonization to which the countries of the region were subjected by the various colonial powers;
3. the different roles played by different factors in the various countries, and their type of dependence, not only on South Africa, but also on the capitalist world-economy;

4. lessons drawn from experiences of the regional cooperation model of market integration in other regions of sub-Saharan Africa.

The experiences of the East African Community and of the PTA led the SADCC member countries to fear the creation of a supranational structure. It was recognized at the Arusha summit that for politically and economically diverse states the model of market integration would lead to unequal distribution of the benefits of regional cooperation. Thus tensions and conflicts could best be avoided by acting collectively to reduce economic dependence. SADCC opted for a decentralized, non-bureaucratic structure, which demands maximum participation from the member states. SADCC's policy and regional program are set down and approved at the annual meetings of the heads of state and in meetings of ministers of the nine countries. The programs are implemented by the country or countries where they are located, and not by SADCC itself.

The conception of SADCC as regards regional cooperation and coordinated development took the form of selected sectoral programs. This conception is not the same as the institutional coordination and planning that are typical of models of market integration and integrated development. Institutional planning requires a supranational element, where the members give up part of their sovereignty in favor of collective economic planning.

Each member state is responsible for the selection, financing, and execution of the projects within its sphere, taking into consideration SADCC priorities. Politically, regional decisions are taken and sustained by consensus at the level of meetings of the Council of Ministers. Administratively, the organization maintains a small secretariat in Gaberone, headed by an executive secretary. This is all so as to avoid a heavy and expensive bureaucracy, typical of supranational organizations. The secretariat does not draw up plans for regional integration. It is simply mandated to coordinate the action program and the foreign finance.

In general SADCC views institutional structures as a means of facilitating its work, and not as ends in themselves. Thus institutional structures have been created merely to serve concrete areas of development. The absence of a complex bureaucratic central apparatus makes possible dynamism in intergovernmental contacts and minimizes administrative expenditure. There exist the following institutions:

1. the summit of heads of state and government, which meets annually;
2. the Council of Ministers, which supervises implementation of the annual program;
3. the standing committee of officials, a body that assists the Council of Ministers, with sub-committees that meet regularly with each country responsible for a sector in order to evaluate results;
4. sectoral commissions to supervise high priority programs, of which up to now only one has been created, the SATCC (Southern African Transport and Communications Commission);
5. a secretariat to coordinate the implementation of the SADCC program and to serve its institutions.

The program of action is divided among the member states, with sectoral responsibilities attributed to each one in the following way:

Angola	Energy
Botswana	Agricultural research and control of animal diseases
Lesotho	Tourism, Soil use and conservation
Malawi	Forestry and wildlife
Mozambique	Transport and communications, Information, and Agriculture (1991)
Swaziland	Manpower development
Tanzania	Industry
Zambia	Mining
Zimbabwe	Food security

Namibia   Fisheries (a sector that was previously Mala-
                    wi's responsibility.

The distribution of sectoral responsibilities to the member countries
was not done on the basis of comparative advantage, but on the
basis of the attributes of the individual members.

It should be considered that this whole concept of organization
also derived from a real analysis of the potential of the group of
countries of the region, which makes SADCC an organization sui
generis.

The Results of Cooperation

In general, despite the severe economic problems caused by recession in the world-economy, lengthy periods of drought, and the
destabilization that plagues the region, SADCC has had positive
results. To a large extent this bears testimony to the political will
and determination that inspire the countries that are its members,
despite their continuing economic vulnerability.

In some of these countries, particularly Angola, Mozambique,
Tanzania, and Zambia, the rate of inflation is higher than 30%.
SADCC's choice of gradual, discontinuous and growing development, based on programs of mutual benefit, has in fact proved
effective. Regional cooperation has become an integral part of the
thinking of the countries of the region (see Table 1).

Although overall dependence on South Africa has not been
reduced, some significant successes have been achieved towards this
goal. Many of SADCC's aims have been achieved, and two in
particular should be stressed, namely:

· the mobilization of resources to implement national, interstate and regional policies;
· concerted action to guarantee international cooperation in
  the context of a strategy for economic liberation.

The spirit of cooperation among the SADCC countries can also
be seen in the coordination among the countries in mobilizing

resources to solve the problems of each corridor. Complementing this is the implementation of the projects and a relative increase in the volume of traffic. Of particular importance is the positive evolution in the upgrading and development of the corridors and regional airports (Dar es Salaam, Gaberone, Kilimanjaro, Lilongwe, Maseru, and Matsapa), as well as in carrying out the energy programs.

But there remain problems that still limit any substantial increase in traffic (Table 2) through the corridors, such as a shortage of wagons and locomotives, the poor state of conservation of the lines, and security conditions in the corridors. This is the reverse of what has happened with air links which have been considerably improved (Table 3).

It should be noted that in the analysis of regional cooperation special stress was and is laid on the transport and communications sector, since, as stated above, it is a determinant factor for the development of the countries of the region. Thus we will take a more detailed look at this sector, so as to understand its origins in depth, based not only on its historical development but also on the current dynamics of the sector.

In southern Africa there is an extensive network of roads and railways linked to seaports, which received its current configuration during the colonial period. Of the nine SADCC countries, six are landlocked, and the major transport routes of the three coastal countries link the ports to areas of great economic activity in the region's interior.

In the SADCC area there are five traditional transit systems with the following corridors:

1. The Maputo Corridors
   for South Africa, Swaziland, and Zimbabwe, with links for Botswana, Zambia, and Zaire;
2. The Beira Corridor
   for Zimbabwe, with links to Botswana, Zambia, and Zaire, and a connection with Malawi;
3. The Nacala Corridor
   for Malawi;

Table 2-D-1
SADCC Project Financing Status by Sector ($ Million), 1989–90

Sector	No. of Projects	Total Amount	Foreign		Local		Secured		Negotiated		Gap	
			Amount	%	Amount	%	Amount	%	Amount	%	Amount	%
Energy	92	670.90	651.22	97.07	19.68	2.93	182.29	27.17	0.00	0.00	488.61	72.83
Food, Agriculture, Natural Resources												
Agricultural research and training	17	259.23	246.40	95.05	12.83	4.95	74.85	28.87	0.00	0.00	184.38	71.13
Fisheries, forestry and wildlife	56	364.48	352.10	96.60	12.38	3.40	123.84	33.98	10.95	3.00	229.69	63.02
Food security	36	186.58	148.89	79.80	37.69	20.20	62.58	33.54	1.47	0.79	122.53	65.67
Livestock production and animal disease control	15	111.67	65.19	58.38	46.48	41.62	76.08	68.13	0.00	0.00	35.59	31.87
Soil & water conservation and land use	13	65.13	54.86	84.23	10.27	15.77	22.43	34.44	0.00	0.00	42.70	65.56

Table 2-D-1 (continued)

Sector	No. of Projects	Total Amount	Foreign Amount	Foreign %	Local Amount	Local %	Secured Amount	Secured %	Negotiated Amount	Negotiated %	Gap Amount	Gap %
Industry and Trade	15	23.72	23.30	98.23	0.42	1.77	5.68	23.95	0.39	1.64	17.65	74.41
Manpower Development	33	22.50	22.23	98.80	0.27	1.20	13.83	61.47	0.00	0.00	8.67	38.53
Mining	43	81.81	77.86	95.17	3.95	4.83	39.08	47.77	0.00	0.00	42.73	52.23
Tourism	8	10.49	10.27	97.90	0.22	2.10	2.56	24.40	0.00	0.00	7.93	75.60
Transportation and Communication	218	6078.60	5349.70	88.01	728.90	11.99	2423.60	39.87	358.10	5.89	3296.90	54.24
GRAND TOTAL	546	7875.11	7002.02	88.91	873.09	11.09	3026.82	38.44	370.91	4.71	4477.38	56.85

Notes:
1. The column "secured" includes both local and foreign resources.
2. The column "negotiation" refers to resources for which there is a clearly identified funding source and a high probability of concluding a funding with in a specified period.

Source: SADCC (1990)

Table 2-D-2
Total Traffic Entering and Leaving Zimbabwe To and From
Contiguous Railway Systems

Via	1987		1988	
	Imports	Exports	Imports	Exports
Beit Bridge	760,000	1,275,000	1,300,000	1,110,000
Limpopo Corridor	NIL	15,000	NIL	40,000
Beira Corridor	95,000	302,000	110,000	283,500
Plumtree/Mafeking	470,000	680,000	450,000	635,000
Victoria Falls/Zambia	235,000	380,000	350,000	730,000

Source: SADCC (1989: 47).

Table 2-D-3
Number of Civil Flight Services per Week Between the SADCC
Member States

Year	1985	1986	1987	1988	1989
No. of Services	133	136	198	224	258
% Increase		2%	46%	13%	15%

Source: SADCC (1989: 49).

4. The Dar es Salaam Corridor
  for Zambia and Zaire;
5. The Lobito Corridor
  for Zambia and Zaire.

With their systems of land transport and 60 regular or semi-regular international or coastal shipping lines, the SADCC ports possess facilities to link the region with all the significant zones of world maritime trade. Other important transit lines in southern

Africa are Durban-Zimbabwe, Durban-Botswana, and Richards Bay-Zimbabwe or Botswana. The ports of East London, Port Elizabeth, Cape Town, and Saldanha also have links with the neighboring countries via Johannesburg. Walvis Bay and the secondary ports of Swakopmund and Luderitz in Namibia are linked to the railways of South Africa. Table 4 shows the total volume of cargo handled in the ports of the region.

In expectation of general and rapid economic growth, as from 1970 South Africa carried out major investments to containerize its transport system. In the 1980's it found itself with excess capacity on its ports and railways. In 1976 Mozambique closed its border with Rhodesia, thus implementing United Nations sanctions against the Ian Smith regime. The South African companies operating there, and the rest of the Rhodesian economy, used, however, the alternative routes in South Africa that had meanwhile been completed. At the same time actions were begun to destabilize transport

Table 2-D-4
Cargo Handled in Ports in 1987 (Millions of Tons)

Dar es Salaam	3.6
Nacala	0.1[1]
Beira	1.7[1]
Maputo	2.3[1]
Lobito	0.3[2]
Durban	48.4
Richards Bay	47.5
East London	1.8
Port Elizabeth	3.5
Cape Town	4.1

Notes:
1. Does not include coastal shipping.
2. Figure is for 1986 and does not include shipping.

Source: Southern African Development Coordinating Conference (1988); South Africa (1989). Calculated on the basis on tonnage.

in the region, particularly attacks by Rhodesian commandos and later by Renamo against the transit corridors in Mozambique.

The location of the SADCC ports is geographically advantageous. In comparison with the South African ports, they are only a short distance from some of the most important economic zones in the region (see Table 5). SADCC policy consists in trying to convert geographical advantage into economic advantages. But South Africa is also strongly interested in attracting the cargo of its neighbors and uses every possibility to link the countries of the region to its own transport systems. The SADCC countries affected by the policy of destabilization are thus concentrating a large part of their material and financial resources on the revitalization and modernization of the transport sector. The transit corridors play a special role here. In 1986–87 the SADCC countries sent 62% of their exports to, and received 56% of their imports from, partners overseas. All the countries of the interior depend on the transit corridors in coastal and other countries. On their journey between the port and the point of origin or destination, 73.1% of the total foreign trade of Zambia, 49.5% of Zimbabwe, 49.5% of Malawi, 45.1% of Swaziland, and 14.3% of Botswana passed through one

Table 2-D-5
Selected Rail Distances between Economic Centers and Ports
(in Kilometers)

	Dar es Salaam	Nacala	Beira	Maputo	Richards Bay	Durban	Lobito
Blantyre		807	648	2,519	2,368	2,567	
Lilongwe		1,007	1,024	2,895	2,712		
Harare	3,468		602	1,481	1,986	2,066	
Lusaka	2,042		2,025	2,020	2,737	2,817	2,494
Gaborone	3,556		1,710	1,715	(a)	1,168	
Johannesburg				584	659	835	
Matsapha				275		540	

Note:
(a) Via Zimbabwe

or more countries of the region. The maritime trade of these countries always generates transit transport. The second largest group of cargo flows are those between SADCC and South Africa, where imports dominate. In third place comes transport within SADCC, and finally transport between SADCC and other African countries.

Destabilization of the corridors and of other communication routes by military acts and by trading measures (such as tariff wars, and secret transport contracts) causes serious difficulties both for the transit countries and for the countries of the interior. Apart from the loss of life and the damage caused by war, there are interruptions to the circulation of goods, and stoppages of productive activities. This and the use of alternative routes adds to the costs and the time of transport. As a result, the terms of trade deteriorate, and so does the balance of payments.

At times of conflict, the major routes for transit trade are the preferred targets for attacks and sabotage. Through the destruction of infrastructure, it is easily possible to paralyse or make difficult the economic life of one or more countries and to create economic dependence on the opposing political force.

South Africa took advantage of this possibility as part of its regional policy, and not only for political motives. For the transit of cargo from neighboring countries to South African ports produced important foreign exchange earnings. While the countries of SADCC have made efforts to develop their own transport systems and to increase their independence from external factors, South Africa has done all in its power to maintain dependence in the interest of its national economy and regional policy.

The Situation in the 1980's

Under normal conditions, the shortest corridors could also be the most economic ones for the countries of the interior. That means the Nacala Corridor for Malawi, the Beira Corridor for Zimbabwe and partly for Zambia, the Limpopo Corridor again for Zimbabwe, for Zambia and for parts of Botswana, the Ressano Garcia line for the Transvaal, and the Goba line for Swaziland and for the Johannesburg area. But the policy of destabilization, with its constant attacks on the SADCC corridors, has resulted in considerable displacement of cargo flows. In Mozambique, between 1979 and 1988 the amount of transit cargo handled dropped from 6 million to 2.7 million tons, while in Angola transit traffic came to a complete halt. A large part of these cargoes was diverted to ports that are much further away (see Table 6).

In 1988, the landlocked countries of SADCC transported about 50% of their maritime foreign trade (by tonnage) through South African ports. Prior to Mozambican independence, all of the maritime traffic of Malawi, maritime traffic, 90% of Zimbabwe, 90% of Swaziland, and over 65% cent of that from the eastern Transvaal passed through Mozambican ports (*Estudos Moçambicanos,* Nos. 5/6). The data mentioned above clearly reflect the

Table 2-D-6
Effective Use of Transit Ports by Countries of the Interior
(Percentage of Maritime Foreign Trade Cargoes)

	Port	1984	1987
Zambia	Dar es Salaam	60	99
	RSA Ports	40	1
Malawi	RSA Ports	70	78
	Nacala	23	0
	Beira	5	17
	Dar es Salaam	2	5
Zimbabwe	RSA Ports	51	36
	Beira	28	48
	Maputo	21	16
Botswana	RSA Ports	100	100
Swaziland	Maputo	70	56
	RSA Ports	30	44

Source: Southern African Development Coordination Conference (1988). Calculated on tonnage basis.

situation created by the policy of destabilization by the end of the 1980's. Despite this, governments and carriers, even the South Africans, have continually stated their interest in the "natural outlets to the sea," particularly through Mozambique. In fact, transit traffic has always increased in those periods when the lines have been successfully protected against Renamo actions.

A report from the South African Foreign Trade Organization (SAFTO) noted a new increase in South African exports through Maputo between 1988 and 1989, after a reduction from 6.8 million tons in 1973 to 0.45 million tons in 1988 (*Weekly Mail*, 1/12–19/1989). The last two years of this period, almost to the end of 1988, were characterized by intensive Renamo activity.

In 1984 the then South African Transport Minister Schoeman described Maputo as the natural port for the Transvaal and called on private businessmen to invest there (*Rand Daily Mail*, 8/14/1984). Even in 1977, two years after Mozambican independence, 43% of all cargo handled in Maputo came from South Africa. In 1986, R.F. Botha stressed in Parliament the importance of Maputo for the exports of the eastern Transvaal, and said the possibility should be studied of South Africa participating in the modernization of the port (*The Star*, 5/7/1986).

Despite the special significance of Maputo port for South Africa and particularly for the Transvaal, it should be borne in mind that this country does possess its own modern ports. In 1988 South African ports handled a total of 88 million tons of overseas trade, and almost two million tons of coastal traffic. In that overseas trade there also figured exports from the Transvaal.

Thus interruptions to traffic along the transit routes between the Transvaal and Maputo caused by Renamo activity did cause real economic losses for the carriers, but they were not so hard to bear for the South African economy as a whole. Finally the difference in the distance in the routes to Maputo and to South African ports is not very large.

But for Mozambique, where income from transport services provides almost 20% of the assets on the balance of payments, interruptions caused substantial foreign currency losses. In many of these cases, apart from the cargoes, the ships too, originally headed for Maputo or other Mozambican ports, were diverted to South African ports. Under such circumstances, the high fixed costs of transport infrastructures were not covered, and still further costs resulted from the necessary repairs to sabotaged lines.

The great advantage in terms of distance provided by the port of Beira was evidently the reason why Zimbabwean troops were sent into Mozambican territory to protect the railway, road, and pipeline of the Beira Corridor against Renamo attacks. This measure taken by the two governments, as well as the work on rebuilding and extending the port and the railway, have made Beira once again an attractive proposition for Zimbabwean carriers. From 1986 onwards they exported and imported more goods each year than the previous one through Beira. In 1988 this reached a transit volume of 1.28 million tons. The figure rose further in the years 1989–90, as can be observed from Table 7.

In 1988 Zimbabwe exported about 300,000 tons through the port of Maputo, about 25% less than in the previous year. The route to Beira is much cheaper for Zimbabwe than the route via Durban. Despite the reduced tariffs charged by South Africa for many cargoes, the Beira route only costs half as much as the Durban one (comparing 1985 prices for overland transport of fertilizers, steel, and containers loaded with general cargo and tobacco).

South Africa's destabilization policy also led the other countries to a similar situation. In 1988, Malawi was obliged to spend 43% of its export earnings just on transporting its foreign trade cargoes on the lengthy route to the South African ports (*Beira Corridor Group Bulletin,* No.13, 1989). A paradoxical situation, given that the distance from Malawi to Nacala is only one-third as long as that to Durban. Extremely complicated transport conditions arose for Zambia. Zambia's geographical situation is not very favorable, and so it depends for its maritime trade entirely on transit through other countries. Because of the war in Angola, Zambia had to cease using its traditional route to the port of Lobito, and instead export its copper via the east African coast. But the Beira and Maputo corridors also did not offer complete and permanent security, while the Tazara railway between Zambia and Dar es Salaam struggled with organizational and technical difficulties.

South Africa has viewed the SADCC transit corridors in two ways: on the one hand, as a locus of destabilization and economic and political pressure, and on the other as an opportunity to play "big brother".

Through its own military actions, and through its support for Unita and Renamo, South Africa has waged war against the corridors and other transport infrastructures that are of vital interest for the countries of the region. Sabotaging the transit trade through the corridors was accompanied by loss of confidence by the carriers, who always had to divert their cargos to the railways and roads of South Africa.

Constant interruptions to the transit routes, the resulting delays in circulation, and the destruction of and damage to means of transport led to an additional shortage of locomotives and wagons. In this situation the countries of the region found themselves forced to hire rolling stock from South Africa.

But the South African corridors also had a role to play in the framework of South Africa's regional policy. South African advisors in 1981 set out a list of possible measures against neighboring countries which could be applied in South Africa's political interests. Among them were "limiting or prohibiting the use of South Africa's railway and harbor facilities," and "ignoring or infringing the rights of adjacent land-locked states under the Law of the Sea (U.N.)" (Geldenhuys, 1981). By using its support for military actions against the SADCC corridors and the possible closure of its own transit routes at the same time, South Africa tried to cut off the neighboring countries from overseas markets, and made use of the situation thus created in favor of its own regional policy.

In the forced situation in which several of the region's transport companies found themselves, South Africa offered to play "big brother". For A. Moolman, the 1989 General Manager of South African Transport Services (SATS), this meant technical assistance, maintenance, and servicing, hiring out planes and locomotives as desired by the neighboring countries, at market prices and under flexible conditions. "The purpose then will not be an immediate return, but the potential of doing profitable business later." And he

Table 2-D-7
National Ports and Railway Company of Mozambique Commercial and Planning Directorate Port Handling 1989–90 (in thousands of tons)

Indicators	1 1989 Actual	2 1990 Actual	3 Planned	4 Ratio 2:3	5 Ratio 2:1
Tons/Port Total	6,387.1	5,979.7	7,006.4	85.3%	93.6%
National	1,100.0	1,031.3	1,302.8	79.2%	93.8%
International	5,287.1	4,948.4	5,703.6	86.8%	93.6%
Imports	1,536.9	1,440.3	1,885.7	76.4%	93.7%
Exports	219.8	255.6	377.2	67.8%	116.3%
Transit	3,530.4	3,252.5	3,440.7	94.5%	92.1%
S. Africa	1,134.2	667.3	965.0	69.2%	58.8%
Swaziland	346.4	431.3	391.0	110.3%	124.5%
Zimbabwe	1,868.7	1,977.7	1,944.5	101.7%	105.8%
Malawi	39.8	67.6	32.4	208.6%	169.8%
Zambia	119.5	98.9	105.8	93.5%	82.8%
Others	21.8	9.7	2.0	485.0%	44.5%
Maputo Port	3,133.2	2,955.5	3,104.5	95.2%	94.3%
National	343.2	413.7	361.9	114.3%	120.5%
International	2,790.0	2,541.8	2,742.6	92.7%	91.1%
Imports	876.4	965.7	952.2	101.4%	110.2%
Exports	151.7	190.6	159.4	119.6%	125.6%
Transit	1,761.9	1,383.5	1,631.0	84.9%	78.6%
S. Africa	1,134.2	667.3	965.0	69.2%	58.8%
Zimbabwe	259.5	286.9	275.0	104.3%	110.6%
Swaziland	346.4	431.3	391.0	110.3%	124.5%
Others	21.8	0.0	0.0	0.0%	0.0%
Beira Port	2,503.9	2,529.9	2,788.6	90.7%	101.1%
National	292.7	304.6	329.0	92.6%	104.1%
International	2,211.2	2,225.3	2,459.6	90.5%	100.6%
Imports	393.3	320.7	553.1	58.0%	81.5%
Exports	50.4	45.6	101.6	44.9%	90.5%
Transit	1,767.5	1,859.0	1,804.9	103.0%	105.2%
Zimbabwe	1,609.2	1,690.8	1,669.5	101.3%	105.1%
Malawi	38.8	59.6	27.6	215.9%	153.6%
Zambia	119.5	98.9	105.8	93.5%	82.8%
Others	0.0	9.7	2.0	485.0%	—

Table 2-D-7 (continued)

Indicators	1 1989 Actual	2 1990 Actual	3 Planned	4 Ratio 2:3	5 Ratio 2:1
Nacala Port	420.2	267.5	734.8	36.4%	63.7%
National	177.6	116.3	300.1	38.8%	65.5%
International	242.6	151.2	434.7	34.8%	62.3%
Imports	234.9	136.7	330.4	41.4%	58.2%
Exports	6.7	6.5	99.5	6.5%	97.0%
Transit	1.0	8.0	4.8	166.7%	800.0%
Malawi	1.0	8.0	4.8	166.7%	800.0%
Quelimane Port	200.4	174.1	266.6	65.3%	86.9%
National	161.8	156.4	213.5	73.3%	96.7%
International	38.6	17.7	53.1	33.3%	45.9%
Imports	31.8	11.4	43.9	26.0%	35.8%
Exports	6.8	6.3	9.2	68.5%	92.6%
Pemba Port	59.6	24.8	62.4	39.7%	41.6%
National	54.9	12.4	48.8	25.4%	22.6%
International	4.7	12.4	13.6	91.2%	263.8%
Imports	0.5	5.8	6.1	95.1%	1,160.0%
Exports	4.2	6.6	7.5	88.0%	157.1%
Imhambane Port	69.8	27.9	49.5	56.4%	40.0%

added: "Eventually we may even become members of the Southern African Development Coordination Conference" (*Financial Mail,* 11/17/1989).

Here one notes the continuation of the "transport diplomacy" of J. Loubser:

Transport diplomacy can be seen in this context as the strongest and most strategic antidote to isolation and for the realization of the RSA's potential for creating prosperity and bringing about stability in the subcontinent. The establishment and maintenance of communication by means of railways, airways and harbors can be seen as South Africa's key to Africa (Loubser, 1980).

"Transport diplomacy" was one side of South Africa's regional policy in the 1980's. The other was destabilization. In 1989, G. Babb, then South Africa's Deputy Director of Foreign Affairs, confirmed the two aspects: "It is true that we previously supported Renamo, but we are not doing so now, and we would like to make this clear" (BBC interview, *Noticias,* 3/17/1989).

The object was now clear. "South Africa, as a SADCC member, could help boost African economies in power generation, transport, agriculture, and technology. . . . After years of enmity, sanctions and other pressures against the country, many African states now see South Africa as a potential partner" (*Financial Mail,* 7/7/1989).

The events of the 1980's left deep marks on regional transport. Between 1982 and 1985 the port of Maputo alone lost $ 534 million because of the decline in South African traffic. Over the same period Mozambique Railways lost $ 260.5 million in freight income (Johnson & Martin, 1989). The condition of the infrastructure and the loss of means of transport led to a great demand in the SADCC countries for rolling stock and maintenance services.

The change in South African regional policy at the end of the 1980's has been not just a simple expression of good will, but the result of the balance of forces inside South Africa, and of the processes under way in the region after Cuito Cuanavale.

"Transport diplomacy" has adapted to the new situations. We cite A. Moolman from 1989 again: "Transport diplomacy may have started with an element of altruism, but it's being conducted on a very strict business basis now. . . . It has been profitable. SATS earned more than R30m in the six months ending July 31 playing the role of big brother" (BBC interview, *Noticias,* 3/17/1989).

At the same time, South Africa has used the last few years to improve its own position in the struggle for cargo, particularly through other investments in transport and technological innovations, and a marketing thrust in the region and in the rest of the world by South African agencies and transport companies. According to the *International Herald Tribune,* the result is that "South Africa earns about R270 million a year from the use of its rail and harbour facilities by neigbouring countries" (9/29/1989: 9).

From the start, "transport diplomacy" was in harmony with the intentions of the handful of large-scale transport companies who operate in most of the region's transport corridors, and in maritime transport. They are dominated by South African capital and are interlinked. Their firms possess ships, land transport and maintenance resources, their own containers, and a vast network of highly experienced agencies and representations. They control much of the transit traffic in southern Africa.

The "market leader" is Manica Holdings Ltd. with its freight service. This South African group has 40 representations, in all the countries of SADCC with the exception of Angola. Manica Freight Services offers a package of various services, such as transport, cargo operations, warehousing, consultancy, agency work, and a "Total Freight Management" service. In Mozambique, Manica controls between 70–80% of cargo in transit, and represents 50% of the ships that stop at the country's ports. Manica and other transport and agency firms, representations, and "Offshore Companies" have at their disposal an extensive and efficient system for transport management in southern Africa. The group has in itself the power to dominate the transport market. It has, at the same time, many years of valuable experience, the knowhow and the necessary means of transport, as well as the ability to make competitive offers, to dictate prices and conditions, and to direct cargo along various overland and maritime routes according to tariff and contractual maneuvers. In this situation, a large part of the freight charges and commissions deriving from the SADCC corridors flow into South African bank accounts. The current level of transport monopolization in southern Africa links substantial numbers of clients to the companies that have traditionally dominated the sector.

Based on the principles of the Lusaka Declaration, the SADCC member countries agreed in 1980 on the establishment of a "Southern African Transport and Communications Commission" with the task "to reduce economic dependency, particularly, but not only, on the Republic of South Africa. . . ." In the transport and communications sector SADCC is carrying out a vast program of restoring and extending the network of connections, and of revitalizing services. The program involves 201 projects with a total value in 1989 of over $5 billion. Despite stepped-up Renamo activities in the second half of the 1980's, initial results have already been obtained, particularly in the Mozambican corridors.

Taking the Beira Corridor as an example, one can see that by the end of 1990, a total of 24 projects had been concluded, 25 were under implementation (with contracts already signed), 19 were in various stages of preparation with their finance guaranteed, while eight were still on the drawing board, without finance, or with the finance under negotiation. More than 85% of the external financing needs had been assured.

As for port traffic in this same corridor, one can note a moderate increase of around 4%, from 1.755 million metric tons in 1989 to 1.83 million tons in 1990. Rail traffic in the corridor experienced a growth of 30% (taking both national and international traffic into account), although the rail lines have operated under extremely difficult conditions.

Apart from the security problems in the Angolan and Mozambican corridors, SADCC transit traffic has also suffered from a shortage of locomotives and wagons, management and communications difficulties, and some technical shortcomings in the roads and railways. The SADCC annual report stated: "This situation compelled land-locked member states to continue to rely heavily on the transport routes through South Africa for their overseas trade. It is, therefore, absolutely necessary that implementation of SATCC programs in the regional corridors be vigorously pursued to enable one of the basic goals of SADCC, reduction of dependence on South Africa, to be achieved" (SADCC, 1989).

Problems of the Future

The physical vulnerability of transport routes remains the same at all times. But the real risk of being attacked depends on the balance of internal and regional forces and on the general political climate. The ending of military tension within individual countries and throughout the region would facilitate the normal circulation of people and goods. But the correct use of modern installations and routes also requires modern techniques for managing complex processes.

In transport, the struggle between the corridors for transit cargo, as well as the introduction of multimode technologies, leads on to the need to create new forms of cooperation both between transport and the rest of the economy, and between the various participants in the transport process. Such cooperation would have two major aims: to guarantee transport from door to door, or at least between "dry ports," that suffers from little or no interruption; and to enter into stable long-term relations between transport and its main users which allows the application of multimode technologies.

Containerization and other technologies which go beyond the limits of just one branch of transport are based on major infrastructural investments, which demand a high rate of future use of installed capacity. Only in this way will it be possible to reach a reasonable level of transport costs and tariffs that stimulates trade.

Cooperation in multimode transport creates interdependence among the participants. In containerized transport and other forms of multimode transport all the partial processes depend technologically on each other, and taken together they form a transport chain. Each company participating takes responsibility for the final result, and its financial situation is influenced by the costs and income of the entire cooperative system. This, as well as the general possibility of transport linking zones, countries and peoples and of opening access to markets, could become factors of political stability.

The contradiction that will remain significant for regional cooperation lies in the desire of the SADCC member countries to take sovereign decisions over their transport without any discrimination and the economic and political interests of the South African state and South African capital, especially the transport companies who are already operating in the region together with foreign firms.

In the coming period important areas of transport in southern Africa will remain under direct or indirect South African control. But the cooperation of the SADCC member countries with the major transport companies has traditions and seems indispensable for the future. It should be incorporated into the general context of regional cooperation including South Africa.

> For the region to attain true independence in transport and communications, it must provide alternatives that are efficient, reliable, and financially viable. The size of the South African transport system permits it to take advantage of network and scale economies not available to individual SADCC countries. Thus, it is through collective action that the SADCC countries can improve the competitive position of their network (SADDC, 1988).

This policy started from the competitive situation existing between the various transport systems in the region, and the great possibilities for collective action. Transport should stimulate the trade and development of each one of the countries. To achieve this, state sovereignty had to be maintained over the most important transport routes, particularly the transit corridors, even under conditions where they are being used by companies of other ownership.

To struggle for just conditions also meant defending the interests of the national carriers against monopoly pricing policies, in this way protecting the terms of foreign trade. There is a permanent contradiction between the interest of the transit countries in receiving foreign exchange from transport charges, and the desire of the countries of the interior for low transport costs for their exports and imports. It is the task of a coordinated tariff policy to deal with this problem in favor of the economic development of all the countries concerned.

Apart from the coordination of projects for the development of their transport systems, the SADCC countries have other possibilities in the struggle for just conditions in regional transport:

· the acquisition of cargo by collective institutions, and "cargo sharing" on the basis of the 40/40/20 UNCTAD formula or some other proportion agreed between the selling and buying countries;

· the consolidation of cargo in containers and other cargo

units so as to permit the extension of multimode transport in the region;
- improved management of the means of transport and of procedures, including the application of systems of modern communication;
- the establishment of regional cooperation organizations between transport companies, transport companies and carriers, participants in multimode transport, and companies that act as middlemen (forwarding, shipbroking, chartering, etc.); and
- cooperation in commercial and transport legislation.

The two sides in the current conflict are well aware of the importance of transport for southern Africa. The efforts of the democratic forces of the region and the world for a peaceful solution involve transport as a factor of communication and development.

When the goals for each SADCC sector were defined, reference was made to the need as well to expand the regional system of telecommunications. By the year 1988–89, 38 telecommunications projects had already been drawn up, whose cost was estimated at $ 744.1 million; 45% of the necessary finance had been guaranteed (Beira Corridor Authority, 1990).

Several of the projects on the list, including the microwave links Mbeya-Mzuzu-Blantyre, Blantyre-Tete-Harare, Harare-Mutare, and Beira-Chimoio, as well as the integration of Mozambique and Swaziland into the international telecommunications network, were completed during the 1988–89 period.

But one also notes in this area difficulty in implementing some projects along certain corridors in Angola and to some extent in Mozambique, due partly to security questions, and partly to lack of the necessary funds. Table 8 gives us a picture of telecommunications flows in the region and the respective circuits from 1980 to 1987. This subsector is important, in an unobtrusive way, in SADCC sectors overall, because it has great influence not only for the reduction of dependence of some member countries (Swaziland and Lesotho) on South Africa, but also for efficiency in coordinat-

Table 2-D-8
Outgoing Traffic Analysis (thousands of paid minutes)
Summary of five countries

	1980–81	1982–83	1984–85	1986–87	Cumulative Annual Growth
Botswana	355	544	875	1049	19.8
Malawi	265	365	505	822	20.8
Tanzania	101	203	304	341	22.5
Zambia	526	754	1005	1622	20.6
Zimbabwe	555	802	1061	2117	25
Total: SADCC Region	1802	2668	3750	5951	22
RSA	14742	17670	14423	16709	2.1
Other destin.	5383	8680	11762	17118	21.3
Total: World	21927	29018	29935	39778	10.4
% of total traffic					
to SADCC countries	8.2	9.2	12.5	15.0	
to RSA	67.2	60.9	48.2	42.0	
to other destin.	24.5	29.9	39.3	43.0	
% of total traffic					
using satellite[1]	40.5	38.4	40.0	44.7	
% of SADCC traffic					
Direct Routes[2]	88.7	85.7	86.7	92.7	
Transit PANAFTEL[3]	0.9	1.8	1.1	0.8	
Transit RSA	9.0	9.0	7.2	4.1	
Transit Satellite (regional)	0.0	0.0	0.0	0.0	
Transit out of region[4]	1.4	3.5	4.9	2.5	

Notes:
1. Represents only traffic using the in-country earth stations. Does not, therefore, include traffic patched through a neighboring country's earth station.
2. Circuits hardpatched at a transit location within the SADCC region are considered direct.
3. This figure includes Kenya.
4. Usually via European locations.

ing and developing projected actions as a whole.

There is no doubt that SADCC came as a severe blow to the CONSAS plan launched by Pretoria. Suddenly South Africa saw its most dependent neighbors and its allies in the region become members of a project that was implicitly hostile towards it. Within South Africa, SADCC was, and is, regarded as a threat. Deon Geldenhuys stated that SADCC's success could increase South Africa's isolation, and could lead the countries of the region to become further involved in the liberation struggle against apartheid.

Thus the South African response was to promote and develop the policy of destabilization. While economic and diplomatic factors are important in destabilization, the principal means used by South Africa were military. South Africa promoted and support-ed terrorist groups acting in particular in Angola, Mozambique, Lesotho, and Zimbabwe. Their main targets were precisely develop-ment projects and transport and communications links. In fact, transport and communications, a vital area for the SADCC coun-tries, are still the preferred targets for destabilization. There are continual acts of sabotage and destruction of railways, roads, and bridges.

South African destabilization has already caused the SADCC member countries extremely high losses which the EEC, for exam-ple, now calculates at around 60 billion dollars. Faced with this situation, the SADCC countries have undertaken joint efforts in order to develop and consolidate unity and solidarity through coordinated activities in defence of their sovereignty and territorial integrity, as well as in protecting regional economic projects and interests. Examples of this cooperation and coordination include not only the presence of Zimbabwean and Malawian soldiers in Mozambique supporting the defence of the Beira and Nacala Corridors respectively, but also the material support given by Angola and Botswana, and cooperation in controlling the frontier with Zambia. South Africa will continue to promote acts of destabilization at various levels in southern Africa, limiting the success of SADCC being one of its goals.

The success or failure of the SADCC project would necessarily be determined by the involvement, or the distancing, of investors or donors, since finance is basic for implementing the region's programs. Thus all SADCC countries encourage foreign private investment, while there are certainly differences in their investment codes; in general the SADCC countries prefer joint ventures. In all the countries one factor is common—state control. Regardless of their political leanings, the state has been present in the placing of capital and the extraction of profits. SADCC defends the principle that private investment should be in accordance with the political and economic goals of the region.

A large part of the investment for SADCC projects comes from the World Bank, the European Community, and the Nordic countries. But the most significant investments are made bilaterally, mainly in the form of private investment. The countries of eastern Europe were never very involved in SADCC, and gave priority to bilateral cooperation with some individual SADCC members. Given the current political context in eastern Europe, these countries will be in no condition to carry on providing "solidarity aid" to Africa. They will become potential competitors for aid and for private investment.

One also notes that SADCC's conception of regional cooperation, that is, selected sectoral planning, attracted the interest of Western donor countries, probably after they had realized that traditional models of regional integration are not practical. One may consider that, due to the current attention given by the Western countries to eastern Europe, there will be some alteration in investment priorities. This would oblige the SADCC countries also to develop investment at the regional level so as to allow relative and positive development of their programs.

SADCC has to pay special attention to the volume and quality of Western investments, so that a reduction in dependence on South Africa does not become the consolidation of dependence on the West. This situation would create a serious conflict between the goals of SADCC of ensuring international cooperation in the framework of the Lusaka Declaration on the one hand, and on the other the creation of a new form of multilateral dependence in the region.

Despite all the difficulties, it can safely be stated that SADCC has managed to win the confidence of investors and donors. The growing acceptance of, and support for, the regional needs and priorities as defined by SADCC, also reflect the confidence that donors and investors have in SADCC.

The political will for economic cooperation has proved very strong. Above all, common opposition to the apartheid system and to South Africa's policy of regional dominance has served to strengthen this political will for economic cooperation. But after ten years of intense activity, directed essentially towards establishing the foundations for solid regional cooperation, through the creation and upgrading of decisive economic infrastructures, SADCC projected new development strategies for the 1990's. These include increasing agricultural production, and the production of consumer goods and raw materials, which will help stimulate trade. This master line in SADCC philosophy for the next ten years was laid down at the Harare summit of August 1989.

Among the various aims of this philosophy, it is worth stressing the decision to prepare the formalization of SADCC, giving it an appropriate legal status, taking into account the need to replace the organization's memorandum of understanding with a written agreement or treaty.

SADCC has also expanded the areas of collaboration among its members, so that it now covers social sectors such as information and culture. These facts allow us to conclude that SADCC is gradually implementing its project of building a network of regional cooperation and integration, which is likely to prove increasingly efficient and effective.

A new development in SADCC was the integration of Namibia as the organization's tenth member, after its independence. The participation of an independent Namibia in SADCC could relieve the economic dependence of this territory on South Africa. With this membership, SADCC will strengthen its organization and improve its capacities. This could constitute an unequivocal advance for the organization.

Despite the political transformations in southern Africa, and particularly the imminent end of apartheid and the start of a genuine democratization process in South Africa, there remains concern at the nature of the integration into SADCC of a post-apartheid South Africa. While there may be no ideological motives for a collision between the interests of the South African economy and of the economies of the SADCC countries, it is legitimate to consider that South African membership of SADCC will of necessity depend on the character and essential nature of the future South African government, and on its genuine concern for the well-being and economic development of the neighboring countries.

The model of market integration will not be ideal for a SADCC with 11 members, given the economic superiority of South Africa, since this would certainly lead to unequal development, with a strong tendency towards polarization. This leads one to conclude that, based on the specific quality of the type of relationships among the SADCC member states, the development model of integrated cooperation would be ideal, for it would allow that the countries of the region as a whole could, in a balanced manner, take due profit from the potential that it has.

In fact, the prospect of peaceful change in the South African political system presents the appearance of an economy with important infrastructures, and endowed with advanced technology, in the southern region of Africa. While receptive to regional cooperation, it is reasonable to think that a democratic South Africa will regard as its priority improving the well-being of its own people, through economic growth that allows the elimination of the current imbalance between the average wage in the Black community, and in the other communities.

As was stated during the summit marking the tenth anniversary of SADCC, a democratic South Africa could become a member of the organization. But this integration should contribute towards the establishment of sub-regional cooperation based on relations of interdependence, promoting the agricultural, industrial, technological, and infrastructural development of each one of the member countries, and of the entire region. This takes into account the fact that interdependence strengthens, whereas dependency implies a reduction in, the freedom and capacity for autonomous action for each country or group of countries working together.

Considering the specificity and the heterogenous nature of the countries of the region, one can state that the cooperation model that characterizes it—"think SADCC"—has proved to be the most appropriate, and constitutes a model for regional cooperation that will have to be treated with consideration and respect in the future.

South Africa's Economic Trajectory: South African Crisis or World-Economic Crisis?

Statement of the Problem

A s the Second World War came to a close, a period of seemingly unprecedented prosperity and growth spread across the world-economy. As the 1960's came to a close the realities of yet another worldwide stagnation emerged. Since then, the world-economy has been marked by decelerating growth, the redivision of tasks across the global division of labor, and generalized uncertainty in state economic policies. Neither the North nor South, East nor West has been spared. Parallel convulsions are evident in the interstate system as well. On the one hand, the United States has been dethroned from its unchallenged hegemonic position, and forced to respond more vigorous and innovative forces located in Europe and Asia. On the other hand, non-core political regimes, previously formed and cemented by conditions of expansion and the stability of the cold war, have been collapsing.

One of the most dramatic loci of such world-systemic cycles and trends has been states located in the semiperipheral zone—including South Africa. Changes in the global division of labor have generated ever higher levels of industrialization across the semiperiphery. Indeed, the early evidence from selected semiperipheral states led many to assert that crisis in core areas would provide the opportunity for semiperipheral states to expand continuously their growth

167

rates, productivity, and competitiveness on the world market. In more recent years, however, the semiperiphery has been marked as a whole by declining economic performance and prospects. Key factors here have been the shrinkage of international markets, protectionist measures imposed by core states, technological advances and challenges emanating from core areas, and the effects of mounting debt crises. Meanwhile we have witnessed the emergence of stronger social, political, and especially labor movements. In contrast to initial expectations, longer-term evidence would suggest that semiperipheral states are marked by endemic accumulation and political crises.

Given the distinctiveness of apartheid, few have placed South Africa within these changing global relationships, cycles and trends. Yet even the most ephemeral evidence would indicate that South Africa is no exception to the forces and conjunctural shifts evident across the semiperipheral zone. Take for example the simplest criterion, that of economic growth. On the basis of purely national data it has long been asserted that South Africa's rate of growth was among the highest in the world throughout the post–1945 period. As Graph 1 indicates, crude economic measures did indeed rise rapidly. Rising prices for gold in the 1970's only served to sustain such beliefs.

As the steam ran out of the gold boom, however, it became more commonplace to hear voices of uncertainty. By the mid–1980's a broad consensus emerged that South Africa was in the midst of a deep and intractable economic crisis. When this "crisis" began has been a matter of some dispute. While the cloud of speculative activity surrounding the spectacular rise in the price of gold in the mid–1970's and especially 1980–1981 momentarily obscured the emergence of this crisis, by the late 1980's many observers were arguing that the turning point of economic life occurred in the early or mid–1970's. As the Governor of the South African Reserve Bank argues, "the structural slowdown of South Africa's real rate of growth began around 1974, and not in 1981" (cited in Gelb, 1987: 33).

This was a most ambiguous turning-point. For in matching a variety of reversals on several different terrains, it permits quite

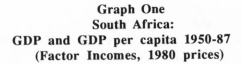

Graph One
South Africa:
GDP and GDP per capita 1950-87
(Factor Incomes, 1980 prices)

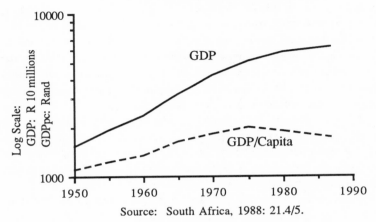

Source: South Africa, 1988: 21.4/5.

contradictory readings of the course and causes of what has come to be called South Africa's "organic crisis."[1] For South African economists the origins of the crisis is primarily to be analyzed in terms of internal economic imbalances,[2] and, as one moves into the 1970's, political struggles inside South Africa. For those conversant with the region of southern Africa, the early and mid–1970's have equal importance. It was during this period that Portuguese colonialism was overthrown and the struggle against minority rule in Namibia, Zimbabwe, and South Africa intensified. The growth of this political struggle on the regional terrain has entailed a massive direct economic cost for frontline states. At the same time the unproductive expenditures by the South African state associated with the defense of apartheid escalated, while South African capital saw the opportunity for expansion on regional and world markets foreclosed. Finally, if one moves beyond South and southern Africa, the mid–1970's signify, as argued above, no less a transition: it was precisely in this period that the full transition from seemingly endless expansion to stagnation in the world-economy took place.

If South Africa entered an economic and political crisis in the early 1970's, one may thus trace it on several different levels and to quite different roots. In contemporary accounts these roots are intermingled, leaving it uncertain whether and to what extent South Africa's crisis is due to political struggles in southern Africa or wider economic transformations. The implications of different possibilities, particularly as we move towards a majority-ruled South Africa, are considerable. What might, for example, be the economic effects of the demise of the apartheid state for both South and southern Africa, particularly in light of the continuing effects of the world depression, stabilization policies, etc.?

In order to begin to approach this issue we pose a key question: to what degree are the changes in South Africa's situation since the 1970's accounted for by a cyclical shift in the world-economy? And to what degree is it accounted for by the special political conflict of southern Africa?

Such a question cannot be approached by examining South or southern Africa alone. If the high level of political and military conflict particular to southern Africa is central, then a marked divergence in key aspects should be noted between the trajectory of South Africa and countries similarly located in the world-economy at the beginning of the 1970's. Thus while the world-economy's effects should be noted in the evolution of all comparable countries, we are particularly interested in the degree to which South Africa's economic vectors may have changed differently from those of comparable countries in the post–1970 period.

In order to estimate different trajectories we first need to select a set of countries similarly situated in the world-economy in the early 1970's. We have chosen nine countries which may be presumed to have been of comparable rank to South Africa in terms of strictly economic criteria: GNP per capita (GNPpc) plus a manufacturing sector of some significance. The list crosses Africa, Asia, and Latin America: Portugal, Mexico, Brazil, Chile, Taiwan, Peru, Turkey, Algeria, and Malaysia.[3] We have added to this list for comparative purposes two old Commonwealth and White settler states with high GNPpc (Australia and New Zealand), Zimbabwe (with a lower GNPpc, but a neighbor with a significant manufacturing sector), and South Korea (typical of the Newly Industrializing Countries of the 1980's, with a much lower GNPpc as of 1970 but a higher one as of the late 1980's).

Taking this group the question remains: to what extent does South Africa diverge from the common effects of the world-economic downturn after the early 1970's?

South Africa's Changing Position in the World-Economy

South Africa vis-à-vis the core
We explore this question first at a most basic level: to what extent has South Africa's command over world-economic resources changed over recent phases of world-economic expansion and contraction?

Graph 2 charts South Africa's distance from core areas by comparing GNPpc for South Africa as a percentage of the GNPpc average for four "organic members" of the core (France, Great Britain, F.R. Germany, and the United States). To the extent the

Graph Two
South African GNP/Capita as a
Percentage of Organic Core GNP/Capita

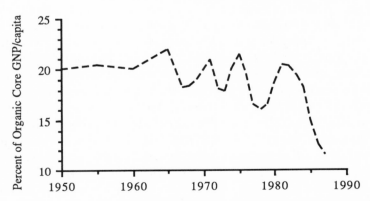

Sources: For 1967-87: from World Bank (1989a). Pre-1967 figures from World Bank (1976, 1980, 1984).

percentage increases, South Africa may be said to have moved upward within the global division of labor (or closed the "gap" between itself and core countries); to the extent the percentage falls so too has South Africa declined. This is one might note, a very different procedure than simply estimating—or even comparing— national growth rates (see the purely South African trends in Graph 1). As Graph 2 shows, during the period from 1965 to 1975 South Africa's position steadily revolved between 17–22% of the core average. A sharp fall after a peak in 1975 was broken by the gold fevers of 1980–81; since that time the trend has been steadily and disastrously downward, reaching a level of 11% in 1987.[4]

South Africa in comparative perspective
Such evidence suggests that the phenomenon of national economic decline is heightened at the world level, for even as stagnation has marked core countries since the early 1970's, South Africa has fallen even further. This leaves open, however, the degree to which South Africa has fallen further or faster than other countries outside our "organic core" group.

In order to approach this area we have measured, in Graphs 3– 5, our comparative countries' GNPpc as percentage of South Africa's GNPpc, i.e., our comparative cases are placed on an index of South Africa = 100. To fall below 100 indicates a position below South Africa's trajectory; to be above it indicates wealth and command of world-economic resources above South Africa's level.

South Africa versus the Exceptional Cases. Graph 3 places our exceptional comparative cases of Australia, New Zealand, South Korea, and Zimbabwe against the South African standard (i.e., South Africa=100). As might be expected, both Australia and New Zealand stand well above South Africa's position from 1950 onward. From the mid–1970's onward, however, the gap between them and South Africa clearly widens: here at least is further evidence of the growing gap between South Africa and core countries. If one examines the periphery, in this instance South Korea and Zimbabwe, quite different results emerge. From sharing a very similar position in 1975, South Korea has accelerated past South Africa, in stark contrast to Zimbabwe's movement down-

Graph Three
Core and Peripheral Competitors as a
Percentage of South African GNP/Capita

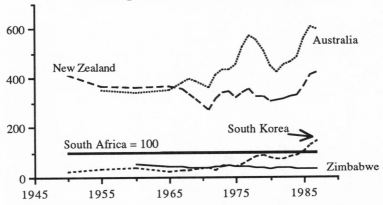

Sources: For 1967-87 from World Bank (1989a), except for Taiwan from
OECD (1967, 1984, 1989). Pre-1967 figures from World Bank
(1976, 1980, 1984).

Graph Four
Selected Countries as a
Percentage of South African GNP/Capita

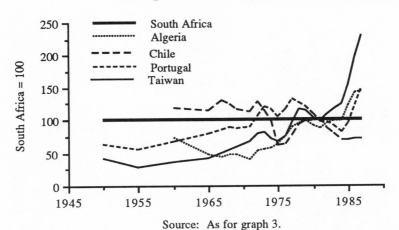

Source: As for graph 3.

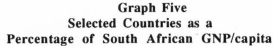

Graph Five
Selected Countries as a
Percentage of South African GNP/capita

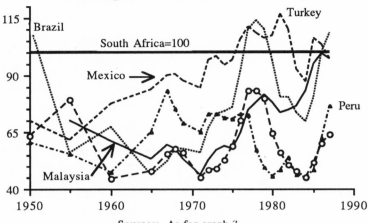

Sources: As for graph 3.

ward. While suggestive of a tied South African-Zimbabwean (if not regional) trajectory, such evidence is too limited to draw conclusions regarding South Africa's distinctiveness by comparison to similarly-situated countries as of the mid–1970's.

South Africa vis-à-vis the semiperiphery: What differences? To pursue this latter issue moves us to the comparison of South Africa with other semiperipheral states. This has been broken down into two graphs (Graphs 4 and 5) for clarity of presentation.

Taken individually, each case contains different turning-points. Several distinctive cases, may, however, be noted at the outset. On the one hand, Chile, alone above South Africa in 1960, has fallen significantly below South Africa since the outbreak of the world depression (and the rule of Pinochet and the Chicago economists). On the other hand, Taiwan has dramatically escalated from well below South Africa to well above it—following the pattern emblematic of South Korea in Graph 3 and the East Asian newly industrializing countries (NIC's) in general. More temperate cases of overtaking South Africa are to be found in the steady advance of Portugal and the better performance of Algeria since the early 1970's.

Adding these trends to those indicated in Graph 5 reveals more common patterns amidst the welter of individual paths. If one examines the period 1965–1975, it is evident that all our cases, with the sole exception of Chile, began to close the gap with South Africa. And while South Africa's high figures associated with the gold boom of 1980–81 distort the picture, the same general trend held from 1975 to 1987. In short, South Africa, even by comparison to states similarly situated within the global division of labor, has been falling further and faster.

One must note, however, the magnitude and pace of this slide. First, with the exceptions of Algeria, South Korea, and Taiwan, the gap between our core standard and all the states observed so far (including Australia, New Zealand, etc.) has widened since 1975. Second, the pace of South Africa's decline has indeed been more rapid, but only marginally so—although one may temper this statement if one examines only the 1981–1987 period.

First Conclusions. From this first set of macro-comparisons one may thus conclude that South Africa's decline in world-economic terms pre-dated the outbreak of the great depression in the early 1970's. Since that time South Africa's movement downward in the international division of labor has however accelerated, moving in concert with—but at a slightly more rapid pace than—the vast bulk of semiperipheral states.

It remains, however, to disaggregate both South Africa's profile and the differences between its trajectory and those suggested above. This is the task of the following sections.

The Structure, Pace, and Timing of Advance and Decline in the Current Great Stagnation

Growth and fluctuations

Evidence of a widely shared transition from boom to stagnation is charted in Table 1. Over the course of the 1950's and 1960's domestic production accelerated for all the countries under review here. The rate of the growth of South Africa's GDP during the

Table 3-1
Gross Domestic Product Average Annual Real Growth Rates

	1950–60	1960–70	1970–80	1980–87	1975	1987
Algeria	2.1	4.3	7.0	3.8	5.2	1.3
Brazil	3.1	5.4	8.4	3.3	5.2	3.0
Chile	2.2	4.5	2.4	1.0	-13.2	5.7
Malaysia	2.5	6.5	7.8	4.5	0.8	5.5
Mexico	3.2	7.2	5.2	0.5	5.7	1.4
Peru	2.6	4.9	3.0	1.2	3.5	6.9
Portugal	0.7	6.2	4.6	1.4	1.2	5.0
South Africa	3.0	6.3	3.6	1.0	2.4[a]	2.6[b]
Taiwan	7.6	9.2			4.8	12.4
Turkey	2.8	6.0	5.9	5.2	8.9	7.2
Australia	2.3	5.6	3.0	3.2		
New Zealand	2.2	3.9	2.3	2.9		
South Korea	2.0	8.6	9.5	8.6	7.5	11.1
Zimbabwe	4.1	4.3[c]	1.6	2.4	-2.1	-0.1

Notes:
a. South Africa, 1982.
b. 1961–70, not 1960–79.
c. SAIRR, 1989, 406.

Sources:
1950–60: World Bank, 1980.
1960–70, 1970–80: World Bank, 1982.
1975, 1980–87: World Bank, 1989a.
Taiwan: Asian Development Bank, 1986 & 1989.

1950's and 1960's was higher than most, but not spectacularly so—in contrast to some accounts which state that only Japan exceeded South Africa's pace in this period. In this period, at least, a rising world-economy lifted all boats.

In the 1970's such shared fortunes diverged. Stagnation and economic uncertainty in the core was matched for most of our cases by a substantially slower rate of GDP growth. The turning point—as measured by the annual rate of GDP growth (World

Bank, 1989a: Table 6)—occurred in almost all cases in 1973–74. The decline in growth rates attenuated in the late 1970's, due largely to the short-lived commodities boom, only to fall yet again to even negative rates in the 1980's. From the mid–1970's onward South Africa's fall was among the sharpest, paralleling or exceeding that of the worst Latin American cases. Zimbabwe's record amidst war and sanctions was erratic, but overall fell in the 1970's and 1980's. South Korea and Taiwan by contrast maintained and even exceeded (although erratically so) the pace they established in the 1950's and 1960's. If the world crisis was evident among all cases, clearly responses were divergent.

Sectoral patterns

Hiding beneath these decelerations and accelerations in growth rates were, however, significant transformations in the structures and distribution of economic activity. As many have noted, the capitalist world-economy's transition to stagnation marked more than simply a decline in growth rates: it signalled and propelled forward a remaking of the global division of labor as core areas shed competitive manufacturing production processes to the semiperiphery. If one examines the sectoral division of GDP over time for our cases this process *and its unevenness* is evident.

No great agrarian transformation is evident at the level of agriculture's share of GDP after the mid–1970's (see Tables 2 and 3). By the mid–1970's, the figure for agriculture in most of the countries concerned was already below 15%, although one might note that only South Africa and Chile were below this figure fifteen years earlier. Higher figures in the mid–1970's for South Korea, Turkey, and marginally Zimbabwe fell over the next decade and a half.

The path of manufacturing by contrast is intriguing. Between 1970 and 1987 the weight of the manufacturing sector increased in every country (reaching hyperindustrilizaton rates in South Korea) with the exception of South Africa, Algeria, and Australia (and probably New Zealand if data from the same sources were readily available). To explain these exceptions one might note Algeria's role as oil exporter, and Australia's more core-like path

Table 3-2
Percentage of GDP: Agriculture

	1955	1960	1970	1975	1980[a]	1987[b]
Algeria		16	10	9	6	12
Brazil	21	16	10	9	10	*11*
Chile		9	7	7	7	
Malaysia	36	36	31	28[c]	23	25[c]
Mexico	18	16	1	11	*10*	9
Peru	24	18	16	14	8	11
Portugal	30	25	18	14	13	9
South Africa	15[d]	12	8	8	7	6
Taiwan	29	28	15	11	8	5
Turkey	43	41	30	27	23	17
Australia		12	6	6		4
New Zealand				10	13	8
South Korea		37	27	24	16	11
Zimbabwe		18	15	16	*12*	11

Notes:
a. Figures in italics are for 1979, not 1980.
b. Figures in italics for years other than shown.
c. Asian Development Bank, 1986 for 1975 figure, 1989 for 1987 figure.
d. South Africa, 1982.

Sources:
1955, 1960, 1970: World Bank, 1984, with exception of Taiwan, from World Bank, 1980.
1975: United Nations, 1986: 122–139.
1980: World Bank, 1982.
1987: World Bank, 1989c.

(as substantiated in Graphs 3 and 4 where the gap between South African and Australian GNPpc increased).

Further confirmation of such divergent trends is provided by the distribution of the economically active laborforce (Table 4): Australia and New Zealand from 1960 onward have had few

Table 3-3
Percentage of GDP: Manufacturing

	1955	1960	1970	1975	1980[a]	1987[b]
Algeria		8	14	10	14	12
Brazil	2	26	27	24		28
Chile		21	26	20	21	
Malaysia	9	9	13	16[c]	24	23[c]
Mexico	24	19	24	23	24	25
Peru	23	24	24	25	27	23
Portugal	26	29	33	31	36	
South Africa	20[d]	21	23	22	23	23
Taiwan	19	212	33	35	35	39
Turkey	11	13	17	19	21	26
Australia		28	27	21		17
New Zealand			22	23	21	
South Korea		14	21	26	28	30
Zimbabwe		17	21	22	25	31

Notes:
a. Figures in italics are for 1979, not 1980.
b. Figures in italics for years other than shown.
c. Asian Development Bank, 1986 for 1975 figure, 1989 for 1987 figure.
d. South Africa, 1982.

Sources: as for Table 3-2.

workers committed to agriculture, while the percentage accounted for by industry has remained steady or fallen slightly. South Africa's reported percentage of the labor force in industry and agriculture has remained almost constant between 1960 and 1980, and at much higher levels in agriculture. In all the semiperipheral cases, by contrast, the percentage of agriculture has fallen while the percentage of industry has risen (or remained steady as for Peru and Chile). In several cases this crossing of paths has been dramatic, suggestive of the group of rapid industrializers (South Korea, Brazil, and Taiwan). If South Africa thus entered the period of the

Table 3-4
Distribution of Labor Force: Agriculture and Industry

	1960		1970		1975		1980	
	Agr	Ind	Agr	Ind	Agr	Ind	Agr	Ind
Algeria		12[a]	50[a]	13[a]	41		27[b]	31[b]
Brazil	52[a]	15[a]	44[a]	18[a]	38		31[b]	27[b]
Chile	28[a]	28[a]	21[a]	25[a]	20		17[b]	25[b]
Malaysia	63	12	56	14	53	15	50	16
Mexico	55	20	45	23	40	24	36	26
Peru	53	20	48	18	44	19	40	19
Portugal	44	29	33	33	31	34	28	35
South Africa	32	30	31	29	31	29	30	29
Taiwan	50	18	37[c]	30[c]	30[c]	36[c]	19[c]	42[c]
Turkey	70	11	68	12	61	13	54	13
Australia	11	40	8	37	7	35	33	6
New Zealand	15	37	12	36	10	36	9	35
South Korea	66	9	50	17	42	23	34	29
Zimbabwe	69	11	64	12	62	14	60	15

Sources:
World Bank, 1984, II, except:
a. World Bank, 1976.
b. World Bank, 1988.
c. Taiwan, 1988.

world-economic crisis with a relatively strong manufacturing sector, it has failed to advance further than almost all comparable cases.

Changing relationships of trade, production, and unequal exchange

During the interwar depression the world market in commodities and capital flows was shattered and brought to a standstill. This has not happened during the present world stagnation. During the last fifteen years significant ruptures and transformations in these relationship have however taken place. As Tables 5 and 6 on the structure of imports reveal, upward leaps in oil prices (1973–4,

1979–80) dramatically raised the percentage of imports accounted for by fuels (with the exception of our oil exporters), which then fell as oil prices declined in the 1980's. While data are completely unreliable due to the oil boycott, there is little doubt that this held true for South Africa as well. Meanwhile industrial goods maintained their overwhelming and surprisingly steady proportion of the value of imports over the 1970's and 1980's—although the volume of imports became increasingly constrained due to the debt crisis (see below). More significant is the overall trend in the terms of trade, which has been declining, often quite sharply, especially after the short-lived commodity boom of the 1970's (see Table 7). Gold prices—always countercyclical—alleviated this trend for South Africa only momentarily, as prices peaked first in 1974 ($194) and again in early 1980 ($850), only each time to fall substantially thereafter.

Deindustrialization in the core (and much of the periphery as well) and expansion of trade during this great stagnation did open up specific export opportunities for semiperipheral countries. As Tables 8 and 9 on export structures indicate, most of our countries expanded manufacturing exports during the 1970's and 1980's. Chile did not, based upon the politically-constructed resurgence of export production by large agricultural producers. South Korea's and Taiwan's export profile has become dominated to an unprecedented degree by manufactured goods, including a high proportion of the heavier and more technologically advanced "machinery and transport equipment" group. By contrast Zimbabwe's manufacturing exports are heavily weighted by semi-processed mineral and agricultural products (see chapter 2a).

Against this pattern of manufacturing and export orientation one must set South Africa. South African figures as reported by international agencies are almost useless because of the manipulation of figures due to sanctions and boycotts. It is common knowledge, however, that South Africa has had a difficult time in exporting even relatively simple manufactured goods beyond the regional market.[5] By comparison to Taiwan or South Korea, or even Brazil and Mexico, South Africa has not managed to enter into the process of capturing industrial production being shed by core

Table 3-5
Percentage Share of Merchandise Imports: Food, Fuels, Other Primary Commodities

	1960	1970	1975	1980	1987
Algeria	26	13		21	27
Food	4	2	2	3	2
Fuels	2	6		5	7
Other primary					
Brazil					
Food	14	11		10	9
Fuels	19	12	26	43	27
Other primary	13	7		6	8
Chile					
Food		15		14	12
Fuels		6	20	21	10
Other primary		7		4	4
Malaysia					
Food	29	22		12	10
Fuels	16	12	12	15	6
Other primary	13	8		6	4
Mexico					
Food	4	7		8	11
Fuels	2	3	6	2	1
Other primary	10	9		7	8
Peru					
Food	16	20		20	13
Fuels	5	2	12	2	1
Other primary	5	5		5	3
Portugal					
Food	15	14		14	13
Fuels	10	9	15	24	12
Other primary	28	13		11	8
South Africa					
Food	6	6		5	2
Fuels	7	5	0.25	0.6	0
Other primary	9	4		4	4

Table 3-5 (continued)

	1960	1970	1975	1980	1987
Taiwan					
Food		9	10	7	6
Fuels		5	14	26	11
Other primary		1	17	14	12
Turkey					
Food	7	8		4	4
Fuels	11	8	18	49	22
Other primary	16	8		5	13
Australia					
Food	6	6		5	5
Fuels	10	6	10	14	5
Other primary	16	7		5	4
New Zealand					
Food	8	15		15	7
Fuels	8	11	12	24	7
Other primary	16	10		7	4
South Korea					
Food	10	17		10	6
Fuels	7	7	19	30	15
Other primary	25	21		17	17
Zimbabwe					
Food				15[a]	10[a]
Fuels			23	17[a]	8[a]
Other primary				3[a]	3[a]

Sources:
1960: World Bank, 1982;
1970, 1980: World Bank, 1984;
1987: World Bank, 1989c;
1975: United Nations, 1983.
Taiwan: from Taiwan, 1988.
a. World Bank, 1989b.

Table 3-6
Percentage Share of Merchandise Imports: Machinery & Transport Equipment; Other Manufactures

	1960	1970	1975	1980	1987
Algeria					
Machinery & trans.	14	37	40	37	29
Other manufactures	54	42		35	35
Brazil					
Machinery & trans.	36	35	32	20	28
Other manufactures	18	34		21	28
Chile					
Machinery & trans.		43	33	28	33
Other manufactures		30		34	34
Malaysia					
Machinery & trans.	14		33		50
Other manufactures	28				30
Mexico					
Machinery & trans.	52	50	45	50	46
Other manufactures	32	31		33	34
Peru					
Machinery & trans.	37	35	32	41	47
Other manufactures	37	38		32	37
Portugal					
Machinery & trans.	26	30	25	25	33
Other manufactures	21	34		27	34
South Africa					
Machinery & trans.	37	46	53	52	46
Other manufactures	41	37		36	34
Taiwan					
Machinery & trans.		35	32	28	35
Other manufactures		21	28	26	34
Turkey					
Machinery & trans.	42	41	35	18	39
Other manufactures	24	36		25	43
Australia					
Machinery & trans.	31	41		36	39
Other manufactures	37	42		40	47
New Zealand					
Machinery & trans.	29	34	34	30	39
Other manufactures	39	43		36	44

Table 3-6 (continued)

	1960	1970	1975	1980	1987
South Korea					
Machinery & trans.		30	26	22	34
Other manufactures		25		21	28
Zimbabwe					
Machinery & trans.			29	30[a]	36[a]
Other manufactures				35[a]	43[a]

Sources:
1960: World Bank, 1982.   1970, 1980: World Bank, 1984.
1975: United Nations, 1983.   1987: World Bank, 1989c.
Taiwan: Taiwan, 1988.   a. World Bank, 1989b.

Table 3-7
Terms of Trade, 1980=100

	1967	1970	1975	1980	1987
Algeria	18	19	57	100	54
Brazil	190	189	126	100	97
Chile	227	237	107	100	84
Malaysia	161	103	75	100	72
Mexico	97	108	94	100	70
Peru	129	131	94	100	69
Portugal	129	132	107	100	100
South Africa	126	122	115	100	71
Taiwan[a] (1981=100)	147	157	124	104	106
Turkey	167	160	110	100	101
Australia	141	121	109	100	72
New Zealand	156	141	96	100	98
South Korea	149	122	115	100	71
Zimbabwe	161	178	111	100	84

Sources:
World Bank, 1989a.   a. Taiwan, 1988.

Table 3-8
Percentage Share of Merchandise Exports: Machinery & Transport Equipment and Other Manufactures

	1960	1970	1975	1980	1987
Algeria					
Machinery & trans.	1	2	1	0	0
Other manufactures	6	5	0.7	0	1
Brazil					
Machinery & trans.		4	10	17	17
Other manufactures	3	11	13	22	28
Chile					
Machinery & trans.	0	1	1	1	3
Other manufactures	4	4	7	19	6
Malaysia					
Machinery & trans.		2	6	12	27
Other manufactures	6	7	11	8	13
Mexico					
Machinery & trans.	1	11	9	19	28
Other manufactures	11	22	20	21	19
Peru					
Machinery & trans.	0	0	1	2	3
Other manufactures	1	1	2	15	16
Portugal					
Machinery & trans.	3	8	13	13	16
Other manufactures	52	56	55	58	64
South Africa					
Machinery & trans.	4	7	6	5	3
Other manufactures	24	34	19	4	75
Taiwan					
Machinery & trans.	2	17	20	25	32
Other manufactures		60	62	63	60
Turkey					
Machinery & trans.	0	0	1	3	7
Other manufactures	3	9	21	9	60
Australia					
Machinery & trans.	3	6	6	5	8
Other manufactures	5	14	7	21	17
New Zealand					
Machinery & trans.	0	2	3	4	
Other manufactures	3	10	10	17	

Table 3-8 (continued)

	1960	1970	1975	1980	1987
South Korea		7	14	20	33
Machinery & trans.	3	70	63	70	59
Other manufactures					
Zimbabwe					
Machinery & trans.			3	2[a]	3[a]
Other manufactures	3		11	26[a]	37[a]

Sources:
1960, 1970: World Bank, 1980.   1975: United Nations, 1983.
1980: World Bank, 1984.   1987: World Bank, 1989c.
Taiwan: Except 1960, Taiwan, 1988.
a. World Bank, 1989b.

Table 3-9
**Percentage Share of Merchandise Exports: Fuels, Minerals &
Metals, and Other Primary Commodities**

	1960	1970	1975	1980	1987
Algeria					
Fuels, minerals, metals	12	73	94	99	98
Other primary commodities	81	21	5	1	0
Brazil					
Fuels, minerals, metals	8	11	15	11	22
Other primary commodities	89	75	58	50	33
Chile					
Fuels, minerals, metals	92	88	75	59	69
Other primary commodities	4	7	17	21	23
Malaysia					
Fuels, minerals, metals	20	29	25	35	25
Other primary commodities	74	61	57	46	36
Mexico					
Fuels, minerals, metals	24	19	35	39	44
Other primary commodities	64	49	38	22	9

Table 3-9 (continued)

	1960	1970	1975	1980	1987
Peru					
Fuels, minerals, metals	49	49	47	64	71
Other primary commodities	50	49	50	19	11
Portugal					
Fuels, minerals, metals	8	5	6	7	3
Other primary commodities	37	31	26	21	16
South Africa					
Fuels, minerals, metals	28	27	26	23	12
Other primary commodities	42	32	40	23	9
Taiwan					
Fuels, minerals, metals		2	1	2	1
Other primary commodities		22	17	10	7
Turkey					
Fuels, minerals, metals	8	8	12	9	6
Other primary commodities	89	83	66	65	27
Australia					
Fuels, minerals, metals	13	27	38	29	37
Other primary commodities	79	52	47	45	38
New Zealand					
Fuels, minerals, metals		1	6	6	6
Other primary commodities	97	80	80	74	69
South Korea					
Fuels, minerals, metals		7	8	1	2
Other primary commodities	56	17	15	9	5
Zimbabwe					
Fuels, minerals, metals	71		41	22[a]	17[a]
Other primary commodities	25		45	0.49[a]	43[a]

Sources:
1960: World Bank, 1982.
1970: World Bank, 1980.
1975: United Nations, 1983.
1980: World Bank, 1989
1987: World Bank, 1989c.
Taiwan: Taiwan, 1988.
a. World Bank, 1989b.

countries, an outcome suggested earlier by the data on the weight and labor force of the manufacturing sector. In the face of even stiffer competition on the world market and pressures for trade liberalization, South Africa's industrial future cannot be considered bright.

The debt nexus

The growing attention paid to exports, and especially that of higher-rewarding manufactured goods, reflects the emergence of the drastic need to earn foreign currency to pay off foreign liabilities well ahead of even the provisioning of minimal national investment funds. The debt crisis is a phenomenon primarily of the 1980's. The basic patterns have been visible across all of our countries, reflecting changes in the world-economy: As the world-economy slid into stagnation, direct investment to the semiperiphery and periphery declined as a source of capital, while short-term outflows to safe havens in the core, especially from the private sector in the semiperiphery, has accelerated. This led the public and private sector in the semiperiphery to turn to the petrodollars so aggressively marketed by core banks; short-term loans thus accelerated. Rising international interest rates in the face of the stagnation of the early 1980's subsequent triggered a massive debt crisis, as levels of repayment rose while new funds were cut off. This dictated in turn an urgent need for a surplus on the current account line of the balance of payments.

It has been estimated that the twin shocks of declining terms of trade and rising interest rates hit South Africa harder by the mid–1980's than countries such as Brazil, Mexico, and South Korea (but not Peru) (Holden, 1989: 25). While figures on South Africa's debt are absent from all standard international compilations, it would appear however that neither the timing nor path of South Africa's debt burden varies significantly from the rest of the semiperiphery. While the Asian Nic's, due to their different export profile and volume, have been able to service their debt, a severe debt crisis including the rescheduling of debt payments, has marked the rest of the semiperiphery from 1982 onward. South Africa's debt standstill and rescheduling of 1985, for example, followed hard on the heels of similar occurrences in Latin America in the previous three years.

Where South Africa does stand out, however, is in its ability and willingness to service its rising debt burden (facilitated in no small part by the non-democratic distribution of associated costs). As far as can be estimated (see e.g., Table 10), this burden is a lesser percentage of GNP than for many comparable countries, while South Africa's historically high level of exports (as a share of GDP) provides a strong base for debt servicing. South Africa's standstill in 1985, capital flight, and a continuing shortage of loans thus appears overly dramatic. It is here that the political situation in South and southern Africa figures centrally. For the addition to economic stagnation of political instability and a growing anti-

Table 3-10
Total External Debt: Percentage of GNP

	1970	1980	1983	1986	1987	1988
Algeria	*19.3*	46.8	33.7	34.1	39.4	47.6
Brazil	*12.2*	30.6	50.1	41.7	39.4	30.7
Chile	*32.1*	45.2	98.9	141.6	123.8	96.6
Malaysia	*10.8*	28.0	63.6	85.3	75.9	66.0
Mexico	*16.2*	30.1	66.4	87.3	77.8	58.0
Peru	*37.3*	51.0	63.5	61.0	41.5	47.3
Portugal	*12.1*	40.4	74.0	58.4	51.3	42.3
South Africa		27.6	32.3		36.3	
Turkey	*15.0*	34.4	40.8	58.0	62.0	57.7
South Korea	*22.3*	48.7	50.8	45.5	31.5	22.0
Zimbabwe		14.9	39.2	53.0	51.5	43.5

Note: Figures are only approximate for comparisons.

Sources:
South Africa: Hirsch, 1990; percentages calculated with GNP figures from World Bank, 1989a.
1970: World Bank, 1989c; refers to only long-term debt only, i.e., excludes IMF credits, short-term debt; see text.
All others: from World Bank, 1990b.

apartheid movement has pushed foreign investors and banks to close off the flow of capital more than narrowly-construed economic circumstances might warrant. Meanwhile local investors are either fleeing or exporting capital. In short, an unstable economic situation turned critical as international financial links have been politicized. And this rebounds upon the internal political and economic situation, as the government is prevented from sustaining economic growth, and its reform program, as it is forced to cut imports and tighten capital markets whenever the economy begins to advance—in order to maintain a balance in the current account to service the debt burden. The feedback between long-term economic vulnerability and the contemporary political struggle is now enclosed within a circle.

Innovation and Regional Restructuring: Divergent Paths

As the preceding sections indicate, South Africa has been at a competitive disadvantage during the current stagnation by comparison to other semiperipheral states. As suggested in different ways along different dimensions, this derives in part from long-term patterns of accumulation fostered by apartheid as well as more contemporary political struggles. State policies tied to apartheid and monopolized enterprises and markets have worked strongly to deter the pursuit of new technology, more advanced production and labor processes, and the skilled labor force required to compete with advancing semiperipheral states. At the interstate level state responses have also been limited by apartheid, which has dictated willing acquiescence under unfavorable conditions in such bodies as GATT and the confrontations and constraints imposed by necessity to defend against sanctions, divestment, and boycotts.

Selected semiperipheral states have by contrast been able to deploy innovative state policies in order to increase their command over world resources during the initial phase of global stagnation and ensuing restructuring of production processes. Such advantages for some—but clearly not all—selected states continue into the most recent period. This is especially evident if one examines emergent patterns of technological innovation and regional/global economic blocs. Here the contrast between southern Africa, Latin America, and the Asian Pacific basin is especially instructive. While contraction and instability is evident in the first two areas, the Asian Pacific basin promises to advance its rapid industrial growth through a combination of innovation in productive arenas and enhanced regional linkages.

Take for example the issue of trade, an especially critical one in this as in past great depressions. At this juncture, Taiwan, South Korea, Malaysia, Mexico, and Brazil are faced with the prospect with graduating out of various "preferential" trade relationships with the United States and, most notably, into GATT in the middle 1990's.[6] Although the current Uruguay Rounds of GATT have been broken off by an U.S.-European dispute over farm subsidies, the newly industrialized countries in the Third World will be under intense pressure to open up their markets, curtail protectionism, "respect" the intellectual property of Western multinational corporations, and operate their service sector—in fields ranging from finance to telecommunication and construction and investments—within the framework established by advanced capitalist states. On this score, there is consensus among the United States, Western Europe, and Japan (Weissman, 1991: 336). In the Asian Pacific rim there are however forces and alternatives which may offset these negative trends by integrating this region to a far greater degree than has hitherto been the case in the postwar period.

At the center of this process stand the increased demand by Japan and China for manufactured goods from across this area, and current policy reforms designed to support industrial restructuring and innovation based on resource complementarity. This has created opportunities for cooperation between the Asian Nic's (South Korea, Taiwan, Hong Kong, and Singapore)[7] and members of the Association of South-East Asian Nations (ASEAN)— Indonesia, Malaysia, the Philippines, and Thailand. During the 1980–87 period, the growth rate of Manufacturing Value Added (MVA) in the South-East Asian region averaged 9.8% annually despite the world stagnation (UNIDO, 1990: 76).[8] In 1988 substantial gains occurred in the share of world MVA in Asian developing countries as well as Japan. Declines were registered in Latin America and the Caribbean region. Western Europe, sub-Saharan Africa, and North America maintained approximately their same shares. The most recent report continues this assessment:

> The Latin America and Caribbean region recorded MVA growth of only 1.7% for 1988, as MVA in Brazil declined by 2.5% and Argentina registered a bare 0.3% increase.... The debt crisis, particularly in Argentina and Brazil, is in large measure responsible for the poor performance, as producers struggle to maintain operations in the face of deteriorating infrastructure, including power supplies and transport facilities, and difficulties in obtaining inputs and keeping machinery in operation (UNIDO, 1990: 8).

For semiperipheral states in the Asian Pacific rim, the leading industrial branches now include electrical and non-electrical machinery, fabricated metal products, transport equipment, professional and scientific equipment, non-ferrous metals, plastic products, footware, and other manufactures. By contrast, in Latin America and southern Africa as late as 1987 output levels in most of these branches had not recovered from the impact of the 1980–82 world recession.

Moving forward from these different positions augurs different responses by semiperipheral states to the technological challenges of the 1990's. As semiperipheral states seek to supersede past technological/production mixes, they have all come under increasing pressure to facilitate and manage technological transfers as well as endogenous technological development (Castells & Tyson, 1989: 22). In so proceeding semiperipheral states are caught between lower-wage competitors and the need to match increasing technological sophistication of the core areas as older production processes and technologies are retired and new ones usher forth. This forces a move into more complex and higher value-added traditional products as well as into newer high-technology products—which weaker semiperipheral and peripheral competitors have more difficulty producing. Moreover, as semiperipheral states try to move up the ladder toward more complex manufacturing, they will run into more opposition from core countries. For Latin America the debt crisis and structural adjustment reveal severe obstacles to any favorable response to these challenges, while sanctions, labor conflict, and political instability limits the capacity of South Africa to compete in these areas.

Responses and capabilities in the Asian-Pacific Rim would seem to follow a different path. In order to move beyond labor-intensive assembly operations, the capital, new technology and managerial skills needed to serve local markets were obtained from Japan and the United States. Over a relatively short period of time, however, indigenous producers in this zone joined with foreign-funded ventures to develop the new technologies and skills required to produce and export increasingly complex manufactured goods. This then provided the basis for the replacement of imports via the expansion of the assembly operations of intermediate inputs. In such a manner significant increases in higher levels of value-added manufacturing have been achieved.

Under the impact of the soaring value of the yen both large and small Japanese manufacturers have sought to obtain inputs from neighboring countries, including most notably Asian Nic's and ASEAN countries that offer substantial cost advantages. U.S. enterprises have been forced to follow as a result of the increased competition with their own firms. Semiperipheral states from the Asian-Pacific Rim have in many instances welcomed direct investment from Japan and the United States as part of a strategy of upgrading their industrial base from tradition activities such as apparel, footware, leather goods, and toys. In a similar fashion the appreciation of the Korean won and the Taiwan dollar, as well as their graduation out of the group enjoying the benefits of the Generalized System of Preferences has forced many enterprises of the Republic of Korea and Taiwan Province to migrate to Indonesia, the Philippines, Malaysia, Singapore, and Thailand (UNIDO, 1990: 78–80). The prospects are good for the future penetration of Vietnam and other states in South Asia.

This movement of labor-intensive branches of industry from established Nic's in Asia to lower-cost neighbors has enabled the

former to upgrade their industry towards higher-technology production. The Asian-Pacific Rim is thus poised—if not assured—for
a fundamental restructuring and integration that will increase
economic interaction and cooperation between Japan, China, the
Asian Nic's, and ASEAN. Prospects for a similar movement in Latin
America remain by contrast most clouded. Whatever the results of
trade negotiations with the United States and Canada, there remains
the fundamental task of resolving debt and structural adjustment
problems. Unless the transition to a majority-ruled era is peaceful
and prompt, South and southern Africa will have a very difficult
time indeed in adjusting to ongoing technological and regional
challenges that have now become competitive on a global scale.

Reprise

South Africa's economic crisis is without doubt part and parcel of
a similar pattern across the semiperipheral zone. As the discussions
of debt and industrial restructuring suggest, however, the economic
structure created by the state and capital during the apartheid years
left South Africa ill-prepared to face the full flowering of the world-
economic crisis. These entrenched patterns in alliance with the drive
to defend apartheid account in turn for a large part of South
Africa's increasing slippage within the semiperiphery as the world-
economy has evolved in the last fifteen years. Unlike the Asian
Nic's, or even Brazil and Mexico, the structure of accumulation in
South Africa has not managed the transition to higher-rewarding
forms of production. Indeed—as foreshadowed by Chile perhaps—
South Africa's future on the basis of current trends is one of
decline, as other semiperipheral countries utilize this period to
move away from primary production and simple (and highly
competitive) manufacturing production.

That this weakness has provided the pressure points for political
attacks by the opponents of apartheid, as the debt issue illustrates
(Hirsch, 1989), should hardly surprise us; political struggles have
indeed considerably complicated the effects of the world-economic
downturn—but they did not inaugurate them, or sustain them
alone. Still, as everyone from the head of Anglo-American to the

Governor of the South African Reserve Bank now realizes, there can be no economic revival without majority rule. Yet the converse of the opportunities provided by a common semiperipheral fate are its implications for the future. As the evidence indicates, a post-apartheid South Africa will continue to face a hostile world climate, the impoverished economic legacy of apartheid, and a highly competitive struggle amongst semiperipheral states.

Notes

1. On the notion of an "organic crisis," see the seminal monograph by Saul & Gelb (1981).

2. See for example Volkskas Bank (1990), as well as Gelb (1987), whose argument is challenged, however, on the basis of manufacturing profit rate comparisons by Nattrass (1989).

3. This list was generated by taking all countries within 50 percent (above or below) of South Africa's GNPpc circa 1973, and then eliminating: small countries with a population below 10 million, oil-exporting countries, and members of COMECON (data absent, and different class and state structures). Algeria might have been excluded as an oil exporter, but is included nonetheless because of the size of its manufacturing sector.

4. A similar trend in the 1970's and 1980's, one might notice, holds for the region as well (see chapter 2(A) on trade flows).

5. See chapter 2(A) for a discussion of this and a breakdown of related data.

6. Each semiperipheral state has negotiated a different date for graduating into GATT and the new status as "Advanced Developing Country."

7. The following section draws upon UNIDO (1990). The report includes both Hong Kong and Singapore. We have excluded these two city-states from our own calculations below due to the size of their populations and their political classifications as micro-states.

8. UNIDO's South-East Asia region includes: Oceania, Brunei Darussalam, Fiji, French Polynesia, Hong Kong, Indonesia, Malaysia, New Caledonia, Papua New Guinea, Philippines, Republic of Korea, Samoa, Singapore, Taiwan, Thailand, Tonga, Tuvalu, and Vanuatu.

Chapter 4

The Region as a Zone of Geostrategical Struggle

Sergio Vieira and Thomas Ohlson
assisted by Gulamu Taju and Ana Xavier

Over the last three decades southern Africa has been the stage for conflicts that have destroyed lives and property and have turned the region into a major concern for Africa and for the international community. The final act in the decolonization of the continent has been played out in southern Africa. This scene began in 1975 with the decolonization of Angola and Mozambique, followed five years later, in 1980, with the end of the Rhodesian rebellion and the birth of Zimbabwe, and culminating in 1990 with the independence of the last African colony, Namibia, the release of Nelson Mandela, and the legalization of the South African liberation movement.

Underlying the various conflicts in the region was the question of colonialism and racism. Successively, Portuguese colonialism and the racist minorities in Rhodesia, Namibia, and South Africa tried by force of arms to preserve their political, economic, social, and military hegemony. There remains as the focus of attention, and as the epilogue, the question of apartheid.

In recent years, regardless of their political, economic and social regimes, of their diplomatic relationships, of their strategic and tactical alignments, all the states of southern Africa, with the exception of Tanzania, have been the target for either direct aggression or destabilization by South Africa. The scale of the loss of life and destruction of property since 1980 is unparalleled and unprecedented in local history.

Unlike other regions of tension, the facts point towards a single source of violence, namely South Africa and its regime. In its regional relations, the South African government has systematically, and in violation of the most basic norms of international law, resorted to the threat or use of force or of economic sanctions. In this activity, it has sometimes invoked a "right to hot pursuit," or "the right to retaliation."

Military and economic measures have been combined together as integral parts of the model of aggression, designed to mould the victim to the wishes of Pretoria. Despite declarations from the Afrikaner community that it waged the first liberation struggle on the continent, at the start of the century, the reality is that ever since then the authorities in Pretoria have systematically placed themselves on the side of European powers against the emancipation of colonized peoples. The South African government supported the Katanga and Biafra secessions, a long way from its own borders, with the purpose of blocking the decolonization process. The same goal had already been revealed in the 1950's, when South Africa contributed to the repression of Mau-Mau (the patriotic movement in Kenya), and to maintain the Central African Federation of the two Rhodesias and Nyasaland. The Portuguese colonial wars, particularly in Angola and Mozambique, and the rebellion of the Salisbury regime, all benefited from military, financial and other support from Pretoria. The independence of Mozambique in 1975 destroyed the viability of the project of holding back the national liberation process and majority governments north of the Rovuma, Zambezi, and Limpopo rivers.

As part of its efforts to maintain the southern African countries as satellites through its new policy of the "Constellation of States" (CONSAS), and also reacting to the policy of detente advocated by the continent after the 1969 Lusaka Manifesto, Pretoria, faced with the collapse of the Portuguese empire, promised not to interfere in the decolonization of Mozambique, to promote the release of Zimbabwean political prisoners, to convince Ian Smith to negotiate with the liberation movement, and to withdraw its own forces from Southern Rhodesia.

The failure of the Victoria Falls and Geneva talks led to the resurgence of war in Rhodesia. Prime Minister Johannes Vorster, however, refused to intervene openly on Smith's side against Mozambique. This was due, among other things, to the involvement of his forces on the western front, in Namibia and Angola.

But it should be noted that the South African government did start imposing economic sanctions against Mozambique. It drastically reduced the number of Mozambican miners in South Africa from close to 120,000 to about 40,000; it abolished the gold clause in the arrangements over deferred wages; and it cut South African traffic through the Maputo rail and port system from over 10 million tons a year to little more than one million. However, South African armed aggression in Mozambique did not take place during the period of the Rhodesian war.

South Africa's military invasion and occupation of Angola as from August 1975 determined the internationalization of the conflict in the sub-continent. Troops from Nigeria, Guinea-Bissau, Guinea-Conakry, and Congo sanctioned with their presence the massive Cuban intervention. The O.A.U., the non-aligned countries, and the international community in general, faced with a conflict between South Africa and Angola, sided with Luanda, even when they expressed reticence about the participation of the Cuban contingents. In January 1976, the extraordinary O.A.U. summit on the Angolan question ended in an impasse: half the members supported Luanda; the other half, reluctant to give their blessing to the Cuban forces, were opposed. But rapidly the balance swung towards Luanda, precisely because Pretoria's intervention drove the African community, the non-aligned countries, and the concert of nations as a whole, with the exception of the United States, to recognize the MPLA government.

White Rhodesia, under pressure from the armed struggle waged by ZANU and the worsening of its international isolation, was forced to abandon the principle of racial supremacy, and installed a Black government, led by Bishop Muzorewa, although this had support neither internally nor abroad. South Africa noted that it was inevitable that the White frontier would retreat from the north to the Limpopo. The failure of the South African strategy to hold back the liberation struggle, in the context of the cold war then prevailing, opened the path towards the sharpening of extremist positions. The regime set up a scenario of "total onslaught" by Moscow, and in 1977 advocated the adoption of a Total Strategy that, while claiming to be defensive, affirmed the right to intervene in any African state south of the equator.

The starting-point has two interlinked dimensions. The majority of the South African population, like the neighboring countries, wanted the abolition of apartheid, regarding it as the cause of instability and conflict, while the ruling South African elite wanted to preserve minority and racist hegemony. South Africa presented itself as the regional representative of the dominant economic order in the world, while its opponents were part of the tendency that proposed building a new economic order with a balanced relationship between North and South, a growing cooperation among the countries of the South, and a balanced and equal relationship with Pretoria.

In one way or another, the perception of the two dimensions to the conflict could lead to identifying opposition to apartheid as a confrontation with the capitalist economic system in the southern African region.

The South African government resorted to the most varied of methods to impose its dominance. Actions ranged from open intervention by its own armed forces, to economic blockades, to the organization and control of subversive and terrorist movements, to the occupation of parts of other countries' territory, to flagrant violations and refusals to comply with agreements and with the norms of international law.

A good example to illustrate this is Lesotho. In the 1970's South Africa took action to install and maintain in power a government that it believed would best serve its interests. It supported Leabua Jonathan's coup d'etat to prevent the opposition from reaping the fruits of its electoral victory. In the 1980's the Jonathan government diversified its international relations and tried to some extent to free the country from the overly suffocating embrace of the giant surrounding it. Pretoria then sponsored the organization and operations of the so-called Lesotho Liberation Army (LLA), which carried out some terrorist activities. When the Lesotho government did not submit, there was an escalation of threats and retaliations that culminated in late 1985 and early 1986 in a blockade of the territory, preventing the entry of goods, particularly foodstuffs, and hindering the cross-border movements of Sotho citizens, most of whom work in South Africa. On January 20, 1986 there was a military coup that overthrew the Jonathan government and with it its efforts to act independently (*Southern African Dossier,* 1986).

These are the kind of phenomena that characterized and gave the scale of the tension and conflicts in the southern part of the African continent. All the independent states of southern Africa rejected the principle of racial discrimination and colonial rule. They all knew the experience of being colonized and suffering discrimination. They were all born from patriotic forces that opposed these evils. The colonial racist experience was very recent in the region, so that it was still the generation of the freedom movements that dominated in the leadership of these states. Therefore the goals of South Africa—political, economic and military hegemony—were not acceptable. In opposition there arose a different conceptualization, intrinsically different from the South African one, of how regional relations should be structured.

The line of demarcation was drawn by apartheid, the principal cause of conflict in the region. Besides this, at least in the political declarations of the Front Line States and SADCC members, independence meant more than political independence—it was also the right to formulate and implement an independent strategy of socio-economic development. Development meant more than economic growth—it was also the reduction of inequalities and injustices inside and between nations. Peace meant more than the absence of physical violence and war—it was also the absence of structural violence and exploitation within and between states. Finally, security meant more than the military capacity to remove foreign threats to basic national values—it also included the broader vision that underdevelopment, the poor use of resources, the polarization of wealth within and between nations, violations of human rights, illiteracy, malnutrition, disease, and other non-military aspects of security contribute towards tensions, conflicts, and insecurity. Thus national security should be viewed in the broader context of collective or common security. National security measures which threatened these wider interests were considered illegitimate.

While these general goals functioned as a substitute for a commonly-held ideology, they did not, however, guarantee the cooperation that was advocated. The truth is that common opposition to apartheid, and commitment to freeing these states from dependence on South Africa, was of great importance, particularly as a unifying factor in regional cooperation.

Achieving the aims set out was, however, conditioned by the position of the region in the international division of labor, by the dependence inherited from colonialism, and by the politically and economically heterogeneous nature of the states concerned. Since the nineteenth century both Portuguese and British colonialism had institutionalized a structure wherein the territories they held operated as satellites of South Africa, with the occupation of Angola, Tanganyika, and South West Africa by the end of the First World War.

Thus strategic cooperation between the members of the Front Line States and of SADCC was situated within a complex context of driving and inhibiting forces. They constituted a group of recently independent, economically weak, and politically diverse states that were trying to follow together a difficult strategy—containing diplomatic, political, economic and military components—against a series of continual and growing external threats to their political and economic stability (Ohlson, 1990).

Apartheid—Source of the Conflict

The basic and constant goal of South Africa's regional strategy has been that of preserving minority rule in the country, and its regional dominance. To achieve these central aims, the South African leadership constantly and increasingly engaged in both internal repression and external warmongering. These took shape step by step in the banning of political organizations and the declaration of the state of emergency internally, while in the region the Total Strategy unfolded. This determined the militarization of the regime, and the creation of a new center of power based on the State Security Council.

Apartheid was a strategy for capitalist accumulation in the colonial framework, and its preservation determined increasing levels of coercion and state repression. To achieve this goal, a politico-ideological structure, and a police and military apparatus had to be set up that would be capable of justifying super-exploitation and of maintaining social order. This situation obviously had negative repercussions for the regime, regionally and internationally, given the priority accorded to strengthening the military apparatus so as to prevent regional solidarity against apartheid, and to ensure, by force if necessary. Their objectives in the region were viable, in the context of coercive diplomacy. This posture in defence of racism and a warlike regional attitude isolated Pretoria internationally, turning the country into a "pariah state," against which sanctions and embargoes were launched, and thus the government, through the increasing militarization of the state, and the establishment of a securocratic regime, tried to find the strategic and tactical response for confrontation. But in the international context then prevailing, this policy demanded an open or a tacit alliance with centers of power in the North—an alliance with financial centers as well as with military centers and intelligence services. The cold war ensured that this alliance was with the West.

The development of the internal struggle against apartheid, which involved new sectors of the population, including Whites and even Afrikaans-speakers, the inefficiency of the system as far as capitalist development of the country was concerned, the growth of international pressure and the application of sanctions, disinvestment by foreign capital, the reluctance of banks to renegotiate South Africa's debts, the collapse of the colonial and racist empire which pushed racial equality to the very borders of South Africa, political, and diplomatic isolation—all these factors came together cumulatively to force the regime officially to abandon its ideology, and to start a process of reforms in the period when P.W. Botha was still head of state.

The initial behavior of the new alliance in power in South Africa was characterized by the forced replacement of P.W. Botha by F.W. de Klerk, the apparent marginalization of the "securo-crats" which then followed, a move towards closer relations with big capital, and a greater flexibility in regional and international dialogue (*Southern Africa Dossier,* 1989b & 1990).

This was the context for the independence of Namibia, the release of political prisoners, and the legalization of formerly banned organizations. The measures taken restored the status quo prior to 1960, but up until the end of 1990, despite announcing that it had abandoned the ideology of apartheid, the regime persisted in rejecting the principle of majority government, to be established democratically and not racially. Proposals for power sharing and the parameters put forward by the government up until then sought to safeguard in new forms the internal and regional dominance of the White minority. In practice this meant privatizing apartheid, ruling out in advance the means to implement an affirmative policy of integration and of correcting the severe existing economic and social imbalances. Under cover of democrat-ic phraseology, such as "the right of association," "no oppression of minorities," and "the right to property," attempts are being made to entrench the right to discriminate in the future constitution (Davies, 1990).

But a new dynamic was arising. When the system retreats, this does not lead inevitably to the demobilization of the forces in control of profound transformations. With the passing of the initial euphoria at the release of the best-known political prisoners, and the legalization of banned organizations, the demand for substan-tive changes was now heard both inside South Africa and interna-tionally. The Lusaka Declaration from the O.A.U.'s Ad-Hoc Committee on southern Africa, on March 19, 1990, posed again the basic questions. These were taken up by the 1990 O.A.U. summit, and by the special session of the United Nations General Assembly.

The negotiation process and its results depend on a number of parameters which will establish the balance between what is possible and what is desirable. Unity in a negotiating platform of the forces opposed to apartheid; international pressure; the capacity of the neighboring countries and the Front Line States to bear additional sacrifices; the reactions of the extreme right, particularly among the securocrats; the evolution of White opinion—these are among the many variables that condition the exact political balance that can be reached in the phase now beginning. The switch of international attention towards the Persian Gulf, and the collapse of the eastern bloc, have to some extent pushed the balance towards the right.

It is quite evident that any solution based on the defence of racist dominance, reformed or otherwise, will merely result in continued violence, domestic repression and regional warmongering. The less balanced the solution, and the longer it takes, the greater will be the frustration, and the seeds will have been sown for new conflicts.

Strategies in Conflict

Taking into consideration the expressions of the conflict, the interests of the parties concerned, the resources and doctrines involved, the activities undertaken and their effects, three important periods can be identified in the unfolding of the southern African conflict.

For White power south of the Zambezi (1960–1974)

In the 1960's most African countries achieved their political independence. But in contrast to events in the rest of the continent, South Africa saw the strengthening of "internal colonialism," with the banning of mass political organizations and increased measures of repression. In Rhodesia, the settler community led by the Rhodesian Front declared, in 1965, unilateral independence from the British crown, also strengthening internal colonialism. In Angola and Mozambique, Portugal persisted in its colonial presence, thus bringing about colonial wars that opposed the colonizing power to the national liberation movement. In Namibia, South Africa refused to accept decolonization. Under normal circumstances, this territory should have acceded to independence in the 1960's, just as had the other former African colonies of Imperial Germany—Togo, Cameroon, and Tanganyika. Faced with the refusal of the mandated power to discharge its duty, in 1966 the United Nations withdrew the mandate from Pretoria, and charged the Council for Namibia with guaranteeing the right of its people to self-determination. The colonial power maintained its administration illegally, and obstructed the activity of the Council.

Facing this wave of decolonization and African independence, the White powers of southern Africa allied together in an effort to hold back national liberation and majority rule to north of the Zambezi. South Africa, Rhodesia and Portugal supported each other in the colonial wars in Angola and Mozambique, in Salisbury's rebellion, and in violating the sanctions imposed by the U.N. Security Council. This activity continued in the 1970's, although the 1969 Lusaka Manifesto had offered a lessening of tension through dialogue between the White powers of the region and the nationalist movements.

For its part, starting from the informal cooperation between Tanzania and Zambia in supporting the liberation movements in Angola, Mozambique, Zimbabwe, Namibia, and South Africa, the O.A.U. decided, at the beginning of the 1970's, on the composition of the "Front Line States" grouping, consisting of these two countries plus Congo-Brazzaville and Zaire (bordering on Angola), and Botswana (bordering on Namibia, Zimbabwe, and South Africa).

But the Front Line States never presented themselves as a homogenous group. Based on their own concerns, these countries united, but without posing a common strategy above national interests. In the initial period of its activity, the Front Line States had differing positions on Angola. Tanzania supported only the MPLA, as did Congo-Brazzaville. Although Zambia supported the MPLA, it was also backing UNITA, while Zaire was the only state to back only the FNLA. In the period immediately prior to Angolan independence, Zaire supported mercenaries and sent its own forces to invade Angolan territory from the north. While Congo-Brazzaville supported the MPLA during this period, it was also to some extent trying to promote Cabindan secession. As from late 1974, the Front Line States, now with Frelimo among its members, took multiple initiatives to ensure that the Alvor Accords concerning

Angola were respected. Faced with Zaire's attempt to impose its own dominance through the FNLA, the group tried, in vain, to facilitate an alliance between the MPLA and UNITA. The MPLA's feeling of victory after it had militarily defeated its opponents in Luanda blocked the initiative. The invasions by the FNLA in the north, with the support of Zaire and mercenary forces, and of South Africa, with mercenaries from the group of Chipenda, at that time an MPLA dissident, redefined alliances and interests. In particular, Zambia broke the alliance, realigning itself alongside South African and U.S. interests in the Angolan question, and later in the Zimbabwean conflict.

Military cooperation was another important aspect in regional strategy. Such cooperation dates back to the early 1960's and the beginning of the armed liberation struggle in the Portuguese colonies. Zambia and Tanzania provided rearguard bases and training for the liberation movements. There was also direct cooperation between the liberation movements, for instance, in the program of guerrilla training and logistical support given to ZANU fighters inside Mozambique in the mid–1970's, even though at the time Frelimo still considered ZAPU as its political ally among the Zimbabwean liberation movements.

The search for a regional constellation and the anti-apartheid responses (1975–1980)

After the 1974 Lusaka Accord, signed between Portugal and Frelimo, the South African government promised not to interfere in the decolonization of Mozambique, and in fact, when ultra-colonialist and racist circles tried to stage a rebellion on September 7, 1974, the regime abstained from providing support to its ideological allies—even though they had requested help, and even though Ian Smith's regime was favorably disposed towards this request. For South Africa, there was a great risk of facing a Luso-Mozambican alliance, in a context in which international opinion would, almost in its entirety, have supported the defence of Mozambique against a seizure of power. Unlike the Angolan situation, in Mozambique the liberation movement appeared coherent, united, and prestigious. In the Rhodesian case, Pretoria promised to convince Smith to negotiate with the national liberation movement, to ensure the release of Zimbabwean political prisoners, and to withdraw its own forces from southern Rhodesia.

The fall of the Portuguese colonial regime in 1975 altered the regional balance of forces, and gave fresh impulse to the liberation struggle in Rhodesia, Namibia, and inside South Africa. In an attempt to preserve its dominance, Pretoria proposed the establishment of a Constellation of Southern African States (CONSAS). The Vorster government vacillated between a policy of regional detente, and its concern to ensure military control over Angola, a country that it invaded in 1975 with U.S. support. That support was withdrawn with the Soweto uprising of 1976, and the following U.N. Security Council mandatory arms embargo in 1977. Vorster was then removed in 1978 in a palace coup staged by P.W. Botha with the support of the securocrats.

Botha's policy, known as the "Total Strategy," was defined in 1977. It was based on mobilizing all available resources, economic, political, socio-psychological, and military, to promote the interests of South Africa at domestic and regional level. Starting from the concept of a "total onslaught"orchestrated by Moscow, using as its instruments the nationalist organizations and the neighboring countries, the Total Strategy proposed to act in three directions:

  · To relaunch, in new forms, the concept of a Constellation of States, ensuring Pretoria's dominance, and neutralizing any socialist experiments. The constellation was conceived of as both an economic and a security alliance. Coercive methods, such as the application of economic pressure or of military action, would be used to force reluctant states to accept it. Thus, for example, South Africa was to make an agreement with Lesotho on use of the waters of the Orange River conditional on signing a security accord. A similar position was adopted towards Botswana.
  · A second aspect was the direct use of force, either through open interventions by the South African Defence Forces (SADF), or by forces who, though consisting of nationals of the target state, were recruited, trained, equipped, and led by

Pretoria. They were, however, presented as armed opposi-
tions to the regimes concerned.

· Thirdly, the decision-taking process was restructured, and
power was centralized at first in the hands of the Prime
Minister and later (after 1984) in those of the Executive
State President. At the same time a national security management system was built up, at various levels, as an effective
organ for taking decisions beyond cabinet or parliamentary
control.

The preferred targets for the South African strategy of violence
were Mozambique and Angola. More important than ideological
and other differences, and quite apart from the attacks that Pretoria
claimed to fear would be launched from these two states, the
essential reason for this policy lay in Pretoria's desire to knock out
the region's overall effort to free itself from South African dominance.

The choice of Marxism by Angola and Mozambique ran
counter to Western interests, and could be interpreted as favoring
Soviet designs globally at a moment when the Indochina and
Watergate disasters had forced retreats on the United States. This
was the background explaining the indifference or sympathy
towards Pretoria's intentions in the power centers of the North. In
Angola, invasion and occupation of parts of the country began in
August 1975, while Portugal was still ruling the territory. The
invasion of Angola internationalized the regional conflict. Troops
from Cuba, Guinea-Bissau, Congo, and Nigeria intervened in the
Angolan conflict.

As for the Namibian question, with the agreement of South
Africa, and following the activity of the so-called "Contact Group"
of the five Western powers, the United Nations Security Council
approved Resolution 435/78. SWAPO, the Front Line States, and
Nigeria had been consulted and had given their approval. But when
it came to applying the resolution, the Pretoria government, for the
first time, raised the question of the Cuban troops in Angola. Since
the Namibian question had dragged on for twelve years, ever since
1966, while there had only been a Cuban presence for three years,

since 1975, the regional perception was that this position was put forward merely to disguise a new obstructionist maneuver, and to provide a basis for readjusting interests between the superpowers who were making use of the Namibian and Angolan questions.

At the same time, alliances and interests were redefined among the Front Line States. After seeing the FNLA collapse, Zaire withdrew for a time from the Angolan question. Tanzania, Mozambique, and Congo-Brazzaville remained thoroughly committed to the MPLA. The basic justification for this was the need to neutralize South African interference in Angola. Zambia was however now openly opposed to the government in Luanda. The Angolan crisis paralysed the Front Line. Only after Zambia recognized the Angolan government was it possible to resume normal relations, now concentrated on the Rhodesian question. But the Rhodesian issue once again rent relations among the Front Line States asunder, insofar as Zambia gave some support to Nkomo's plan to marginalize ZANU, even through a unilateral agreement with the Smith regime. Angola's relationship with the Soviet Union also to some extent led that country to a greater alignment with ZAPU. Zambia's economic difficulties led its government to reopen the trade route through Rhodesia, and to initiatives towards the Smith regime and towards South Africa that were not always well received by its other partners in the Front Line States.

With the independence of Angola and Mozambique, Congo-Brazzaville and Zaire stopped participating in the group of Front Line States. They were replaced by the two newly independent states; Zimbabwe was added in 1980 after its independence. The modus operandi of the Front Line States consisted of ad-hoc summits of a functional nature, instead of setting up a large permanent secretariat and other fixed structures, and this has remained the prevailing method of cooperation. Probably this may be the only functional way of working, given the inhibiting factors already mentioned. Thus each Chairman of the Front Line States has in effect continued the foreign policy of his own country, and at the same time the summits allowed flexibility, pragmatism, and speed in collective responses to questions that were vitally important for common goals. The modus operandi set out for the

Rhodesian question continued throughout the Lancaster House negotiations, and was then transplanted to three other major questions in which the Front Line States were diplomatically active, namely Namibia, the war in Angola, and the problem of sanctions against South Africa.

After the formation of the Patriotic Front, the Front Line decided to support the forces of a united guerrilla army. But when the unity project failed, Mozambique and Tanzania supported the ZANU guerrillas. Zambia and Angola provided base and logistical facilities to ZAPU. In general, the U.S.S.R. gave support in equipment and training to ZAPU, while China did the same for ZANU. Libya and Ethiopia trained significant contingents of ZANU and also some of ZAPU. Mozambique also sent a contingent of 500 volunteers to fight alongside ZANU as from 1978.

This cooperation was also shown in the Mozambican support for Tanzania, when the latter country defended itself against the annexation of Kaguera by the Idi Amin regime, and then fought to bring about Amin's downfall. A particularly important individual role was played by Mozambique in supporting ZANU and applying sanctions against Rhodesia. The failure of the Victoria Falls and Geneva negotiations led to the resurgence of the war in Rhodesia. Intensified warfare and international isolation then forced Smith to abandon the principle of racial supremacy and to install a Black government with Muzorewa at its head.

Over the past fifteen years, in terms of diplomacy and international policy, the Front Line States have won considerable standing in very broad forums, such as the O.A.U., the Commonwealth, the Non-Aligned Movement, and the United Nations. They played a key role in the negotiations for Zimbabwean independence. They also collaborated in the process taking place at roughly the same time which led to the adoption by the U.N. Security Council of Resolution 435/78 on the independence of Namibia. The Front Line States also played an important role in influencing Western public opinion and political leaders as regards sanctions against South Africa.

"Total Strategy" versus SADCC (1980–1988)

South Africa promoted the "Total Strategy" in the region, while internally it decreed the State of Emergency, it restructured the decision-making system by concentrating power in the hands of the Prime Minister (and later of the State President), and it built a securocratic regime. It strengthened its military might in order to hinder regional solidarity. As part of its "coercive diplomacy," it sought to intimidate the neighboring countries, and intervened directly through the use of its own regular forces, or indirectly through puppet armies.

It was intended that the Total Strategy should be 20% military and 80% economic and political. But right from the start the strategy was condemned by events, and the proportions were inverted in favor of military action rather than economic or political activity. The determining events were the independence of Zimbabwe under ZANU leadership, and the creation of SADCC by the nine sovereign states of the region.

The Total Strategy then concentrated on open or secret acts of intimidation against the neighboring states aimed at removing SWAPO and ANC forces from the South African border. At the same time, military actions, particularly the sabotage and destruction of the communications systems, were designed to weaken the states of the region, prevent them reducing their dependence on South Africa, and indeed even to increase that dependence.

Significant military events were acts such as the air raid against exclusively civilian and Mozambican targets in the city of Matola in May 1983; and the simultaneous raids against Harare, Gaborone, and Lusaka, again against purely civilian and local targets, in 1986, which deliberately coincided with, and therefore wrecked, the mission by the Commonwealth Eminent Persons Group (EPG). The blockade against Lesotho, the terrorist campaign of assassinating opponents of apartheid, even in Western European capitals, the mercenary invasion of the Seychelles, the military sponsorship of the conspiracy against Saõ Tomé—these are various examples of the warlike policy of the so-called Total Strategy.

South Africa's relationship to Mozambique sums up its position towards the region, and illustrates the range of measures of various kinds that Pretoria has used against its neighbors. Following ZANU's election victory, and as part of the Total Strategy, South African Military Intelligence sheltered Rhodesian special forces, in order to reorganize them and use them against Mozambique. These forces were composed of former common criminals and war criminals, mainly of Mozambican or Portuguese origin (Taju, 1988; Hall, 1990).

At the core of these forces were groups of "Flechas," militarized forces of the Portuguese political police, the PIDE/DGS, who, during the colonial war, with Rhodesian and South African assistance, trained and operated in the Chimoio area, bordering Rhodesia. On June 2, 1974, these forces, led by Major Oscar Cardoso, fearful of the Portuguese MFA (Armed Forces Movement), which had already detained some of their colleagues, and fearing possible reprisals for their involvement in particularly frightful crimes, crossed the border into Rhodesia, and were taken into the Odzi military camp.

Ken Flower, then director of Salisbury's intelligence services, integrated them, strengthened their group by adding other war criminals and mercenaries, and recruited new members for this group forcibly inside Mozambique. The Rhodesians particularly used helicopter-borne raids against re-education centers, where criminals and delinquents were being held, notably those who had been in the police and armed forces. To disguise its origins, this melange was given various names, "Magaia," "Africa Livre," "Mocambique Livre," "MNR," and finally, in the 1980's, "Renamo."

Rhodesian intelligence and later special units of the Rhodesian army used this group for reconnaissance missions, for sabotage, and even in massacres such as that at Nyazonia. It was this group that Ken Flower handed over to General van der Westhuysen, director of South African Military Intelligence, in 1980. It was reorganized and used to carry out the new missions determined by the Total Strategy.

In this process, those individuals who did not guarantee their loyalty to the new designs and procedures were eliminated, even by murder. Such were the cases of "Secretary-General" Orlando

Cristina, who represented the interests of the Portuguese capitalist Jorge Jardim, and of settler circles, of the Bomba brothers and many others. Unlike the Rhodesian project, Pretoria wanted complete command over the operation, and refused to share its goals with any other of the existing components.

The change in command determined a change in strategy and aims. The Rhodesian regime had pursued limited objectives of a military nature, to ensure room for maneuver in the final phase of the breakup of its system. This was quite compatible with the ambitions of those circles nostalgic for Portuguese colonialism, who had proposed a Rhodesian style "independence" for Mozambique.

The South African regime, knowing that it was militarily and politically impossible to turn Mozambique into a Bantustan, tried to make the existence and functioning of any organized society inviable. It defined its strategy as the devastation of Mozambican society and of its capacity for later recovery. Under South African sponsorship this armed activity did not propose to set up an alternative to the existing power, nor to implement any political project, however conservative or right-wing it might be. Apart from ritual statements, for outside consumption, about "anti-communism," "free elections," "a free press," "democracy," "power of the chiefs," and "religious freedom," there was not the slightest program for the political mobilization, either of the people under their control, or indeed of the very people recruited by Pretoria themselves.

Practice showed that privately-owned tractors, trucks, warehouses, or production units were just as much targets for looting and destruction as were goods belong to state companies or cooperatives. Religious establishments belonging to the most varied denominations were also looted and destroyed, and priests of various nationalities were kidnapped and murdered. It is only as part of a foreign project of devastation that one can understand how the pregnant woman and the school student, the maternity ward and the school, the storehouse and the peasant hut, all become priority targets for armed attacks. In fact, the principal targets for armed attack are the most vulnerable strata of the population, the peasants and their few belongings, and the education and health infrastructures.

The war has already resulted in a million deaths, of whom more than half are children. A thousand settlements, over a million rural homes, about 3,000 schools, almost a thousand health posts and rural hospitals, have been looted, destroyed, burnt down. A third of the population has been displaced, deprived of their homes, and prevented from cultivating their fields. Assistance to the victims was deliberately blocked as part of a plan to use famine in the breakup and destruction of society. The material losses resulting directly or indirectly from aggression and the prevention of productive activity have amounted to 15,000 million dollars.

After South Africa had begun large-scale destabilization of Mozambique in 1980, Zimbabwe and Tanzania provided military training for the Mozambican armed forces. As from the same year—and in part as a result of the SADF raid against Matola in January 1981—an agreement came into force between Mozambique and Zimbabwe on the exchange of defence and security information and intelligence, as was already the case with Tanzania, Zambia, and Angola. As from that moment, a Front Line Defence and Security Committee in practice took institutional shape. With the escalation of South African aggression through Renamo, Zimbabwean and Tanzanian troops were sent in 1985 into Mozambican territory, and collaboration was also established with the Zambian army along the Zambian frontier with Tete province. In 1987, Malawi sent troops to defend the Nacala Corridor in Mozambique.

To some extent, the Front Line States, through regional collaboration, wanted to avoid an internationalization of the conflict such as had happened in Angola. Even countries that had no border with Mozambique, such as Botswana and Angola, contributed to the joint effort with weapons, ammunition, and equipment.

Economic cooperation was the last, but not the least important form of strategic cooperation against the aspirations of South Africa in the region. As was mentioned earlier, Pretoria's CONSAS plan was designed to block the advance of "Marxism" in the region, to increase economic dependence on South Africa, and to halt or limit the activities of the ANC and SWAPO. This plan was unacceptable to most of South Africa's neighbors. The experience of political cooperation developed among the Front Line States made it feel necessary to develop economic cooperation, both against dependence on South Africa, and for national and regional economic development.

Economic cooperation among the Front Line States developed from a small secretariat set up in Gaberone, Botswana, in early 1979. The lines that would guide SADCC were adopted at Arusha that same year. The formal creation of SADCC took place on April 1, 1980 in Lusaka; its prospects had improved greatly with the result of the liberation struggle in Rhodesia and the ZANU victory in the elections (see chapter 2d).

The Positions of Actors from Outside the Region

Until recently southern Africa was, for various reasons, an area of traditional British, and to some extent Portuguese, dominance. The Berlin Conference gave the region largely to Great Britain, recognized London's ally, Portugal, as the sovereign power in Angola and Mozambique, and, in a balancing exercise, conceded Tanganyika and Namibia (Southwest Africa) to Imperial Germany.

The British ultimatum to Portugal over the annexation of the territories in between Angola and Mozambique, which had been claimed by Portugal in the "rose-colored map" controversy at the end of the nineteenth century, and the MacMahon arbitration over the port of Lourenço Marques, showed that the Berlin shareout had not fully satisfied Great Britain's expansionist appetites. The Anglo-Boer War, and the First World War, which allowed Great Britain to acquire the German territories, consolidated British supremacy.

The breakup of British power followed the Second World War. In South Africa, the Afrikaner population won political power, and began a process of self-rule and rupture with London. The national liberation movements led various countries successively to independence in the decades between 1960 and 1990. With the weakening of Britain, U.S. capital appeared in the region, and took on a dominant role in South Africa. More recently Japanese and (West)

German capital have been tending to take pride of place (see chapter 2c).

Historically, China, the Soviet Union and the various countries of eastern Europe were absent from the continent. Their entry was in support of colonial emancipation. The European countries other than Britain and Portugal were only marginally represented, through consular missions, some trading arrangements, and this or that investment in the economic sphere. The Second World War, however, led to a flood of immigrants, and so there arose, particularly in South Africa and Rhodesia, communities of Italian, Jewish, Greek, and eastern European origin.

The liberation struggles in Angola, Mozambique, and Zimbabwe, and the Namibian and South African conflicts introduced new interests and solidarities onto the southern African scene. Portugal's participation in the Atlantic alliance, Lisbon's special links with Madrid and (after the installation of the military regime) with Brazil, and French diplomatic embarrassment arising from the war in Algeria, guaranteed that Portugal would receive more or less open support for its colonial wars. This complicity, occasionally shame-faced, tried to find a raison d'etre in the imperatives of the cold war.

It should be noted, however, that the United States, during the Kennedy administration, was opposed to Portuguese colonial policy, imposed an arms embargo against Portugal, and voted in favor of the colonized peoples at the United Nations. But the following administrations, embroiled in the Vietnam conflict, and concerned with the role of the Azores as a logistical springboard for flights to the Middle East, diluted the position of principle. They thus supported various supplies for Portugal and broke the links established in the 1960's. The Pretoria-Lisbon-Salisbury axis furthermore used the argument that White supremacy was the guarantee of the values of Christian and Western civilization.

All the African countries, the non-aligned movement, and the countries of the then socialist community declared in favor of the movement for the independence of the Portuguese colonies, though with differing motivations. In this context, and with rare exceptions determined by strategic national interests, all these countries broke off diplomatic and consular relations with Portugal, or refused to establish them, and applied various sanctions against Lisbon. From an early date, certain NATO countries, such as the Netherlands, together with Sweden and Finland, provided non-lethal support to the national liberation struggles. Morocco, Algeria, and Egypt provided military support, as did the socialist countries, particularly the U.S.S.R. and China, both through training and military supplies.

The neighboring countries agreed to act as rear bases for the armed liberation struggles, accepting sacrifices and sometimes suffering military and other forms of retaliation: this was the case of Guinea and Senegal in relation to Guinea-Bissau, Congo and Zaire in relation to Angola, Tanzania and Zambia in relation to Mozambique, and also Zambia to Angola.

These alignments were to some extent repeated during the Rhodesian conflict, transporting into the region the contradiction and global rivalry between the superpowers. Despite the will and the effort of the local actors, their concerns were read almost exclusively in the light of the tensions prevailing in the North. But crucial differences arose in Rhodesia arising from the nature of the rebellion against the crown. In 1965, Great Britain took the initiative of requesting the U.N. Security Council to impose mandatory sanctions. In public, only Portugal and South Africa declared that they had no intention of applying them (Jardim, 1978).

In reality, these sanctions only began to take effect after an independent Mozambique enforced effectively this international decision. An enormous second operational front opened for the liberation movement, which had begun to benefit from logistical facilities as soon as Frelimo succeeded in crossing the Zambezi in 1970. The progress of the armed struggle brought fresh impetus to the international front in support of the liberation of Zimbabwe, and drastically worsened the Rhodesian regime's isolation.

The nascent international detente at Helsinki; the lesson learned of the waste and uselessness of the colonial wars in Portugal and Rhodesia; the increased importance of public opinion in the struggle against apartheid and the occupation of Namibia; the growing political, financial, diplomatic, and military costs implied by the insistence on obsolete warlike methods that promised no way out of the impasse; the understanding that colonialism and racism throttled the development of a market economy—all this contributed decisively towards a realignment of forces internally, regionally, and internationally, which allowed Namibia to become independent, and gave prospects for the end of the discriminatory regime in Pretoria.

National liberation allowed the diversification of the political, diplomatic, economic, commercial, and cultural relations of the new states. Although independence has not always meant cutting the umbilical cord of subordination (including psychological subordination) to the former metropoles, the fact is that it imposed an autonomous presence in the international arena, and thus opened new channels of communications and interests. Other states joined Great Britain and Portugal.

Countries such as the U.S.S.R., China, and the German Democratic Republic appeared on the subcontinent, and became important economic partners of Angola, Mozambique, Tanzania, Zambia, and Zimbabwe. In the social field, Cuba was one of the most significant countries, particularly in education and health. Many thousands of Angolan, Mozambican, and Namibian students achieved their secondary and mid-level education in specially-built schools on Cuba's Isle of Youth.

The main Western European countries, France, Italy, West Germany, and the European Community as a whole, had a growing presence in the areas of transport, energy, agriculture and fisheries. Spain discovered a new area for participation, particularly in fisheries. The European Community has come to represent assistance on the order of 5 billion dollars to SADCC, quite aside from bilateral programs of support between the Community (and its member states and the countries of the region). The Nordic countries and the Netherlands had long-standing relations with the national liberation movements. The links forged in the early days now took shape in economic and social development projects. Sweden in particular has provided one of the greatest flows of aid to the states of southern Africa. The United States and Japan appeared as donors of food, and other, aid, and also in the economic area. This was also the case of industrializing Third World countries, such as Brazil, the two Koreas, China, and Pakistan.

In the area of military cooperation, there was a significant diversification of suppliers. During the wars of liberation, in general, Portugal, South Africa, and Rhodesia found support and supplies in the West, while the countries of the East, notably the U.S.S.R. and China, provided training and supplied equipment to the national liberation movements. The colonial and racist powers supplied themselves from the West, though as from the 1980's, weapons from the East were transferred commercially to South Africa. However, no state, with the exception of Israel, collaborated officially with South Africa in the military field, or publicly authorized the sale of military equipment to Pretoria.

The socialist countries, particularly the U.S.S.R., China, and the Democratic Rep. of Korea became important suppliers of equipment and training, and in certain cases even sent military advisers to ensure the training of new national armies. Today it is these countries, together with Great Britain, that supply the greater part of the supplies, training, and assistance to the majority of the states in the region. In this field, it is also important to mention the role of Israel and Taiwan in Malawi and Swaziland. France, Spain, and Italy have also provided some equipment and training to Mozambique.

It is important to note that the depolarization of the conflict and east-west rivalries in southern Africa have allowed diversified military assistance, in various forms, to the Front Line States. The U.S.S.R. and China, for instance, joined Great Britain in supporting Botswana, Lesotho, Tanzania, and Zambia, while Great Britain, Spain, France, and Italy joined the traditional partners of Angola, Mozambique, and Zimbabwe in the military sphere.

This last aspect took on a symbolic importance, and expressed the content of the political about-turn in perceptions and actions in the southern part of the continent. The ideological history of the United States and of the coalition of European forces that fought against Nazism and fascism should have been favorable to the cause of the emancipation of peoples and of equality between human beings. The United States was born of a war of liberation against colonialism. Anti-fascist Europe was the bearer of the democratic ideals of the French Revolution. Its combat was supported by the sacrifice of African and Asian troops from the colonies. All experienced the horrors and holocaust caused by racism. The Afrikaner community was dominated by people who, during the Second World War, had declared themselves in favor of Hitler's cause. The defeat of fascism left Salazar's Portugal rather isolated in the concert of democratic nations, given its political philosophy, and the sympathies that its leading circles had shown towards the Axis powers.

The cold war in Europe, the involvement of democratic powers such as France and Great Britain in armed colonial conflicts, the situations arising from the defeat of the Kuomintang in China, the war in Korea, the Indochinese and Middle East problems—in practice, all these factors determined an overall colonialist position of the Western countries towards the cause of the liberation of the Portuguese colonies, Namibia, and South Africa. NATO did not ostracize the Lisbon and Pretoria regimes. Instead it integrated Salazarist Portugal into the military defence of the "ideals of freedom."

This development ensured that the socialist camp, regarded as "the global adversary," found itself alone in the cause of solidarity with the struggle of colonial peoples. More important still, this dichotomy made easier the positions of repressive intransigence taken by the colonial and racist forces, which resulted in the bellicose adventures of the colonial wars. In the West, the weaponry and training given by the socialist countries to the cause of liberation were understood only as part of the "communist onslaught." It was on this Manichean perception that support, open or disguised, for the Lisbon, Salisbury, and Pretoria regimes was based.

African efforts, the efforts of the Front Line States, and particularly of Mozambique, were to try to depolarize the conflict, to bring Western governments and opinions to identify the real causes of the prevailing tensions, and thus to replace confrontation with consensus. Samora Machel was to say that in the Rhodesian question, the Front Line States, Great Britain, and the liberation movements were allies because they were all equally interested in ending the racist and colonial rebellion against the crown. This new way of thinking made possible the Lancaster House negotiations, the end of the war, and the victory of common sense.

Placing the southern African conflict within concrete parameters resulting from a specific reality opened prospects among the protagonists, both those within and those outside the region, conducive to the convergence of views so indispensable for dialogue, the re-establishment of a climate of trust, and cooperation for mutual benefits. Apartheid was isolated as the fundamental and determinant cause of tension.

This approach also resulted in further cooperation and lessening of tensions among the SADCC member countries. It reduced the growing tension between Malawi and the Front Line, that had derived from the use of Malawi in the South African aggression against Mozambique. Following this, a contingent of Malawian troops joined Mozambican forces in the defence of the Nacala Corridor. Efforts at detente also resulted in a lessening of the friction between Kinshasa and Lusaka on the one hand, and Luanda on the other. (The death of Samora Machel on October 19, 1986 took place on his return flight from Mbala where once more efforts had been made to calm the tensions between those three capitals.)

Regional strategy was concentrated on pursuing those goals defined as priorities—the end of the aggression and occupation of Angolan territory by South African forces, the implementation of U.N. Resolution 435 on Namibian independence, the elimination of the South African policy of regional destabilization and the devastation of Mozambique, and the removal of apartheid and the democratic access of the majority to power in South Africa.

Sanctions against South Africa

The period 1984–87 saw a wave of new sanctions legislation. At the level of official measures, there were four main packages: the Nordic Program of Action; the Joint European Community (EC) policy; the Commonwealth package; and the 1986 U.S. "Comprehensive Anti-Apartheid Act." While these vary in scope, those adopted by South Africa's major trading partners and foreign investors were far from comprehensive. Neither the Commonwealth nor the EC packages were binding on individual member states. Great Britain, in particular, refused to implement more than a few token measures. The U.S. Congressional Act did not prohibit imports of strategic minerals, agricultural produce, or bank loans, nor did it prevent transfers of technology (except computer technology to government agencies enforcing apartheid).

In February 1987, the U.S., Great Britain and (F.R.) Germany all voted in the U.N. Security Council to block an attempt to make mandatory measures identical to those in the U.S. Act. Great Britain, West Germany, and Portugal had all earlier combined to block a proposed EC ban on coal imports. Loans (except those to the government) were not banned under the EC package, and in the case of Great Britain the EC ban on new investments was voluntary. A 1984 U.S. Act did oblige the Administration to oppose new IMF loans, but provided for a number of exceptions. As one study put it, U.S. legislation provided the administration with plenty of "wiggle room" (Padayachee, 1987).

The first point that needs to be made in assessing the impact of sanctions on South Africa is then that sanctions packages applicable to South Africa's major trading partners were limited and partial in scope. They did not restrict imports of strategic minerals; nor did they, in themselves, seriously affect financial links or transfers of technology. They were thus full of crucial loopholes. Nevertheless, as the Commonwealth Expert Study Group on sanctions concluded, "partial sanctions have been a partial success" (*South Africa: The Sanctions Report*, 1989: ch.3). They forced some concessions and, combined with other pressures, have been part of the process of creating the climate which led to changes in Pretoria's stance on regional and domestic issues perceptible at the beginning of the 1990's.

The sanctions measures which can be identified as having had the most impact have been financial sanctions, the oil boycott, and the arms embargo. Trade sanctions in general have also had a more limited impact, being responsible for an estimated 7% cut in export earnings since 1985.

Financial sanctions and disinvestment

As far as what may be termed "financial sanctions" are concerned, as indicated above, a major input emerged from the changing perceptions of international bankers acting not out of a sense of solidarity with the people of South or southern Africa, but in their own material interests. The onset of the crisis of the apartheid system in the mid–1970's greatly affected the pattern of foreign investment in South Africa. The growing perception on the part of foreign investors that long-term capital investment in South Africa might be risky initially contributed towards the emergence of a pattern in which loans to government, the banking sector, and state corporations increasingly replaced long-term direct investments in the private sector as the major form of foreign investment (see chapter 2c and chapter 3).

P.W. Botha's August 1985 "Rubicon speech" provoked the next major change. Received as it was as an indication that the Botha administration did not have a program capable of guaranteeing long-term stability, it led to a run on the Rand and a decision by foreign bankers (led initially by Chase Manhattan) not to "roll over" (renew) a number of short-term credits, which theoretically fell due for repayment. Although a debt standstill agreement was subsequently negotiated with creditors in January 1986, this provided for repayment on relatively stiff terms and created a situation in which South Africa has found it increasingly difficult to raise new loans since then.

Although large amounts of foreign debt were repaid between 1985 and 1988 and all obligations have thus far been honored, South Africa faced a situation at the end of the 1980's in which about $22 billion was owed to foreign bank creditors (Preece, 1989). Under "normal" circumstances, this would not be an excessive burden for an economy the size of South Africa's, but given the restrictions on obtaining new loans and "rollover" facilities, South Africa found itself forced to export capital to repay its debts. Of the $22 billion owed, about $11 billion remained at the end of the decade inside the "standstill net." This amount fell subject to the rescheduling agreement negotiated in 1986, providing for repayment in various segments. However, beyond this lay the $11 billion outside the "standstill net" falling due for repayment over the course of the 1990's.

At the same time, the South African economy found itself having to sustain a number of important disinvestment, partly prompted by the generalized lack of confidence on the part of foreign investors and partly by pressures from anti-apartheid campaigns in Western countries. Although many of these did not involve the breaking of all ties, they nonetheless did result in substantial outflows of funds despite the fact that disinvestors had to accept an unfavorable rate of exchange under the "financial rand" system. Another, less publicized, development was the effective disinvestment by major South African conglomerates. Almost all the major corporations began in the late 1970's to acquire large external holdings, financed at least in part by withdrawals of funds from South Africa.

The combined effect of all these factors has been that since 1985 South Africa has had a consistently negative balance on both the long-term and short-term capital accounts of its balance of payments. With foreign reserves lower by the late 1980's than those of Botswana,[1] the only way available to the authorities in Pretoria to finance the consistent deficit on capital account was to run large surpluses on current account. More specifically, imports had to be curtailed in order to build up a surplus sufficient to meet debt repayment schedules. Since industrial growth in South Africa depends on importing various inputs, this has meant intervening in such a way that industrial growth was deliberately curtailed. The deleterious impact of the debt squeeze on growth became starkly apparent in the third quarter of 1988 when the monetary authorities of Pretoria found themselves compelled to intervene to abort a 3.2% mini-boom in order to build up reserves to meet a punishing repayment schedule. Under the circumstances of the debt squeeze, the South African economy could not afford to sustain a growth rate only half that achieved during the "boom" years of the 1960's.

Oil sanctions

While the oil embargo has clearly not had the effect of shutting down the engine of the apartheid economy, its effects too have been significant. Even though Pretoria has succeeded in finding suppliers willing to sell it oil, it has had to do so "through the back door" under circumstances in which each tightening of the screws of the formal embargo has raised the costs of circumventing it. Among the extra costs the South African economy had to bear were those arising from the premium prices that have had to be paid to "backdoor" suppliers, the costs of creating huge strategic reserves, and the substantial funds that have been diverted to uneconomic oil exploration projects like Mossgas. P. W. Botha himself estimated the cost of evading the oil embargo between 1973 and 1984 at $25 billion (*South Africa: The Sanctions Report,* 1989: 15, 144–47). Like financial sanctions and disinvestment, the oil embargo thus became a significant obstacle to apartheid prosperity and, moreover, a major potential Achilles heel in any possible situation of tightening sanctions.

The arms embargo

The third form of sanctions with major significance for developments in the region has been the arms embargo. The arms embargo decreed by the United Nations, of which the 1977 mandatory prohibition on the sale of weaponry and related equipment to South Africa was the most important aspect, was only achieved after a long struggle (since 1956) in the U.N. Those who were the most reluctant—and who vetoed all prior proposals for a mandatory arms embargo—were the Western powers with important financial interests in South Africa. Thus, for the bloc of African and other Third World states, the arms embargo finally agreed to by the Western powers was in fact considered to be a compromise. Arms embargoes were an alternative to general economic sanctions. What then were the circumstances and specific reasons which led to the 1977 embargo? Four general reasons can be indicated.

The so-called oil shock of 1973–74 to a certain extent raised the political profile of Third World countries in the international system. Many of these states were profoundly committed to the anti-apartheid cause. For those Western countries deeply involved in economic relations with South Africa, the 1977 embargo offered an alternative through which they could soothe those newly-rich Third World countries that were both economically important and anti-apartheid, without having to reduce greatly their own activities in South Africa.

The arms market was prospering in the second half of the 1970's. There was little or no danger of underutilization of the capacity of the armaments industries of the industrialized countries due to the loss of South Africa as a client. Instead of this, there was the possibility that anti-apartheid African and Middle Eastern governments—some of whom were among the largest arms importers in the world—might boycott purchases from companies or countries that wanted to supply military equipment to South Africa.

The 1975–76 invasions of Angola, and the 1976 Soweto massacre forced measures against apartheid onto the international political agenda.

Finally, in some key countries—which could have been important suppliers of weaponry and military technology to South Africa, or which had played that role—political power passed into the hands of governments that took a more or less firm anti-apartheid position. This happened not only with the Carter administration in the United States, with its ambassador Andrew Young at the United Nations, but also with the British labor government of James Callaghan, and the Social-Democratic government of (F.R.) Germany. The conservative government in France would have had problems with its principal African clients if it had chosen to vote against the mandatory embargo.

Thus the mandatory arms embargo against South Africa did not result merely from moral indignation over the apartheid system, but to a large extent from careful calculations as to what behavior would best serve the national economic and political interests of the major Western arms exporting countries. Such calculations also facilitated the continued flow of arms and equipment to South Africa, particularly from the major Western powers. Therefore the arms embargo enjoyed only partial success. It did not achieve its basic goals such as the end of apartheid and of South Africa's regional aggression. One important reason for this partial failure were the vague formulations contained in the 1977 mandatory arms embargo. These made it easy to interpret the embargo in a minimalist way and led to a notable growth in the South African arms industry (Landgren, 1989; Brzoska & Ohlson, 1986; Minty, 1986).

There were two basic ways of not implementing the embargo: violations and loopholes.[2] There are also two basic categories of articles covered by the embargo—*weapons* and *others* (which means all goods and services, other than actual weapons, that may contribute to the South African military effort). This can be illustrated in the following way:

	Violation	Loophole
Weapons	I	III
Others	II	IV

This schema offers a useful framework for what could be described as a "typology of non-implementation." It also helps evaluate what are the most important methods of non-implementation for the South African arms industry. The categorization follows the definition that most governments used in applying the 1977 embargo, particularly the double usage of articles considered as civilian in nature unless proved otherwise. This is in accordance with prevailing international definitions about weapons of war. The other possible definition is that all articles with a double usage should be considered as military, unless it is proved that their use is exclusively civilian. This is the interpretation chosen by most Western and other countries when it comes to the sale of sophisticated technology to states of the Eastern bloc (the so-called COCOM rules).

In accordance with the interpretation above, *violations* are illegal deals involving smuggling and other Black market operations. The number of known cases of arms smuggling (method I) has been very small. They included, for instance, the cases of G5 ammunition, rifle barrels, and Centurion tanks. To this category of contraband could be added the latest Israeli RESHEF missile-launching vessel, built in Israel in 1978, the alleged resupply of two FI Mirages from France in 1979, and the alleged entry of Mirage 3 combat aircraft from Argentina in mid–1978. There were also various cases of the smuggling of small arms. South Africa has bought large quantities of small arms such as rifles, pistols, mortars, hand grenades, and ammunition, both of Western and of Eastern origin, from private weapons suppliers and even from state export organizations, particularly in order to equip the forces trained to operate in Angola, Mozambique, and other countries.

Similarly, smuggling of articles other than actual weapons (method II) included examples such as G5 technology, blueprints for IKL/HDW submarines, missile guidance systems from private suppliers in the United States, and the sale of a German ammunition factory by (Rheinmetal). It also included the delivery of military electronic equipment for converted Boeing refuelling planes, acquired from Israel.

The South African authorities and their foreign collaborators used a wide range of methods to violate the arms embargo. These included the creation of dummy companies, domestically and abroad, bribing officials of companies or of governments, the use of obscure arms suppliers, transport agencies and shipping companies, false boarding documents, alteration of the routes used by ships, false end-user certificates, smuggling photographs of blueprints for projects or factories via the diplomatic bag, etc. It has been difficult to estimate the importance of these deals for South Africa's military industries. Due to its extremely secret nature, only part of this clandestine trade has become public knowledge. However, contraband is an expensive and uncertain method of acquisition, and it may be assumed that ithas been a complementary method subordinate to the legal acquisition of articles of military-industrial value.

Apart from this, the South African concept of "total engineering," that is, the ability to master the technology used in the weapons and in the military subsystems that are acquired so as to be able to repair and develop them without outside help, required a level of access to technology that very rarely could be obtained just through illegal trade operations. Thus, contraband in technology (method II) seemed to be preferred to contraband in weapons (method I).

Loopholes basically means using ambiguities in the embargo. Cases of the direct import of weapons classified as civilian by the exporter (method III) were obviously rare. It might be said that this category included some equipment for the South African police force and for the defence of the "independent" Bantustans. The most important and most frequent loophole was the acquisition of goods and services described as "others" (method IV). This included the following:

1. Finished products classified as civilian by the exporter, but with possible military applications, such as computers, radars, telecommunications equipment, trucks, and jeeps;
2. Various inputs for the arms industry, such as electronic parts, motors, gearboxes, spare parts, and pre-fabricated equipment for the maintenance and improvement of existing weapons factories;
3. Machinery that could be used for the manufacture of weaponry;
4. The transfer of technology, such as blueprints for projects or for factories for the production of articles with military applications, or of machinery used in the production of these articles;
5. The transfer of brain power and knowhow in the form of visits of foreign experts to South Africa, exchange of staff between research institutes, joint research and development efforts, etc.

The lowest common denominator for all the transfers described above is that they all concerned articles with double usage. In most cases they were acquired openly, usually in the major industrialized countries, such as the United States, (F.R.) Germany, Great Britain, France, and Japan. These countries only restricted the transfer of some of the articles and technology necessary for the South African arms industry, but allowed others. The principal source was through transnational companies: through direct imports, purchase of production licenses, deliveries of subsidiaries operating in South Africa, co-production or control of those subsidiaries, direct investment in foreign companies outside the country, etc. A large part of the technology also came from countries or governments who wanted to cooperate with South Africa for one or other "particular" reason, such as the so-called "pariah states" of Israel and Taiwan. The importance of the pariah link has been increasing, since the Western governments and the transnational companies are under growing pressure to stop investing in and halt cooperation with South Africa.

Why has South Africa been authorized to gain access to military technology, despite the condemnation of its apartheid policies, and its aggressive regional behavior? There were some general reasons why arms embargoes are difficult to implement comprehensively. First, there was no United Nations body that could enforce a mandatory arms embargo. Instead of this, the logical measure against a member who violated the embargo would be to appeal to the other member states to impose an embargo against the offender. To have some practical value, a United Nations mandatory arms embargo must be translated into national laws and regulations by the member states (if national legislation does not already conform with the embargo).

Secondly, a number of industrial, economic, military and political interests and forces were opposed to the moral and judicial reasons that underlay the arms embargo, and most of the arms exporting states did not have legislation that covered arms exports. Transfers of weaponry tended to be approved or prohibited in an ad hoc way, based on short term economic and political interests.

Thirdly, today's abundance of producers and suppliers of military equipment made it inconceivable that an international embargo could be totally effective, even with the maximum of legislation in most arms exporting countries, unless sanctions were to be accompanied with an air, sea, and land blockade, as in the case of Iraq.

Fourthly, the international arms market today was essentially a buyer's market. There was a general excess of capacity in the international arms industry—supply was greater than demand. Increasingly governments considered the economic forces behind arms exports so strong that they approved of the business, even though they might have liked to avoid it for political reasons. This situations sapped the will of governments to adopt legislation that might have later reduced the prospects of the arms industry obtaining lucrative export contracts.

Fifthly, with the growing technological complexity of modern weapons systems, the distinction between military and civilian articles, inputs and prefabricated equipment, became less than clear. Articles of double technology—i.e., that can be used both for military and civilian purposes—were abundant. From the viewpoint of implementing the embargo this brought innumerable problems that were difficult to resolve, and they increased with the level of scrutiny applied.

Finally, alongside the open trading of goods and services on the world market, there was the international Black market, where illegal or semi-legal transactions took place. If all other methods failed, the embargoed state could always—despite the great cost involved—opt to use the Black market for many of its needs.

In evaluating the impact of the arms embargo, the conclusion must be that if it was expected that the embargo would lead to the immediate eradication of apartheid, or to the end of the process of militarization in South Africa, and that it would seriously restrict South Africa's capacity for regional aggression, then such expectations were wrong. If, on the other hand, the embargo is regarded as one method amongst various of bringing pressure to bear on South Africa to change its policies, then the results appear less negative.

It may be considered that the 1977 arms embargo did have an impact. It deprived South Africa of access to the major systems for importing arms then in existence. South Africa came to have great difficulties in acquiring modern combat aircraft, military helicopters, warships, submarines, battle tanks, and other tracked vehicles, as well as anti-tank and ground-to-air missiles. In various ways the 1977 embargo hit at South Africa's efforts to obtain the latest military technology, and increased South Africa's expenditure on components, spare parts and technology. Clandestine trade always imposes extra costs.

It should be noted that the factors mentioned above worked in favor of the 1988 ceasefire agreement in Angola, and the implementation of U.N. Security Council Resolution 435 on Namibian independence. To some extent they caused the loss of South Africa's military superiority over its Angolan and Cuban opponents. This was largely due to the arms embargo. This fact argues in favor of the efficiency of sanctions. Apart from this, even if arms embargoes did not have an immediate effect on South Africa's actual military capacity in the regional context, they curbed or made more expensive the acquisition of financial and manpower resources. There are no figures on this expenditure, but one of the themes in the White South African journals on defence and arms supplies is that the domestic production of weaponry has been very expensive.

Progress in arms production is frequently cited in the South African press as a way of calming down public opinion and South Africa's Whites. But the military experts and those dealing with expenditure must have serious grounds for concern. The government presents the state-controlled company Armscor as the most powerful arms producing industry, but the quantitative costs of Armscor have been questioned by the opposition in parliament. For years rationalization and adjustment measures have been announced to improve the work of Armscor. In 1984 a special investigating committee, led by General J.J. Geldenhuys, presented a series of proposals on how to rationalize weapons production. However the report did not solve the dilemma that the South African market is too small for economically viable production of such a large range of armaments.[3]

South African weapons production is a victim of self-sufficiency. Self-sufficiency is a form of isolation, whether self-imposed or imported. This approach offers employment and prosperity for some during a short period, but stagnation in the long run. If the country protects itself and its industries from international competition, then it ceases to be stimulated by competitive prices and international markets. The cost is enormous. In the case of the

South African arms industry, there is no other solution, given the embargoes and the overall goal of preserving apartheid and regional dominance. It is here that the embargo has had—and continues to have—its effects.

Countersanctions imposed by South Africa

Sanctions imposed by South Africa against its neighbors have been the other major form in which sanctions have been significant in the evolving struggle for southern Africa. South African sanctions against regional states can be recognized as falling into two interconnected categories.

First, there have been measures implemented as part of Pretoria's overall destabilization campaign. In a widely quoted paper written for Pretoria University's Institute of Strategic Studies, Deon Geldenhuys (1981) identified thirteen ways in which Pretoria could potentially apply "disincentive economic levers" in pursuit of its regional policy goals. They ranged from manipulating trade and transport flows, through prohibitions on migrant labor recruitment and the movement of persons to outright economic blockades. Most of the options identified by Geldenhuys were applied in practice in one form or another during the 1980's, often to complement aggressive military action. Pretoria's involvement in actions of this type belied its protestations that it was opposed to sanctions on principle (SARDC, 1986). Throughout the 1980's, an increasing list of regional states found themselves victims of sanctions imposed against them by Pretoria.

With the intensification of the sanctions campaign against Pretoria, a new dimension was added to Pretoria's own sanctions campaign. It threatened to respond to any tightening of sanctions against it by imposing what became known as "countersanctions" against regional states. The objective of "countersanctions" appeared to be to pressure regional states into withdrawing support for sanctions and perhaps even into giving tacit support to Pretoria's campaign against sanctions; and also to provide a "disincentive" to the international community, by taking steps to give credence to its assertion that the principal victims of sanctions against South Africa would be Blacks in South African and in neighboring states.

In June 1985, the then South African Deputy Minister of Foreign Affairs, Louis Nel, and State President P.W, Botha both made speeches threatening to expel foreign migrant workers if sanctions were imposed (*Financial Times*, 7/31/1985). By November 1985 it was reported that preparations for a major "counter-sanctions" campaign had been discussed by the State Security Council, which had formulated plans for, inter alia, the expulsion of foreign migrant workers (*Business Day*, 11/11/1985). As some form of tightened sanctions became inevitable, attention among Pretoria's strategists shifted to questions of targeting and timing of "countersanctions." By early August 1986, "senior South African sources" were quoted in the press as saying that Pretoria's reaction to sanctions would be "graduated but potentially massive defensive and appropriate." High on the priority list was a trade "tit for tat" against neighboring states, and the imposition of a new licensing regulation on Zimbabwean imports on August 1st was described as the "opening shot" in the "sanctions war." The "second leg" would involve the repatriation of foreign refugees and migrant workers (*Sunday Times*, 8/3/1986). On October 8 1986, a ban on Mozambican migrant workers was announced less than a fortnight before President Samora Machel died in highly suspicious circumstances in a plane crash on South African territory. There were several factors underlying the labor ban and other actions taken against Mozambique at the time, including the openly aggressive posture of Malawi. But it was no coincidence that the ban came less than a week after the passage of the U.S. sanctions bill.

The implementation by Pretoria of sanctions against the region has without doubt been costly. It has been estimated that boycotts and embargoes imposed by South Africa cost SADCC member states the equivalent of $260 million between 1980 and 1984 (see Hanlon, 1986a: Appendix 1). In the case of Mozambique alone, the National Planning Commission estimated that the reduction in the volume of South African traffic passing through Mozambican ports and the cutback in recruitment of Mozambican mine workers cost the equivalent of $816 million between 1975 and 1983 (Mozambique. National Planning Commission, 1984: 41). The costs of diverting South African traffic away from Maputo port alone have been calculated at $534 million for the decade 1976–1986.[4]

While South African sanctions and "countersanctions" have imposed costs on the region, their effects have not all been negative. The threat and later reality of "countersanctions" in the mid-1980's provided a real spur to the SADCC program. The threat of a squeeze on traffic to and from landlocked countries, in particular, formed the background to the January 1986 SADCC summit which launched the current Beira corridor program. Similarly, the climate of sanctions with the threat of "countersanctions" was one of the major factors leading a number of donors seriously to contemplate becoming involved in supporting SADCC projects. These included a number of countries whose governments were opposed to sanctions against Pretoria, who became involved in order to show that they were nevertheless "doing something positive" in southern Africa.

The Costs of the Conflict

South Africa

It is clear that the enormous growth in the amounts spent by South Africa in the military area over the past 30 years (escalating from 44 million rands in 1960–61 to 9,937 million rands in 1989–90) is something that the South African government has sought to disguise and to minimize. On average these numbers represent about 15% of government expenditure and about 3–4% of GDP. In fact, these sums are not so very high when compared with those of other countries. However, there are at least three important points on this matter to be borne in mind.

The comparison between state expenditure and the general GDP is of limited relevance in itself. A growing economy does not automatically imply a growth in military needs. The fact was that military expenditure grew and often exceeded the growth in overall state expenditure. This is noteworthy given the stagnation of the South African economy over the same period.

Actual expenditure was much greater than what is budgeted. The defense budget represented only part of what can be called "security expenditure." As a first step in approaching the real level of security expenditure in South Africa, the "protective services" must be referred to, that is, expenses on defence, police, the judiciary, and prisons (Table 1).

Table 4-1
Expenditure on "Protective Services" in 1988–89 and 1989–90 (in millions of rands)

	A Budget 1988–89	B Budget 1988–89	C Budget 1989–90	% increase of C over A	% increase of C over B
Defence	8,196.0	8,742.8	9,937.4	21.2	13.7
Police	1,940.0	2,130.5	2,496.3	28.7	17.2
Judiciary	277.4	307.5	348.6	25.7	13.4
Prisons	630.4	673.0	751.0	19.1	11.6
Total	11,043.8	11,853.9	13,533.3	22.5	14.2

Sources:
Financial Mail, March 17, 1989; *Weekly Mail,* March 17, 1989; *Star Weekly,* March 22, 1989.

The general budget for 1989–90 was 65 billion rands. The defense budget was 937 million rands, 15.3% of the total. The inclusion of the other "protective services" raises security expenditure to 13.5 billion rands, or 22.6 percent. Even so, this leaves out some substantial expenses related to security, including:

- a large part of the expenses of the SWATF and of the SWAPOL forces in Namibia (up to independence);
- part of military intelligence and the secret services (Finance);
- the Bantustan armies (Development Aid);
- the construction of military bases, including accommodation and defense buildings (Public Services);
- part of military medical expenditure and wages (health and the private sector);
- part of the armament and other military equipment, research

and development expenditure (Education, Special Defense Account and the private sector);

- costs related to the joint management center and other parts of the national security management system (various departments).

It is calculated that if all the security-related costs mentioned above are included, then total expenditure on defense and security would be between 20–24 billion rands, or between 31–37% of total expenditure. This would probably amount to between 8–9% of GDP (*Weekly Mail*, 4/7–13/1989). Since security expenditure is a valid indicator of the level of militarization in South Africa, theoretically we may consider that South Africa is at least twice as militarized as the defense figures alone might initially suggest.

Recent substantial increases in security expenditure (despite the peace agreement with Angola and Cuba and the poor state of the South African economy) indicates that peace is apparently more expensive than war. This is not such a paradox as it might appear, given the absolute priority that the security apparatuses in apartheid South Africa enjoy. The geographical shrinking of South Africa's external defense perimeter could lead to an increase in security expenditure for the following reasons: modernization and growth in conventional arsenals (the need for this was underscored by the Cuito Cuanavale experience), and later stress on conventional rather than guerrilla warfare; greater need for professional soldiers, arms, and other equipment along the borders; increase in internal security.

Military and defense expenditure consumes resources, and contributes little to the growth of an economy's productive potential. This becomes a problem when the civilian sectors of the economy do not generate growth, which is precisely what has characterized the South African economy since the mid–1980's. The South African manufacturing sector is not a source of foreign exchange: the country is dependent on the export of minerals, and the import of essential goods. Gerhard de Kock, former governor of the South African Reserve Bank, calculated that about 80% of South Africa's imports are essential equipment and intermediate goods without which the economy cannot support itself (*South African Barometer*, 3/27/1987: 20). The foreign exchange to pay for these imports comes from two main sources: exports of primary goods and minerals, and foreign investment (loans, risk capital, or the transfer of technology).

Since Western commercial bankers in 1985 expressed their deep lack of confidence in the prospects for the South African economy, the freezing of new loans was accompanied with a reluctance to renew credits. This had a snowball effect, which began to be felt immediately inside South Africa. With the prospects for enormous gains rapidly disappearing, private investors began to disinvest. They were followed by public creditors who refused new loans and debt renegotiations. Trade sanctions were introduced by many more countries. As Alan Hirsch remarked "The ease with which the West took a moral position in the 1980's was helped by the sickness of the goose that laid the golden eggs" (*Weekly Mail*, 8/18–24/1989: 14).

Rescheduling its debts thus became a major problem for the South African government. The hostility of international financial markets led to deficits from 1985 on, both in the long and the short term. With limited foreign exchange reserves, South Africa had no option but to finance these deficits with a surplus on current account, i.e., mainly through an increase in the export of gold and other minerals. The shortage of new capital from abroad, and the growing debt forced the decision-making centers to put the brakes on demand, limiting both private expenditure and economic growth. The annual growth rate of five percent thought necessary in order to overcome economic problems, pay the debt, support security costs, pay for improved living standards in the cities etc. cannot now be sustained with the overheated economy.[5]

The SADCC member states

The economic effects of the war of destabilization on SADCC member states are well documented, and can be clearly seen in the statistical data published in recent years in four areas: deaths due to the war, refugees and displaced people, the impact on education and health, and regional losses in GDP due to the war of aggression waged by South Africa. It should be borne in mind that the demographic and economic statistics, particularly in Angola and Mozambique, are not exact.

UNICEF has calculated that at least 1.3 million people have died in Angola and Mozambique as a direct or indirect result of the war between 1980 and 1988. At least 850,000 of these deaths were of children less than five years old. The concept of "death due to war" includes deaths directly caused by military action, deaths due to hunger caused by insecurity, and deaths resulting from the combined effects of malnutrition, illness, and destruction of the rural health network (1989: 10, 24–25). The inhuman massacres of civilians by Renamo in Mozambique has led high-ranking officials of the U.S. State Department to compare Renamo to the Khmers Rouges of Cambodia, and to describe the situation in Mozambique as "one of the most brutal holocausts against ordinary human beings since World War II."[6]

In Angola and Mozambique, more than 11 million people—from the rural population of both countries—have been displaced from their homes and their land. About nine million of these are displaced inside their own countries, while 1.5–2 million have been forced to seek refuge in neighboring countries. This imposes great burdens on the countries of refuge (UNICEF, 1989: 20).

It is impossible to speak of real and sustainable socio-economic development without a healthy and reasonably well-educated population. After independence, priority was given to these sectors in most of the southern African states, and in many cases these public sector programs achieved considerable success. This was particularly the case in Mozambique whose vaccination and literacy programs became models for the international community. Destabilization changed all this. By mid–1989 more than 2,655 primary schools, or about 45% of the total, had been destroyed or closed in Mozambique. This affected over half a million children, and more than 7,000 teachers. Similarly, about 850 health posts, and 10 of the 27 rural hospitals were destroyed or seriously damaged. In 1981, the health budget amounted to $5.40 for each Mozambican. By 1988 this sum had fallen to less than one dollar per capita (Frelimo, 1989: 212, 238; Martin & Johnson, 1989:

MO28–31).

The first overall estimate of the regional GDP loss due to war and destabilization was presented by SADCC to the 1984 O.A.U. summit. This estimate covered the period 1980–84, and it came to more than ten billion U.S. dollars (SADCC, 1986c: Annex B). At that time, this was equal to 10% of the combined GDP of the nine SADCC member states over the same period. This estimate was divided into the following categories: direct losses due to war, additional defense expenditure, extra transport and energy costs, contraband, refugees, lost export and tourism income, boycotts and embargoes, drops in production, and lost economic growth and trading conditions. The most recent estimate made by the UNICEF experts group covers the period 1980–88 (UNICEF, 1989: Annex A). Using basically the same methodology as the SADCC study, and making adjustments in the calculations and exchange rates, they came to the estimate in Table 4-2 which indicates a GDP loss more than three times the total foreign debt of all the SADCC member states (North/South Roundtable, 1988: 14).

Table 4-2

State	Billions of U.S. dollars
Angola	30
Mozambique	13.5
Other SADCC members	17
SADCC total 1980–88	60.5

In addition to the three kinds of costs listed above, there are others of a more political nature. These costs, which are interconnected, result primarily from the war of destabilization, as well as from efforts to alleviate the adverse effects of the conflict. One is a heavy dependence on donor countries, which is particularly the case with Mozambique. Another is the loss of economic freedom. Certain negative (though necessary) consequences arise from the changes in economic policy. This is obvious in Mozambique, where the

Economic Recovery Program, commonly known by the acronym PRE, has lessened the capacity of the state to channel resources to the health and education sectors, and has as well as cut the living standards of the poorest strata in the urban areas.

Furthermore, as a result of destabilization, interaction with and dependence on South Africa have not been reduced, and neither has intra-SADCC economic cooperation increased as would have been expected under conditions of peace. As had been noted, some of these changes in economic policy result from errors in formulating and implementing development policies. However, the current lack of room for economic maneuver is to be explained principally by the war of destabilization waged by South Africa.

Institutionalizing the emergency: the case of Mozambique

Mozambican society has been particularly devastated by the combined effects of the various forms of destabilization. From this point of view, it is important to analyze the actions carried out both because of their almost unique character, and because of their future effects in terms restoring a matrix of progress and development.

The goal of destabilization is to make it impossible for Mozambican society to function. This activity in Mozambique is not aimed at creating any alternative or parallel power. Any Mozambican government, no matter how conservative or anti-Communist it might be, would be obliged to make the rail and port system linking the landlocked countries to the sea functional, thus depriving Pretoria of one of its most important means of pressure against the region, and also taking from it the financial profits that it gains from this exercise.

If we look at the data referring to the targets of destabilization, then we can note that systematically it is the most vulnerable sectors of society who came under the heaviest attack. Since Pretoria took control of Renamo about 3,000 primary schools have been destroyed, and 400 teachers kidnapped, mutilated or killed. Half a million children have been deprived of formal education. More than 800 health posts and rural hospitals have been looted, destroyed or burnt down. With enormous effort, between 1975 and

1980 the country built one health unit for every 9,700 in-habitants—this health coverage has now dropped to one unit for every 13,000 inhabitants. About 1,000 private shops and coopera-tives that guaranteed agricultural marketing and supplied the peasantry have been looted and burnt. Hundreds of thousands of houses and stores have been burnt down in thousands of villages. To obtain the best results from their destabilization and to render Mozambican society inviable, South Africa has made use of natural disasters (floods, cyclones, and droughts), ordering its forces to obstruct the systems supporting the victims of the emergency, thus preventing them from reorganizing their lives.

Convoys of clearly-identified vehicles of the Red Cross and other humanitarian organizations have been attacked, set on fire and destroyed, while the drivers have been murdered or kidnapped. This activity is designed to institutionalize hunger, endemic disease, and the disintegration of communities forced to live a nomadic existence. It has led to the displacement of a quarter of the Mozam-bican population, and has forced over a million Mozambicans to take refuge in neighboring countries. Aggression has directly caused the deaths of 100,000 civilians, according to the most conservative of estimates. If we add to these the indirect deaths, resulting from the attempt to institutionalize hunger and disease, the destruction of homes and of organized life, the number of victims may possible approach a million.

A report published by the U.S. State Department, written by Robert Gersony (1988) at the request of that department, provides us with data that draw our attention to the methods and effects of the conflict in Mozambique. Summing up his conclusions, the author of the report writes:

> First, the level of violence reported to be conducted by RENAMO against the civilian population of rural Mozam-bique is extraordinarily high. . . . If the population estimates reported in the introduction to this report are correct, there are roughly 200,000—250,000 refugee and displaced fami-lies in Mozambique and in the neighboring countries, the majority of whom are conflict victims. If the refugee reports

are generally accurate and the sample reasonably representative, it is conservatively estimated that 100,000 civilians may have been murdered by RENAMO in this manner.

The same 170 refugees report many hundreds of cases of systematic forced portering, beatings, rape, looting, burning of villages, abductions and mutilations. These patterns of systematic abuse represent many hundreds, if not thousands, of individual instances reported by this small sample. Conservative projections based on this data would yield extremely high levels of abuse.

That the accounts are so strikingly similar by refugees who have fled from northern, central and southern Mozambique suggests that the violence is systematic and coordinated and not a series of spontaneous, isolated incidents by undisciplined combatants.

Second, the relationship between RENAMO and the civilian population, according to the refugee accounts, revolves almost exclusively around a harsh extraction of labor and food. If these reports are accurate, it appears that the only reciprocity provided by RENAMO for the efforts of the civilians is the possibility of remaining alive. There are virtually no reports of attempts to win the loyalty—or even the neutrality—of the villagers. The refugees report virtually no effort by RENAMO to explain to the civilians the purpose of the insurgency, its proposed program, or its aspirations. If there is a significant sector of the population which is sympathetic to this organization, it was not reflected in the refugee accounts.

When quantifying the violence against the local population, the author of the report attempted to determined who was responsible and reached the conclusions found in Table 4-3 for the 1985–88 period. On the basis of the information obtained, the report also notes that acts of violence attributed to the government forces, are isolated acts of indiscipline and are subject to punishment.

Of the refugees interviewed, the report declares that 91% had a "very negative" opinion of Renamo, 5% a "somewhat negative"

Table 4-3

	Renamo	Government	Unknown
Deaths	94%	3%	3%
Deaths of children	96%	4%	0
Kidnap of civilians	94%	3%	3%
Percentage reporting rape	15%	1 case	0
Houses burnt	A third of the refugees had their homes burnt down by Renamo		
Looting of property	93%	6%	1%
Mutilations	5% of refugees testi-fied to mutilations carried out by Renamo		

opinion, while 83% held positive views of, or were not critical towards, the government.

Despite the burdensome inheritance from Portuguese colonialism and the war of aggression, Mozambique overcame the destruction caused by Rhodesia and by natural disasters, overcame the losses resulting from the implementation of sanctions against Smith and from world inflation, and somehow managed to increase Gross Social Product by 11.6% between 1977 and 1981. Successes were achieved in education, health, and living conditions.

In 1970 less than 1% of the population had completed primary education, and 93% of the population over seven years old was illiterate. Yet in 1981 there were 1,300,000 children in primary schools. Between 1975 and 1982, 430,000 children completed their primary education. It was possible to claim then that one out of every ten Mozambicans was attending some form of formal education. The percentage of people who were illiterate dropped by 30 percent.

Vaccination coverage in Mozambique reached 95.7 percent. In the first five years of independence infant mortality dropped from

150 to 80 per 1,000. 49% of all pregnant women received pre-
natal assistance. In 1970, three per cent of homes had their own
sanitation, but in 1980 the number had reached 40 percent.
Between independence and 1980, 700,000 families in the rural
areas gained access to sources of clean water, while in the urban
areas 300,000 families benefitted from piped water as against
45,000 in the colonial period.

The destructive character of the aggression put an end to this
process of transforming the lives of the people, and the development activities resulting from this enormous effort.

As from 1982 progress was halted, and the economy and the
social services together went into decline. The destruction of
workplaces, the sabotage of communications and of the energy
distribution system, the systematic attacks against villages, the
looting and burning of peasant stores and huts, the mining of
cultivated fields, all this generalized an offensive against the development efforts of Mozambican society.

Once peace is re-established, the accumulated effects of material
and human devastation will require gigantic efforts at repair which
will be difficult for a country in a state of complete exhaustion.
Furthermore, it is doubtful whether international cooperation will
be capable of providing significant support at a time when attention is being redirected eastwards.

More serious than the physical destruction have been the human
traumas, and the fact that a considerable number of children in the
rural areas have been deprived of access to schooling, and of the
minimum diet needed to prevent physical and mental problems. A
significant proportion of future generations will appear ignorant,
and physically and perhaps mentally stunted. This will certainly
prolong in time the effects of destabilization, long after the destabilization itself has ended.

Some data beginning to emerge about hunger, cholera, and
displacement in Angola, lead one to think that a similar scenario
can be detected in that country.

Conclusion

The Soviet-American relationship, now centered on the search for areas of agreement, made positive action by the superpowers viable in solving regional conflicts. These were no longer viewed in the light of a confrontation of interests, and instead became the object of a concerted search for stable solutions. The presence of the Cuban contingent, as part of the Angolan strategy for defending its sovereignty and territorial integrity, became unnecessary with the South African withdrawal from Angola and the subsequent independence of Namibia. The undertaking given by South Africa to cease its interference in the internal affairs of Angola through its support for UNITA opened the prospect for internal reconciliation, since Savimbi's group was losing its character as an instrument of apartheid aggression against the Luanda government. The closure of the ANC's reception and training centers in Angola, and the evacuation of the ANC fighters, eliminated the real or imagined danger of an external and violent onslaught against South African Whites. These premises ensured the necessary trust for the implementation of Resolution 435 on Namibia.

The tendency in the United States and the Soviet Union has become, to some extent, to put the brake on the arms race as regards systems of mass destruction. The difficulty that the U.S. and the U.S.S.R. are experiencing in controlling events and in disciplining their allies and friends leads one to the perception that regional conflicts in an interdependent world threaten the stability of the global security system. But the end of confrontation between the superpowers allows a new understanding of regional conflicts, stripping them of their ideological nature.

The U.S.S.R. has tried to present parameters for this new conception, placing human values above class values, prioritizing areas of interest, rather than areas of divergence, and advocating political solutions for all regional conflicts.

Political solutions for all regional conflicts reassert the principle that, however localized the tension may be, it has repercussions globally on international relations. These concepts, which had already been expressed at the Helsinki Conference, allow a pragmatic approach to conflicts and make solutions easier. However, there is still the risk that once again regional conflicts may be viewed in the abstract, and in the search for a solution, the merits of the parties to the conflict may be ignored, thus consolidating flagrant injustices that will generate new conflicts.

Soviet concerns are also based on internal factors that demand the revitalization of the Soviet economy, and a halt to the breakup of power, relegating to a secondary position foreign policy and solidarity. These positive concerns are still not evident in U.S. policy, which seems to want to exploit for tactical purposes the current weakness of its one-time global adversary in order to impose a "Pax Americana" on the planet.

In this context, southern Africa, despite everything, benefits from the end of bipolar confrontation. For certain Western circles, opposition to apartheid used to be viewed as a smokescreen hiding Soviet expansionism in the subcontinent. But now, as the events in Namibia show, this opposition is the common position of all the powers. On the other hand, the end of the bipolar system may facilitate the triumph in the region, even if only temporarily, of the interests that are identified with the preservation of White dominance, though under new forms. This variant is made possible by the reduction in the anti-imperialist capacity to conceive its interests and defend its conceptions.

Present developments are nonetheless favorable on the whole for the re-establishment of peace and stability in the region, although numerous obstacles may arise in the processes now under way. In South Africa, the question of reconciliation among races and ethnic groups, long conditioned to conflict, has become sharply posed. The abolition of apartheid is not simply a political or legal question, but implies positive actions to re-establish effective equality of opportunities in society between the various races. This affirmative action may eventually imply a certain decline in the administrative and even the economic efficiency of the apparatuses, and some destabilizing effect among those sectors of the population reluctant to accept racial equality or who, because of maximalist demands, are incapable of supporting the gradual transformation of society.

Problems of national reconciliation also arise in Mozambique and Angola where, regardless of the nature of destabilization, it has to be recognized that several thousand nationals of the two countries were used to carry out this destabilization. There are psychological problems to be overcome, and the moral wounds to be healed of a conflict which, in many ways, is similar to classic civil wars. In a period when to some extent, and for various reasons, support from countries of the north for the south is likely to decline, there will be serious obstacles.

The liberalization of economies, their opening to market strategies, will have to bear in mind (for they will suffer grave risks if they do not) the slight or even zero capacity for accumulation in societies such as that of Mozambique where about a quarter of the population is displaced, and living below the absolute threshold of physical survival.

The democratization of societies, the creation of truly pluralist spaces, the transformation of citizens into the subjects of the history of their societies, holding rulers politically responsible before their societies—these are complex problems to which there is no simplistic answer. No one doubts that these are imperative vectors of development, just as many people are fully aware that the forms and the processes must be found within the society itself, reserving for imported solutions the character of mere reference points.

Regional cooperation, with the transformation of SADCC into a motor of development, integrating a democratic South Africa, is a plausible and desirable scenario, capable of stimulating the recovery of an area that contains ample natural and human resources. Attempts to make use of SADCC as an instrument to consolidate, in a new form, South African hegemony, however, is something that could introduce new variants and tensions into the scenario that could put at risk the aims of development and harmony. International aid and cooperation could overcome the weakness of the countries of the region in relation to South Africa and allow a balanced relationship.

From this point of view, the greatest effort for South-South relations and a perspective of aid and cooperation with the North destined to ensure greater local self-sufficiency in the valuing of resources could be considered key elements.

Notes

1. Botswana's foreign reserves at the beginning of 1989 stood at $2.26 billion (equivalent to around R5.6 billion). Those of South Africa in December 1988 were R4.93 billion (*The Star International Airmail Weekly* 1/3/1989). In 1980, South Africa's foreign reserves were R16.6 billion (*Financial Mail* 17/3/1989).

2. This analysis is taken from an earlier paper: Ohlson, 1988.

3. A summary of the findings and recommendations of the Geldenhuys Commmitee is given in South Africa, *Ministry of Defence,* (1986: part 1, 1–11).

4. See the draft chapter for *South Africa: the Sanctions Report* (1989). This statement which appears on page 22 of what is described as the "final draft" of the section on Mozambique did not appear in the published version.

5. For a thorough discussion of the emergency, extent, and implications of current economic crisis in South Africa, see *Southern Africa Dossier,* 1989a.

6. Deputy Assistant Secretary of State for Africa Roy Stacy speaking at a donors' conference in Maputo, quoted in James Brooke, "U.S. Assails 'Holocaust' by Mozambicans Rebels," *International Herald Tribune,* April 26, 1988. The reference to the Khmers Rouges was made by Assistant Secretary of State Charles Freeman during a visit to Brazil in March 1989, quoted in *Noticias,* March 14, 1989.

Chapter 5

Evolving Class-Race Stratification in the Region

A. Introduction to Issues of Class and Race

The ways in which class and race are intermeshed as social realities—in terms of social stratification, in terms of political struggle, in terms of consciousness—have been a central locus of political and intellectual debate in the world-system for over a century. This has been especially true in relation to southern Africa where, for particular historical reasons, understanding this nexus has been of fundamental importance for analysts and activists.

Capitalism as an historical system has created a correlation everywhere and at all points in time between class status and racial/ethnic group affiliation. Those at the bottom of one hierarchy tend to be at the bottom of the other. But the correlation is always imperfect. It is never true that *all* those at the bottom of the class hierarchy are at the bottom of the race/ethnicity hierarchy. And it is seldom true that all those at the bottom of the race/ethnicity hierarchy are at the bottom of the class hierarchy (although this was in fact one of the historic objectives of the apartheid system).

This "imperfect correlation" of class and race/ethnicity has two general consequences. The first is that the confusion in categories thus created can be extremely stabilizing for the capitalist system. The creation of groups of persons with "status inconsistency" leads to the phenomenon of such people defending the system in order to defend their relative position in the overall hierarchy, even if this position is relatively low. This is an old and familiar point about the political divisiveness such category "confusion" creates among the lower strata—old and familiar, but still correct. The history of the political role of "poor Whites" in South Africa is a classic instance of this general phenomenon.

The second consequence of the "imperfect correlation" is the emergence of two separate, overlapping, and contradictory consciousnesses—class consciousness and race/ethnic group consciousness. This poses a fundamental problem for antisystemic movements—of which string to play. The history of these movements in southern Africa has been replete with debate over the strategy to follow. Indeed, the deepest splits within the movements have occurred over this issue.

The structures and their interrelations, as they have developed in southern Africa, are of course historically specific to the region. Nonetheless, since they fall within a pattern that is everywhere to be observed in the modern world, there are several questions to be addressed. Once we distinguish the ways in which southern Africa's class-race stratification is typical and the ways in which it is different (even exceptional), we must address the issue of the origins of the differences. We shall also want to know how the particular configuration has been caused by the developing "regionality" of southern Africa, and how it has in turn affected the degree of economic and political integration of the region. Finally, we shall want to project in the next chapter what this portends for a post-apartheid southern Africa. Will the political transformation merely bring southern Africa to a more "typical" form of class-race stratification? Or will the fact that southern Africa has a past of "exaggerated" class-race stratification have the political consequence of a rebound, towards the radical reduction of a class-race stratification system?

B. Historical Development of Social Base of Class

In this section analyzing the region's changing social hierarchy, the focus is on socio-economic location rather than position; in Marxian terms, class-in-itself rather than class-for-itself. This structure, and location within it, is in fact more often discussed in terms of occupations and economic sectors, than of social classes. This choice, partially imposed upon us, as for example when the relevant data has only been collected in sectoral categories, originates primarily in a desire to avoid entering into the debates over which occupations belong to which social classes.

Regional Wage-Labor and Economic Growth

Formal sector employment as a whole for southern Africa stagnated between 1975 and 1985 (see Table 5-B-1); as the population grew (see Table 5-B-2), the percentage of the working age population with formal sector jobs plummeted. In the second half of the 1970's, the rate of growth of employment declined in almost every country, while in the 1980's many countries registered an absolute decline. Total regional employment outside of Angola and Mozambique increased less than 6% in the ten years after 1975. If the figures from the ex-Portuguese colonies were available, their

257

Table 5-B-1
Total Formal Sector Employment in Various Countries of the Region

	1955	1960	1965	1970	1975	1980	1985
South Africa							
Black			2296	2455	2882	2946	2848
White			948	1073	1253	1345	1351
Coloured			411	492	597	672	678
Asian			99	125	157	178	186
Total			3754	4145	4889	5141	5063
Zimbabwe							
Black	517	546	560	637	808		877
Other	73	89	90	104	120		60
Total	590	635	650	747	924	902	937
Zambia							
Black	224	208	233	310	365		
Other	29	33	34	27	34		
Total	253	241	267	347	399	379	362
Botswana				41	57	83	117
Malawi				160	246	370	395
Lesotho			2	15	30	40	40
Namibia				60	87	125	150
Swaziland				42	65	75	73
TOTAL (8 countries)				5599	6762	7190	7210
TOTAL (4 countries)			4673	5254	6242	6462	6402

Note: Domestic service is not included in these totals. South African figures listed under 1965 are for 1966.

Sources: See page 291.

inclusion would no doubt nullify even this increase.

The experience of these ten years stands in very striking contrast to that of the the immediately preceding ten years, when formal sector employment grew rapidly. The employment figures for South Africa, Lesotho, Zambia, and Zimbabwe, for example, indicate an increase of 50% in employment between 1965 and 1975, compared to a 2% total increase in the decade following 1975. In Mozambique and Angola, too, the contrast in net employment creation

Table 5-B-2
Southern African Population and Population Growth Rates,
1955–1987

	Average Yearly Population Growth			Total Population (in millions)			
	1965–73	1973–80	1980–87	1955	1965	1975	1980
Angola	2.0	3.5	2.5	4.4	5.3	6.7	7.6
Mozambique	2.3	2.6	2.7	6.7	8.4	10.6	12.1
Swaziland	2.6	3.1	3.4	0.3	0.4	0.5	0.6
Zimbabwe	3.5	2.9	3.7	3.0	4.3	6.1	7.0
Malawi	2.8	3.0	3.8	3.0	3.9	5.2	6.1
Lesotho	2.1	2.5	2.7	0.8	1.0	1.2	1.4
Botswana	3.1	3.7	3.4	0.5	0.6	0.8	0.9
Zambia	3.0	3.1	3.6	2.8	3.6	4.8	5.6
South Africa	2.4[a]	2.8[b]		15.4	19.5	25.3	28.3
Namibia				0.5	0.6	0.9	1.0
TOTAL				37.4	47.6	62.1	70.6

Notes:
a. 1960–69   b. 1970–79

Sources: See page 291.

between the two decades is striking, although the exact figures are
unknown.

When pre- and post-1975 formal sector employment performances in the ex-Portuguese colonies are contrasted here, as when
other aspects of their economic performances are analyzed below,
the temporal dividing line is really the economic peak immediately
prior to the transition crisis. The point is that the mid–1970's was
a real watershed, not only for southern Africa but for the world-
economy as a whole. Five years later (or ten years or fifteen years),
there was still less total employment in Angola and Mozambique
than there had been in the early 1970's. This fact of course is
consistent with experience across southern Africa.

The contrast in employment creation between these two decades is directly correlated to the contrasting economic experience of the region before and after 1975. Without exception the countries of southern Africa in the 1960's experienced economic growth in excess of population increase; every country in the region, including Botswana, grew faster in the 1960's and the first half of the 1970's than it did in the 1980's (see Table 5-B-3, but also World Bank, 1989b: 222).

For Angola, Mozambique, Zimbabwe, Zambia, and Namibia, the break came in the mid–1970's. A transition crisis in the newly independent Portuguese colonies led to precipitous economic decline in Mozambique and economic collapse in Angola. Despite a modest recovery in both countries in the late–1970's, GDP in 1980 was far below what it had been in 1973–74. In Zimbabwe and Zambia, there was an absolute decline in GDP in the mid–1970's, followed by a recovery, and by 1980 GDP stood approximately where it had in 1975. From 1977, Namibia had slipped into

Table 5-B-3
Index of Real GDP Growth for Countries in the Region: 1960–1985

	1960	1965	1970	1975	1980	1985	High Year 1970–81	Low Year 1970–81
South Africa	71	97	128	161	189	199	1981:198	1970:128
Swaziland	31	59	86	119	152	177	1981:171	1970:86
Botswana	50	59	94	209	359	624	1981:385	1970:232
Malawi	20	25	32	44	58	64	1981:58	1970:32
Lesotho	32	46	53	70	110	116	1981:117	1970:53
Angola	29	39	47	30	31	36	1973:61	1976:27
Mozambique	32	36	53	47	48	40	1973:61	1976:45
Zimbabwe	62	74	98	134	132	156	1981:141	1978:114
Zambia	84	112	127	144	137	135	1974:149	1974:127

Note: Each country in this table has a separate index. Absolute GDP comparisons not possible; the table is intended to facilitate comparisons in relative growth.

Sources: See page 291.

a deep recession that by 1984 had translated into a 20% real reduction in production per capita (*Africa South of the Sahara, 1990*: 737). South Africa's economy went into the doldrums in the mid–1970's, but then picked up again by the end of the decade, GDP peaking in 1981. The relatively small GDPs of Botswana, Malawi, Swaziland, and Lesotho grew right through the decade (see Table 5-B-3).

After 1981, the South African economy entered a period of stagnation, but this was an apt description for all of the region in the 1980's outside of Botswana, and to a much lesser extent Zimbabwe. The Mozambican economy declined precipitously after 1980–81 until 1986 when economic restructuring resulted in a mild upturn. The Angolan GDP grew slightly in the 1980's, although it was increasingly made up—35% in 1988 (*Africa South of the Sahara, 1990*: 240)—of oil. For the region as a whole, the 1980's were even worse than the second half of the 1970's (see Table 5-B-3).

Urban Wage-Laborers

Urban employment did not suffer quite as much as overall formal sector employment, because the sector that experienced the largest fall in employment was commercial agriculture. Increased mechanization on the commercial farms in South Africa (Nattrass, 1977) had meant a steady attrition in farm labor since the 1960's, but the pace of the fall was much greater after 1975. The pace of mechanization in agriculture in Zimbabwe had also picked up in the 1960's (Clarke, 1977a), but decline in the total of those employed in the sector did not set in until the mid–1970's. In South Africa the total agricultural wage-labor force fell by one-third between 1976 and 1986 (Davies, 1988: 18); the fall in Zimbabwe in these years was approximately 100,000, or from 34.6% to 26.2% of the total work force (Zimbabwe CSO, 1989a: 9).

In Angola and Mozambique, two of the other centers of commercial agriculture in the region prior to 1975, production declined drastically with independence in both the White plantation sector and the peasant sector. This simultaneous collapse was brought on by the flight of the Portuguese owners of the plantations and the private traders. The state in Angola and Mozambique stepped in to try to fill the void thus created in trade and large-scale commercial agriculture.

Results in terms of marketed agricultural production were mildly encouraging in Mozambique in the late–1970's and early–1980's, and probably meant temporarily saving tens, or even hundreds, of thousands of jobs in the sector (Isaacman, 1983). However, the war with South Africa-sponsored Renamo in the 1980's meant a second collapse, both of production and employment, as the drying up of agricultural exports and wide-spread famine attest. In Angola the attempts to revive agriculture met with even less success; in fact the real value of agricultural production declined on a per annum average of 9.7% between 1973 and 1980 (World Bank, 1989b: 222). As the war with UNITA spread and intensified the situation only got worse.

The only country in the region whose experience went counter to this trend of falling absolute and relative employment in agriculture was Malawi (ILO, 1979: 169; 1987: 341), but its wage-labor force is too small to effect the regional trend set by the far larger economies of South Africa, Zimbabwe, Angola, and Mozambique.

In other words, during the decade after 1975 there was a small growth in non-agricultural wage-labor (see Table 5-B-4), paralleling a rapid decline in agricultural employment. In contrast during the decade preceding (1965–75) regional non-agricultural wage-labor increased more than 50% in South Africa and Zimbabwe combined and at the same rate between 1970–75 in Zimbabwe, Zambia, Botswana, Malawi, Swaziland, and South Africa combined (see Table 5-B-4).

Industrial Wage-Laborers

And what of industrial[1] wage-laborers, what is normally thought of as the heart of the working class? In the post-1975 period there was an absolute decrease in regional employment in this field, if not quite as dramatic a one as in agriculture. For those countries for which statistical data are available, the 1975 and 1985 com-

Table 5-B-4
Non-Agricultural Employment in the Region: Industrial (I) vs. Service (S)

	1955 I	1955 S	1960 I	1960 S	1965 I	1965 S	1970 I	1970 S	1975 I	1975 S	1980 I	1980 S	1985 I	1985 S
South Africa														
Black					947	651	1037	747	1306	974	1376	1022	1275	1074
White					374	588	374	685	429	811	440	891	450	886
Coloured					189	117	240	155	290	210	304	263	294	272
Asian					53	40	71	50	92	62	100	75	97	87
Total					1536	1396	1722	1637	2117	2057	2220	2251	2116	2319
Zimbabwe														
Black	195	94	189	117	147	124	204	142	264	201			256	355
Other	25	44	28	57	26	60	32	68	37	78			20	40
Total	220	138	217	174	173	184	236	210	301	279	275	300	276	405
Zambia														
Black	129	60	97	65	115	88	152	125	186	171	163	184	143	183
Other	14	16	14	19	13	21	12	17	18	35	28	52	31	82
Total	143	76	111	84	128	109	164	142						
Botswana							11	26	16	20	19	26	18	32
Swaziland							11	13						
Malawi							39	67	56	96	77	111	71	134
TOTALS														
6 countries:					1837	1689	2183	2095	2694	2668	2782	2924	2655	3155
Zambia, Zimbabwe, & South Africa only:							2122	1989	2604	2517	2658	2735	2535	2907
TOTAL Industrial and Service Combined														
6 countries					3526		4295		5352		5706		5810	
Zambia, Zimbabwe, & South Africa only:							4111		5121		5393		5442	

Notes: Domestic service is not included in these figures. I=Industrial, S=Service.

Sources: See page 292.

bined totals are almost identical (see Table 5-B-1).

While there are no comprehensive statistics on industrial employment in Mozambique and Angola immediately prior to and after the transition crisis, the evidence that exists suggests that the number of industrial workers in the independent countries never reached pre-independence totals. In Angola, manufacturing employment fell from 125,000 in 1973 to approximately 39,000 in 1981 (Bhagavan, 1983: 25); employment in construction, too, undoubtedly followed the same path of decline. Only oil workers kept industrial employment from falling further than it did.

In Mozambique, industrial employment decline is certainly indicated by the precipitous fall in industrial production, which declined approximately by two-thirds in value between 1974 and 1985 (World Bank, 1984: I, 126–27; 1989a: 413); however, Frelimo policy in the abandoned enterprises that it took over was to keep the employees on even when production declined, thus reducing what would otherwise have been a more disastrous employment drop (personal communication by S. Vieira).

The post-1975 period of declining industrial employment contrasts with a period in the 1960's and early–1970's of particularly strong growth. In both Zambia and South Africa the number of industrial workers increased by approximately 45% between 1965 and 1975; and in Zimbabwe the number jumped some 74% (see Table 5-B-4).

The size of the increase in Mozambique is indicated by the growth between 1960 and 1975 in the percentage of the labor force[2] in industry from 8% to 15.3% (World Bank, 1984: II, 413), during a period of rapid overall increase in employment. By independence the value of production in manufacturing placed Mozambique among the eight most industrialized countries in Africa (Torp, 1989: 41). An indication of the size increase in Angola is the average per annum real growth of industry between 1965 and 1973 of 20.2% percent (World Bank, 1989b: 222).[3] By the time of independence, Angola too was among the most industrialized countries on the continent.

The fall in industrial employment in the region in the post-1975 period, just as its rapid rise in the ten to fifteen years before 1975, is closely correlated with the regional rhythm of industrialization. However, growth in industrial employment always lagged behind growth in the value of industrial production; and falls in the value of industrial production often precipitated greater falls in the level of industrial employment.

In South Africa, for example, between 1975 and 1980 the real value of manufacturing increased by approximately one-quarter (IMF, 1989b: 645), while the increase in manufacturing employment was no more than 7% in these five years (IMF, 1989b: 645). The value of industry in general increased by approximately 8% (World Bank, 1989a: 513), while the increase in industrial wage-labor was less than 5 percent (Schneier & Abedian 1987: Table 1, Appendices 3–6). The reason for this discrepancy lies in the capital-intensive nature of industrial (particularly manufacturing) investment in southern Africa during the post-1945 boom (for tropical Africa as a whole see Arrighi & Saul, 1973: 11–43; for South Africa, see Wolpe, 1988: 85–86; for Zambia, see Seidman, 1974: 604; for Zimbabwe, see Stoneman, 1978: 67, and Arrighi, 1970: 223).

The Service or Tertiary Sector[4]

One of the major changes in regional patterns of production, investment and employment in the post-1975, but particularly the post-1980, period has been the shift in the economic center of gravity from the productive spheres, i.e., the primary and secondary sectors, to the service sphere, the tertiary sector. Thus, for the period 1980–87, for example, the average real annual percentage growth (in value) of services surpassed, and often quite significantly, that of industry in all but one of the countries in the region (Botswana) for which data is available (data was not available for Namibia and Angola; for South Africa see World Bank, 1989a: 512–13; for all seven other countries see World Bank, 1989b: 222–23).

Between 1975 and 1985 there was a decline of 2% in the combined total industrial employment in Zimbabwe, Zambia, South Africa, Malawi, Botswana, and Swaziland (see Table 5-B-4).

In that same decade there was an increase of 18% in the total service employment in these same countries (see Table 5-B-4; for the structural shift towards tertiary employment in Angola, see Santos, 1984, and Dilolwa, 1978). During the industrialization boom prior to 1975 services grew even faster absolutely, but were often outpaced by growth in industry, as was the case, for example, in Zimbabwe, where service employment between 1965 and 1975 rose by 42%, but industrial employment grew by 74 percent (see Table 5-B-4).

When we combine the industrial totals with those from agriculture where, as we have seen, employment was plummeting after 1975; in other words, when we contrast the primary and secondary sectors with the tertiary, instead of the industrial with the tertiary, the shift in the economic center of gravity is all the more dramatic.

Overall in the region during the 30 years since 1960 there has been considerable absolute, as well as important relative, growth in services. That this growth was more pronounced prior to 1975 corresponds with experience in every other sector. In the post-1975 period the absolute growth has been much more uneven and on average has been much slower, but it has still been significant, and up to at least the mid–1980's was systematically outpacing any growth in the productive sectors. Namibia was an extreme case, where service employment in 1988 was 3.5 times that of industrial employment (Omar, 1990: 6).

Expansion of the tertiary sphere has meant the growth of two occupational categories in particular: first, professional, semiprofessional, and technical workers; and secondly, clerical and white-collar workers. Growth in the tertiary sector is often used as an indicator of growth in these occupations, and in fact in this case does provide an indicator of the rising number of workers in these occupational categories. Growth in capital-intensive productive enterprise has also contributed to a rapid increase in these occupations, although this increase is harder to document because few governments outside of South Africa collect information in occupational categories.

The South African data allows us to see directly the growth in these occupations. The overall growth in the clerical/white-collar workforce was quite impressive, both before and after 1975. Between 1969 and 1985 the overall growth in employment of this occupation was approximately 78%; the growth after 1975, while slower, i.e., only 27% (SALDRU, 1986: 93, 96, 101), was still fairly high. The professional, semiprofessional, and technical category expanded 114% in these sixteen years (SALDRU 1986: 93, 96, 101).

Public Sector Employment

Since the 1960's a growth pole for both of these occupations has been the public sector, which has expanded particularly rapidly. In Angola, public administration and defence expenditure went up following the colonial reforms initiated by Portugal in 1961, rising by an average annual rate of 7.7% in real terms between 1960 and 1973 (see World Bank, 1984: I, 6–7). In Mozambique it did not climb significantly until the mid–1960's, but climbed by two-thirds between 1965 and 1973 (World Bank, 1984: I, 126–27).

Employment in the public sector in Zambia increased to such an extent that, by the early–1980's, 75% of all Zambian employees were either in the public or parastatal sector (EIU, 1989b: 15).

In Zimbabwe the intensification of the war and a late decision by the regime to try to find Black allies led to a jump in public administration costs[5], and their share of the country's total GDP rose from 5.6% to 9.7% between 1974 and 1978 (Zimbabwe CSO, 1986b: 5). Public administration employment went up approximately 40% between 1974 and 1977 (Rhodesia CSO, 1978: 6–7).[6]

In South Africa between 1973 and 1987 the public sector grew by 4% per annum, while the private sector grew by less than one percent (from Business Day, as quoted in SAIRR, 1988: 326). Public sector employment between 1965 and 1975 grew by 42% (Standish, 1987: 78–79).

The rate of expansion of the public sector systematically slowed from the mid–1970's in what seems to have been a direct consequence of deteriorating economic conditions. With the end of the regional economic boom of the 1960's and early 1970's, a squeeze was put on government expenditure.

Public administration and defence in Zambia, so strong up to 1976, slowed down thereafter; the average per annum growth rate for the 1970's was only 1.7 percent (World Bank, 1984: I, 201). In Botswana the growth rate of public administration and defence averaged 13.9% per annum in the 1970's but it averaged 27.7% in the 1960's (World Bank, 1984: I, 21). In South Africa the growth in public sector (not necessarily the same as public administration and defence) employment totaled only 16% in the decade after 1975 (Standish, 1987: 77).

In the Portuguese colonies, public administration and defence expenditures plummeted with independence and the transition crises. The result was that public administration expenditure in Angola, which had risen at an average per annum rate of 7.7% between 1960 and 1973, fell by an average 1.5% annually in the 1970's (World Bank, 1984: I, 6–7). After rising in Mozambique at an average per annum rate of 6.4% in the 1960's and slightly better in the early–1970's, expenditure on public administration and defence fell by an average 1.7% in the 1970's (World Bank, 1984: I, 126–27).

However, if stalled economic growth and falling government revenues put limitations on growth in the public sector, the fall in the rate of growth of government expenditure was lessened by governments allowing budget deficits to mount and decreasing public sector productive investment in favor of current expenditure. The result was that while there was a slowdown in the rate of increase of expenditure, post-1975 growth in the public sector tended to outpace that in the private sector (until very recently; see below), just as growth in services has tended to outpace growth in the productive sphere of the economy (see above).

In spite of the cuts, in other words, many governments in the region have resisted cutting public expenditures to the lowly level of private economic activity and government revenue. This resistance, a frequent target of World Bank and IMF criticisms, has meant that public sector employment (comprised mostly of office and professional workers), fared better between 1975 and 1985 than did private sector employment (a larger component of which was made up of production workers).

The Urban Reserve Army

The urban reserve army, what Sandbrook (1982: 156) refers to as the "laboring poor" among the urban masses, is a relatively recent phenomenon in southern Africa. Southern Africa of the labor reserves has historically been characterized by Blacks who were supposed to be formally working in the "White" economy or else subsisting and waiting on standby in the reserves; an urban informal economy meant squatters and a "leakage of labor." As a result, relative to West Africa, informal sector[7] activities in southern Africa have been invisible: both less numerous and less visible (Mkandawire, 1986: 73).

The late–1970's and 1980's were a period of rapid growth in and visibility of the informal sector in cities across the region. The increasingly fast rate of population growth (see Table 5-B-2) in the post-1945 subcontinent, but particularly the increasing rate of urbanization (paralleling industrialization) in some parts of the region during the 1960's (see Table 5-B-5), was the start of change in this regard. The real change came with post-1975 economic stagnation and an increased rate of urbanization, whether induced by war, as in the ex-Portuguese colonies; or by the breakdown of urban influx control, as in Rhodesia in the 1970's and South Africa in the 1980's; or by the growing poverty in the rural areas most everywhere.

At the top of the informal-sector social scale there are private entrepreneurs (which I will consider in the next section), but below them are the far more numerous laboring poor. They survive in what could be called marginal occupations, and for capital provide a reserve in the case of economic expansion.

They do not comprise a single class, and certainly not a single occupation. Casual laborers, petty producers with their apprentices, more often petty traders or providers of services, the laboring poor move in and out of work, in and out of official unemployment statistics.[8] Domestic laborers, because of the nature of their work relation with their employers, their low pay, the irregularity and insecurity of their employment, etc., should also be, and often are, placed in this category. Statistics on domestic laborers are notori-

Table 5-B-5
Percentage of National Populations Living in Urban Centers, 1960–1987

	1960	1965	1970	1975	1980	1987
Lesotho	1.5	2.0	2.6	3.5	11.5	
		6.0			14.0	19.0
Malawi	4.4	4.9	6.4	8.0	9.6	
		5.0			10.0	13.0
Botswana	1.8	3.9	9.5	14.0	18.8	
		4.0			19.0	21.0
Zimbabwe	12.6	14.4	16.9	19.8	23.0	
		14.0			22.0	26.0
Zambia	23.1	26.4	30.0	33.9	43.0	
		23.0			43.0	53.0
Mozambique	3.7	4.6	5.7	7.1	8.7	
		5.0			13.0	23.0
Angola	10.4	12.5	15.0	17.8	21.0	
		13.0			21.0	26.0
South Africa	46.6	47.2	47.8	48.4	49.6	54.0
Swaziland	3.9	6.4	7.5	8.1	14.3	
		7.0			14.0	30.0

Note: The second row of figures for each country has been calculated on the basis of a slightly different definition of urban center. There is much recent evidence to suggest that the Zimbabwean figures for the 1960's are highly suspect (Zinyama & Whitlow, 1986; Davies, 1987; Kay, 1971). The consensus today seems to be that during the 1960's Zimbabwe underwent a degree of deurbanization.

Sources: See page 292.

ously unreliable and Zimbabwe is unusual in including them in its sectoral and overall employment statistics.

It is hard to determine the size of the informal sector or its constituent elements, but there have been various estimates made in countries around the region (but mostly in South Africa) of the size of the informal sector in general and the laboring poor specifically. In South Africa a study done in 1985 suggested that the total number of Africans involved in informal sector activities in that country was approximately two million, including 55% in trading and hawking, 16% in services, and 23% in production and construction (SAIRR, 1989: 357). These proportions seem typical of the informal sector. A 1969 study of the Zambian informal sector, for example, revealed that 60% of the workers were in the retail sector and 27% in manufacturing and construction (Fry, 1979: 62).

Another study estimated that the total participation in the South African informal economy, full-time or part-time, was approximately 3.5–4 million.[9] The important hawking contingent of the laboring poor now has its own organization, i.e., the African Council of Hawkers and Informal Business (ACHIB); the number of hawkers in the country was estimated at more than one million in 1988 (SAIRR, 1989: 358).

In Zimbabwe in 1986 the government estimated the number of people working in the informal sector to be approximately 500,000, and categorized another 200,000 as unemployed, while admitting that it is hard to distinguish between those in the two categories (Zimbabwe CSO 1986b: 25). In Zambia in 1969, there was an estimated 201,000 urban unemployed and informal sector workers; by 1974 the number was estimated to have risen to 298,000 (Mwanza, 1979: 31).

To get a rough idea of the size of the informal sector for the region as a whole or at least of the rhythm of its expansion and contraction, one need only compare rates of demographic growth, urbanization and formal sector employment. To disaggregate from this total the number of laboring poor, one need only assume that their number always vastly outnumber the number of informal petty entrepreneurs. Using these guidelines, it is safe to say that the number of laboring poor in southern Africa is skyrocketing.

The average annual rate of population growth has increased in every country of the region, except for Zimbabwe, during each successive decade from the 1950's through the 1970's, and even in Zimbabwe stood at 3.2% in the 1970's (World Bank, 1984: I, 203, for Zimbabwe). At present the rate of growth for the region as a whole must be near 3%, since the only three countries with rates below that in the 1980's are Angola (2.5%), Mozambique (2.7%), and Lesotho (2.7%) (see Table 5-B-2).

The pace of urbanization had been slow in this part of the continent until recently but since the mid–1970's it has picked up considerably. Zambia, was already in 1960 an extraordinarily urbanized country relative to others in the region. The ensuing seven years brought independence (and the end of restrictions on Black movement), economic growth, and an expansion in education and in the public sector. There was a clear post-independence change from male to family migration to the cities (O'Connor, 1983: 70). By 1970 Zambia was "the most highly urbanized country of middle Africa" (*Africa South of the Sahara 1971*: 892), with 28% of its population classified urban.[10] Employment opportunities probably accounted for the continued climb into the 1970's, but even after the economy's downturn thereafter the inflow to the cities never slackened. By 1985 approximately half of the population was living in urban areas (EIU, 1989b: 8).

A comparison of the 1962 and 1969 censuses in Rhodesia indicates a rate of urbanization in the 1960's slow enough to constitute a real deurbanization (22.8% intercensal growth), but between 1969 and 1982 growth of the urban population was on the order of 122% (Zinyama 1986, 372). The urban influx of the late 1960's and early 1970's, although limited for Blacks by the continued partial efficacy of influx control, was fueled by the attraction of urban employment in a growing economy. During the boom years of 1969–74 the population of Salisbury (both Black and White) grew from 386,000 to 545,000 (*Africa South of the Sahara, 1979–80*: 1154).

In the late–1970's, war-related disruptions and growing poverty in the rural areas created strains on the urban influx control machinery and squatting in the vicinity of Harare grew rapidly (O'Connor, 1983: 145). With independence influx control laws were repealed and by 1982 Harare's population was 656,000, and if Chitungwiza, with a population of 173,000, and other "satellite" cities created in the 1970's are included, the capital's population was closer to one million (*Africa South of the Sahara, 1984–85*: 999). Most observers assume that the rate of flow into Harare has picked up further since 1982, as the rapidly growing number of secondary-school leavers crowd into the city to escape rural poverty and to compete for the fast-dwindling number of new jobs.

In South Africa, the country in the region that has long had by far the highest urbanization rate, the rate of growth between 1960 and 1980 was very slow, officially increasing from 46.6% to 49.6% (see Table 5-B-5). A partial explanation of this stagnation lies, as it does to an extent in Zimbabwe, in the regime's policy of urban influx control, the efficacy of which could be seen in the high urban sex ratios of males to females (Simkins, 1981c: 3; for Zimbabwe, see O'Connor, 1983: 80). The South African regime's relatively effective implementation of urban influx control and their massive resettlement of the Black population to the reserves resulted in a dramatically disproportionate growth of the reserves relative to the "White" areas during these twenty years (Simkins, 1981c: 3).

In the second place, the creation of satellite Black cities within the borders of equally artificial "homelands," adjacent to cities in the White areas, meant not only an increase in the number of commuters, but in a real sense an increase in the urban population that was not officially considered urban because of its location on the other side of the border. This urbanization within the Bantustans and adjacent to urban areas within "White" South Africa has been labelled "displaced urbanization" (Murray, 1987a: 311). Thus, the only major city officially to register a large growth of population between 1970 and 1985 was metropolitan Cape Town, which has no adjacent reserve. Growth here was from 1,097,000 (*Africa South of the Sahara, 1984–85*: 793) to 1,912,000 (*Africa South of the Sahara, 1989*: 937).

In the Portuguese colonies in the 1950's the low rate of urbanization, especially among Blacks, had more to do with lack of development than urban influx control. An indicator and leading edge of the growth in the urban population since was the growth of Lourenço Marques. In 1960 its population was 178,000 (*Africa South of the Sahara, 1984–85*: 611); by 1970 it had increased to 355,000 (*Africa South of the Sahara, 1979–80*: 679); then by 1980 it had doubled again to 755,000 (*Africa South of the Sahara*,

1984–85: 611), in spite of the exodus of well over a 100,000 Portuguese from the capital following independence.

With the war against South Africa-sponsored Renamo intensifying and drought setting in, the 1980's witnessed a further flood of immigrants to the capital; by 1987 Maputo's population was estimated to be over one million (*Africa South of the Sahara, 1989*: 733). The 1980's inflow occurred despite stepped up government efforts to curb it, notably in Operation Production in the early 1980's. In less than thirty years the population of the capital had increased almost sixfold.

In Angola, the percentage of those living in urban areas rose during the economic expansion of the 1960's under the Portuguese, as it did under very different conditions after independence. Although with independence there was a tremendous exodus abroad of mostly urban-dwelling Portuguese and, in addition, an exodus to the countryside of urban-dwelling Blacks to pursue subsistence agriculture, neither phenomenon had any medium-term effect on the rate of urbanization.

The exodus from the cities was short-lived; the war soon drove people back. So, too, did the possibility of employment, since the only employer of note, outside the oil companies, was the state. Huambo, in the heart of the war-torn highlands, grew from 62,000 in 1970 to 203,000 in 1983; Lobito from 60,000 to 150,000; and Benguela from 41,000 to 155,000 (EIU, 1989c: 10). Returning refugees from Kinshasa, Zaire, poured into Luanda, and the population there grew from 450,000 in 1976 to approximately 1.2 million by 1980 (Bhagavan, 1986: 24).

Southern Africa over the last fifteen to twenty years has undergone, as in much of Africa, a process of involution "in which a growing [urban] population shares a relatively fixed pool of jobs and goods" (Coquery-Vidovitch, 1988: 306, describing the situation in sub-Saharan Africa as a whole). What makes it worse is that real wages from formal sector employment are declining across much of the region in the 1980's (for South Africa, see Schneier & Abedian, 1987: Table 5-B-2, Appendices 3–6; for Zimbabwe, see Schaefer, 1988: 17). As real wages have fallen, even many people with full-time employment have entered the informal sector.

Nor are the laboring poor and informal sector petty entrepreneurs necessarily the uneducated. One study in South Africa indicates, for example, that "township manufacturers are not unsuccessful job-seekers; rather they tend to be relatively skilled, well-educated workers who voluntarily left their previous employers" (Rogerson, 1987: 415). The number of school-leavers is multiplying; they are usually very reluctant to stay in the rural areas (even if jobs existed); and the formal sector is simply not capable of absorbing them. In Zimbabwe at the end of the 1980's, their number was approaching 300,000 per year (Chidzero, 1988), while net employment growth stood at about zero.

Private Entrepreneurs

Our period did not open auspiciously for private entrepreneurs in southern Africa.[11] Economic stagnation or decline was setting in in most parts of southern Africa, an indicator of which, but also a contributing element of which, was the waning interest in the region on the part of international capital. Investments from all sources were on the decline. Gross domestic investment as a percentage of GDP peaked in most southern African countries sometime in the 1970's and declined thereafter (see Table 3 in World Bank, 1989a, as well as chapter 2). The investments that were made were increasingly made in the public sector. In South Africa, for example, between 1970 and 1985, 64% of all net fixed investment was made in government services or state corporations (SAIRR, 1989: 347).

In Mozambique and Angola, the economies were crumbling in the mid–1970's, and many key economic actors were fleeing abroad. The states stepped in to take over and manage abandoned property. In Zambia between 1969 and 1972 there had been a wave of nationalizations; more were soon to come in independent Zimbabwe. More generally, the world economic and political climate up to 1981 was conducive to an expanding state role.

However, private entrepreneurial activity never disappeared and in the 1980's there was a resurgence, paralleling a changing world climate of opinion regarding the role of the state. The opportunities were there: restrictions on Black business activities began to be lifted in South Africa from the mid–1970's following Soweto, and far more swiftly in independent Zambia and Zimbabwe; in Angola and Mozambique, because of the Portuguese flight, there was a void that the state attempted to fill, but in Mozambique, at least, it was prepared partially to cede its place once private economic agents reappeared—thus, in 1979–80 much of retail trade was privatized (Hanlon, 1984a: 195–96).

As the economic slump settled in, government revenues declined, and budget deficits and foreign debt mounted, governments tended to withdraw from some of the areas in which they had previously been active, such as fixed capital investment (see above). Whether at the behest of the World Bank and the IMF or not, several governments in the region (South Africa, Angola, Mozambique, Zambia) began to take steps to privatize parts of the public and parastatal sector and otherwise to cut public expenditure.

In Mozambique, for example, restructuring led to a 10% cut in the civil service wage bill in 1987 (*Africa South of the Sahara, 1990*: 714). But even before official restructuring, a process of contraction of the state's role had begun in Mozambique. In 1979–80, much of retail trade was privatized, as was a much smaller percentage of agriculture (Hanlon, 1984a: 195–98). Further steps were taken towards privatization and market determination of prices in 1983 at the Fourth Congress of Frelimo, but particularly after a program of restructuring (ERP) had been worked out with the IMF in 1987. In Zambia an IMF-backed austerity program was implemented in 1983 and led to a 13% reduction of the civil service (EIU, 1989b: 15). In South Africa privatization from the mid–1980's touched everything from sorghum beer to iron and steel. By 1987, President dos Santos of Angola had announced that the government would seek an accord with the World Bank and the IMF as part of a planned economic restructuring. The state in southern Africa, as elsewhere in the 1980's, was "rolled back."

Zimbabwe presents an interesting partial exception to this trend. Although Mugabe's government has recently worked out a trade liberalization program with the World Bank, it has bucked the Bank's advice in other areas, for example, in privatization. In recent years the government has nationalized important South African firms in the productive fields, including Delta, the biggest company in the country and a subsidiary of Anglo American (Schaefer, 1988: 12).

In any case the large firms in the region, whether public or private, have for the most part not been expanding production. Mergers and buyouts have been common in the 1980's but not productive investments (for the tendency towards concentration in South Africa, see Wolpe, 1988: 85; for the drop in productive investment in Zimbabwe in the 1980's, see Bond, 1990: 11; for the collapse of public sector investment in Namibia see *Africa South of the Sahara*, 1990: 737). Nor are there many new enterprises. The international markets for the plantations and mines of the region (except oil and diamonds) have been stagnant. The local and regional markets for large-scale and medium-scale manufacturers, markets comprised for the most part of the privileged White enclaves, were stagnant in general and declining in the ex-Portuguese colonies.

What has been growing significantly is the number of small firms and individual business endeavors, often within the informal sector. They require little capital to get started (and none for the smallest-scale undertakings); the number of those available to start them has been continually replenished by the fast rising number of urban underemployed and unemployed; and they service a Black market (local or national) that grew enormously during the boom and is often not served by the manufacturing giants.

In the early 1980's, an observor could still write that in Lusaka, Bulawayo, Harare, and other "ex-European" cities of the region "the large-scale [i.e., formal] sector still employs most of the workforce and is totally dominant in terms of the amount of business conducted" (O'Connor, 1983: 143). It is doubtful whether this is still true, at least in terms of employment.

In South Africa, for example, the business community is structurally divided between a very large number of small-scale firms (not even including the myriad number in the informal sector) and a handful of private firms (seven conglomerates) that along with the state dominate the economy. In 1982 it was estimated that there were 75,000 small businesses in the formal sector in South Africa. In the commercial sector approximately 90% of all firms are small; approximately 80% in industry. The small businesses dominate the Black consumer market, which although it is enormously expanded over what it was in the 1960's, is largely restricted to nondurables and semidurables (Libby, 1987: 299).

The dramatic change in attitude of the apartheid regime towards the informal sector and small businesses since the mid–1970's has facilitated the growth of small entrepreneurs. The number of recorded businesses in African townships in 1962 stood at 7,850; by 1984 it had grown to 40,000, and by 1986 60,000 (Pityana, 1988: 8). The growth in the informal sector has been even faster. Various studies estimated the value of this unmeasured South African economy between 25% and 40% of that of the formal economy, and a growth rate five to seven times faster. Approximately 26% of total African income was presumed accounted for by informal sector earnings. The number of businesses run from households was estimated in 1987 at 1.8 million (SAIRR, 1989: 357–58).

Zambian economic reforms of the early 1970's led to the proliferation of small-scale businesses, mostly in trade, transport, and construction. Concerning this development Baylies and Szeftel (1982: 187) contend that "the most significant structural change in Zambian society since independence has been the rapid proliferation and increasing political importance of an indigenous owning class." Most of this activity was in the informal sector, but even among those who chose to register the name of their company, the majority were involved in small-scale operations in which the owner and other family members make up most of the labor.

In Angola, the flight of the Portuguese and the destruction and disruption of war between 1974 and 1976 dealt the economy in general and private enterprise in particular a crushing blow. Urban manufacturing industry, except the tiniest informal-sector endeavors, has dwindled since independence. In 1972, there were 5,561 functioning manufacturing enterprises; by 1981, there were 148 (Bhagavan, 1986: 25). The plantation economy was all but destroyed, with coffee (the biggest pre-independence export crop) production falling more than 90 percent (*Africa South of the Sahara*, 1989: 238). The MPLA stepped in to take over some of the many abandoned plantations and factories; some two-thirds of the functioning manufacturing firms in 1981 were in production only because the state was running them (Bhagavan, 1986: 25). Nationalized coffee plantations account for some 60% of coffee production (*Africa South of the Sahara, 1989:* 238).

Oil is the lifeblood of the regime and the national economy. With most oil originating in offshore drilling stations in Cabinda, the oil industry is largely sheltered from the war on the mainland. Sale of oil and oil derivatives accounted for over 95% of total exports in 1985, and an average 40% of state revenues and 35% of GDP. Angolan oil production is second only to Nigeria in sub-Saharan Africa. Because of it, Angola is one of the rare countries in southern Africa to have attracted foreign investment in the 1980's; between 1985–1990 total investment in the oil sector is expected to reach U.S $3 billion. In this sector nationalization was intended as a means of garnering a larger share of the money to made from a valuable asset. The state now controls all fuel production and distribution and, through the Sociedade Nacional de Combustiveis de Angola (SONANGOL), owns a majority of the shares in the Cabinda Gulf Oil Company (*Africa South of the Sahara, 1989:* 240).

The flight of the Portuguese meant a collapse of the national trade network, which they dominated. Prior to independence some two-thirds of the resident Portuguese had been dependent on commerce for a living (Bender, 1978: 233), and they had dominated even petty and rural ventures. Here, too, the state stepped in to fill a void, but in this case was less successful. Its resources were spread too thin; unlike oil, the trade network linking rural and urban areas was extremely vulnerable to war disruption; an overvalued currency and rationing encouraged speculation rather than orderly trade; and a lack of consumer goods meant that peasants were extremely reluctant to grow for the market.

A new class of Angolan private traders began to emerge who managed to get the peasants to trade with them by providing, not worthless local currency, but goods they obtained in town from people queuing at the "people' shops," factory workers who had access to goods at subsidized prices, and people of all social strata who had stolen goods (Bhagavan, 1986: 23). By the mid–1980's a "thriving free-market economy" (Birmingham, 1988: 3) had developed in urban parts of the country.

No matter how widespread was the growth in the small business sector after 1975 or how significant the growth of oil and diamond operations, they paled in comparison to overall private sector growth in the pre-1975 period. The 1960's and early 1970's were characterized by the rapid growth in medium-sized and large-scale business enterprises; it was their expansion that accounted for most of the growth in GDP during these years.

Small-scale entrepreneurs in this earlier period, benefitting from the rapid growth of national production and local buying power, undoubtedly also grew rapidly in number and aggregate wealth. What makes the small-scale entrepreneurs of particular significance after 1975 is the fact that theirs for the most part was the only show in town.

Rural Producers

The most important trend in agriculture in southern Africa from the mid–1970's was the marginalization of peasant production and a "crisis of access to subsistence" (Bush, 1986: 297) in the reserves; in the 1980's there was a weaker countertrend, most notably in Zimbabwe, towards consolidation of a commercially-oriented section of the peasantry, but the social differentiation that this entailed merely accentuated the subsistence crisis for most reserve dwellers.

Observers have commented on the overcrowding, environmental deterioration, and fall in reserve production in southern Africa since at least the interwar period. The present situation is partly a result of cumulative problems of neglect (the peasant sectors looked upon more as labor reserves than sources of crops), overpopulation (a function of limited and poor quality land), and slow social differentiation through commercialization.

There are also more immediate causes. The worker-peasant

households that made ends meet by combining subsistence production with wage employment, that were the basis of the region's cheap labor (Wolpe, 1972), and that were so common a feature in southern Africa have been seriously squeezed from the urban end by the stagnation in formal sector employment, and from the rural end by falling terms of trade on the world market and low fixed prices on the local market.

For those migrants who had worked in South Africa and sent their remittances back to their households in countries across the region, the period after the mid–1970's was particularly bleak. Mechanization of production in mining and agriculture, a policy of internalization of the labor supply, and general economic stagnation meant that South Africa did not need nor was it accepting the same number of foreigners, especially the unskilled, that it had up to that point.

The normal strains on conjugal relations inherent in the worker-peasant household, i.e., the economic necessity to separate for long periods and the difficulty of maintaining the conjugal relation in these conditions (Murray, 1981: 64), was aggravated by the increasing difficulty of finding employment and the increasing insecurity of remittances, as well as the cumulative problems, referred to above, in the reserves themselves. The result has been an increasing number of women-headed households (ca. 30% of total rural households in the region: see Bush, 1986: 298), cut off completely from remittances and having less security of access to reserve land because of the gender of the household head.

Women-headed rural households have become synonomous with "poor peasant" households (for Zambia, see Cliffe, 1979: 161–64; for Zimbabwe, see Bonnevie, 1987: 82; for South Africa, see Greenberg & Giliomee, 1987: 319, and Murray, 1981: 98). Left without remittances, the women and sometimes the children of these women-headed households have had to seek out employment themselves, often as seasonal farm laborers, as they have increasingly done, for example, in South Africa, Zimbabwe, Malawi, and Swaziland (see Bush, 1986: 295; for South Africa, see Cock, 1981: 285). These jobs are among the lowest-paying. Combined with reproductive tasks, they leave many women no time for productive work on their land, and no means to employ others to do it. This often results in the need to their purchase basic food supply at inflated prices from local shops.

Eventually and increasingly, women have chosen to leave the rural areas, even if entry into the cities has usually been illegal for them—they were one of the prime targets of urban influx control—and to look for work in domestic labor, industry, or the informal sector (for South Africa, see Greenberg & Giliomee, 1987: 318). Those left behind, often older women and children, are likely to be even more destitute.

By far the most important cause of the subsistence crisis in the rural areas in some countries of the region was the disruption and dislocation caused by war. This was certainly the case in Angola and to a lesser extent Namibia throughout our period; in Mozambique in the 1980's; and in Zimbabwe in the late 1970's. Such disruption of course lowered crop yields, but also meant large numbers of refugees, and stepped up rates of urbanization. In countries such as Mozambique and Angola it is questionable how many of the uprooted peasants living on the fringes of the cities will return to the rural areas when security conditions allow it. Drought, too, has been a significant cause of the subsistence crisis, especially in the early 1980's, and particularly in Mozambique.

By the 1980's, food imports into the region were becoming commonplace. The peasant sectors were not only not producing enough to feed the cities; there was a net import of food into many of the peasant areas (Bush, 1986: 297). This does not mean that no one in the reserves was making money in agriculture, but rather that the money made was garnered by a very few.

In the South African reserves, "structured and massive labor surpluses preclude any subsistence functions" (Greenberg & Giliomee, 1987: 309). The decline of aggregate production and of yields/hectare in the reserves became precipitous from the 1950's (Simkins, 1981a: 262–63), and the massive resettlement of hundreds of thousands of Blacks into them between 1960 and 1980 (Simkins, 1981c: 5) extinguished any possibility of food self-subsistence for the majority.

Consistent with this development is the rapidly growing number of so-called "commuters" in South Africa, who travel daily between their residences in the reserves and their work places in the White urban areas. Although they are officially domiciled in the home-lands and thus presumably have maintained a foot in the peasant arena, they and their families are usually packed into the densely populated border townships. They have no more involvement with agriculture than do most permanent urban-dwellers. Although they are officially migrants, they are "taking on the characteristics of a settled, landless proletariat" (Southall, 1986: 170).

With the labor market tightening and the market hierarchy becoming more rigid, residents of the reserves have also become increasingly marginalized as potential workers. "Large portions of the Bantustans...simply fall outside the institutional labor market, as there is no legal recruiting or requisitioning of labor. For those who can reach the rural labor market, there are sometimes oppor-tunities for wage employment, but almost always within the lowest-paid, most unskilled and 'undesirable' sectors of the economy" (Greenberg & Giliomee, 1987: 319).

In Angola, agriculture has been massively disrupted from at least the 1960's. During their war against the guerrillas, the Portuguese resettled more than one million peasants into fortified villages, resulting in "a marked decline in economic productivity and food supplies" (Bender, 1978: 195). The war also caused hundreds of thousands of Africans to flee to Zaire; according to the United Nations there were approximately 250,000 Angolan refugees in Zaire already in 1966 and 400,000 by 1972 (Kibreab, 1983: 25, 27).

Then came the transition crisis of 1974–76 and the collapse of both plantation and peasant market production. The average annual real rate of growth of agricultural production in the 1970's was negative 8.3% (World Bank, 1984: I, 6–7). Since independence the urban population has been fed mostly with imports (Bhagavan, 1986: 21).

The post-independence civil war drove the number of refugees up to approximately 620,000 by 1979. It then declined consider-ably to 215,000 by 1982 but then, with the war against UNITA becoming more intense, it rose to an estimated 261,000 by 1986, with an additional 94,000 estimated to be taking refuge in Zambia (Bariagaber, 1988: 4.1.33–36).

Within the country by 1981 some half a million Ovimbundu had been resettled into fortified villages by the MPLA as part of their war effort against UNITA (*Africa South of the Sahara, 1983–84*: 189), and another 300,000 were displaced in the south, as they fled South African raids. There were also concentrations of "internal refugees, totaling over 600,000 people, fleeing combats on the central plateaux and the drought-ridden areas" (*Africa South of the Sahara, 1988*: 219).

Peasants from the Central High Plateau, which has been the area most effected by the war, flooded into the local cities of Huambo, Benguela, and Bié, whose post-independence populations soared (see above). Disruption also prevented the peasants here, in what had been regarded as the "breadbasket" of the country in the colonial period, from feeding themselves, much less the local urban population (Bhagavan, 1986: 21).

Until the 1980's, however, when the spreading civil war caused a new wave of urbanization (*Africa South of the Sahara, 1988*: 219), disruption was probably not the major obstacle to peasant production for the market in most of the country. The Portuguese-run shops in the African residential areas and the whole Portuguese-dominated trade network that fed these shops collapsed soon after independence and with it most incentive for the peasants to market their crops. The new regime offered no incentive, neither prices nor goods available to purchase, to produce for the market. En masse the peasants retreated back to subsistence agriculture, while some of those living close to urban areas availed themselves of the emerging parallel market (see section on private entrepreneurs).

While there had been considerable commercialization of agriculture among the peasantry in pre-independence Angola (Kaplan, 1978: 212–13), it had become widespread only during the last fifteen years of the colonial era, when there there was an influx of Portuguese settlers and soldiers (Bhagavan, 1986: 13). Eighty-five percent of all households in the country still produced their own food (Bhagavan, 1986: 18), and it was easy to stop growing the surplus intended for market. The social differentiation of the peasantry that had begun in the 1960's (Kaplan, 1978: 207) was considerably limited by this return to subsistence farming.

As the war spread in the 1980's the danger was increasingly to peasant subsistence production. Serious food shortages were reported in central and southern Angola in 1981–82 and the situation became dramatic between 1983 and 1986 (*Africa South of the Sahara, 1988*: 220).

Agriculture in Mozambique was also disrupted by the war of independence and the refugees it caused, but there was a large difference in degree. The number of refugees in 1966 was minimal, and by 1972 was only about 60,000, most of them taking refuge in Tanzania (Kibreab, 1983: 25, 27). The post-independence experience was also different in this regard. There was no war inside Mozambique in the late 1970's and so the number of refugees was minimal.

With the war with South Africa-sponsored Renamo, however, there was an unprecedented growth in the number of refugees, to over 300,000 by 1987, mostly to Malawi (Bariagaber, 1988: 4.1.36), and over a million by late 1988, including 630,000 in Malawi and at least 150,000 in Zimbabwe (Goliber, 1989: 10). There were other reports that by the mid–1980's some 200,000 refugees from southern Mozambique had established themselves in the Gazankulu "homeland" in South Africa (*Africa South of the Sahara, 1990*: 708). Thus, the decline of total agricultural production (comprising both the peasant, cooperative and state sectors), while significant during the mid–1970's crisis—making for a 1970's average decline of approximately 1.5% per annum (World Bank, 1984: I, 127)—was much more drastic in the 1980's, dropping in value by almost 50% between 1980 and 1985 (World Bank, 1989a: 413).

As in Angola the post-independence flight of the Portuguese (and Indian) operators of the trade network in Mozambique led to a collapse of the network and the withdrawal of most of the peasants back into subsistence production. Mozambique is a much more densely populated country than Angola and the percentage of the population living in urban centers in the 1960's and 1970's was far lower than in Angola (see above). The commercialization of peasant agriculture had a long history, but far more in cotton, cashews, and other crops for export than in foodstuffs for the cities, in contrast to Angola, where maize was the biggest pre-independence cash crop among the peasantry (Kaplan, 1978: 213).

In the heartland of peasant cash-cropping in the north of Mozambique, there were very few urban centers and cotton cash-cropping had long been combined with subsistence agriculture; the disappearance of rural transport and traders here led to withdrawal into subsistence agriculture. In 1982, the Minister of Agriculture stated that in Cabo Delgado less cashews were being sold than were exported from the liberated zones during the war (Hanlon, 1984a: 111). Cotton production fell as well.

Private traders managed to provide an outlet and motivation for considerable peasant production for the urban parallel market, especially around Maputo. The rapid growth of the population here and the flight of the settler farmers who had fed the city in colonial times provided a market and an opening. Changes in policy in the 1980's allowed much of this illegal trade to enter legal channels, and presumably gave the peasants more incentive to grow a marketable surplus and for traders to gather it.

In the south, cash-cropping had often been combined with wage-labor in South Africa, the combination of which had led to the formation of a market-oriented middle-peasant class (First, 1983, and Hermele, 1988: 52–54). Higher wages for mine labor in South Africa and a reduction in the number of those hired since independence, and privatization in the 1980's that clearly favored the better-off farmers, whether classified as peasants or as private farmers, combined to accentuate social differentiation and boost productivity, at least in Chokwe (Hermele, 1988: 53–55). In secure areas near urban markets there has been a considerable rise in production for sale, at first for the parallel, but increasingly for the official, market. Thus, for example, the production of vegetables for the market, the product of the so-called "green zones," multiplied five-fold between 1981 and 1986 (Torp, 1989: 40).

The war has of course geographically limited these developments in the 1980's as overall levels of agricultural production attest. Between 1981 and 1983 the marketing of cash crops from the family sector fell by two-thirds and by 1986 was still only 40% of what it had been in 1981 (the "non-family" sector stood at approximately 45%) (Torp, 1989: 40). Thus, while in some areas of the south and other pockets around the country there is evidence of market-oriented agriculture and growing social differentiation among the peasantry and other agriculturalists, most of the country is typified by either subsistence or sub-subsistence (due to war, disruption and drought) agriculture or even the abandonment of agriculture altogether.

In Zambia differentiation of the peasantry, especially those within reach of the Copperbelt towns, had begun long before independence, but the post-independence extension of credit and services to the peasant areas had a differential impact that exaccerbated this inequality (Cliffe, 1979: 160; Momba, 1989: 339–40). The most successful "graduated" to the ranks of the "commercial" farmers, a category monopolized by Whites before independence. White farmers continued to receive a disproportionate amount of state support to agriculture (Momba 1989, 342–43). Nevertheless, growing urbanization and the economic boom provided a market, also, for the so-called "emergent farmers" among the peasantry, and many of them regularly produced for the market, while drawing on their less prosperous neighbors for labor (Cliffe, 1979: 164–65).

The big change in the rural areas came in the 1980's with a change of government policy towards agriculture generally and the "traditional" sector in particular (see EIU, 1989b: 45). The government tried to induce those in the reserves to increase staple production and the commercial farmers to concentrate on export crops. Both goals have met with some success. The emergent farmers now produce two-thirds of an expanding maize crop, while production in the commercial sector is increasing even faster (EIU, 1989b: 18–19, 45).

The big success story has been peasant agriculture in independent Zimbabwe; the peasant sector there has been producing on aggregate a very significant percentage of total agricultural produce in that country with a relatively large class of middle peasants producing most of the marketed grain (Mumbengegwi, 1986).

Commercialization of Black agriculture had a long history in Rhodesia, both in the African Purchase Areas (private tenure) and the Tribal Trust Lands (communal tenure). Whenever there has been an opening or any incentive offered, peasant farmers have responded with large increases in marketed production (Shopo, 1985: 39–44). Productivity in the reserves held up through the 1950's (Mosley, 1983: 71–72).

During UDI the conditions were not very propitious for peasant agriculture, with the settlers erecting various disincentives to Black commercial agriculture. In the second half of the 1970's, a declining economy and an intensified war reduced the chances of successful peasant farming, whether subsistence or commercial. "An estimated third of the three million head of cattle in the TTLs was lost through disease, theft and forced sales or slaughter. Half a million people were herded by the government into some 230 fortified 'protected' or consolidated villages. Thousands fled into the towns, and between 100,000 and 150,000 across the borders into neighboring territories " (Brand, 1981: 49).

With independence, the new government made improvements for the peasants in the areas of credit, marketing facilities, agricultural extension services, and especially output pricing. The result was that by the mid–1980's peasant production accounted for more than half of all maize sales and nearly as high a proportion of cotton sales through the marketing boards. A large number, but probably less than 20% (Moyo, 1986: 168), of the peasants profited from the new opportunities and produced most of the marketed surplus.

The new policies sped up a process of geographical and social differentiation that had been well under way in the 1950's but that had been slowed somewhat by settler policies of the Rhodesia Front government. As in Mozambique and Zambia, many of the succesful farmers had or have had access to wage remittances from the private sector (for Zimbabwe, see Bonnevie, 1983: 101; for Zambia, see Cliffe, 1979: 160). The stagnation in formal sector employment has simply accentuated the privileged position of those households with access to the remittances originating in such employment. Some of these same households have solidified their position by getting involved in transport or trade ventures (for Zambia, see Momba, 1989: 340; for an older example of the polyvalence of successful peasant farmers in Zimbabwe, see Weinrich, 1975: 63, 80).

However, even in Zimbabwe the trend in the rural areas for most rural households was marginalization. They were increasingly cut off from urban remittances; they had insufficient resources to ensure subsistence much less a regular marketable surplus; in some countries the security situation was such that they could not be sure of being able to plant or to harvest what they did plant; individuals and whole households were increasingly abandoning the rural areas.

Notes

1. In line with International Labor Office classification, I define industrial as the total of mining, manufacturing, construction, and utilities.

2. The labor force, or economically active population, is a much broader category than employees. It includes employees (and the unemployed), but, as well, employers, own-account workers, unpaid family workers, and members of producer cooperatives (ILO, 1988: 3–4).

3. There was no comparable increase in industrial employment, because some of the average annual growth rate of industry is accounted for by the rising value of Angola's oil in this period. Nevertheless, manufacturing alone increased by an average 15% per annum between 1962 and 1967, and 20% per annum from 1968 to independence (World Bank, 1990c).

4. The category of services is used in different ways by different authors and organizations. I follow the usage of the World Bank, rather than that of the International Labor Office, in defining services broadly to cover ILO sectors six, seven, eight and nine, i.e., trade, restaurants and hotels, transport, storage, communication, finance, insurance, real estate, and community, social, and personal services.

5. It should be noted however that the importance of the state in running the economy was established long before either independence or the intensification of the war. In the Federation period the government engaged in price-setting and made considerable infrastructural investments. Under Rhodesia Front rule, the state increased its intervention through new

nationalizations, import control via currency allocation, and numerous new administrative bodies and powers to steer the economy through international sanctions. In South Africa, too, the government had for a long time intervened extensively in the economy. The increases that I am describing were on top of this already high baseline.

6. Of course some of these employees were soldiers, as were an important percentage of the new public sector employees in Angola and Mozambique in the early 1970's, but an important percentage of them were not. There was, for example, a significant expansion of education in these countries in the periods mentioned (see below).

7. Writing about the informal sector in sub-Saharan African cities, Coquery-Vidrovitch writes: "The informal sector operates a market of commodities and services providing an irregular and unverifiable income, in which the dividing line between the licit and the illicit is often difficult to discern. . . . Their activities are generally small-scale, usually run by a family or a single individual, rarely employing more than ten people, and drawing on local, not external resources. They make up for lack of capital and technological equipment by a relatively abundant informal labor force that is recruited for work by the day or by the job. . . . Little analyzable data is available, since these informal establishments normally elude current criteria of statistical investigation such as a fixed location, a license, payment of taxes, and eligibility for state assistance" (Coquery-Vidrovitch, 1988: 301).

8. It is often difficult to distinguish conceptually and practically between those in the informal sector from the unemployed for several reasons: the degree of underemployment or at least under pay of those in the informal sector makes them in essence unemployed; those in the informal sector often register as unemployed; and they are in this sector on standby and as a last resort (see discussion in Zimbabwe, CSO, 1986a).

9. The discrepancy between this estimate and the one quoted in the preceding sentence is to be accounted for, I think, by the absence in the smaller estimate of the participation of non-Blacks, the significance of which has been attested to by other studies (SAIRR, 1989: 357).

10. The definition used at this time by the government of Zambia was "people living in centers of 5,000 or more." These definitions vary in different countries, and thus are not comparable. Nevertheless, they can give us an idea of what was happening within each country.

11. From the perspective of Black businessmen the picture was very different. In fact the growth of Black business is a major theme of the post-1975 period. This story, however, including the sub-themes of the role of the states in furthering Black business interests and the question of who is benefitting from privatization belongs to the next section.

Sources for Tables

Table 5-B-1: South Africa: 1965–85 (Schneier & Abedian, 1987: Table 1, Appendices 3–6). Zimbabwe: 1956, 1960 (*Africa South of the Sahara, 1971:* 599); 1965–75 (*Africa South of the Sahara, 1979–80:* 1167); 1980 (*Africa South of the Sahara, 1983–84:* 957); 1984 (Zimbabwe CSO, 1989b: 9). Zambia: 1966, 1960 (Fry, 1979: 34, 42); 1965–75 (Fry 1979: 63–64); 1980, 1985 (ILO, 1987: 345). Botswana: 1972, 1975 (ILO, 1980: 160); 1980, 1985 (ILO, 1987: 337). Malawi: 1970, 1975 (ILO, 1979: 169); 1980, 1985 (ILO, 1987: 341). Lesotho: 1965 (*Africa South of the Sahara, 1971:* 435); 1972 (*Africa South of the Sahara, 1974:* 448); 1977 (*Africa South of the Sahara, 1979–80:* 538); 1980 (*Africa South of the Sahara, 1981–82:* 561). Swaziland: 1970, 1975 (ILO, 1979: 171); 1980, 1985 (ILO, 1987: 344). Namibia: 1971 (Omar, 1990: 8); 1974 (*Africa South of the Sahara, 1979–80:* 700); 1980, 1985 (estimates based on Omar, 1990: 6, 11; SAIRR, 1983: 606; and 1977–84 depression).

Table 5-B-2: Columns 1, 2 and 3: World Bank, 1989b: 269: Angola, Mozambique, Swaziland, Zimbabwe, Malawi, Lesotho, Botswana, Zambia. South Africa, column 1 and 2: World Bank, 1984, I, 163. Columns 4 and 5: World Bank, 1984, I: same as in Table 1, columns 1–5, etc. Namibia, column 4: ILO, 1958: 665; column 5: *Africa South of the Sahara, 1971:* 762. Columns 6, 7 and 8: World Bank, 1989a: same as in Table 1, column 6. Namibia, columns 6 and 7: *Africa South of the Sahara, 1981–82:* 731; Column 8: *Africa South of the Sahara, 1988:* 731. Angola, columns 6 and 7: World Bank, 1984, I: 7; Column 8: World Bank, 1989b: 269. Mozambique totals in columns 4 and 5 adjusted upwards on basis of general raise made in past totals as of late 1980's (see World Bank, 1989a: 413).

Table 5-B-3: Columns 1–5, 7 and 8 (constant market prices): World Bank, 1984, I: Angola, 6–7; Botswana, 20–21; Lesotho, 104–05; Malawi, 110–11; Mozambique, 126–27; Swaziland, 170–71; South Africa, 162–63; Zambia, 200–01; Zimbabwe, 202–03. Column 6 (constant factor prices):

my estimate based on material in World Bank, 1989a: South Africa, 513; Swaziland, 545; Mozambique, 413; Malawi, 381; Lesotho, 361; Botswana, 153; Zimbabwe, 641; Zambia, 637. Angolan estimate based on 1980's per annum growth rates in *Africa South of the Sahara, 1990,* Angolan section.

Table 5-B-4: Same as Table 5-B-1, except Lesotho and Namibia, which are not included in Table 5-B-4.

Table 5-B-5: The first row of figures for each country except South Africa are from World Bank, 1984, I: Mozambique, 65; Angola, 4; Swaziland, 86: Zimbabwe, 103; Malawi, 57; Lesotho, 54; Botswana, 12; and Zambia, 102. The South African row of figures is from World Bank, 1989a: 512–13 and SAIRR, 1988: 452. The second row of figures for each country is World Bank, 1989b: 278.

C. Historical Stratification by Race

Race, even more than class, has been socially constructed. Black and White have come to be regarded worldwide as categories of social attribution. Other categories, such as mulattos, have been utilized at some places and times, but less universally. Southern Africa as a region has had a particularly long and exaggerated tradition of social classification by race.

For one thing, racial terms have been official legal categories with specific legal consequences. They have been reflected in the censuses, not however consistently from census to census. During the early part of the century, racial categories were being added to the censuses in South Africa. In the 1892 Cape Colony census the only distinction was between "European or White" and "Coloured," a category comprising "all non-European people." The next census in 1904 distinguished three "clearly defined race groups in the colony: White, Bantu, and Coloured," the latter now used to comprise "all intermediate shades between the first two" (quoted by Goldin, 1989: 242–43). These categories, plus an Asiatic category, were those employed in the first South African census of 1911. A mixed category was added to the Southern Rhodesian census in 1911, and in Northern Rhodesia in 1921.

The new category of "Coloured" was clearly considered an intermediate one in the official race hierarchy. Thus, the criteria used, besides skin color, included notions of European-like (i.e., "civilized") behavior. In the British colonies of southern Africa, for example, the censuses defined a person of mixed race as one whose parents were of different race and who lived in a European manner (Shaul, 1960: 38). While state officials thus distinguished between this new group and the Blacks (or Bantus or Natives) beneath them, and awarded them correspondingly greater political rights, the line between White and non-White was simultaneously made sharper. Thus, in South Africa:

> The development of a distinct Coloured identity at the turn of the century was associated with the ossification of the colour line. The ability of light-skinned people to "pass for white" by 1904 was being greatly restricted (Goldin, 1989: 246).

During the 1920's and 1930's differential treatment of the variously ranked races was exacerbated.

In the Portuguese colonies between 1926 and 1933 a new social policy was established that paralleled much of what was happening in the British sphere. Known as the *Indigenato,* the new policy distinguished legally between the indigenous and the non-indigenous population. Only the latter were granted the protection of Portuguese law; the former, defined as Africans or their descendants governed by native custom and without sufficient culture or civilization to come under the same laws as the Portuguese, were issued passbooks (if male) and made subject to the government's labor codes, manpower needs, and vagrancy laws (Wheeler & Pelissier, 1971: 131).

While the possibility was held open of selective assimilation (*assimilado* status) for some of the indigenous population, the earlier idea of the gradual assimilation of the entire Black population was set aside (Wheeler & Pelissier, 1971: 130). In any case, by the 1950's only 1% of Angolan Blacks were deemed civilized and classified as *assimilados* (Bender, 1978: 151); there were even fewer in Mozambique (Henriksen, 1978: 126). Of course Whites did not need to be assimilated; they were all assumed to be civilized. Some 90% of Angolan *mestiços* (mulattos) were classified in 1950 as *assimilados* and thus presumably were on an equal legal footing with Whites, but it in fact assured them of only an intermediate status (Bender, 1978: 151). During the decades of the deterioration of the African legal position (culminating and formalized in the *Indigenato*), the position of the *mestiços* (for more than a century a socially-recognized and relatively privileged group) was also considerably downgraded (Bender, 1978: 53–54).

Official racist policies began to be challenged after 1945. There was some change in the British sphere already within the Federation, and eventually the complete rejection of official racism upon independence in Malawi, Zambia, Lesotho, Swaziland, and Botswana. By 1961, the Portuguese felt obliged to drop their *Indigenato* system, and with it the distinction between civilized and uncivilized people. The government of Southern Rhodesia resisted the tide between 1965 and 1979 but eventually had to yield. In the 1980's some legal reforms concerning race were implemented in Namibia and then independence led to the scrapping of official racism altogether. The South African state was the only one to move in the other direction, adding dramatically to its racist legal framework in 1948.

The political changes were reflected in changes in census categories, where enumeration by race began to end. The last censuses to use race in Angola and Mozambique were those of 1960; in Lesotho and Swaziland, 1976; in Botswana, 1984; in Malawi, 1977. In Zambia, while the 1969 census still distinguished between Africans and non-Africans, subsequent ones distinguished only citizens and non-citizens. Post-independence Zimbabwe ceased to record government data by racial or ethnic category, although the 1982 census still retained such categories. Namibia, under South African rule, used South African categories in the 1970 census. For political reasons, in 1981, the categories were expanded to twelve: Whites, Coloured and various African group names such as Ovambo and Herero, but all of them were now labeled ethnic groups.

Whatever the present legal framework regarding race in each country in southern Africa, there remains the social fact of a colonially constructed three-tiered racial hierarchy: White; Coloured, or *mestiço* (and Asian or Indian if present); Black. Different liberation movements in the region have reacted in different ways to this social reality. In Mozambique, Frelimo has always taken a non-racial position, distinguishing only between Mozambicans and non-Mozambicans. The position of the ANC in South Africa is also non-racial, in contrast to the position, for example, of the PAC. Both the ANC and the PAC, however, seem to agree today on a usage of the term of Blacks to include Indians and Coloureds, as well as the vast majority of the population (a category the ANC and PAC call Africans, the South African state has historically labelled Bantus, and I am calling Blacks in this text to conform to usage in other parts of southern Africa).

In Zimbabwe, the governing party, ZANU-PF, has always distinguished between, on the one hand, Blacks or Africans, and, on the other hand, Whites, including therein Asians and Coloureds; the Smith regime, interestingly, made the same distinction between what they labelled as Africans and non-Africans, the latter including Asians and Coloureds, as well as Whites (Clarke, 1977a: 14). The movements seem united in either wanting everybody in one camp or else reducing divisions to two camps, although this has caused some debate among at least some Coloured anti-Apartheid activists in South Africa (see the discussion in Wallerstein, 1987).

In any case, the focus of this paper is on the three-tiered racial hierarchy that remains a crucial socio-economic characteristic of southern Africa, whether or not legally recognized or enforced.

The White Presence within the Region

In the 1970's White-settler/colonial southern Africa shrunk not only politically and militarily but also demographically. By 1980 more than 94% of the region's White population resided in South Africa and they represented less than 7% of the region's population (see Table 5-B-3). This was a dramatic change from the early 1970's when 20% of the region's White population still lived outside the borders of South Africa, and the Whites represented more than 9% of the region's population (see Table 5-B-3). By the 1980's, the situation had returned to that of the 1930's when the only significant number of Whites in the region to be found outside South Africa were in Southern Rhodesia (Freund, 1984: 193).

From the time of southern Africa's incorporation into the world-economy (see Martin, 1987), the overall White presence in the region outside of South Africa (and to a lesser extent Zimbabwe) has followed a rhythm of expansion and contraction, corresponding roughly to swings in the world-economy: rising into the 1920's, falling in the 1930's, rising again after 1945, and falling once again in the 1970's. The direction of net migration would be strongly into the region in one period, strongly out of the region at another.

The first wave of White immigration into the subcontinent was into the Transvaal in the late nineteenth and early twentieth centuries; it spread into Southern Rhodesia and the Katanga province of the Belgian Congo before the First World War, into Angola in the 1920's, and into Northern Rhodesia after 1925. An ebb tide in the 1930's dried up White immigration into Southern Rhodesia and led to an absolute fall in the White population in several southern African countries, including Nyasaland, Mozambique, Northern Rhodesia, and Angola, particularly dramatic in the latter two (for Northern Rhodesia, see Shaul, 1960: 42; for Nyasaland, see Shaul, 1960: 46; for Angola, see Clarence-Smith, 1983: 180, and Freund, 1984: 193; for Mozambique, see Henriksen, 1978: 135 and Freund, 1984: 193).

With Africa's "second colonial occupation"[1] after 1945 and the boom in tropical agricultural commodities that had already begun, there ensued an unprecedented wave of new White immigration into southern Africa in the late 1940's and 1950's. Most of the immigrants crowded into the burgeoning cities, but a significant number settled onto the best farm land, ousting resident Africans from the fertile plateaus of Angola and Southern Rhodesia, the highlands in Nyasaland, and along the Limpopo and elsewhere in Mozambique, in order to cash in on the rapidly rising prices for coffee, tobacco, tea, etc. In Mashonaland in Southern Rhodesia, for example, this period is known as the "second occupation of Mashonaland," the first following the 1896 rebellion, to signify the degree of displacement of rural Africans by newly arrived White settlers.

Between 1946 and 1950 there was a net White immigration into South Africa of over 100,000 persons (Minter, 1986: 75). More significant was the growth in the White settler population in other countries of the region. Southern Rhodesia gained 50,000 Whites through immigration during these same years (Minter, 1986: 77), and another 30,000 in the mid–1950's (Angola Comite, 1975: 9), by which time only one-third of the White population had been born in the country (Minter, 1986: 77). At its peak between 1951–56, net immigration of Whites into Northern Rhodesia totalled over 23,000 (Ohadike, 1974: 396). Mozambique's White population more than tripled between 1940 and 1960 (Henriksen, 1978: 135), most of it through immigration; Angola's population increased fourfold in these same twenty years, with the net immigration reaching 10,000 per annum by the mid–1950's (Wheeler & Pelissier, 1971: 138).

Rising African nationalism temporarily reversed this settler flood tide in the early 1960's, but it quickly resumed, with rising White immigration into the Portuguese colonies and Southern Rhodesia during the rest of the 1960's and the early 1970's, which more than compensated for emigration from Zambia and Malawi (Table 5-B-3). In spite of an enormous influx of White immigrants into South Africa in this period, averaging 30,000 net migrants yearly (SAIRR, 1989: 155), by the early 1970's almost 20% of the region's White settlers lived outside of the borders of the Republic (Table 5-B-3).

The White settler governments in Southern Rhodesia, the Federation of the Rhodesias and Nyasaland, and of course in South Africa worked hard to entice new White immigration into their territories. During the late 1940's and 1950's this corresponded to British policy in the region (Freund, 1984,: 195), and probably that of most other European powers. However, Harold Macmillan's "winds of change" speech in 1960 heralded a change in British policy, in the face of rising African nationalism, that made the settlers in the British sphere dispensable. Metropolitan encouragement for White emigration to the colonies fell off.

The political situation in Portuguese Africa was completely different. There were no autonomous White settler governments in

Angola or Mozambique, and rising African nationalism only made the Portuguese government redouble its efforts to increase emigration to the colonies. To bring about emigration to Mozambique, in particular, the Portuguese government felt obliged to offer all sorts of incentives, including the complete organization and financing of agricultural communities composed of transplanted Portuguese peasants (Henriksen, 1978: 136).

The real retreat of White settlers from the region has occurred only since the onset of the region's economic crisis and political upheaval in the mid–1970's. The liberation of Angola, Mozambique, Zimbabwe, and Namibia has broken White settler political power and made legal race privilege a thing of the past. The 1970's and especially the 1980's have brought a severe economic downturn. Many settlers have chosen to leave or else to retreat to South Africa (see below); others remained but refused citizenship in the new Black-majority ruled countries.

Outside of South Africa, and to a lesser extent Zimbabwe, the region's White population was largely a post–1945 phenomenon and did not have very deep roots. In Zambia (and previously in Northern Rhodesia):

> The [White] population has, in fact, always consisted largely of temporary immigrants. . . . People have always been arriving and departing in large numbers, and even during the mid-fifties, when the total population was expanding very rapidly, emigrants amounted to between one-third and one-half the number of immigrants (Kay, 1967: 28–29).

In Angola, which was far more of a settler colony than Mozambique (both in number and percentage of Whites, as well as their rate of turnover and occupational dispersal in the economy), only 20% of the White population in 1960 was native-born (Wheeler and & Pelissier, 1971: 143). Even in Southern Rhodesia only one-third of the White population in the mid–1950's had been born in the country (Minter, 1986: 77).

South Africa's White population, in contrast, especially its Afrikaner community, had roots that went back centuries. In 1960 some 90% of White South Africans were native-born (SAIRR, 1965: 110). Nevertheless, continuing White immigration into South Africa, too, has been considered crucially important by the Pretoria government. First, the rate of natural increase among the non-White population in southern Africa has risen steadily since 1945, and is now much greater than that of the Whites. In the 1970's, for example, the increase of the South African White population was only 20%, in spite of enormous numbers of immigrants (*Africa South of the Sahara, 1982:* 43). The increase of the Coloured population was 28%; for Asians it was 30%; and for Blacks, it was 38 % in spite of a significant net emigration from the country (*Africa South of the Sahara, 1982:* 43).

Secondly, the reproduction of South Africa's economy, given its race/class stratification, formally required White immigrants to fill its skilled labor requirements. Finally, and in consequence of the first two phenomena, net White migration statistics were seen as a gauge of White confidence in the settler structure (Raftapoulos, 1986: 304, writing about Southern Rhodesia, where the situation was the same). This confidence has at times been shaken. The three brief periods of net emigration from South Africa between 1955 and 1987 were 1960 (Sharpeville), 1977–78 (Soweto), and 1986–87 (renewed militance in the townships) (SAIRR, 1989: 155).

Similarly, in Southern Rhodesia, the periods of net emigration between 1955 and 1976 were 1961–64 (breakup of Federation), 1966 (UDI, and the beginning of the international sanctions), and 1976 (intensification of the guerilla war) (EIU, *Rhodesia:* 1977: Table One; Angola comite, 1975: 9). During the last few years of the war and the first few years of independence, Zimbabwe's White population declined by half. In countries with a less rooted White population, and where the Whites had less confidence in the post-colonial state, such as Angola and Mozambique, independence led to even more dramatic White exodus (Table 5-B-3).

The unbroken growth of South Africa's White population camouflages to some extent the White demographic rhythm of contraction and expansion in the region as a whole. In fact, the rhythm in South Africa has sometimes been countercyclical to that of the region because of the nature of geographical expansion and con-

traction of White presence in the region. South Africa has historically served both as the origin of White settlers in other parts of the
region, and as a refuge for White settlers from other parts of the
region fleeing changed economic or political circumstances. South
Africans were among the first settlers in Zimbabwe, Zambia,
Namibia, and even far-off Kenya (Bender, 1978: 48). Since the
early 1930's, South Africa has been the principal source of immigrants into Northern Rhodesia. In 1956, people born in South
Africa accounted for over 40% of Northern Rhodesia's White
population; another 10% came from Southern Rhodesia (Kay,
1967: 29), which could be considered a regional subcenter. South
Africa was always a major source of immigrants into Southern
Rhodesia. During the mid–1950's, immigrants to the Federation
from South Africa matched those from Great Britain, together
constituting better than 80% of the immigrant total (Minter, 1986:
77).

In 1979, on the other hand, when White rule in Zimbabwe was
drawing to a close, some 50% of the total immigration into South
Africa originated in Zimbabwe (SAIRR, 1980: 70). And in the
1960's, when there was a net emigration of over 30,000 White
Zambians, most of them moved to South Africa or Southern
Rhodesia (Ohadike, 1974: 398).

A significant shift in the composition of the region's White
population during this latest contraction has been the replacement
of foreign South Africans and Southern Rhodesians, as well as
"local" Whites, by White expatriates from Europe and North
America (for Zambia, see Ohadike, 1974: 399, 409; for Mozambique, see Kaplan, 1984: 95). This shift clearly strengthens the
reorientation of countries in southern Africa away from South
Africa and towards overseas core countries, a reorientation corresponding to what we know about trade and investment ties in the
1970's and 1980's (see chapters 2a and 2c).[2]

Mixed-race presence in the region depended on natural increase
among members of this category, as well as continued miscegena-
tion. Immigration, except for a limited number of Cape Verdians
into Angola, was not a source of increase. Asian presence in the
region, on the other hand, owed much to immigration. The Goans

in Mozambique are the Asian group with the longest history in southern Africa; they played a significant part in the economy and administration of Portuguese East Africa since the seventeenth century (Kaplan, 1984: 95). The vast majority of the region's Asians are descendants of people from the Gujerati region of the Indian sub-continent,[3] whether Hindu or Muslim, who came to southern Africa as indentured workers or settlers in the late-nineteenth and early-twentieth centuries, before further "Indian" immigration was blocked in South Africa and Southern Rhodesia. Their population growth since then has been due mostly to natural increase, although until Federation the door was open to their immigration into Northern Rhodesia and Nyasaland. In the period 1945–1955, the small Indian communities in these two territories increased more than threefold (Shaul, 1960: 44, 46).

The rise and fall in the rate of Indian emigration has paralleled that of White emigration, except when it has been a result of legislation either disproportionally effecting the Indian population, such as that passed in Zambia and Malawi after independence reserving all rural trade to Africans, or directly targeting Indians, such as the expulsions from Mozambique following India's take-over of Goa in 1961. However, Asians in general and Indians in particular have shown themselves to be much more rooted in the region than Whites (Table 5-B-3).

Black Migration within the Region

While there has historically been very little movement of Africans into the region from without, except a little from Tanzania and parts of Zaire, the region has been typified by migrant flows of Black labor across the region. These flows, when permanent, have affected population totals in the countries involved. Thus, for example, the 1946 census in Lesotho indicated an absolute decline of the Black population since the previous census in 1936. Demographers agree that the only possible explanation of this phenomenon has to have been a massive emigration of Basotho into neighboring South Africa (as related in Martin, 1992: 16).

Whether permanent or oscillating they have contributed in no small way to the creation of the regional ethnic/occupational hierarchy. With rare exceptions, such as on the Zambian Copper-belt (Daniel, 1979: 105), extra-territorial migrants were employed in relatively low-wage sectors (relative, that is, to that of other sectors in the host country), especially if they were only working seasonally. Urban influx control measures exacerbated this inequali-ty between native-born and foreign-born Africans in countries across the region, as well as that between labor-supplying and labor-receiving parts of the region.

Host countries such as South Africa and Rhodesia have system-atically tried to channel foreign migrants into low-paying sectors, such as the mines and farms. In 1990 in Zimbabwe, ten years after the lifting of influx control, and at least twenty years since any significant influx of foreign migrant work-seekers, a large percent-age of farm workers continued to be Malawian.

Prior to the 1970's regional labor flows of oscillating migrants were both heavy and multi-vectored (Leistner, 1967: 55). In the 1950's there were three important regional centers of employment for extra-territorial migrant labor: the Copperbelt, the mines and farms of Southern Rhodesia, and the mines and farms in South Africa. The Copperbelt drew in labor from Tanzania, Angola, Southern Rhodesia, and especially Nyasaland. Southern Rhodesia depended on Nyasaland, Mozambique, and Northern Rhodesia. South African farms often relied on labor from immediately neighboring countries, such as Botswana, Lesotho, Swaziland, and southern Mozambique. The Transvaal mines drew in labor from across the region, but more from southern Mozambique than anywhere else.

By the early 1970's there was only one real pole of attraction for extra-territorial migrant labor. In Southern Rhodesia laborers of foreign origin continued to be an important source of labor on the mines and the farms, but the annual flow into and out of the country was drying up (Kay, 1971: 65). On the Zambian Copper-belt, the post-independence policy of Zambianization led to a fall in the Black non-Zambian labor force, declining from approximate-ly 25% of the total in 1964 to approximately 12% in 1971 (Daniel, 1979: 105); meanwhile a company stabilization policy begun more than fifteen years before had put a virtual stop to the migrant flows (Ohadike, 1974: 401–8).

In South Africa, the gold mines were relying more than ever on foreign labor, particularly from southern Mozambique and Malawi. South African farms, on the other hand, while still drawing on their traditional foreign sources, had cut their manpower needs and now relied on the homelands for the bulk of their labor (Stahl, 1981: 28). Nevertheless, the total number of foreign migrants in the economy remained very high and looked particularly big relative to the numbers moving into any other part of the region (Wilson, 1976: 453, 462).

In the early 1970's, South Africa began to implement a policy of internalization of the mine labor force (see, for example, SAIRR, 1982: 85, but also chapter 2b) following the implementation in the 1960's of a similar policy regarding farm labor. To the degree that the mines on the Rand still depend on foreign labor, it came to be migrants from Lesotho or the TVBC "independent" homelands, or else southern Mozambique (SAIRR, 1989: 421).

That doesn't mean that there are less migrant workers in South Africa today. On the contrary, a corollary of internalization has been an increase in the number of migrants and commuters travelling between the homelands and the "White" cities; even industry is now served by homeland contract workers. This was made possible by the resettlement of countless Blacks into the homelands and the strengthening of the influx control machinery during the 1960's and 1970's (see Simkins, 1981c). By the mid–1980's, over half of all Black workers in "White" South Africa were migrants or commuters (Southall, 1986: 165).

Southall identifies seven statuses of Black labor in the country ranging down from urban insiders, through commuters, to foreign migrants (Southall, 1986: 167–68). This segmentation and hierarchicalization of the Black labor force intersects with ethnic divisions and homeland/urban divisions, as well as native-born/foreign-born divisions. The ethnic/national contradictions and hierarchicalization of the region have been reproduced in concentrated form in South Africa; internalization, perhaps, is the culmination of this process.

In addition to these oscillating flows of male migrants there have been more permanent cross-territorial movements of Africans within the region. The relative attractiveness of urban/manufacturing wages and the simultaneous decline of the African rural areas in the 1940's meant a flow of would-be urban-dwellers, particularly pronounced in South Africa where industrialization and reserve deterioration had proceeded the furthest. White authorities in South Africa from the late 1930's and in Southern Rhodesia from the late 1940's tried to control this urban influx, without much initial success. The cross-territorial movement of Africans towards South Africa and to a lesser extent Southern Rhodesia reached a peak in the late 1940's and early 1950's.

By the 1960's, South Africa's urban influx-control mechanisms were working quite effectively: the proportion of foreign-born Africans was declining and the urbanized proportion of the African population had stabilized, even falling slightly during the next twenty years (Savage, 1985: 191). Urban influx control was never as effective in Southern Rhodesia as it was in South Africa, but then it never had the pull on regional labor either.

However, this bottling up of Africans in the reserves within South Africa and Southern Rhodesia, and in the other countries (two variants of the same policy) was only effective in the short term. The rate of urbanization in the 1970's was greater all over sub-Saharan Africa than it had been in the 1960's (Davies 1987: 20). In Zimbabwe, the de-urbanization of the 1960's (see notes to Table 5-B-5) had already been reversed by the early 1970's (Davies, 1987: 20), and in South Africa, the official scrapping of urban-influx control in 1986 was preceded by years of rising clandestine urbanization. Urbanization was driven not only by deteriorating conditions in the rural areas due to long-term structural problems, but, increasingly, in the 1970's and 1980's by war and famine (see chapter 5b).

Rural dislocation, resettlement and the profusion of refugee populations, all consequences of the economic and political crisis from the mid–1970's, were dramatic indications of the rising volume of a less orderly, permanent (or at least indeterminant) Black migration in this period that dwarfed the flow of oscillating

306 _____ *Chapter 5*

migrant labor. The extent to which these new migrants were crossing national borders was clearly massive, but the pattern of movement was much less clear, both because the crossings were clandestine (since illegal), and because the movement was more or less anarchic. The extent to which these flows were influencing regional stratification was even less clear (but see chapter 2b).

Overall, Urban, and Industrial Employment Disaggregated by Race

During the economic boom of the 1960's and early 1970's, the growth in formal sector employment across the region seemed to benefit all the racial groups, although judging by South Africa it was the Coloureds and the Asians who benefitted disproportionally[4] (Table 5-B–1, but see also Clarke, 1977b: 18, 22–28, 46–47 for some evidence supporting a similar trend in Zimbabwe). For the three countries for which we have a White-Black breakdown, it was Zambia that had the highest rate of growth in overall Black employment, followed by Zimbabwe and then South Africa.

Setting aside agricultural employment, a sector in which the generation of employment did not match that in other sectors, the trend was particularly propitious for the non-White groups, outpacing that of the Whites, at least in Zimbabwe and South Africa. In South Africa Black non-agricultural (i.e., urban) employment grew by 45%, but the White 33%, while in Zimbabwe Black employment grew by 65%, almost twice as much as White urban employment growth (Table 5-B–4). Within South Africa Coloured and Asian urban employment, however, grew still faster than did Black (Table 5-B–4).

During the decade beginning in the mid–1970's, there was very little growth in overall formal sector employment growth for any racial group, with some few exceptions. The exodus of Whites from Zimbabwe resulted in a small increase in employment there among Blacks, Asians, and Coloureds, just as the exodus of Whites from Zambia in the 1960's boosted the growth of non-White Zambian employment between 1965 and 1975. In South Africa, there was an increase of approximately 15–20% in Coloured and Asian employment (Table 5-B–1) during the decade of slow economic growth.

Between 1975 and 1985, non-agricultural employment growth was not very different for South Africa than overall employment growth: negligible among Whites and Blacks, small but not insignificant among Asians and Coloureds (Table 5-B–4). Urban Black employment growth in Zimbabwe, however, was surprisingly high, at about one-third, and was particularly significant because it was concentrated into a few years after independence (Table 5-B–4).

The greatest disparity in the growth of White and non-White employment was in the industrial sector. In the two biggest industrial countries in the region, South Africa and Zimbabwe, growth in non-White industrial employment was double that of Whites between 1965 and 1975 (Table 5-B–4). The paucity of growth in White industrial employment during the South African industrial boom, approximately 23% (Table 5-B–4), lends support to the thesis that in the 1960's and 1970's there was a structural shift of White labor away from blue-collar jobs (Meth, 1981 193; Pachai, 1979: 234; Wolpe, 1988: 86). Although White industrial employment grew faster than in South Africa, it was still dwarfed by the increase in Black industrial employment and was perhaps indicative of a structural shift similar to that in South Africa (Clarke, 1977a: 18). Leading the way in this surge of non-White industrial employment, at least in South Africa, were again the Coloured and Asian groups (Table 5-B–4). The gains of Asians and Coloureds, who were very little engaged in mining, were concentrated in construction and manufacture. Between 1960 and 1970 the percentage of the total Coloured employees in manufacturing increased from 17% to 24%, while the percentage of the total Indian population rose from 27% to 35% (Pachai, 1979: 275).

Between 1975 and 1985 there was no growth to speak of in industrial employment in any of these three countries. This fact seems in obvious contradiction to what is apparent to the most casual observer of South Africa, i.e., the growing strength and importance of the South African working class, and especially the industrial working class. Of course, much of this change has to do more with organization and consciousness than increasing numbers. There were, for example, 2 Black unions and 16,000 Black union members in 1969; in 1977 there were 25 unions and 70,000 members; and by 1984 there were 55 unions and 400,000 members (Lipton, 1985: 340). Growing militancy and political consciousness have been manifested in the increasing number and effectiveness of strikes, and the nature of the demands put forward.

There are, however, some material factors that are not unimportant in explaining labor's growing strength in South Africa. In the first place, between 1960 and 1975 there was, as noted, a tremendous growth in the number of Black, Coloured, and Asian nonagricultural, and particularly industrial, wage-laborers, both in absolute numbers and relative to White employment. While employment growth in general slowed way down after 1975, in some areas it grew rapidly between 1978 and 1982, for example, among non-White workers in manufacturing (Schneier & Abedian, 1987: Table 1, Appendices 3, 4, 5).

In the second place, the households of which the Black urban laborers were a part were less and less likely to have a split worker/peasant vocation and consciousness. This more thorough proletarianization was due to the collapse of the reserves as agriculturally productive sites, a process whose speed picked up enormously beginning in the 1950's (Simkins, 1981a: 262–63) and which could only have been aggravated by the enormous resettling of the Black population into the reserves in the 1960's and 1970's. In 1960, some 36% of Black South African males and 43% of Black South African females lived in the reserves; by 1980 the percentage of Black males living in the reserves had risen to 50%, while the percentage of Black females had risen to 58% (Simkins, 1981c: 3).

The family of a Black urban wage-laborer might still very well live in the rural area, but it was increasingly likely to be simply an address and not a site of even subsistence production.[5] This situation certainly contrasts with, for example, that of the peasant miracle in independent Zimbabwe.

In the third place, from the 1960's the increasing capital intensity of investment in mining and manufacture (not to mention agriculture) and the change in the labor process, including the fragmentation of jobs, that has gone with it has paved the way for a structural shift in industrial needs from unskilled to semi-skilled workers (Wolpe, 1988: 86). For example, between 1969 and 1985 the percentage of the total Black South African workforce in the semi-skilled category rose from 16.7% to 30.5% (Schneier & Abedian, 1987: 17). These better-educated, more skilled workers were less easily replaced (Wolpe, 1988: 82) and collectively enjoyed more "work-place bargaining power" (Beittel, 1988) than did their less skilled counterparts working in a different work-place environment in the 1950's.

In the fourth place, the expansion of the non-White semi-skilled working class was preceded by the fragmentation of White skilled jobs. The Whites made redundant were taking on supervisory roles or moving elsewhere. Thus, the percentage of supervisors among the White workforce almost doubled between 1969 and 1985, while the semi-skilled working class percentage fell by half and the overall working class percentage fell by 20 percent (Schneier & Abedian, 1987: 34). The crumbling of job reservation (see Wolpe, 1988: 86–87) is both cause and consequence of the declining role of the South African White working class.

Of course, South Africa was not unique in these various ways. There was a rapid change as well on the Copperbelt in the labor process and the manpower needs of industry (from unskilled to semiskilled), for example, in the 1960's and early 1970's (Daniel, 1979: 101, 111; Cliffe, 1979: 154); the same could be said in Zimbabwe for mining (Clarke, 1976: 65–66), and to a lesser extent for industry (Harris, 1975: 147). Still, while there are similarities between processes in South Africa and the rest of the region with regard to working-class formation, the intense confluence of factors in South Africa goes some way towards explaining the working class phenomenon there.

Office and Professional Workers

While during the 1960's and early 1970's, many Blacks across southern Africa had been drawn into or upgraded in production jobs within the burgeoning industrial structures, for the last 30 years, it has been office and professional/technical work that has provided the biggest and most significant opening to Black and other non-White workers. In South Africa, for example, while total employment in clerical, sales and service (in the narrow sense of the word; see note 4 in chapter 5a) jobs increased by 78% between 1969 and 1985, the growth was approximately 139% for non-Whites (SALDRU, 1986: 93, 96, 101). During these same years, the percentage of the non-White workforce occupationally classified as clerical, white-collar, or technical grew in a continuous way from approximately 6% to 12% of the Black workforce, 11% to 21% of the Coloured, and 28% to 37% of the Asian (Schneier & Abedian, 1987: 17, 24, 29, 34). In Zambia, Africanization on the Copperbelt meant a large increase not only in Black semi-skilled production jobs but also in Black office and technical employment (see Daniel, 1979, 110–11). In Zimbabwe, surveys indicated that, between 1981 and 1985 the percentage of non-Whites in the national economy's professional and technical posts rose from 56% to almost 90% (*Herald,* 8/10/89: 8).

Such evidence as exists suggests that non-White employment in the tertiary sphere, where office and professional jobs are concentrated, has been growing particularly fast. Service sector employment growth in South Africa has disproportionally benefitted non-Whites, increasing by more than 75% (Blacks increased by 65%) between 1965 and 1985, as opposed to 50% for Whites, and has outpaced industry as a growth source for non-White employment (Table 5-B–4). In Zimbabwe, Blacks have benefitted from a rise of almost 200% in service sector employment since 1965 (Table 5-B–4). The particularly rapid increase in the 1980's was due not only to the pace of growth in overall service sector employment, but the exodus of many Whites from service sector jobs after independence (Table 5-C–1).

In Zambia, too, Black service sector employment has grown faster than Black industrial employment (see 1955–70 in Table 5-B–4). In Angola, given the flight of the Whites in the mid–1970's and the structural shift of the economy towards tertiary employment (Santos, 1984; Dilolwa, 1978), it is logical to assume that it is the tertiary sphere, and thus office and professional/technical work, that has provided the most opportunity for non-White advance. The same could probably be said for Mozambique.

The public sector, which is also strongly correlated to office and professional/technical work, has historically in settler countries been a bastion of White employment. Consisting largely of white-collar posts requiring education and experience that historically were difficult for Blacks to obtain, government service could also serve as a haven for poorly educated or unskilled Whites that the private sector might let go by the way side (see, for example, Clarke, 1977a: 21).

When Whites left a country following independence, the largest labor force void they left behind was usually in the public sector. Educated members of non-White race categories were quick to fill these new openings. Even when Whites stayed, post-independence, Black-majority ruled countries usually instituted some form of Africanization, and the public sector was the easiest and thus fastest sphere to be Africanized, at least in administrative posts and up through middle-level technical positions. White flight from Mozambique, Angola and Zimbabwe, plus a policy of Africanization in Zimbabwe, resulted in a dramatic color change in the public sectors in these countries. In Zimbabwe, for example, by the mid–1980's, the percentage of Whites in the civil service was down to approximately 3%, or more or less equal to their proportion of the national population (*Herald*, 8/10/89: 8).

Non-White opportunity in the public sector has not been simply a function of how many Whites were replaced by the post-independence governments; expansion, too, meant new job openings. More hospitals and schools meant more non-White nurses and teachers. More social services, planning structures, etc. meant more Black, Asian, and Coloured office workers. Employment in the public sector (including the parastatals) in Zambia increased by almost 200% in the course of a post-independence expansion of social services and a wave of nationalizations between 1966 and 1976 (Fry, 1979: 63–64).

Independence and Black majority rule were not the only sources of growth in the number of non-White public sector jobs. In Zimbabwe the number of Blacks in public administration, for example, rose by 75% between 1964 and 1974 (*Africa South of the Sahara, 1979–80:* 1167). In South Africa, the apartheid regime's

Table 5-C-1
Population by Racial Category: 1955–1985 (in thousands)

	1955	1960	1965	1970	1975	1980	1985
South Africa							
Black	10900	12250	13800	16060	18136	20863	24901
White	2856	3080	3395	3751	4240	4500	4961
Coloured	1242	1509	1742	2018	2368	2600	2881
Asian	410	477	533	620	727	821	878
Zimbabwe							
Black	2775	3365	4020	4847	6110	7321	
White	167	222	219	230	278	148	100
Coloured	8	10	13	15	31	22	
Asian	5	7	8	9		11	
Zambia							
Black	2750	3120	3560	3999	4800		
White	65	75	70	43	29	22	14
Coloured	2	2	3	4	16		
Asian	5	8	10	11			
Angola							
Black	4290	4604	5135	5535		7366	
White	110	172	180	290	350	35	35
Coloured	30	53	80	110		180	
Asian	—	—	—	—		—	
Mozambique							
Black	6620	7410	8268		10300	12000	
White	72	97	110	150	200	15	15
Coloured	28	31	50		45	50	
Asian	17	19			23	23	
Swaziland							
Black	302		383		483		
White	6	9	8		8		<8
Coloured	2		4		4		
Asian							
Malawi							
Black	3040		4021		5532		
White	6	10	7		6		
Coloured	1		11		3		
Asian	9				6		

Table 5-C-1 (continued)

	1955	1960	1965	1970	1975	1980	1985
Lesotho							
Black	797		967		1212		
White	2		2		2	2	
Coloured	1		1		<1		
Asian							
Botswana							
Black	472		550	620			
White	3		4		6		
Coloured	2		3	11			
Asian			1				
Namibia							
Black	403	429	475	578	687	847	1058
White	55	73	87	91	100	76	78
Coloured	50	59	69	78	90	119	134
Asian	—	—	—	—	—	—	—
TOTAL WHITE (millions)	3.3		4.1		5.2	4.8	5.2
TOTAL POP- ULATION (millions)	37.4		47.6		62.1	70.8	80.9

Sources: See page 324.

"homelands" policy beginning in the 1960's had a similar effect. The gist of the new policy was "the superimposition onto the reserve economy of the apparatus of an Africanized state" (Southall, 1982: 176). These new entities expanded quickly as the authorities delegated to run them had an interest in solidifying their social bases by responding to some of the most pressing demands of their constituencies for services and jobs.

In the Transkei, for example, by the time "independence" was granted, the number of central government bureaucrats working for the Transkei civil service numbered some 10,000; there were an equal number of official employees in more distant spheres of administration (Southall, 1982: 178). Between "independence" in 1976 and 1980, the number of employees of the Transkei central authorities doubled (Standish, 1987: 75).

In the 1980's, the apartheid regime's attempts to find allies resulted in increasing numbers of non-Whites in central government positions (SAIRR, 1988: 326). Similar attempts to build a social base for its "internal settlement" in Namibia had similar results. Numerous administrative functions were shifted from Pretoria to Windhoek. State spending went up rapidly, increasing by 75% between 1979 and 1982, and reaching a level equal to 60% of Namibia's GDP by 1984–85 (*Africa South of the Sahara, 1989:* 751). Money was spent to expand the central and "ethnic" administrations, the number of civil servants rising from 35,000 to 44,000 between 1980 and 1985, "while major increases in the pay of black teachers, nurse and civil servants" were made (*Africa South of the Sahara, 1989:* 751). Education expanded rapidly in the 1980's: between 1980 and 1986 the number of enrolled Black primary and secondary students increased from 181,000 to 345,000 (*Africa South of the Sahara, 1984–85:* 638; *1989:* 758). The whole thing was bankrolled by the South African regime.

Educational expansion was as closely correlated with economic as political factors. In the first place, as with other sectors of the public domain, education had to be financed by government revenues and thus was ultimately linked to the state of the economy. More specifically, the growth in the demand for office workers and professionals during the regional economic boom necessitated a better-educated workforce. Thus, regional enrollment in primary schools increased by 80% prior to 1975 and by 45% afterwards; regional enrollment in secondary schools increased by 300% prior to 1975 and by 150% afterwards (see Table 5-C–2).

South Africa's development had started earlier and proceeded further than other countries in the region and relative educational development reflected this difference (see Table 5-C–2, especially in 1960 before any countries in the region had achieved independence). South Africa was a regional educational, as well as economic, center that attracted students, as well as job hunters. In the

1940's, long before Rhodesia had a university, much less one open to non-Whites, Fort Hare ran advertisements in Southern Rhodesia's *Bantu Mirror* inviting Black applicants. The regional nature of education in southern Africa is nicely captured in an autobiographical work by Lawrence Vambe. He describes attending a teacher training school in the 1930's in Southern Rhodesia, a school that drew in Black students from Northern Rhodesia, Nyasaland, and Bechuanaland (Vambe, 1976: 108). However, if Southern Rhodesia's "pull" corresponded to its role as a regional sub-center (see how this is reflected in educational statistics in 1960 in Table 5-C–2), the fact that the school recruited its Black teachers in South Africa indicates the real center of the region (Vambe, 1976: 108).

Among the non-White race groups across the region, it was the Coloureds and Asians who under settler rule were better educated, faced fewer legal obstacles, and were generally higher up the occupational ladder. Not surprisingly they were the ones to derive greater benefit from the new office and professional job opportunities that White retreat opened up.

The Upper Echelons

Blacks and other non-Whites have not, for the most part, penetrated the upper echelons of the economic hierarchy. In South Africa it appears that during the 1970's and 1980's there was an increase in the percentage of the White workforce in "bourgeois" categories (including owners and executives in small private firms; executives and administrators in all medium-sized and large-scale organizations and firms, including the civil service: see Schneier & Abedian, 1987: 15), while in the other three racial groups there has been either no change or else a decline (Schneier & Abedian, 1987: 17, 24, 29, 34).

Although, by the mid–1980's, the South African state had become a major employer of non-White labor, the top posts were still reserved for Whites. Of the nearly 3,000 people in the top five levels of government, more than 98% of them were White, and the 38 non-Whites (of whom 17 were Blacks) were all in the two lowest rungs of this five-tiered leadership hierarchy (SAIRR, 1988: 326–27).

Table 5-C-2
Primary (P) and Secondary (S) Education in the Region, 1960–85
Number of Students (in thousands) and Percent of School-age Population in School

	1960 P	1960 S	1965 P	1965 S	1970 P	1970 S	1975 P	1975 S	1980 P	1980 S	1985 P	1985 S
Angola												
Number	21	2	218	15	434	44	516[b]	59[b]	1301	186	870	145
Percent[a]			39	5		7						
Botswana												
Number	42	1	66	1	83	4	116	12	172	18	224	32
Percent[a]			65	3	65	7		16	91	19	100	29
Lesotho												
Number	83	3	168	3	183	6	222	16	245	23	314	34
Percent[a]			94	4	87	7	100	13	100	17	100	22
Malawi												
Number			337	8	363	10	642	14	810	18	942	25
Percent[a]		1		2	35	2	56	4	61	4	62	4
Mozambique												
Number	48	2	354	9	497	27	578[b]	36[b]	1387	90	1248	135
Percent[a]			37	3	47	5			75	5	84	7
Namibia[c]			72 [1962]		113 [1968]					228		331
South Africa												
Number for Black			1885	67	2615	122	3379	319	4233	826	4820	2193
White			482[d]	231[d]	[574]	[287]	[602]	[301]	614	354	571	399
Coloured			395	40	474	62	557	95	615	143	600	191
Asian			109	24	123	44	137	49	152	71	145	87

Table 5-C-2 (continued)

	1960 P	1960 S	1965 P	1965 S	1970 P	1970 S	1975 P	1975 S	1980 P	1980 S	1985 P	1985 S
South Africa[e]												
Number			2871	362	3786	515	4675	764	5614	1394	6136	1870
Percent[a]	89	15	90	15	99	18						
Zimbabwe												
Number			676	34	737	50	863	69	1235	74	2215	482
Percent[a]	96	6	100	6	74	7	73	9	88	8	100	43
Swaziland												
Number			50	3	69	8	90	17	112	23	139	30
Percent[a]	58	5	74	8	87	18	99	32	100	39	100	44
Zambia												
Number			410	17	695	53	872	66	1042	96	1348	132
Percent[a]	42	2	53	7	90	13	97	15	98	17	100	19
TOTAL (excludes Namibia)			5151	452	6847	717	8574	1053	11918	1922	13436	2885

Notes:

a. These numbers represent the percentage of the school-age population actually attending school. For example, 5% of the population of secondary school-age children attended school in Angola in 1965.

b. 1972.

c. Namibia figures combine primary and secondary.

d. 1963.

e. All students.

Sources: See page 326.

In spite of the obvious growth in small Black businesses in South Africa, "evidence that Black business is an awakening giant is hardly overwhelming. Black business, according to one estimate, contributes only 1% to the gross domestic product. There is only one Black-owned company on the Johannesburg Stock Exchange. The economy's key sectors, mining, manufacturing and finance, are still white-owned. And the taxi industry might be growing but the major bus companies are still in white hands" (quoted in SAIRR, 1989: 370). Nor does privatization of the state's huge productive assets offer any realistic opportunity for advancement among Black business people.

The situation is better in countries that have achieved Black majority rule, especially regarding Africanization of the state, but the successes have been more in the middle-level than top-level positions (with the exception of purely political posts). A problem particularly acute in Angola and Mozambique was that the exodus of the Whites was so abrupt, and their domination of the occupational hierarchy until that time had reached down so far, that there were not enough trained non-Whites to fill the void thus created, especially in the upper ranks. But even in a country such as Zambia, which won its independence without much disruption and in the middle of the economic boom, and immediately implemented a policy of Africanization, Black advancement to the upper echelons has been quite limited.

A way of visualizing the problem is to see White retreat in the face of Black advance from the 1960's as up (occupationally); even when the retreat was out (geographically), the result at least at the top was often simply a replacement of White settlers by White expatriates (not an insignificant change but meaningless in terms of non-White advance). In Zambia, the government nationalized the copper industry, but even before that a process of Zambianization had been initiated. In spite of nationalization the number of expatriates[6] on the mines stabilized from 1966 until at least 1976 (Daniel, 1979: 107). Between 1965 and 1975, the semi-skilled and most of the skilled/junior supervisory positions were taken over by Zambian Blacks, but some of the supervisory positions, two-thirds of the officials and all the senior officials remained expatriates

(Daniel, 1979: 108).

In Zimbabwe, Africanization of the civil service had proceeded to the point by 1984 that 86% of the permanent Secretaries and 78% of the Under-Secretaries were non-White (Raftapoulos, 1986: 312). Of course, the country's White population (about 3% of the total) was still vastly overrepresented, but the change after independence was dramatic; in 1981 only 43% of the Permanent Secretaries and 47% of the Under-Secretaries were non-White (Raftapoulos, 1986: 312). The private sector of the economy still belongs to the settlers and foreigners, and "in the important managerial and administrative group in the private sector, there has been little meaningful Africanization" (Raftapoulos, 1986, 313). A survey carried out in Zimbabwe in 1986 by the Confederation of Zimbabwean Industry indicated that almost two-thirds of senior management, one-third of middle management, and a quarter of junior management was White. In addition, many Black chairmen and chief executives felt that they had the "glory" but not the "power" of a top post (*Herald,* 8/10/89: 8).

In recent years, the Zimbabwean state has gone against the regional and global current and embarked on an ambitious expansion of the state productive sector, taking advantage in particular of present South African companies' willingness to disinvest (see chapter 2c), but also purchasing important settler companies, e.g., Traeger Industries (actually purchased by ZANU-PF). State ownership of the companies does not guarantee Africanization of executive-level and managament-level positions, nor does it guarantee their continuing importance and profitability as productive enterprises. But, given the sluggishness of the private sector, it seems to be the only immediate way to further Black Zimbabwean business interests. By reducing the economic hold of the settlers and South Africans, more than that of the core powers, this policy has contributed to an economic reorientation that is also noticeable in the country's evolving pattern of trade and the origin and links of its White labor (see above).

If Blacks have had more success Africanizing the states that they have taken over, than the economies that they find themselves in, that is hardly surprising. In other words, they have had more success against settlers than expatriates; more success against settler capital than international capital. Meanwhile, many of them have been able to use the state to establish themselves in the private sector in niches left open by departing Whites. Economic domination by foreigners and to an extent by settlers (in some countries) has made this avenue of accumulation a common one in Africa (Raftapoulos, 1986: 313, who claims that this is a "feature to be encountered in [all] developing countries"). This "use" of the state has taken many forms.

Partly it was simply a matter of previously established private entrepreneurs taking advantage of lifted restrictions, departing White property-owners, and various African advancement policies. In this way a few hundred of the more prosperous Zambian peasant farmers graduated to private tenure commercial farmers after independence (see Momba, 1989: 342). Similarly, the proliferation of small Black enterprises in Zambia after independence seemed to be the result of people of small means drawing on work experience, formal sector wages and new opportunities (Baylies & Szeftel, 1982: 194–95).

However, the biggest beneficiaries of the Zambian economic reforms were not "the existing petty bourgeoisie but rather the incumbents of high office or high salary positions" (Baylies & Szeftel, 1982: 196). There was a close correlation between the emerging Zambian capitalist class and high office in the Party, government, and parastatals. They have been able to use their high salaries, their skills and contacts, and at times corruption to gain them entry into the class of big private owners (Baylies & Szeftel, 1982: 196–97).

In Zimbabwe, the state has offered similar opportunities to those wanting to engage in private accumulation. Trade, a longtime niche for Black capital, and commercial farming, long a settler preserve, both offered possibilities. There has been an addition of 400 Black farmers to the heretofore exclusively White club of commercial farmers. Black trade and transport operations are expanding. Import and currency restrictions has opened the door to illegal market trading in currency and commodities, although not on the scale of operations in Angola and Mozambique, where shortages and currency overvaluations have been much sharper.

The presence of many Black politicians in the middle of all this money-making has been at the origin of numerous student protests and denunciations of corruption. Another way of "using" the state has been for Black cadres to get their training and experience within the civil service or parastatals and then to take positions in the higher-paying private sector; this flow has caused an internal brain drain of skilled personnel and executives (Raftapoulos, 1986: 287).

In prosperous Botswana, the state has also provided the means for private accumulation. At the root of the process of enrichment has been a land grab, which "has centrally involved a capitalist class in the ownership of cattle and in positions in the state, using the state to advance [their own interests]" (Parson, 1981: 238), by spearheading a drive to privatize land tenure.

> The benefits of post-colonial economic growth, based largely upon capital intensive mining, went to an increasingly urbanized elite based in cattle ownership and employment in the upper levels of the public sector (Parson, 1981: 237).

In Mozambique, the avenues to private accumulation were trade, whether in currency or commodities, and, increasingly in the 1980's, in farming. In agriculture, it seems, the prospering private farmers were in most cases successful farmers from the past, not infrequently White (Portuguese), who had accumulated sufficient means to be in a position to benefit from the changed orientation of the 1980's (Hermele, 1988: 53). Their growth, just as that of the private traders, is being intentionally and directly aided by government and international aid organizations alike (Roesch, 1988: 80–81; Hermele, 1988: 54–55).

One observer of the ongoing process in Mozambique has contended that liberalization has meant the enrichment of groups with access to scarce goods, whether merchants, market stall operators, prosperous peasants and private farmers, some state bureaucrats (others are losing their jobs), and migrant laborers who have chosen to use their South African earnings for agricultural accumulation or contraband trade (Roesch, 1988: 88).

The most important means of access to scarce goods is, of course, employment in the international aid organizations. Their hard-currency salaries and hard-to-obtain foreign goods can provide the means for private accumulation. The intended impact (credit or equipment provided to private traders and farmers) as well as the unintended impact of the aid organizations has been highly uneven. In a setting of widespread shortages and rapid privatization, they are probably contributing more than any other factor to social differentiation and private accumulation. They have also been an important internal brain drain on skilled personnel in the government—far more than in Zimbabwe. If the state was a key instrument of private Black capital accumulation in post-independence Africa from the 1960's into the 1980's, privatization, budget cutting, economic collapse, and war in the 1980's has opened the door to other institutions, e.g., international aid organizations, playing that role.

Conclusion

The race/class hierarchy of southern Africa, in spite of the apartheid regime in South Africa, takes a far less exceptional form in the world-system in 1985 than it did in 1965 or 1975. The three-tiered racial hierarchy remains more or less in place, but that socio-economic fact (unlike the legal fact) is not what made southern Africa exceptional. The primary elements in that exceptionalism were, on the hand, the degree to which Blacks were excluded not only from the upper ranks of the occupational ladder, but from the middle ranks as well, and, on the other hand, the degree to which Whites dominated not only the upper, middle and even the better jobs in the lower levels. What has changed is the starkness of this divide. There is today a far greater spread of the majority Black population, especially into middle-level positions, but even into high-level ones; this will of course be more so with the liberation of south Africa. Whites no longer completely monopolize the peaks; outside of South Africa, they have relinquished much of the middle ground; as blue-collar workers, they are becoming insignificant even in South Africa.

The principal White losers have been the settlers. In Mozambique and Angola, and to a lesser extent in Zambia, Malawi, Zimbabwe, and Namibia, settler emigration has paralleled Black advance. That Whites from Europe and North America dominate the local economies and occupy an inordinate number of professional and managerial positions even in the public sector hardly makes southern Africa unique. Nor is it new in the region, although the degree to which the domination has overwhelmed an earlier partial domination by White South Africans and/or local White settlers is new. What remains of the region's old exceptionalism is embodied in the remaining settlers and the entrenched positions of privilege that they occupy—in South Africa of course, but also in Zimbabwe and to a lesser extent elsewhere in the region.

The biggest immediate winners among non-Whites in the wake of the White retreat to date seem to have been members of the mixed race and Indian categories, who were best prepared educationally and materially to do so. Once again, however, the fact that Indians should be disproportionally represented in some middle-level economic positions, especially in commerce but increasingly in office and professional work, is hardly unusual in Africa. Nor is it extraordinary that people considered mixed race (or elsewhere simply light-skinned Blacks) should find themselves, on average, in a position of relative advantage or privilege vis-à-vis more dark-skinned people.

Notes

1. The expression "second colonial occupation" was coined by John Lonsdale and Anthony Low to describe post-war colonial policy in British East Africa (see Freund, 1984: 194), specifically the new growth of colonial government investment in infrastructure and social welfare, the expansion of government agricultural intervention, and the colossal growth of the colonial bureaucracies.

2. Sometimes this shift in status did not mean a change in personnel, but rather, for example, the refusal of a White-settler to take out citizen-

ship in a Black-majority ruled country. Never the less, the result was the same: local and South African ties were cut; core ties were retained or forged.

3. It is presumably because these people come from the Indian subcontinent that they are referred to as "Indians," whether the locale of origin is in fact in present-day India or Pakistan. I use this label, as I use Coloured, because it is the official one.

4. Statistics on Coloured and Asian employment are hard to obtain for Zimbabwe or Zambia, because in neither country are they disaggregated from the general category of non-African. In Angola and Mozambique, moreover, no racial statistics at all were collected after 1960.

5. The importance of this rural change for urban working-class developments was brought to my attention by Mark Beittel.

6. In Zambia the term expatriate was used to cover both settlers, as well as White temporary residents.

Sources for Tables

Table 5-C-1: The basic source used for 1955 was ILO, 1958: 665. Censuses were used when available. Many Black population counts, especially between 1955–70, have been revised upwards when they seemed out of line with present estimates of population totals in the past, as reported in World Bank, 1984, I & II, and World Bank 1989a. The assumption was made that when there was an undercount made, it was the Blacks that were undercounted. The number of non-Blacks have been subtracted from the more recent total population estimates; the remainder are assumed to be Blacks.

South Africa: 1955=ILO, 1958: 665; 1960=Africa South of the Sahara, 1971: 703; 1965=SAIRR, 1965: 110; 1970=SAIRR, 1971: 59; 1975= SAIRR, 1976: 31; 1980=SAIRR, 1982: 43, 45; 1985=SAIRR, 1986: 2.

Namibia: 1955=ILO, 1958: 665; 1960=*Africa South of the Sahara, 1973:* 839 and for Coloureds, Wellington, 1967: 130; 1965=Leistner, 1967: 53 and for Coloureds, *Africa South of the Sahara, 1971:* 762; 1970=*Africa South of the Sahara, 1976–77:* 599; 1975=SAIRR, 1976: 460; 1980= SAIRR, 1982, 608; 1986=*Africa South of the Sahara, 1988:* 731.

Zimbabwe: 1955=for Whites, ILO, 1958: 665; for Asians and Coloureds: Shaul, 1960: 38; Black remainder; 1960=for Whites, Kay, 1971:

59; for Asians and Coloureds, Kay, 1971: 61; Black remainder; 1965=for Blacks and Whites, Leistner, 1967: 53; for Asians and Coloureds, Kay, 1971: 61; 1970=for Whites and Blacks, Kay, 1971: 61; for Asians and Coloureds, Kaplan, 1983: 93; 1975=*Africa South of the Sahara, 1976–77*: 681; 1982=Zimbabwe CSO, 1985b; 1985=for Whites, *Africa South of the Sahara, 1990*: 1108.

Zambia: 1955=for Whites, ILO, 1958: 665; for Asians and Coloureds, Shaul, 1960: 44; Black remainder; 1960=for Whites and Asians, Ohadike, 1974: 396, 399; for Coloureds, Kay, 1967: 40; Black remainder; 1965=for Asians and Coloureds, Kay, 1967: 40; for Whites, Leistner, 1967: 53; Black remainder; 1970=for Whites and Asians, Ohadike, 1974: 396, 399; for Blacks, *Africa South of the Sahara, 1972*: 925; for Coloureds, my subtraction; 1975=for Whites, as well as Asians and Coloureds, *Africa South of the Sahara, 1982–83*: 1180; Black remainder; 1980=for Whites, half the difference between the figures for 1975 and 1985; 1985=for Whites, *Africa South of the Sahara, 1984–85*: 1118.

Angola: 1955=for Whites, Wheeler & Pelissier, 1971: 138; for *mestiços*, ILO, 1958: 665; Black remainder; 1960=Wheeler & Pelissier, 1971: 256; 1965=for Whites, Leistner, 1967: 53; for *mestiços*, estimate based on 1960 and 1970 figures; Black remainder; 1970=for Whites and *mestiços*, Kaplan, 1978: 65, 84; Black remainder; 1975=for Whites, Kaplan, 1978: 65; 1980=for *mestiços*, Kaplan, 1978: 59; White estimate based on Luanda data for 1976, *Africa South of the Sahara, 1979–80*: 130 and Kaplan, 1978: 65; Black remainder; 1985=guestimate.

Mozambique: 1955=White estimate made based on 1950 and 1960 censuses, Henriksen, 1978: 135; *mestiço* and Asian estimates made on the basis of these same two censuses, *Africa South of the Sahara, 1971*: 527 and Clarence-Smith, 1983: 181; Black remainder; 1960=for Whites, *mestiços* and Asians the census (sources listed just above); Black remainder; 1965=for *mestiços* and Asians, Leistner, 1967: 53; White estimate made on basis of 1960 census and 1970 approximation by Henriksen, 1978: 135; Black remainder; 1970=for Whites, Henriksen, 1978: 135; 1975=for Whites, Henriksen, 1978: 135; for Asians, Kaplan, 1984: 95–96; for *mestiços*, an estimate based on information in Kaplan, 1977: xi; Black remainder; 1980=for *mestiços*, Kaplan, 1977: xi; for Whites, Kaplan, 1984: 95; for Asians, Kaplan, 1984: 96; Black remainder; 1985=guestimate.

Swaziland: 1955=for Whites, Coloureds, and Asians, estimate based on

1946 census (ILO, 1958: 665) and mid–1960s census (*Africa South of the Sahara*, 1972: 811); Black remainder; 1960=for Whites, Booth, 1986: 134; 1965=*Africa South of the Sahara*, 1972: 811; 1975=*Africa South of the Sahara*, 1981–82: 1020; 1985=estimate based on information in *Africa South of the Sahara*, 1983–84: 815.

Malawi: 1955=for Whites, ILO, 1958: 665; for Coloureds and Asians, Shaul, 1960: 41 and 46; Black remainder; 1960=for Whites, Nelson, 1975: 84; 1965=*Africa South of the Sahara*, 1973: 521; 1975=*Africa South of the Sahara*, 1982–83: 640.

Lesotho: 1955=for Whites, Coloureds, and Asians, estimate based on 1946 census (ILO, 1958: 665) and 1966 census (*Africa South of the Sahara*, 1972: 426); Black remainder; 1965=*Africa South of the Sahara*, 1972: 426; 1975=*Africa South of the Sahara*, 1977–78: 478; 1980=for Whites, *Africa South of the Sahara*, 1980–81: 551.

Botswana: 1955=for Whites, Coloureds, and Asians, estimate based on 1946 census (ILO, 1958: 665) and 1964 census (*Africa South of the Sahara*, 1972: 170); Black remainder; 1965=for Whites, Coloureds, and Asians, *Africa South of the Sahara*, 1972: 170; Black remainder; 1970=for Whites, Coloureds, and Asians, estimate based on 1971 census (*Africa South of the Sahara*, 1973: 184); Black remainder; 1975=guestimate.

Table 5-C-2: Enrollment percentages: World Bank, 1984, I=Mozambique 1960, 1965 (65); Angola 1960, 1965, 1970 (4); Zimbabwe 1960, 1965 (103); South Africa 1960, 1965 (82); Swaziland 1960, 1965 (86); Malawi 1960–1975 (57); Lesotho 1960, 1965 (54); Botswana 1960, 1965 (12); Zambia 1960, 1965 (102). World Bank, 1989a=Mozambique 1970, 1980, 1985 (412–13); Zimbabwe 1970–1985 (640–41); South Africa 1970 (512–13); Swaziland 1970–1984 (544–45); Malawi 1976, 1980, 1984 (380–81); Lesotho 1970–1984 (360–61); Botswana 1970–1985 (152–53); Zambia 1970–1984 (636–37).

Enrollment totals: UNESCO, 1977=Angola 1965, 1970, 1972 (194, 252); Mozambique 1965, 1970, 1972 (196, 260); Botswana 1965–1975 (194, 252); Zimbabwe 1965–1975 (197, 264); Lesotho 1965–1975 (196, 258); Swaziland 1965–1975 (197, 264); Malawi 1965–1975 (196, 260); Zambia 1965–1975 (198, 268). UNESCO, 1989=Angola 1980, 1985 (3–85, 3–146); Mozambique 1980, 1985 (3–88, 3–155); Botswana 1980, 1985 (3–85, 3–147); Swaziland 1980, 1985 (3–89, 3–159); Lesotho 1980, 1985 (3–89, 3–159); Lesotho 1980, 1985 (3–87, 3–153); Zambia 1980, 1985 (3–

89, 3–161); Malawi 1980, 1985 (3–87, 3–154); Zimbabwe 1980, 1985 (3–89, 3–161).

Enrollment totals, South Africa: 1965=SAIRR, 1966: 236, 251–52; 1970=SAIRR, 1971: 257, 269, 274, 278; 1975=SAIRR, 1976: 329, 341, 348, 352; 1980=SAIRR, 1981: 357, 360, 363–64 and SAIRR, 1982: 473–74; 1985=SAIRR, 1986: 431–32. Enrollment totals, Namibia: 1965= Azevedo, 1980: 196; 1968=*Africa South of the Sahara, 1976–77*: 601; 1975=SAIRR, 1976: 329; 1980=*Africa South of the Sahara, 1982–83*: 745; 1985=*Africa South of the Sahara, 1988*: 734.

Chapter 6

Regional Prospects and Projects: What Futures for Southern Africa?

_____ *Robert Davies and William G. Martin*

A s the 1980's came to a close, a wide variety of events heralded the possibility of a new era across southern Africa. The signals were widespread: Namibia had achieved independence, support for South African destabilization appeared to be declining, negotiations towards the end of war in Angola and Mozambique were emerging, and, most importantly, the apartheid regime had recognized the inevitable and unbanned the ANC, released Nelson Mandela, and initiated a process of transition away from the classic apartheid order.

While these and related changes have been significant and positive from the standpoint of peace and progress in southern Africa, many uncertainties remain. It is not at all certain what precise form a "post-apartheid" order will assume, or what possibilities it offers for the reconstruction of the region of southern Africa. These uncertainties do not derive in any fundamental sense from mere ignorance. They reflect the fact that the shape of southern Africa is contested terrain. There is no single inevitable future for the region. Rather several different self-styled "post-apartheid" projects, with very different implications for both South Africa and southern Africa, are the focus of struggle among divergent social forces in South Africa, in the southern African region, and internationally. The impact of these struggles on the future pattern of relations between South and southern Africa will not be identical.

331

As other contributions to this volume have indicated, any attempt to remold the region will have to confront the historical legacy of the exploitative relationships constructed under colonial and racist minority rule. Incipient changes in these relationships have been underway since the late 1970's. On the one hand, the advances by national liberation movements profoundly changed the political landscape of the region and laid the basis for collaborative projects such as SADCC. On the other hand, the South African regime's response in the form of the destabilization campaign laid waste to much of the productive activity of the region.[1] Furthermore, as a result of changing patterns of capital accumulation in South Africa and destabilization, the period since the mid-1970's saw South Africa withdraw from two important relationships in which it had historically been present as a buyer: migrant labor and transport. At the same time, trade and investment relations across the region also suffered. As indicated in studies above, the combined effect of such changes substantially threatened the cohesion of the region.

Recent events and developments promise not simply to end or reverse these long-term developments, but to lead to a series of struggles over the construction of new regional relationships. To analyze these present struggles and future possibilities one must recognize, furthermore, important shifts in the balance of forces in the region, inside South Africa and at the global level.

At the regional level decisive battles during the late 1980's initially set the stage for the developments of the early 1980's. The most important of these was the setback inflicted on the SADF in battles at Cuito Cuanavale and elsewhere in southern Angola in late 1987 and 1988 (*Southern Africa Dossier,* 1988; Grest, 1989), and the successful diplomatic unmasking of South African destabilization by Mozambique and SADCC. Together such outcomes forced Pretoria to confront the reality of a major shift in the regional military and political balance, and thus the prospect of the end of its ambitions for regional hegemony based upon apartheid.

These changes took place moreover at a time when the apartheid regime became increasingly vulnerable at home. As the threat of regional and international isolation grew, the apartheid regime was confronted by intractable economic stagnation.[2] In addition to all of this, the Pretoria regime had to confront the reality of its continuing failure to produce a viable political solution in the face of growing pressure from the national liberation and mass democratic movements. As the 1980's came to a close, it was apparent that neither "total strategy" nor its successor "Winning Hearts and Minds" (WHAM) could save its position regionally and within South Africa itself.

The impact of such regional and South African factors was such that a significant bloc within the National Party was compelled to begin the search for an alternative response to the shift of forces nationally, regionally, and internationally. This is not the place to analyze in any detail the circumstances or significance of the accession of F.W de Klerk to the leadership first of the governing National Party and later also of the regime (*Southern African Dossier*, 1989c; 1989b; 1990). For present purposes it is sufficient to note that despite his rather improbable track record, de Klerk has emerged as a representative of a bloc of forces (prominent among them domestic monopoly capital) giving priority to reducing South Africa's international isolation and seeking a "political solution" to the crisis of apartheid. The forces grouped around de Klerk appear have recognized that these objectives will not be achieved without credible constitutional negotiations, involving not just existing allies but also acknowledged representatives of the oppressed majority, including the ANC.

The fundamental aim of the de Klerk regime's strategy appears to be to guarantee the continued hegemony both inside South Africa and in the southern African region of a bloc of class forces led by domestic monopoly capital, not necessarily by insisting on an overtly dominant position within government, but by asserting a more subtle and covert "ultimate control" over any process of change. The aim here is nothing less than predetermining the character and capacity of any successor government. While F.W. de Klerk's actions thus indicate a new balance of forces and terrain of struggle, they should not be interpreted as indicating a surrender to the demands to create a non-racial, democratic society in South Africa of the type envisaged by the major organizations of the national liberation alliance and mass democratic movement.

These emergence of these new configurations in South Africa are paralleled, moreover, by trends in the region as a whole. As already suggested above, the structure and shape of the governments that have held power since independence is currently being refashioned in the wake of economic crisis and international economic and political pressure. The alliances forged between national liberation movements during the struggles for independence, and between states of the region since, will surely be reforged as a result of ongoing negotiations and the forceful emergence of multi-party competition in the political arena. We can hardly trace here the sources and patterns of these developments. They indicate however that regional political determinants are even more fluid than the emergence of majority rule alone would suggest.

Assessment of the implications of these developments within southern Africa is further complicated by the significant changes in the broader world-economy and the pattern of major power relations. Ongoing changes in the international division of labor as a consequence of technological revolutions in the spheres of electronics, information technology, and bio-engineering, among others, threaten to marginalize raw material producers of the periphery, including those in southern Africa. The more recent "opening up" of Eastern Europe to Western capital threatens to accelerate this process by diverting potential capital and aid flows to Eastern Europe.

At the level of international political relations, the reduction in major power confrontation following the end of the "cold war" has already had contradictory effects on southern Africa. On the one hand, the fact that "regional conflicts" are no longer seen in "East-West" terms facilitated the negotiations leading to the independence of Namibia and undercut the capacity of the Pretoria regime to present itself as the champion of the West. On the other hand, the evident desire on the part of the socialist countries to extricate themselves from "regional conflicts" has removed a significant counterweight to the exercise of Western power in the region. Meanwhile the emergence of new blocs in the North—as the European Community, Japan, and North America struggle amongst themselves—serves to diminish further Africa's status and power in the international arena, even that of southern Africa.

The collapse of Communist regimes in many of the countries of Eastern Europe has, furthermore, fueled an already evident trend on the part of Western powers and capital to promote more aggressively "free market" prescriptions. Operating on a terrain already prepared to a large extent by fifteen years of economic crisis, country after country in the periphery has found itself cajoled into accepting a now standard "structural adjustment" package involving privatization, a shrinking of the state's capacity to act in the economy, and increasing openness to world financial, capital, and commodity markets. The only solution held out to the countries of the periphery by international capital is to compete more aggressively among themselves for a larger slice of a static if not declining pie.

All of these factors have to be taken into account in looking at possible future scenarios for southern Africa. The complexities of the developments leading to the present change of course, and the fact that so many issues remain contested terrain, only serves to further underline the point that there is no single inevitable future for the region. Different possible combinations of these factors suggest, however, at least the following possible scenarios in the short and medium run.

Scenario One: Regional Restabilization

The central features of this scenario would be constituted by a return to the major tendencies of the 1945–1975 period: It implies a resuscitation of the region as it was formed and operated during most of the last three decades. Here a reliance upon South African-centered relationships would apply, from enhanced dependence upon financial, investment, and commodity markets to transport and communication services. Such a scenario would constitute, in the words of U.S. policy advisors, a "restabilization" of regional relationships.

"Restabilization" would imply a withdrawal from certain existing forms of destabilization, including the termination of support for agents of low-intensity warfare—now within as well as beyond South Africa's borders. At the regional level "restabilization" its emergence would probably create fairly favorable conditions for victims of destabilization to secure a negotiated end to at least organized forms of armed banditry. At the economic level, however, it would tend to reinforce tendencies to reproduce the existing patterns of economic domination and subordination in the region and undercut projects aiming at a transformation of these relations.

Under such conditions a considerable reopening of regional trade, transport, and labor flows would be possible, marking a return in part to the situation of the 1950's and 1960's. Reflecting changes in the region over the last two decades, one would not however expect an exact replication of previous patterns. On the one hand, reduced officially-contracted labor flows to South Africa since the mid–1970's would be unlikely to be reversed significantly, while on the other hand the revival across the region by South African multinational capital could be expected.

A key question in such a context would be the extent to which a new "post-apartheid" government in South Africa aspired to assert itself as a "regional power". Hanlon (1987) has argued that this could indeed make more difference for the region than the general political complexion of a "post-apartheid" government. If a "post-apartheid" South African government did harbor aspirations in this direction it could be expected to act to defend existing patterns of economic and politico-military dominance and could even seek to forge new relations of domination/subordination.

Even if it did not have overt aspirations of domination, a government operating in a political system which severely constrained any possibilities for socio-economic transformation would be unlikely to actively embrace a project of cooperating with other regional states to transform existing patterns of regional relations. As indicated above, the existing pattern of regional relations was forged not by "market forces" alone. State intervention, in the form of tariff policy, trade agreements, and regulations of other kinds, not to mention the application of various forms of coercion to force peasant producers to make themselves available as migrant workers, all played a crucial role in this regard (Martin, 1986). A passive approach by the government of a "post-apartheid" South Africa or one which focused on immediate economic gain at the expense of restructuring, would tend to favor the reproduction of the existing relations of domination/subordination. Local and foreign capitalist classes, as well as leading Western governments, would under these conditions be able to pursue their own agenda. In such a case much of the effort of South Africa in promoting economic interaction with the region might well be devoted to seeking to maximize the potential trade benefits which would presumably follow the ending of South Africa's "pariah" status with the transition to a "post-apartheid" order.

A possible variant within the broad restabilization scenario could occur if the present SADCC member states maintained a perspective of continuing the struggle for a changed regional economic order on their own in organizations which continued to exclude or minimize participation by South Africa. In such a case we could expect to see a continuation of some divide between the SADCC states and South Africa, and the promotion of projects embracing or privileging only the present ten SADCC members. Of course, some possibilities might exist for such an organization to enter into negotiations with South Africa over aspects of regional economic relations. Indeed in a context of probable declining donor interest in promoting projects aimed at delinking from South Africa in a "post-apartheid" period, bodies like SADCC might find themselves focusing their attention on their potential role as a representative of the rest of the region in negotiations with South Africa. SADCC would lose its current anti-apartheid identification. Donors currently supporting projects sponsored by the organization as part of their own attempt to project an anti-apartheid image may thus lose interest after apartheid is officially declared to have ended. Indeed, a significant portion of aid funding currently channeled to the region could well be diverted to support projects in South Africa. It is also possible under such circumstances that the coherence of regional organizations like SADCC would be adversely affected. As Hanlon has argued:

The ending of apartheid will withdraw the common enemy which has been part of the glue that binds SADCC. This will strengthen the hand of those bourgeois (and petty bourgeois and bureaucratic bourgeois) forces which have continued to support trade with, and dependence on, South Africa, despite destabilisation. They would rather have luxury goods from South Africa than support the development of local industry making mass consumer goods and intermediate goods. They will argue that the ending of apartheid removes the need for SADCC, and that it is sensible to allow South African economic dominance (1987: 441).

Such an outcome would of course weaken the position of regional states, leaving them to negotiate on a bilateral basis or accept the terms and conditions laid down by South Africa, capital, or foreign powers.

Scenario Two: Regional Breakup and Peripheralization

A second possible scenario could emerge if trends leading to the unhindered operation by core economic and political powers were to dominate. Here core-peripheral relationships as known throughout the world-economy would emerge to demarcate southern Africa as simply another peripheral zone of the world-economy, an area fully open to the polarizing effects of the operation of the international division of labor. Under this scenario, direct bilateral relationships between overseas core areas and the *individual* states and primary producers of the region would be absolutely privileged at the expense of relations within the region.

Falling levels of industrialization, GNP per capita, terms of trade, exchange rates, etc., indicate pregnant possibilities of such a path in the current conjuncture. Even South Africa, it must be noted, has not escaped such phenomena during the present global crisis. The prospects for the emergence of such a scenario would be considerably enhanced by the collapse of current initiatives to reduce the level of military conflict in the region and bring about a peaceful, negotiated transfer of power in South Africa. If the processes currently underway were to be aborted, and if there were not sufficient countervailing pressure to render the costs prohibitive, a rapid return to the cycle of escalating regional aggression and conflict of the pre-1988 period would be possible.

We would expect however new variations and dangers as we move into the 1990's. As long as the apartheid state and its security and military apparatuses remain intact, a revival of destabilization could witness the selection of major new targets, with Zimbabwe and an independent Namibia coming in for more attention. For Mozambique, such a scenario would mean not only the probability of a continuation of the bandit war in its own territory, but also the possibility that Zimbabwe found itself so tied down by destabilization at home that it was obliged to reduce its commitment to Mozambique. Drawing upon the weakening of regional parties and states, a widening of the stimulation of ethnic-based banditry and conflict might well occur even without central direction from the highest levels of the National Party. Members of the military and security branches of the apartheid state are quite capable of pursuing this path externally and internally. As many have noted, the grounds for a self-sustaining South African Renamo-type organization is already under construction. As in the 1980's, any such development would hinder the prospects of any form of economic cooperation in the region.

Continuing warfare would not be the only basis on which such a scenario could emerge, however. The basic thrust of structural adjustment programs is towards removing controls on trade, weakening the role of the state in the economy, and orienting the economies of African countries towards their relationships with the core countries of the North. Hence, the operation of international institutions such as the World Bank, the IMF, and GATT tends to propel this scenario forward. By coalescing the interests of regional states, SADCC has operated to check such tendencies. Even in the case of SADCC it is evident that overseas powers have seen the organization as an avenue to reopen access to regional markets closed by war and restrictive state policies.

Scenario 3: Towards a Different Kind of Region?

A third scenario, which would be the most favorable for the peoples of the region, would entail a fundamental restructuring of the southern African region. In the short term, such a development would be enhanced if the momentum of the developments which brought about the shift to the present conjuncture were to continue to have a restraining influence on militaristic aggression, while not capitulating to the economic and diplomatic strategies of Pretoria or allowing apartheid to break out of its international isolation. Such a development would amount to keeping the forces of South Africa's military, police, and security branches at bay while simultaneously keeping apartheid weak. For the independent states of southern Africa as a whole, such a scenario would open up a certain space for national reconstruction and, especially, the advance of SADCC projects currently blocked by destabilization. It would also enable the liberation forces inside South Africa to derive maximum benefit from the new regional conjuncture, while minimizing the openings created for the Pretoria regime to overcome its current economic, political, and military vulnerabilities. As the events of 1990–91 reveal, the South African regime will indeed strive to seize any advantages, based on its proclamations that apartheid has ended, to reopen closed doors regionally and internationally.

To the extent that a favorable balance of forces is retained and political strategies of isolation of apartheid remain intact they permit the contemplation of a more favorable,long-term scenario: the emergence of a "post-apartheid" project which recognized the need for political change to be accompanied by socio-economic transformation matched to a radical restructuring of the pattern of relations between South Africa and southern Africa, and of the region as a whole with the world-economy. The emergence in South Africa of a non-racial democratic order, which did not unduly constrain the capacity of a new non-racial government to lead a process of socio-economic transformation, would create at least the possibility for the emergence of a cooperative project between a democratic South Africa and the other states of the region aimed at transforming the pattern of regional economic relations.

Any such project would have to be elaborated through a process of negotiation and many of the details would depend on factors— such as the precise correlation of forces on the regional plane as well as within each major regional state—which remain to be determined, and thus are by definition currently unknown. In very broad terms, however, such a project could be expected to involve agreement by South Africa to provide resources to support a program aimed at transforming the conditions of underdevelopment elsewhere in the region which give rise to dependent and subordinate regional relations. It could also, since any such transformation is likely to be a relatively protracted process, be expected to include South Africa granting reasonable, if not favorable, terms to the rest of the region in as yet untransformed relations which cannot immediately be broken. In return for this, South Africa could expect to receive preference over extra-regional suppliers, for example, in negotiated trade agreements with the other countries of the region.

Regional institutions in a post-apartheid era

Such initiatives would take place within well-established regional agreements. As a number of analysts have stressed, this raises the question of the degree to which existing alliances and institutions such as SADCC (or the PTA) can be utilized to promote or provide models for such a cooperative project.

Let us take here one example, that of trading relationships among the SADCC states. SADCC has not yet been successful in accelerating the low level of intra-SADCC trade.[3] Indeed if projected towards the future, it is possible that the effects of SADCC interventions could be to reorient trade away from South Africa only to relink more firmly with overseas areas.

In part such outcomes reflect the structures of SADCC. Despite early intentions to develop mechanisms to enhance intra-SADCC trade, no movement on this front has taken place. Indeed a 1986 study commissioned by SADCC concluded that SADCC should eschew any attempt to move beyond simple bilateral trade agreements. Emphasis, it was argued, should be placed instead upon efforts to revive and then link production capabilities of SADCC member states. In support of this conclusion, the study properly noted that SADCC members currently lack an industrial base which could quickly serve to replace imports from both South Africa and overseas core areas (SADCC, 1986b: xvi).

This conclusion followed SADCC's professed principle that the building of national productive capacities must be given first priority, which would later permit higher levels of commodity trade across the boundaries of the SADCC states. While any increased level of intra-SADCC trade will certainly depend upon the growth of an industrial base, it bears repeating that unregulated trade with areas of core industrial production will severely restrict the ability to nurture new sites of industrial production in southern Africa. Examining the origins of South Africa's industrialization process indicates this all too well (Martin, 1990a,b). Furthermore, it should not go unnoticed that SADCC has proven far less successful in eliciting funding for industrial projects than for projects related to transport and communications (see chapter 2d), or that underneath inattention to trade relations at a high level lies considerable tension between SADCC states and capital, which finds expression in a variety of trade restrictions in the defense of national production and markets. None of these phenomena augur well for enhanced levels of inter-industry and inter-territorial linkages and regional self-reliance. Indeed an acceleration of the trends of the last fifteen years, namely an exchange of lessened dependence on South Africa for an increased dependence on overseas core areas, would seem a more likely outcome. Even if one assumes South Africa will become a full SADCC member, it would not necessarily follow, for example, that one would find a reversal of accelerated uneven development and peripheralization. An important lesson here is that any further regional development will require confronting the hard reality of dominant class interests and their determinant role in state policies.

These latter forces are imbricated within and without the region, reflecting the chains of uneven development across and within this distinctive region of the world-economy. If one recognizes this, it no longer becomes possible to assume that benefits directly follow from simply the creation of a larger regional market or controlling only extra-regional forces. Here the example of the alternative regional framework provided by the Preferential Trade Area for Eastern and Southern African States (PTA) is instructive. The PTA aims to move towards a free trade area, a common customs union, a common market, and eventually an economic community. Seven SADCC states are members of the PTA (Lesotho, Malawi, Mozambique, Swaziland, Tanzania, Zambia, and Zimbabwe).

The PTA has been structured to a greater extent than SADCC as a mechanism to check multinational capital's penetration of a regional community (Tandon, 1985; Amin et al., 1987). Central here is Article 15 of the PTA treaty, which was intended to deny the benefits of lowered customs duties to foreign producers located within the PTA community. In relation to trade, the PTA forms an alternative to SADCC structures, and one that is much more clearly designed to counter movements toward either the peripheralization or restabilization scenarios. Even the PTA, however, has found it difficult to retain the principles set forth in Article 15, as much of the industrial production of stronger states such as Kenya and Zimbabwe would be precluded due to the foreign multinational ownership. The result has been the dilution of Article 15.

The strength of the forces arrayed against Article 15 serves to indicate the great difficulties entailed in any program designed to restrict the forces of uneven development. The central problem here is not, as the PTA example indicates, the ability to design institutions and alliances of regionalism. As the examples above indicate, attempts to promote wider economic exchanges, based on notions of comparative advantage, immediately confront accumulation processes that entail instead the generation of uneven patterns of accumulation. It is precisely these pressures that have torn apart regional bodies elsewhere in Africa. The end result, of course, has been the buttressing of core-periphery relationships between African states and core states overseas—hardly a beneficial development.

For southern Africa these forces are considerably complicated by already existing patterns of center-hinterland relationships constructed under the longer history of colonial and settler rule.

While the very limitations of SADCC's structure and its program have thus contained overt conflict between governing classes and national capital(s), it has of necessity failed to confront patterns of uneven development within the SADCC region. In large part these conditions reflect the very real constraints imposed by the current global depression, the existence of the apartheid regime, and the related power of overseas capital, states, and financial institutions. Under such constraints, SADCC has aimed at, and succeeded in, preventing more overt support for the apartheid regime and its attacks upon the frontline states. As Mandaza (1988: 127) has argued, "SADCC's value is essentially in the political arena."

With the end of apartheid the conditions for even SADCC's successes, a common front against the apartheid state, may thus disappear. More to the point however is the broader lesson: If more rapid and equitable regional development is to take place, it will require a stronger antisystemic thrust, one capable of restructuring relations within and among regional states, as well as between the region and the rest of the world-economy. The question thus emerges: what are the prospects and possibilities for such developments under post-apartheid conditions, with or without a transition to global economic expansion?

The viability of competing projects
One proceeds here only tentatively, for the political and economic configuration of a post-apartheid southern Africa remains to be determined by the course of the struggle against apartheid.

Of all the forces in a post-apartheid conjuncture, the actions and interests of the deeply entrenched and committed forces of capital may be most readily approached. Here we would make one assertion only: it would be folly to presume that an unfettered hand for local or international capital would advance the region economically. Given the changing conditions of global investment and production, there is little likelihood that multinational capital would naturally flow towards advanced industrial investments in the region and generate regional prosperity, even if one could imagine the existence of the excessively pro-capitalist and authoritarian states necessary for such a scenario.

Unfettered operations by South African monopoly capital deserve an even harsher judgment. South African capital has historically failed to develop innovative production processes upon which the oligopolistic profits of core-like capitals and high-wage jobs have rested. Any long-term comparison to capital located in core or other semiperipheral areas, much less the present activities of capital flight being carried out by such firms as Anglo American and Rembrandt, indicate this all too well. Indeed if South African capital is monopoly capital, it bears this name by living off sheltered markets, guaranteed labor supplies, and a oppressive state. As even the conservative voice of *The Economist* (7/1/1989: 59) has noted: "The Anglo empire has grown to its present size not because it is more efficient than its worldwide competitors, but because it is a master at running cartels and dominating markets."

If one seeks greater wealth, equality, democracy, and social justice across the region, one is thus forced to turn towards a consideration of a political restructuring of the region in the post-apartheid period. As noted above, such a project would be likely to take place, moreover, in a conjuncture marked by substantive transitions in interstate relations and the global division of labor. This rules out in our view several common expectations.

One common model seems to us most improbable: A purely state-led, autarkic delinking on the basis of an alliance with socialist states located outside of the region. Taking a long view, technical programs calling for the assertion of state fiscal and monetary planning can at best alleviate inequality for a short period; they are unlikely over the long run to address either the enduring inequalities forged during the apartheid decades or the deep structural crisis in the region's position in the global division of labor.

Such a conjuncture rules out as well any continuation of at least two other short-term scenarios actively promoted during the late 1970's and 1980's. For quite obvious reasons, the neo-regional reconstruction of an arena dominated by South African and international capital, and buttressed by a repressive apartheid state (CONSAS), would only occur if the national liberation movement had been comprehensively defeated. For similar reasons, the emergence of an exclusively SADCC region is unlikely in a post-apartheid era.

In a post-apartheid situation the pursuit of neo-colonial solutions—the basic trend in the restabilization scenario—would remain of course a strong force. Restaining some degree of regional cohesion would benefit South African, Zimbabwean, and foreign capital. Equally possible, however, is a breakup of the region. Clearly the colonial and settler forces which have served to forge the region historically—the apartheid state in alliance with core powers, South African capital, and multinational capital—will be either absent from the scene or stripped of their politically dominant positions. Under these conditions the forces of regional cohesion could lessen, particularly if world economic trends follow the trajectories sketched above.

At a very minimal level, it is clear however that a shared interest will exist on the part of regional states to retain a SADCC-type body with South Africa as a member. As SADCC illustrates, bargaining with overseas core states and capital is far more effective given a united regional front. Reconstruction of basic economic infrastructures across the region will also entail regional agreements and cooperation. Finally, the much-heralded possibilities of a larger regional market, as opposed to fragmented, nationally-bounded, markets, will attract much attention, due to the economies of scale and its consequent attractiveness for capital investors.

Such formal institutional imperatives and advantages do not, however, assure a movement beyond a low level of regional association. Assertions by nationally-based capitals that the "national interest" is their interest, and the defensive reactions of state elites guarding their own prerogatives and privileges, all work towards preventing initiatives that would restructure regional patterns of accumulation and unequal exchange. As has been apparent throughout the continent, international institutions, agreements, and capital will also continuously operate to divide any strong regional initiative. If regional planning does not challenge bilateral relationships with core areas, or agrees to the creation of a larger economic space within which multinationals (both international and South African) may operate, it may be tolerated or even welcomed by outside forces and large capital. Even the World Bank's latest program for Africa (1989b) permits the encouragement of regional associations. The limits of such actions are however clearly demarcated by insisting that their objective should be to facilitate more open trade and investment across state boundaries, including those that separate the North from the South. More substantive initiatives vis-à-vis the polarizing forces of the world-economy would no doubt be seriously challenged. One need not even raise the possibility of direct political, much less military, retaliation. One needs only to refer to the expected hostility of commercial and international lenders, the withdrawal or denial of direct investment, and the limiting of access to foreign export markets among other economic actions.

In the face of such centrifugal forces, the path of least resistance for post-apartheid states and their leadership might well be to forsake any regional initiatives that challenge deeply the dominant forces on both the regional and global plane. For these states it may offer the illusion of stability; for the petit bourgeoisie it would promise a growing share in the surplus which can be generated under existing forms of accumulation. Over the long term however, such a trajectory—for all the reasons outlined above—promises only an impoverishment of the region and its peoples.

In one respect the post-apartheid future follows the past: even to sustain, much less advance, regional relationships will require a considerable degree of political intervention. Little benefit will flow directly from the actions of dominant classes and economic forces.

This leaves quite open however what policies, for example, a democratic South African government might actually pursue. Similarly, it remains uncertain how other regional post-colonial/settler states, and the petit bourgeoisie that leads them, will evolve. As historically demonstrated, these forces can take quite divergent paths and actions. This leads to a critical, final variable: the degree to which popular, antisystemic forces can engage and propel vacillating state elites and a wavering petit bourgeoisie to pursue the long-term radical transformation of accumulation on a regional basis. If we are to avoid triumphalism, it is imperative to recognize that capital accumulation is inherently uneven and inherently a process marked by ceaseless struggle, and that capturing state power alone does not end either of these fundamental features of the capitalist world-economy. If this is so, any challenge to exploitation within the region, any attempt to construct a more equitable and substantively democratic future, would necessarily be an antisystemic struggle. In relation to overseas core areas this is well-recognized by the movements and peoples across the region. In relation to the intra-regional inequalities and unequal exchange this is often a subject avoided. The result is that weakness and disunity within the region opens the door for the polarizing forces of the world-economy to penetrate and dominate.

To state this is to neither recommend nor expect a cataclysmic attempt, upon the transition to a majority-ruled region, to shatter once and for all capital and capitalism. It is to recognize that a cooperative restructuring of the region will confront serious, cross-national opposition from within the region itself and vacillating forces within post-colonial/settler states. Presume for example that a larger regional association does emerge, for the reasons adumbrated above. Presume furthermore that a considerable commitment is made by the political leadership of key regional states—particularly South Africa, Zimbabwe, Mozambique, Namibia, and Angola. Assume furthermore that such a regional body pays close attention not simply to relationships of unequal exchange with overseas core areas, but also to intra-national and intra-regional sources of uneven development.

From such a configuration collaborative regional policies could emerge to stimulate more equitable regional investment, not only by state structures, but by local and particularly multinational capital. As any study of the NICs would indicate, such interventionist regulation of the domains of national and multinational capital has been essential to advancing more technologically advanced industrial production processes, research and development centers, and expanded employment. For southern Africa such an aggressive process is in our view practical only on a regional scale. It would entail, moreover, not an "autarkic delinking," but a long process of struggle on several fronts: with international capital and core states, with local and particularly South African capital (after a degree of expected de-monopolization), and against intra-regional inequalities due to the historic structuring of the region and the unequal distribution of the benefits of expanded accumulation across the region. Such a regionalization of more advanced industrial production would be more feasible, it should be noted, if a phase of expansion in the world-economy should occur.

To initiate and sustain such a path would require considerable political struggles to obtain the commitment to a regional, socialist agenda. This is not a process that can be carried out only at the level of state decision-making and interstate agreements within the region. Here one should not overlook the long-term strength of antisystemic forces across the region and indeed within the world-economy as a whole—a statement that may seem strange in this period of the celebration of the victories of liberal democracy and capitalism. For it takes but a moment's reflection to realize that the states and peoples of southern Africa recognize well the impoverishment that submission to the dictates of the IMF and the World Bank entail. Similarly, it is already apparent that the forced opening of the market has and will continue to rebound upon the majority of rural producers across the region. In this area as others, the process is one of class formation and class struggle: even as private farming expands, poverty and protest in rural and urban areas is becoming a stark phenomenon. In the formal sector these trends are even more sharply etched: the ever-sharpening edge of anti-capitalist sentiment and organization within South Africa's Mass Democratic Movement, and particularly the trade-union structures, is equally apparent.

Such developments are, moreover, evident across non-core zones of the world-economy, and especially in areas that have achieved, like southern Africa, a degree of industrial development. Dominated by industrial capital, but unable to sustain the high wage structures that underpin the quiescence of labor in core zones, we are witnessing an explosion of resistance to the dictates of the free enterprise system as it has been constructed in the post-1945 era. Equally apparent is the inability of formal parliamentary democracy to contain such forces. In this respect, the movement against apartheid shares key characteristics with other movements in and out of power. To a growing degree it is quite evident that capitalism has brought not prosperity and progress, but institutionalized poverty and underdevelopment. Southern Africa, by virtue of the historical depth of these forces across state boundaries, is a particularly striking locus of such struggles. As we approach the post-apartheid era, the question nevertheless remains: to what degree will the struggle transcend the boundaries of national and capitalist frameworks, and begin an antisystemic restructuring of the region? It is upon this terrain, and not simply the formulation of institutional frameworks, that the future of southern Africa will depend.

Key Issues in the Evolution of a Cooperative Project

Even if such struggles were to sustain a cooperative, transformative project for the region, it remains to be considered how such an agenda might concretely proceed. Here we consider as examples just four key areas—migrant labor, transport, trade, and investment. Any sustained study of this issue would of course have to confront a number of other areas of economic interaction including energy, water resources and food security, to mention just a few.

Migrant labor
The supply of migrant labor to South Africa will without doubt be one of the first and most difficult issues which will have to be confronted in any attempt to forge a new mutually beneficial economic order in Southern Africa. Any new approach to the problem of migrant labor will have to be based on a recognition of the fact that supplier states cannot, without considerable economic and social disruption, immediately withdraw from the migrant labor system. Their capacity to extricate themselves from what is ultimately an exploitative relationship depends on the generation of employment in supplier states and on the transformation of former labor reserve areas in particular. They need stability of earnings and employment from migrant labor during an interim period in which a program of economic regeneration of former labor reserve areas is implemented. This suggests that any new cooperative

approach to this question during a post-apartheid era would have to involve both short term measures and a long term program of reconstruction.

In the short term, new agreements on the supply of migrant labor would have to be negotiated on terms which tilt the balance of advantage towards supplier states. In particular these would have to be based on at least the following principles:

First, "foreign" migrant workers would have to be recognized as having contributed to the creation of wealth in the South African mining industry and therefore as having rights identical to those of South African workers with regard to wages, security of employment, opportunities for promotion, benefits, trade-union membership, etc. In short, such workers should not be penalized in any way for their "foreignness." Indeed certain categories, e.g., long-serving "foreign migrants," ought to be recognized as having the same rights to settle in the industrial areas of South Africa as will presumably be accorded to South African workers (including those from "independent" Bantustans) in a liberated South Africa.

Secondly, the policy of switching on and off the flow from any country at the whim of mining capital will have to be ended. The importance to supplier states of stability of employment and earnings from this source during at least an interim period will have to be recognized. Firm binding agreements on numbers which take account of these interests will have to be negotiated with supplier states.

Thirdly, benefit and compensation payments will have to be re-examined. There are a number of problems in the current administration of these, ranging from bureaucratic delays to the fact that there are a number of ways in which the health services of supplier states bear "hidden" costs of diseases contracted on South African mines.

At the same time the role of migrant labor recruitment in underdeveloping labor reserve areas will have to be recognized as placing an obligation on the South African mining industry to contribute to the regeneration of the productive capacity of those areas. Projects aiming at employment creation and involving significant investments in rehabilitation of labor reserve areas will have to be supported in supplier states. The aim will be eventually to create conditions which will enable the migrant labor system to be phased out in such a way that it benefits both the working class of South Africa (enlarged by an element of former migrants from regional states, who opt to remain in South Africa as permanent mine workers), who will benefit from the establishment of a stabilized labor system in the mining industry, and the populations of former labor reserve areas, who will benefit from the emergence of employment and income generating activities in their home areas. It is inconceivable that this could be achieved without some transfer of investible surplus from South Africa to supplier states. There are a number of ways in which part of the sizable surplus created in the South African mining industry by "foreign" migrant workers could be transferred for such purposes. The mechanisms would depend partly on the ownership patterns existing in a post-apartheid period, but at the very least some kind of levy on mining companies would have to be considered to establish a fund to channel resources to supplier states.

In addition to these considerations regarding officially-sanctioned or recorded migrant flows, one must also consider the possibility of increasing levels of informal migration. Given the ravages of destabilization, considerable flows to South Africa are already taking place. The use of non-South African labor by employers seeking the cheapest and most intimidated workforce is quite apparent,[4] and follows world-wide patterns in this respect. The elimination of the military border fences and patrols associated with apartheid might stimulate these flows further. With unemployment in South Africa now estimated to be running at over 40%,[5] a new government will face a great temptation to adopt a nationalistic response. This would however only exacerbate relationships with surrounding states, and prove no more successful in stemming "illegal" migration that the deployment of such measures by considerably more powerful core states. Such a conclusion only serves to emphasize the recommendations above, namely the need for a strong commitment to region-wide economic reconstruction based on a cooperative regional project.

Transport

There are two dimensions to be considered in examining regional transport relations. The first and most important is the question of the use by regional states of South African ports and railways versus those of SADCC member states—Mozambique, Angola, and Tanzania. The second dimension is the use by South African importers and exporters of facilities in other regional states, particularly Mozambique.

Both these dimensions have been greatly affected by the apartheid regime's destabilization policies. As an integral part of its post-1978 regional strategy, apartheid South Africa sought to secure an effective monopoly over regional traffic. This was partly motivated by economic considerations (the need to recoup the significant investments made in the containerization of South African ports since the 1970's), but there was also a critical strategic dimension (related to gaining additional leverage over regional states). In pursuit of these objectives, the apartheid regime has actively intervened to divert traffic which might otherwise have passed through the ports and railways of independent regional states to South Africa. Alternative routes, particularly through Mozambique and Angola, have been repeatedly sabotaged by South African-backed armed bandits and "special contract rates," offering discounts of up to 50% of the normal rate to clients from regional states, have been offered in an attempt to wean traffic away from alternative routes. South Africa has also been able to take advantage of the fact that regional freight handling services have been largely controlled by South Africa-linked firms, which have made investments in South African ports and, therefore, have themselves a direct interest in ensuring that a substantial proportion of regional traffic passes through South Africa (Stephens, 1986; MacKintosh 1986).

Any approach to a restructuring of regional transport relations in a post-apartheid era will have to proceed from at least the following principles.

- The existing concentration of regional traffic through the ports of South Africa will have to be recognized as the product, in part, of South African economic and military aggression. Restructuring will therefore have to aim at the very least at rectifying and compensating for existing distortions and imbalances.

- SADCC countries must be recognized as the "natural hinterland" for Mozambican ports and transport services.
- SADCC must be able to recoup and benefit from the investments made in transport facilities—investments which were made as part of the struggle against apartheid.

This would mean that the successor to Transnet (ex SATS) would have to abandon its current policy of attempting to "poach" cargo away from Mozambican ports. Rating policy must be structured in such a way that the shorter distances to Mozambican ports from a number of SADCC countries is reflected in real savings for customers using these ports as against South African alternatives. Technical support should be provided to the transport authorities of the region by South Africa on reasonable terms and the successor to Safmarine should ensure that regional ports are covered by adequate shipping services.

At the same time negotiations will have to be initiated to arrive at a mutually acceptable agreement over the use of Maputo harbor by South African concerns. Negotiations of this nature should ideally specify fixed tonnages and should provide for a reasonable mix of high rated as well as bulk cargo.

Trade

It is repeatedly been indicated throughout this volume that the pattern of trade between South Africa and the rest of the southern African region is characterized by a large deficit in South Africa's favor. It was argued earlier that a greater opening of regional markets to South African manufactured exports, at the expense of those currently coming from outside of the region, could be the major way in which a democratic, non-racial South Africa benefits materially from cooperating in the construction of a new regional order. We also noted earlier that the 1980's had seen a decline in South African trade with Africa, although the future development

of the South African economy depended on being able to make the
transition to a situation in which its manufacturing sector became
a more significant earner of foreign exchange. This trajectory may
be undergoing some reversal given the South African political
conjuncture; Foreign Minister Pik Botha recently stated that South
African trade with Africa doubled over the course of 1989/90
(*Cape Times*, 2/6/1991). If South Africa's evident interest in
increasing its sales to the region were to be accommodated through
an indiscriminate opening of regional markets, however, several
adverse consequences could follow. Existing imbalances could be
enhanced, industrial development in the region impeded, and trade
between existing SADCC member states swamped. Any opening up
of the region to South African commodities which seeks to avoid
such consequences would have to proceed on the basis of negotiating specific trade agreements, which take account of the need to
protect local industries and allow trade between existing SADCC
member states to increase.

What would need to be identified more clearly is the kind of
trade with South Africa that could be encouraged at the expense of
trade with countries outside of the region, and not at the expense
of intra-regional trade or of the development of local industries in
SADCC countries. Here only a few very general observations will
be made. First, the markets of the existing SACU members are
already saturated, indeed oversaturated, with South African goods.
It is undoubtedly in these countries' interests to diversify their
sources of supply and in this connection the SACU agreement
would merit serious review not only in respect of its revenue
sharing provisions, but also in respect of the provisions which keep
member states dependent on South African suppliers. The main
prospects for a post-apartheid South Africa to substitute suppliers
from outside the region would thus appear to lie not with those
countries with which trade relations are already well established,
but with those countries of the region with which South Africa
currently has more limited trade relations: Angola and Tanzania,
most notabley, and, in some areas, Mozambique, Zambia, Zimbabwe, and Malawi as well.

Another element which would need to be identified is the types of commodities this trade should embrace. Table 6-1 (taken from Muirhead, 1988: 102, Table 5) shows the current mix of South African exports to Africa by commodity group.

Table 6-1
South African Exports to Africa

Commodity Group	Exports to Africa (thousands of Rand)		Exports to Africa as % of total exports per group	
	1984	1985	1984	1985
1. Animal & products	31,118	43,490	13.0	13.2
2. Vegetable products	64,960	81,366	13.5	11.4
3. Animal & vegetable fats & oils	14,930	17,210	37.6	22.6
4. Prepared foodstuffs	43,941	79,784	7.9	9.9
5. Mineral products	40,551	283,444	1.3	5.7
6. Chemicals & chemical products	223,788	263,674	33.2	28.2
7. Plastics, resins & rubber products	43,333	69,675	45.2	45.8
8. Hides, skins & leather	1,523	1,520	0.8	0.6
9. Wood & wood products	8,090	13,977	13.4	13.1
10. Pulp, paper & products	25,162	50,838	6.4	7.7
11. Textiles	36,253	51,591	4.8	5.0
12. Footwear & millinery	3,020	5,644	40.8	44.7
13. Non-metallic mineral products	19,264	27,193	44.2	33.2
14. Gems & jewelry	871	1,429	-	0.1
15. Base metals & products	147,466	267,320	6.1	6.4
16. Machinery	126,197	190,007	40.8	35.9
17. Vehicles & transport equipment	41,170	96,125	24.3	26.6
18. Optical & other instruments	8,995	13,675	21.8	18.2
19. Miscellaneous manufactured articles	3,237	6,194	17.8	14.0
20. Works of art	164	32	0.9	0.1
21. Unclassified	6,814	13,710	—	0.1
TOTAL	891,213	1,577,900	3.5	4.3

It should be noted that this table is distorted by the fact that South African trade statistics refer to the trade of the whole of the SACU group with the rest of the continent. It thus obscures the trade that takes place between South Africa and the other SACU members and distorts the picture of South African exports to the continent by including those of other SACU members in the totals. Another problem is that the data do not distinguish between manufactured goods and raw materials.

Nevertheless, it can be assumed from the description that categories 4, 6, 7, 10–12, and 14–19 are largely manufactured goods, while the others are raw materials. Also, it would seem likely that categories 16–18 are the major groupings which include manufactured means of production. On the basis of these assumptions, the table shows that those categories likely to be dominated by manufactures accounted for 79 % of SACU exports to Africa in 1984 and 70% in 1985. Of these, about 25% in 1984 and 27% in 1985, representing about 20 and 19% of total exports respectively, were made up of goods in the categories most likely to include manufactured means of production. This compares with the position for South African exports as a whole in which manufactured goods constituted only about 10% of total visible exports in 1985 (*Southern Africa Dossier*, 1989a). Moreover, while sales to Africa constitute a relatively small proportion of the total exports in many of the categories, in some the proportion is quite significant. The table shows that in 1985 sales to Africa constituted 28.2% of total exports of chemical products, 45.8% of total exports of plastic products, 44.7% of total exports of footwear and millinery, 35.9% of exports of machinery and 26.6% of exports of vehicles and transport equipment. Many of these percentages would undoubtedly have been higher had they been for South African trade with all African countries, including other SACU members. Among the major items in some of these categories are mining and agricultural machinery, fertilizers, pharmaceuticals, building materials, tractors, and foodstuffs (Muirhead, 1988: 93).

Such data points ineluctably to one conclusion: any future for South Africa as an exporter of means of production lies in Africa. And, indeed, this is an area in which other countries on the continent and region could benefit from trade with a post-apartheid South Africa in view of the potentially greater accessibility of South African technology in a number of spheres and the advantages of a greater proximity to suppliers. Trade in consumer goods raises more questions and would in principle need to be considered carefully in the light of local industrial development plans and the need not to swamp trade between existing SADCC member states. Nevertheless, here too there would be some prospects for increased trade with a post-apartheid South Africa.

Any restructuring of trade relations in a post-apartheid era would, however, also have to address the problem of the large deficit in South Africa's favor. This could perhaps, in part, be offset by a greater use by South Africa of services from the region—transport, electricity, water. However, the possibilities of South Africa increasing its visible imports from the region would also need to be examined. As indicated earlier, these currently consist largely of agricultural products and raw materials, plus a small quantity of manufactured goods from Zimbabwe. Among the major individual items currently imported by South Africa from the SADCC region are maize from Zimbabwe (depending on the crop in South Africa), cattle, sheep and goats from Botswana, Namibia, and Swaziland, tobacco and tea from Zimbabwe and Malawi, cashew nuts and seafood from Mozambique, and clothing, textiles, furniture, and electrical goods from Zimbabwe (Muirhead, 1988: 92–93). Any restructuring of trade patterns in a post-apartheid era would have to investigate ways in which South Africa could increase its purchases not only of agricultural commodities and raw materials from the SADCC countries, but also of certain manufactured goods—to enlarge the market and create new possibilities for industrial development in these countries. Needless to say, the type of manipulations which have excluded SACU manufactured goods from the South African market despite the formal provisions of the agreement would have to end.

Investment

The prospects of a cooperative regulation of capital flows poses much greater difficulties than migrant labor, transport, or even trade relationships. The reason is quite straightforward: a shortage of investment funds marks the region as a whole. Indeed many states suffer simultaneous capital outflows and debilitating debt repayments.

This situation places considerable bargaining power in the hands of those who command capital resources, including multinational capital, international financial institutions, and South African monopoly capital. These forces have mounted a strong campaign, moreover, designed to demonstrate that economic growth and prosperity require the absence of any local political regulation of the economy and thus the unfettered operation of private enterprise and free markets. The result has been the imposition of structural adjustment programs and the concomitant weakening of integrity and capacities of the states of central and southern Africa.

Any attempt to facilitate region-wide cooperation in the investment field thus immediately confronts strong obstacles. In the absence of any such endeavor, however, one must expect the replication in southern Africa of the now common pattern across the Third World: the ability of investors and lenders to dictate a competitive struggle between states to offer the most "favorable" and exploitative conditions for foreign investors. This applies even—indeed perhaps most importantly—to regionally-based capital. South African capital is already seeking, on the basis of the openings of the late 1980's and early 1990's, to seize existing opportunities created by a decade of economic crisis and war across the landscape of southern Africa.

These efforts are as yet highly selective: they are overwhelmingly located in the fields of commerce, finance, tourism, and the recuperation of existing assets demobilized by war or foreign exchange shortages. In this sense they indicate an attempt to place under South African capital's control past centers of profit. As such they may indeed generate employment in the short-run. Yet over the long run they are likely only to exacerbate regional inequalities as South African capital seeks from the region only the high profits and low wages derived from non-industrial pursuits—and this based upon the stimulation of competitive bidding between the states of the region for investment funds.

A collaborative approach to transnational investors and lenders offers the possibility of countering such competitive struggles. And under post-apartheid conditions of peace and stability, the resources and infrastructure of the region would offer considerable attractions for productive investment.

In this respect one often encounters the recommendation that a common investment code be formulated among member states of a regional association. This in itself is a formidable objective. Such a code may not, however, be even the most important mechanism, particularly if the aim is to reverse the uneven pattern of capital investment in the region. For even a common investment code would allow the potential for the continuation of the pattern by which industrial investment centers in South Africa, while the rest of the region is left with investment in only raw material or extractive production. Such an outcome could only exacerbate the uneven distribution and gains of investment, and thus heighten tensions among regional states. As pointed out in the discussion of post-apartheid trade relationships, collaboration on a regional basis could target a quite different objective: the stimulation of greater inter-industry linkages and markets than could ever be obtained by any single state alone.

In this regard the regulation of investment necessarily overlaps with the manner by which trade agreements could facilitate a greater level of industrial development across the region, for comparative principles could apply to regional agreements on the distribution of complementary investment strategies and opportunities. South Africa's greater attraction for investment capital in the production of the means of production for the region, for example, might be offset by the targeting of much higher levels of investment in consumer goods industries elsewhere for marketing across the region, including South Africa.

Whatever conditions might be formulated to attract investment, such an approach would clearly require mechanisms and agreements to balance investment opportunities across enhanced regional markets. The priority here would be not simply investment capital, but the investment of funds designed to build linked productive sectors across the region—versus say simply separate sites of production to serve overseas demand. Such an approach could only proceed through cooperative political efforts. These would of necessity apply to overseas multinational capital, South African monopoly capital, and South African parastatals. These last two factors indicate the critical character of the process to a post-apartheid era, for we can hardly foretell here the future shape and form of South Africa-based capital and financial markets. To the extent the South African state's resources remain intact, and are not privatized or severely constrained during the transition period, the conditions for cooperative investment arrangements would be substantively enhanced. They might engage in, but not be limited to, the development of infrastructure, energy, and water resources, and consumer goods industries in exchange for the opportunities that a larger regional market would bring to South African producers.

Such efforts would build upon existing linkages and projects, including many subject to state-to-state agreements. The cooperative rehabilitation of the Cahora Bassa project would, for example, be made possible under conditions of peace in the region and majority rule in South Africa. Cahora Bassa could supply 8% of South Africa's electricity supply and, for the first time, lead to significant returns to Mozambique.[6]

Conclusions

The present chapter has examined a number of alternative scenarios for the southern African region in the short-term and the medium-term. We have devoted much effort to trying to identify certain principles which might constitute the basis of a new cooperative relationship between a democratic, non-racial government of a liberated South Africa and its neighbors in the region; and to examining some of the implications of a cooperative project aimed at transforming the existing pattern of regional relations in the spheres of migrant labor, transport, trade, and investment. While this is only one of several possible scenarios in the near future, it is the only one that would place the interests of the peoples of the region above those of existing regional or extra-regional exploiting classes.

A transformation of this type will not come about automatically or through the operation of market forces. The existing patterns of domination and subordination in the region were created by state intervention. State intervention will be necessary to change these patterns. Since these existing relations have been of benefit not only to the apartheid regime narrowly defined but also to a number of powerful capitalist interests, any change is likely to be resisted. The possibilities of achieving such goals in cooperation with a democratic, non-racial South Africa will thus depend to a large extent on the establishment in South Africa of an order in which a degree of democratic control can be asserted over the economy.

What we have tried to argue is that an alternative to the continued subordination of the SADCC member states does exist, that we can struggle for, and that it could lead to a far more prosperous future for the people of southern Africa than would result from the agenda set by capital and the leading Western states. If a genuinely democratic, non-racial order were to emerge in South Africa, a possibility of cooperating with South Africa in the achievement of these goals would be opened up. If, on the other hand, a self styled "post-apartheid" settlement in South Africa places severe restrictions on the prospects of achieving any significant changes in the socio-economic pillars of apartheid, permitting only a change in the complexion of members of the government, SADCC member states will be compelled either to abandon their goals of economic liberation or to continue to struggle for them in a adversarial relationship with South Africa—but under circumstances where apartheid is declared no longer to exist and the level of external aid and potential cohesion of regional organizations is possibly lessened.

Identifying the third of the above discussed scenarios as the optimum alternative from the standpoint of peace, independence, and development in southern Africa is relatively straightforward. It is, however, an alternative calling for active and carefully formulated strategies both in the region and on the part of the international solidarity movement. Such strategies would need to be rooted in an approach which recognizes that success depends on not allowing either Pretoria or its currently estranged western allies to seize the initiative. While some dialogue between regional states and Pretoria is inevitable, this should not be permitted to build legitimacy for the apartheid regime in international fora. Commitment to the SADCC perspective of transforming the historical ties of dependence of regional states on South Africa should be re-enforced and there should be no acceptance of the proposition that the "natural entry" into the region for Western governments and investors is through South Africa. Above all, the central lesson of the transition to the emerging new conjuncture needs to be learnt: Pretoria's rulers changed their course not because they wanted to, but because objective pressures and constraints were such that they had no other realistic option. As we move into the 1990's it will be no less important to apply this lesson. This requires both preventing the Pretoria regime from overcoming the vulnerabilities which led to the present change of course, and preventing it from unilaterally seizing the benefits of changed regional and international conditions. On the contrary all-round pressure needs to be maintained as part of an overall campaign to end apartheid itself and lay a real basis for a cooperative new order in southern Africa. Equally, popular forces within the present SADCC member states will have to have the capacity to assert themselves and their interests in a common project in which the interests of the peoples of the region predominate, and lay a real basis for lasting peace and progress throughout southern Africa.

Notes

1. 1.3 million Angolans and Mozambicans died as a direct or indirect result of Pretoria's destabilization between 1980 and 1988. The losses suffered by the economies of the SADCC members states over the same period stand at $ 60.5 billion (UNICEF, 1989: 10, 24–25, 35–38).

2. Most immediately, at the end of the 1980's, there was the recognition of the effects of financial and other sanctions. By the third quarter of 1988 monetary authorities were forced, for example, to abort a "mini-boom" in order to build reserves to meet punishing debt repayment schedules in the years ahead. For a development of these points see

Southern Africa Dossier (1989c).

3. As the SADCC (1986b: xv-xvi) notes, "In brief, recorded intra SADCC trade represents 4–5% of the SADCC countries' total imports and exports. . . . which is comparable with other groups of developing countries in Africa, but lower than similar groups in Asia and Latin America."

4. The most scandalous reports surround the buying and selling of persons fleeing the war in Mozambique. See the *Weekly Mail,* "This Man is a Slave," November 16–22, 1990, 1, and "Slave Trade Traced to Reef," Nov. 30-Dec. 6 1990, 1.

5. See *The Star,* September 21 1990 (quoting South African Chamber of Business), and *The Star,* September 25, 1990 (quoting the Development Bank of South Africa).

6. See *Mozambiquefile,* No. 151, February 1989, and *Business Day* (October 10, 1989), for a report of a speech by Eskom's Chief Executive on prospects for re-establishing power supplies "within the next few years."

Conclusion

Sergio Vieira and Immanuel Wallerstein

T he southern African region is at a turning-point. All its colonial territories have become independent, and South Africa may soon at last become a democratic state. Apartheid has fulfilled its historic task within the framework of the colonial system as a mechanism of accumulation. It is retiring from the scene like a dinosaur. Its exit and final agony are violent on a scale equal to the size of the place it occupied in people's lives. Its burdensome legacy is located not only in the memories of suffering but also in the desire of the elites to conserve somehow their dominant role, both within South Africa and within the region. This continuing effort to retain privilege is in conflict with the necessary search for spiritual reconciliation that is a precondition for the launching of a new dynamic of cooperation and progress. We note as a symbol that, as of this writing in May 1991, Nelson Mandela does not yet have the right to vote.

We are leaving a historical period in which White domination seemed unassailable and the political, military, economic, and financial machines of the allied regimes of Pretoria, Salisbury, and Lisbon, tied as they were into Western networks of complicity, seemed all-powerful.

This is now undone. The Portuguese colonial war had as its outcome the collapse of the Marcello Caetano regime, following which it unleashed the dialectic process that led to the end of the rebellion of the Rhodesian Whites and of South Africa's domina-

367

tion of Namibia, and finally to the abandonment of apartheid as a philosophy and method of governance. But the transition has been difficult. In the process, Angola and Mozambique saw the beneficent project for society's social and economic emancipation launched by the liberation movements more or less wrecked. In terms of human lives and material destruction, there is no doubt that the main cost of ending White and colonial power in the subcontinent was paid by Angola and Mozambique.

We may now hope that a new South Africa will become a factor for regional progress and reconstruction. Such an optimistic scenario should not be completely ruled out, but hopes should be tempered by the following considerations:

- The major South African corporations, while maintaining productive bases in the country, have already transformed themselves into transnationals, as stateless as international capital. The "gold dollar," just like the petrodollar, tends to be recycled in the North and only go South secondarily.
- The privatization policy under way during apartheid's final phase could be a significant limitation on the capacity of a democratic South Africa to carry out an affirmative policy establishing ethnic and social balances. It could also come to restrict the availability of state resources for promoting and economic policy of regional cooperation.
- Given the need of South Africa to absorb internal unemployment, the flow of migrants to South Africa might shrink to the disappearing-point.
- The system of domination awoke antagonisms whose solution is profoundly destabilizing, both for the previously privileged sector and for the sector that is now motivated by its expectations, apart from having repercussions on economic efficiency and even on the efficiency of state management and administration. At the heart of this problem are questions of the ownership and control of land, and the ethnic makeup of the administration and the defence and security forces.
- The violence racial domination inculcates in society brings in

its train prejudice and frustration. Fear and the desire for revenge will have an important influence on the shape of social relations and work against efforts to create a climate of trust.

SADCC member countries have to this point expressed no strong views on the question of admitting a post-apartheid South Africa to the group. When SADCC was founded, the primary concern was to establish a balanced relationship between Pretoria's economy and the rest of the region. The world economic stagnation, the devastation of Angola and Mozambique, and the effects of destabilization on the various national economies have all contributed to the removal of this objective from the agenda. The search for stable relations in the region and the legitimate anxiety to achieve a minimum prosperity beyond immediate survival levels perhaps make the alternative of South African integration a realistic and sensible one.

The framework of unequal relations in the region will not disappear overnight, but it could be made at least less suffocating than the previous one. Freed from the condition of apartheid and violence, southern Africa might assert itself as a politically and socially stable zone. This factor, allied to the human and natural resources that continue to be worthy of attention, may mean that the region may remain a zone of interest to the North, particularly with respect to commercial and investment flows.

Once again, the determining factors shaping the North-South relationship must be considered. Structural trends suggest a certain lessening of interest in raw materials, either because some of them are becoming obsolete in view of technological advances, or because the final product uses smaller quantities of them, or because new sources (in particular the seabed) are being developed.

Current events, in their turn, suggest that the core countries may concentrate their immediate attention on the stabilization of eastern Europe and the Middle East, and that this will be done at the detriment of aid and investment finance for the rest of the periphery.

Nonetheless, it is likely that both North Africa and southern

Africa will continue to attract the attention of investors and government agencies, North Africa as an extension of southern Europe and southern Africa because of its combination of human and material resources, and in particular its land, water, hydro-electric, and fossil energy. It is from these diverse strands that the future regional web is being woven.

The political base is in general evolving towards multi-party regimes. Mozambique, South Africa, Namibia, Zambia, Angola, and Botswana have already taken this position. It can be anticipated that Zimbabwe will move in the same direction, and that Malawi, Swaziland, and Lesotho will be impelled towards it, voluntarily or involuntarily. The imperatives of the times and the winds of change will increasingly tend to remove the generation of the liberation odyssey from the political scene, and consign its members to history.

The fragility of the elites, the profound chasms between them and the vast masses of the underprivileged, and the various ethnic splits may however cause instability, and this in its turn may create a demand for tough, dictatorial, and maybe fascistic regimes. The experience of the national liberation process, the presence of some powerful social organizations such as trade unions, traditions of political struggle forged in opposition to monolithic power system might on the other hand provide enough of a positive counter-weight to negative trends and stimulate a climate of debate that would be favorable to the consolidation of a civil and genuinely pluralist society.

Closer regional economic relations, provided they are more egalitarian than in the past, would be favorable to the advance of civil society. The economic relationship would need to take certain vectors into account as essential starting-points:

- The management of water and land, plant disease control, the struggle against animal and vegetable endemic diseases and for agriculture and livestock production and food self-sufficiency, require a community effort.
- Maximizing the use of existing assets and water energy necessarily implies coordinating interests and resources of

the various partners.

· The efficiency of land and sea communications, especially to satisfy the needs of the hinterland, requires the intervention of states and of regional economic agents.

· Absorbing the currently prevalent unemployment, clear evidence of which can be seen in the streams of migrant workers, demands a balanced effort to industrialize on the basis of regional resources.

By the end of the century, the SADCC market plus South Africa will comprise over 100 million people. The question is how to transform this human mass into efficient producers and consumers with a greater effective demand, in order to fend off the specter of economic stagnation and to introduce internal socio-economic growth as a structural factor. Rivalry will persist, especially in the initial stage, between South Africa's interests and the desire of the less competitive Zimbabwean economy to expand. Fears of domination, often well founded, will prevail in the relationship between strong and weak partners. However, in essence the current juncture offers few or no alternative routes than a leap into a cooperative future.

Forty years ago, in Cape Town, the thoroughly conservative voice of Her Gracious Majesty's Prime Minister proclaimed the winds of change. Some social forces tried to hold back the storm, others to ride it. Out of this historic convulsion, we are faced today with decisions that could bring general disillusion or could end up by taking everyone forward towards new horizons. The question is very much open: How fast the wind?

Robert Davies is the Co-director of the Centre for Southern African Studies at the University of the Western Cape in South Africa. He spent 11 years of his exile in Mozambique, where he worked as a researcher at the Centro de Estudos Africanos. From 1982 until 1990 he was head of its Southern Africa Department. He is the author or co-author of a number of books, monographs, and journal articles on the South African state, and is currently contributing to research on the reconstruction of the regional economy.

Helmut Dora was a teacher and researcher in 1989–90 in the Centro de Estudos Africanos. He is a specialist in transport, and possesses great experience in education and research in this area. He has returned to Germany where he is continuing his teaching and research activity.

Alexandrino José has been a researcher at the Centro de Estudos Africanos since 1981. He was trained in history at the Eduardo Mondlane University. Since 1988 he has been the secretary of the scientific council and coordinator of the editorial council of the CEA. His areas of interest are the history of the liberation struggle, migrant labor, and the agrarian question.

William G. Martin is a Senior Research Associate at the Fernand Braudel Center, State University of New York at Binghamton; Associate Professor in the Department of Sociology at the University of Illinois, Urbana-Champaign; and Research Co-Chair of the Association of Concerned Africa

Scholars (U.S.). Among his publications are *Semiperipheral States in the World-Economy* and a wide-ranging set of articles on southern Africa and the world-economy.

Kavazuea Ngaruka, born in Namibia, received his B.A. and Diploma in Adult Education at the University of Sierra Leone (West Africa). He is currently completing his dissertation on the historical patterns of transnational investment in southern Africa in the Sociology Department, State University of New York at Binghamton.

Thomas Ohlson has been a member of the Centro de Estudos Africanos since 1987, and set up the Strategic Studies Department at the Centre. His field of interest is research into problems concerned with peace, development and security. He developed the collection *Dossier-Africa Austral* (Southern Africa Dossiers), edited by the Centro de Estudos Africanos. His main area of research is the study of conflicts and confrontation in southern Africa.

Emmett Schaefer is a doctoral candidate in Sociology at the State University of New York at Binghamton. He has been a participant in the joint Fernand Braudel Center-African Studies Center (CEA), Eduardo Mondlane University project on southern Africa since its inception. His dissertation concerns labor flows and the historical emergence of a southern African regional economy.

Gulamu Taju holds a master's degree from the Maputo Higher Pedagogical Institute. He is a research assistant in the Strategic Studies Department of the Centro de Estudos Africanos. His areas of interest are the history of the nationalist movements, and low intensity conflicts.

Darryl C. Thomas is an Assistant Professor in the Departments of Political Science and Afro-American and African Studies and a Research Associate in the Fernand Braudel Center at the State University of New York at Binghamton. He has written a number of articles dealing with the international relations of the Third World and comparative Black political thought. He is currently completing a book entitled *The Theory and Practice of Third World Solidarity,* forthcoming in 1992.

Sergio Vieira has been Director of the Centro de Estudos Africanos since 1987. He has the advantage of being both a leading protagonist in the liberation struggle in Mozambique and in the southern African region, and an academic in the social sciences. He is the author or co-author of several articles published in various magazines. His current fields of interest are the relations between the North and southern Africa, and strategic studies in the southern African region.

Ismael Valigy has been collaborating with the Centro de Estudos Africanos since 1987. He is a student at the Maputo International Relations Institute (ISRI). He is an ACP/EEC consultant at the Institute for the Development of Local Industry (IDIL) in Maputo. His field of interest is the cooperation between the EEC and the ACP countries in the field of industrial investment.

Immanuel Wallerstein is Distinguished Professor of Sociology and Director of the Fernand Braudel Center at the State University of New York at Binghamton. He is the author of *The Modern World-System* (3 vol.), *Historical Capitalism,* and a number of books on Africa, most recently *Africa and the Modern World.* He was President of the African Studies Association (1972–73) and co-chair of the Association of Concerned Africa Scholars (1977–91).

Gottfried Wellmer worked in Maputo with the Centro de Estudos Africanos from 1983–87 and again in 1989–90, and he remains a collaborator with the CEA. He is a trade-union activist, and a student of southern African affairs, who has followed systematically the liberation war in Namibia, Malawi's behavior in the region, and social and economic developments in South Africa. He currently works in Germany.

Ana Piedade Xavier has been a research assistant since 1988 in the Southern Africa Department of the Centro de Estudos Africanos. She is preparing a thesis for her master's degree to be defended this year at the Higher Pedagogical Institute.

Books and Articles

Amin, Samir, Derrick Chitala, & Ibbo Mandaza, eds. (1987). _SADCC: Prospects for Disengagement and Development in Southern Africa._ London: Zed Press.

Angola Comite, et al. (1975). _White Migration to Southern Africa._ Geneva: Centre Europe-Tiers Monde.

Arrighi, Giovanni (1970). "Labour Supplies in Historical Perspective: A Study of the Proletarianization of the African Peasantry in Rhodesia," _Journal of Development Studies,_ VI, No. 3, April, 197–234.

Arrighi, Giovanni (1977). "Foreign Investment Patterns," in P. C. W. Gutkind & P. Waterman, eds., _African Social Studies: A Radical Reader._ New York: Monthly Review Press, 168–75.

Arrighi, Giovanni (1982). "A Crisis of Hegemony," in S. Amin, G. Arrighi, A. G. Frank, & I. Wallerstein, _Dynamics of Global Crisis._ New York: Monthly Review Press, 55–108.

Arrighi, Giovanni (forthcoming). _The Long Twentieth Century: A Social Theory of Our Times._ London: Verso.

Arrighi, Giovanni & John Saul (1973). "Socialism and Economic Development in Tropical Africa," in _Essays on the Political Economy of Africa._ New York: Monthly Review Press, 11–43.

Arrighi, Giovanni & Jessica Drangel (1986). "The Stratification of the World-Economy: An Exploration of the Semiperipheral Zone," _Review,_ X, 1, Summer, 9–74.

Arrighi, Giovanni & Beverly Silver (1984). "Labor Movements and Capital Migration" in C. Bergquist, ed., *Labor in the Capitalist World-Economy*. Beverly Hills, CA: Sage, 183–216.

Arrighi, Giovanni, Patricio Korzeniewicz, & William G. Martin (1985). "Core-Periphery Relations in the Current and Previous World-Economic Crises." Harare: manuscript.

Asian Development Bank (1986), (1987), (1989). *Key Indicators of Developing Country Members of ADB*. Makati, Philippines: Economic Office, ADB.

Azevedo, Mario (1980). "A Century of Colonial Education in Mozambique," in A. Mugomba & M. Nyaggah, eds., *Independence Without Freedom*. Santa Barbara: ABC-Clio, 191–213.

Bariagaber, Hadgu (1988). "Contemporary Refugee Movements in East and Central Africa and Their Economic Implications," in Union Internationale pour l'Etude Scientifique de la Population (UIESP), et al. *Congrès Africain de Population*. Dakar: UIESP. II, 4.1.17–4.1.39.

Baylies, Carolyn & Morris Szeftel (1982). "The Rise of a Zambian Capitalist Class in the 1970s," *Journal of Southern African Studies*, VIII, No. 2, April, 187–213.

Beira Corridor Authority (1990). *Mozambique: Report No. 14*. Beira, December 31.

Beittel, Mark (1988). "The Radical Interpretation of South African History: A Critical Assessment." Manuscript.

Bender, Gerald J. (1978). *Angola under the Portuguese: The Myth and the Reality*. London: Heinemann.

Bethlehem, Ronald W. (1988). *Economics in a Revolutionary Society. Sanctions and the Transformation of South Africa*. Craighall: A.D. Dunker.

Bhagavan, M. R. (1986). *Angola's Political Economy 1975–1985*. Research Report No. 75. Uppsala: SIAS.

Birmingham, David (1988). "Angola Revisited," *Journal of Southern African Studies*, XV, No. 1, October, 1–14.

Bond, Patrick (1990). "Zimbabwe: Money Makes Money but Investment Drops," *Bulletin of the Association of Concerned Africa Scholars*, No. 30, Spring, 11–14.

Bonnevie, Henriette (1987). *Migration and Malformation—Case Studies from Zimbabwe*. Project Papers A.87.1. Copenhagen: Centre for Development Research.

Booth, Alan R. (1986). "Capitalism and the Competition for Swazi Labour 1945–60," *Journal of Southern African Studies*, XIII, No. 1, October, 125–50.

Bragança, Aquino de (1981). "Savimbi: Itinerário de uma Contra-Revolução," *Estudos Moçambicanos*, No. 2, 87–104.

Bragança, Aquino de (1981). "Independência sem descolonização: A transferência de poder em Moçambique, 1974–75. Notas sobre os seus antecedentes," *Estudos Moçambicanos*, Nos. 5/6, 7–28.

Bragança, Aquino de & Jacques Delpelchin (1989). "Da idealização da FRELIMO á compreensão da História de Moçambique," *Estudos Moçambicanos*, Nos. 5/6, 29–52. ("From the Idealization of Frelimo to the Understanding of Mozambique Recent History," *Review*, XI, 1, Winter 1988, 95–117.)

Brand, Coenraad (1981). "The Anatomy of an Unequal Society," in C. Stoneman, ed., *Zimbabwe's Inheritance*. London: Macmillan, 36–57.

Braudel, Fernand (1984). *The Perspective of the World*. Vol. III of *Civilization & Capitalism, 15th–18th Century*. New York: Harper & Row.

Browne, Robert (1987). "South Africa: Assistance and Aid Programs. " *Third World Quarterly*, IX, No. 2, April, 493–514.

Brzoska, Michael (1986). "South Africa: Evading the Embargo," in M. Brzoska & T. Ohlson, eds., *Arms Production in the Third World*. London: Taylor & Francis, 193–214.

Brzoska, Michael & Thomas Ohlson, eds. (1986). *Arms Production in the Third World*. London: Taylor & Francis.

Bush, Ray, Lionel Cliffe, & Valerey Jansen (1986). "The Crisis in the Reproduction of Labour in Southern Africa," in P. Lawrence, ed., *World Recession and the Food Crisis in Africa*. London: James Currey, 283–99.

Caetano, Marcello (1974). *Depoimentos*. São Paulo: Distribuidora Record.

Castells, Manuel & L. D. Tyson (1989). "High Technology and the Changing International Division of Production: Implications for the U.S. Economy," in R. B. Purcell, ed., *The Newly Industrializing Countries in the World Economy: Challenges for U.S. Policy*. Boulder, CO: Lynne Rienner, 13–50.

Catholic Institute for International Relations (CIIR) (1983). *Mining: Mines and Independence.* A Future for Namibia Series, No. 3. London: CIIR.

Centro de Estudos Africanos (1987). "The South African Mining Industry and Mozambican Migrant Labor in the 1980s." International Migration for Employment Working Paper, No.29. Geneva: ILO, January.

Chamber of Mines of South Africa (1967), (1984). *Annual Report.* Johannesburg: Chamber of Mines.

Chidzero, Bernard (1988). *Budget Speech.* Harare.

Clarence-Smith, W.G. (1983). "Capital Accumulation and Class Formation in Angola," in D. Birmingham & P. M. Martin, eds., *History of Central Africa.* London: Longman, II, 163–99.

Clarke, Duncan (1976). "Structural Trends Affecting Conditions of Labour for African Workers in Rhodesia," *The Rhodesian Journal of Economics,* X, No. 2, June, 59–84.

Clarke, Duncan (1977a). *Agricultural and Plantation Workers in Rhodesia.* Mambo Occasional Papers—Socio-Economic Series, No. 6. Gwelo: Mambo Press.

Clarke, Duncan (1977b). *Distribution of Income and Wealth in Rhodesia.* Mambo Occasional Papers—Socio-Economic Series, No. 7. Gwelo: Mambo Press.

Clarke, Duncan (1980). *Foreign Companies and International Investment in Zimbabwe.* Gwelo: Mambo Press.

Cliffe, Lionel (1979). "Labour Migration and Peasant Differentiation: Zambian Experience," in B. Turok, ed., *Development in Zambia: A Reader.* London: Zed Press, 149–69.

Cock, Jacklyn et al. (1981). "Women and Changing Relations of Control," in *South African Review, 1.* Johannesburg: Ravan Press, 278–99.

Coquery-Vidrovitch, Catherine (1988). *Africa: Endurance and Change South of the Sahara.* Berkeley: Univ. of California Press.

Daniel, Philip (1979). *Africanisation, Nationalisation and Inequality: Mining Labour and the Copperbelt in Zambian Development.* Cambridge: Cambridge Univ. Press.

Davies, D. Hywel (1987). "Population Growth, Distribution and Density Changes, and Urbanization in Zimbabwe," *African Urban Quarterly,* II, No. 1, February, 13–23.

Davies, Robert (1981). "África austral pela libertação económica," *Estudos Moçambicanos,* No. 2, 79–86.

Davies, Robert (1986). "O 'Apartheid' em fúria," *Estudos Moçambicanos,* Nos. 5/6, 173–183.

Davies, Robert (1988). "Notes Towards a Country Report of South Africa." Unpublished paper prepared for CEA-FBC project.

Davies, Robert (1990). "Algumas implicações dos possíveis cenários pos apartheid para a região da África austral," *Estudos Moçambicanos,* No. 8, 143–192.

Davies, Robert et al. (1984). *The Struggle for South Africa: A Reference Guide to Movements, Organisations and Institutions.* 2 vols. London: Zed Press.

Dilolwa, C. Riehe (1978). *Contribução á Historia Econômica de Angola.* Luanda.

Economist Intelligence Unit (EIU) (1977). *Rhodesia Report 1977.* London: EIU.

Economist Intelligence Unit (EIU) (1989a). *Mozambique Report 1988–89.* London: EIU.

Economist Intelligence Unit (EIU) (1989b). *Zambia Report 1988–89.* London: EIU.

Economist Intelligence Unit (EIU) (1989c). *Gold to 1992.* London: EIU, March.

Economist Intelligence Unit (EIU) (1989d). *Country Profile: Angola.* London: EIU.

Economist Intelligence Unit (EIU) (1990). *Angola, São Tomé and Principe Report 1989–90.* London: EIU.

Egero, Bertil (1987). *Mozambique, A Dream Undone: The Political Economy of Democracy, 1975–84.* Uppsala: Nordiska Afrikainstituet.

The Employment Bureau of Africa (TEBA) (various). *Annual Report.* Johannesburg: Chamber of Mines.

First, Ruth (1983). *Black Gold: The Mozambican Miner, Proletarian and Peasant.* New York: St. Martin's Press.

Frelimo (1989). *Relatório do Comité Central ao V Congresso.* Maputo: CEGRAF.

Freund, Bill (1984). *The Making of Contemporary Africa: The Development of African Society since 1800.* Bloomington: Indiana Univ. Press.

Fry, James (1979). *Employment and Income Distribution in the African Economy.* London: Croom Helm.

Gelb, Steve (1987). "Making Sense of the Crisis." *Transformation,* No. 5, 33–50.

Geldenhuys, Deon (1981). "Some Strategic Implications of Regional Economic Relationships for the Republic of South Africa," *ISSUP Strategic Review,* Jan.

Gersony, Robert (1988). *Summary of Mozambican Refugee Accounts of Principally Conflict-Related Experience in Mozambique.* Report submitted to US Department of State, Bureau of Refugee Programs, April.

Goldin, Ian (1989). "Coloured Identity and Coloured Politics in the Western Cape Region of South Africa," in L. Vail, ed., *The Creation of Tribalism in Southern Africa.* London: James Currey, 241–54.

Goliber, Thomas J. (1989). "Africa's Expanding Population: Old Problems, New Policies," *Population Bulletin,* XLIV, No. 3, November, 5–50.

Greenberg, Stanley B. & Hermann Giliomee (1987). "Managing Class Structures in South Africa: Bantustans and the Underbelly of Privilege," in I. L. Markovitz, ed., *Studies in Power and Class in South Africa.* New York: Oxford Univ. Press, 308–21.

Grest, G. (1989). "The South African Defence Force in Angola," in J. Cock & L. Nathan, eds., *Society at War: The Militarisation of South Africa.* New York: St. Martin's Press, 116–32.

Hall, Margaret (1990). "The Mozambican National Resistance Movement (Renamo): A Study in The Destruction of an African Country," *Africa,* LX, No. 1, 39–68.

Hamer, E. (1964). *Die Industrialisierung Sudafrikas seit dem zweiten Weltkrieg.* Stuttgart: Fischer.

Hanlon, Joseph (1984a). *Mozambique: The Revolution under Fire.* London: Zed Press.

Hanlon, Joseph (1984b). *SADCC: Progress, Projects & Progress.* Special Report No. 182. London: Economist Intelligence Unit.

Hanlon, Joseph (1986a). *Beggar Your Neighbours: Apartheid Power in Southern Africa.* London: James Currey.

Hanlon, Joseph (1986b). *Apartheid's Second Front.* Harmondsworth: Penguin.

Hanlon, Joseph (1986c). "Sanctions," *Capital and Class,* No. 30, Winter, 38–42.

Hanlon, Joseph (1987). "Post-apartheid South Africa and its Neighbours,"

Third World Quarterly, IX, No. 2, April, 437–49.

Harris, P.S. (1975). "Industrial Workers in Rhodesia, 1946–72," *Journal of Southern African Studies,* I, No. 2, April, 139–61.

Henriksen, Thomas H. (1978). *Mozambique: A History.* Cape Town: David Philip.

Hermele, Kenneth (1988). *Land Struggles and Social Differentiation in Southern Mozambique: A Case Study of Chokwe, Limpopo 1950–1987.* Uppsala: Scandinavian Institute of African Studies (SIAS).

Hicks, John (1969). *A Theory of Economic History.* London: Oxford Univ. Press.

Hirsch, Alan (1989). "The paperback which reveals a more likely Commonwealth line," *Weekly Mail,* 18–24 August, p.14.

Holden, Merle (1989). "A Comparative Analysis of Structural Imbalance in the Face of a Debt Crisis," *South African Journal of Economics,* LVII, No.1, March, 22–34.

Hymer, Stephen (1972). "The Multinational Corporation and the Law of Uneven Development," in H. Radice, ed., *International Firms and Modern Imperialism.* Middlesex: Penguin, 37–62.

Hymer, Stephen (1976). *International Operation of National Firms: A Study of Foreign Direct Investment.* Cambridge, MA: MIT Press.

Innes, Duncan (1984). *Anglo American and the Rise of Modern South Africa.* New York: Monthly Review Press.

International Labour Office (ILO) (1958). *African Labour Survey.* Geneva: ILO.

International Labour Office (ILO) (1979, 1980, 1987, 1988). *Yearbook of Labour Statistics.* Geneva: ILO.

International Monetary Fund (IMF) (1985). "Foreign Investment in Developing Countries," Occassional Paper No. 33.

International Monetary Fund (IMF) (1987). *International Financial Statistics (1987).* Washington, DC: IMF.

International Monetary Fund (IMF) (1988). *International Financial Statistics 1984,* Supplement Series, Nos. 4–5. Washington, DC: IMF.

International Monetary Fund (IMF) (1989b). *Government Finance Statistics Yearbook.* Washington, D.C.: IMF.

International Monetary Fund (IMF) (Computer tape, 1984, 1986, 1989a). *Direction of Trade Statistics.* Washington, D.C.: IMF.

Isaacman, Allen (1983). *Mozambique: From Colonialism to Revolution,*

1900–1982. Boulder, CO: Westview.

Jardim, Jorge (1978). *Rodésia: O escándalo das sanções*. Lisboa: Intervenção.

Johnson, Phyllis & David Martin (1989). *Apartheid Terrorism. The Destabilisation Report*. Bloomington: Indiana Univ. Press.

Kanduza, Ackson (1986). *The Political Economy of Underdevelopment in Northern Rhodesia, 1918–1960*. Lanham: Univ. Press of America.

Kaplan, D. (1983). "The Internationalization of South African Capital: South African Direct Investment in the Contemporary Period," *African Affairs*, LXXXII, No. 329, October, 465–94.

Kaplan, Irving, et al. (1977). *Area Handbook for Mozambique*. 2nd ed. Washington, DC: Foreign Area Studies, American Univ.

Kaplan, Irving, ed. (1978). *Angola: A Country Study*. Washington, DC: Foreign Area Studies, American Univ.

Kaplan, Irving, ed. (1979). *Zambia: A Country Study*. Washington, D.C.: Foreign Area Studies, American Univ.

Kaplan, Irving (1983). "The Society and Its Environment," in H. Nelson, *Zimbabwe: A Country Study*. Washington, DC: Foreign Area Studies, American Univ., 71–134.

Kaplan, Irving (1984). "The Society and Its Environment," in H. Nelson, *Mozambique: A Country Study*. Washington, DC: Foreign Area Studies, American Univ., 71–128.

Kay, George (1967). *A Social Geography of Zambia: A Survey of Population Patterns in a Developing Country*. London: Univ. of London Press.

Kay, George (1971). *Rhodesia: A Human Geography*. New York: Africana Publishing Corporation.

Kibreab, Gaim (1983). *Reflections on the African Refugee Problem: A Critical Analysis of Some Basic Assumptions*, Research Report No. 67. Uppsala: SIAS.

Knight, J. B. (1988). "A Comparative Analysis of the South Africa as a Semi-Industrialised Country," *Journal of Modern African Studies*, XXVI, No. 3, 473–93.

Landgren, Signe (1989). *Embargo Disimplemented: South Africa's Military Industry*. London: Oxford Univ. Press.

Leistner, G.M.E. (1967). "Foreign Bantu Workers in South Africa: Their Present Position in the Economy," *South African Journal of Economics*, XXXV, No. 1, 30–56.

Lesotho, Kingdom of (1983). *Annual Statistical Bulletin, 1982.* Maseru: Government Printer.

Libby, Ronald T. (1987). "Transnational Corporations and the National Bourgeoisie: Regional Expansion and Party Realignment in South Africa," in I. L. Markovitz, ed., *Studies in Power and Class in South Africa.* New York: Oxford Univ. Press, 291–307.

Lipton, Merle (1985). *Capitalism and Apartheid.* Totowa, NJ: Rowan & Allanheld.

Loubser, J.G.H. (1980). *Transport Diplomacy with Special Reference to Southern Africa.* Sandton: Southern African Editorial Services, 1980.

MacArthur, D. (1980). "Potential Problems Associated with the Recently Introduced Stabilisation Scheme and Associated Bonus Scheme in the Mining Industry," *Human Resources Laboratory Monitoring Report* (Chamber of Mines Research Organisation), IV, No. 6, June.

Machel, Samora Moises (1974a). "Não se pergunta a um escravo se quer ser livre," *Voz da Revolução,* No. 22, Maio-Junho, 3–4.

Machel, Samora Moises (1974b). "Mensagem aos militantes da FRELIMO e ao povo moçambicano por ocasião do golpe de estado em Portugal," *Voz da Revolução,* No. 21, Janeiro-Abril, 3–6.

Mackintosh, Maureen (1986). "O Capital privado e o estado no sistema de transportes da África austral," *Estudos Moçambicanos,* Nos. 5/6, 83–128.

Makgetla, Neva & Ann Seidman (1980). *Outposts of Monopoly Capitalism: Southern Africa in the Changing Global Economy.* London: Zed Press.

Mandaza, Ibbo (1986a). "The State and Politics in the Post-White Settler Colonial Situation," in I. Mandaza, ed., *Zimbabwe: The Political Economy of Transition, 1980–86.* Dakar: Codesria, 21–74.

Mandaza, Ibbo, ed. (1986b). *Zimbabwe: the Political Economy of Transition, 1980–86.* Dakar: CODESRIA.

Mandaza, Ibbo (1987). "Perspectives on Economic Cooperation and Autonomous Development in Southern Africa," in S. Amin, D. Chitala, & I. Mandaza, eds., *SADCC: Prospects for Disengagement in Southern Africa.* London: Zed Press, 210–30.

Mandaza, Ibbo (1988). "Southern Africa: U.S. Policy and the Struggle for National Independence," in I. Mandaza & B. Magubane, eds., *Whither South Africa?* Trenton, NJ: Africa World Press, 111–35.

Martin, David & Phyllis Johnson (1981). *The Struggle for Zimbabwe.* London: Faber & Faber.

Martin, David & Phyllis Johnson (1989). *A Candle on Kilimanjaro. The Frontline States vs. Apartheid.* Report prepared for the meeting of the Commonwealth Foreign Ministers on Southern Africa, Canberra, August 7–9.

Martin, William G. (1986). "'South Africa First': State Initiatives Towards the Creation of Regional Economic Networks in the Interwar Period," African Studies Seminar paper, Univ. of the Witwatersrand, October.

Martin, William G. (1987). "Incorporation of Southern Africa, 1870–1920," *Review,* X, Nos. 5/6, Summer/Fall, 849–900.

Martin, William G. (1990a). "From Nic to NUC: South Africa's Semi-peripheral Regimes," in W. G. Martin, ed., *Semiperipheral States in the World-Economy.* Westport, CT: Greenwood Press, 203–23.

Martin, William G. (1990b). "The Making of an Industrial South Africa: Trade and Tariff Policies during the Interwar Period," *International Journal of African Historical Studies,* XXIII, No. 2, March, 59–85.

Martin, William G. (1990c). "Region Formation under Crisis Conditions: South versus Southern Africa in the Interwar Period," *Journal of Southern African Studies,* XVI, No. 1, 112–38.

Martin, William G. (1992). "Lesotho: The Creation of the Households," in J. Smith et al., *Creating and Transforming Households: The Constraints of the World-Economy.* Cambridge: Cambridge Univ. Press.

Meth, Charles (1981). "Class Formation: Skill Shortage and Black Advancement," in *South African Review, 1.* Johannesburg: Ravan Press, 193–98.

Middlemass, K. (1975). *Cabora Bassa.* London: Weidenfeld & Nicolson.

Minter, William (1986). *King Solomon's Mines Revisited: Western Interests and the Burdened History of Southern Africa.* New York: Basic Books.

Minty, Abdul (1986). "South Africa's Military Build-up: The Region at War," in D. Martin & P. Johnson, eds., *Destructive Engagement. Southern Africa at War.* Harare: Zimbabwe Publishing House, 171–204.

Mkandawire, Thandika (1986). "The Informal Sector in the Labour Reserve Economies of Southern Africa," *Afrique et Développement,* XI, No. 1, 61–82.

Mkandawire, Thandika (1988). "The Road to Crisis, Adjustment and

Deindustrialisation: the African Case," *Africa Development,* XIII, No. 1, 5–31.

Momba, Jotham (1989). "The State, Rural Class Formation and Peasant Political Participation in Zambia: the Case of Southern Province," *African Affairs,* LXXXVIII, No. 352, July, 331–57.

Mosley, Paul (1983). *The Settler Economies: Studies in the Economic History of Kenya and Southern Rhodesia, 1900–1963.* Cambridge: Cambridge Univ. Press.

Moyo, Sam (1986). "The Land Question," in I. Mandaza, ed., *Zimbabwe: The Political Economy of Transition, 1980–86.* Dakar: Codesria, 165–202.

Mozambique. National Planning Commission (1984). *Economic Report.* Maputo, January.

Mugomba, Agrippah & Mougo Nyaggah, eds. (1980). *Independence Without Freedom: The Political Economy of Colonial Education in Southern Africa.* Santa Barbara: ABC-Clio.

Muirhead, David (1988). "Trade and Trade Promotion," in E. Leistner & P. Esterhysen, eds., *South Africa in Southern Africa: Economic Integration.* Pretoria: Africa Institute, 89–104.

Mumbengegwi, Clever (1986). "Continuity and Change in Agricultural Policy," in I. Mandaza, ed., *Zimbabwe: The Political Economy of Transition, 1980–86.* Dakar: Codesria, 203–222.

Murray, Colin (1980a). "Migrant Labour and the Changing Family Structure in the Rural Periphery of Southern Africa," *Journal of Southern African Studies,* VI, No. 2, April, 139–56.

Murray, Colin (1980b). "Stabilisation and Structural Unemployment," *South African Labour Bulletin,* VI, No. 4, November, 58–61.

Murray, Colin (1981). *Families Divided: the Impact of Migrant Labour in Lesotho.* Cambridge: Cambridge Univ. Press.

Murray, Colin (1987a). "Displaced Urbanization: South Africa's Rural Slums," *African Affairs,* LXXXVI, No. 344, July, 311–29.

Murray, Colin (1987b). "Review Article: Landlords, Tenants and Share-croppers—Agrarian Change in Regional Perspective," *Journal of Southern African Studies,* XIV, No. 1, October, 153–59.

Mwanza, Jacob (1979). "Rural-Urban Migration and Urban Employment in Zambia," in B. Turok, ed., *Development in Zambia: A Reader.* London: Zed Press, 26–45.

Nabudere, Dan (1985). "Transnational and Regional Integration in East Africa," in T. Shaw & Y. Tandon, eds., *Regional Development at the International Level.* Lanham, MD: Univ. Press of America, II, 113–134.

Nattrass, Jill (1977). "Migration Flows in and out of Capitalist Agriculture," in F. Wilson, A. Kooy, & D. Hendrie, eds., *Farm Labour in South Africa.* Cape Town: David Philip, 51–61.

Nattrass, Nicoli (1989). "Post-war Profitability in South Africa." *Transformation,* No. 9, 66–80.

Ndlela, D. B. et al. (1986). *Transnationals in Southern Africa.* Harare: Zimbabwe Publishing House.

Nelson, Harold et al. (1975). *Area Handbook for Malawi,* first edition. Washington, DC: Foreign Area Studies, American Univ.

Nelson, Harold, ed. (1983). *Zimbabwe: A Country Study.* Washington, DC: Foreign Area Studies, American Univ.

Nelson, Harold, ed. (1984). *Mozambique: A Country Study.* Washington, DC: Foreign Area Studies, American Univ.

North/South Roundtable (1988). *Total Response to Total Strategy. Toward Economic Recovery and Development in Southern Africa.* Report from a North/South Roundtable Consultation in Juliasdale, Zimbabwe, 1–3 Dec.

O'Connor, Anthony (1983). *The African City.* London: Hutchinson.

Ohadike, Patrick O. (1974). "Immigrants and Development in Zambia," *International Migration Review,* VIII, No. 3, Fall, 395–411.

Ohadike, Patrick (1981). *Demographic Perspectives in Zambia: Rural-Urban Growth and Social Change.* Zambian Papers No. 15. Manchester: Manchester Univ. Press.

Ohlson, Thomas (1988). "Embargo Non-implemented: 25 Years of South African Arms Procurement in the Shadow of the U.N. Arms Embargoes," Maputo: Centro de Estudos Africanos, December.

Ohlson, Thomas (1990). "Africa do Sul e seus vizinhos: Estratégias regionais em confrontão," *Estudos Moçambicanos,* No. 8, 20–33.

Omar, Gasan (1990). "An Introduction to Namibia's Political Economy," SALDRU Working Paper No. 78. Cape Town: SALDRU.

Organization for Economic Development and Cooperation (OECD) (1967–1991). *Geographical Distribution of Financial Flows to Developing Countries.* Paris: OECD.

Organization for Economic Development and Cooperation (OECD)

(1987b). *International Investment and Mutinational Enterprises: Recent Trends in International Direct Investment.* Paris: CEDEX.

Østergaard, Tom (1989). *SADCC: Beyond Transportation, the Challenge of Industrial Cooperation.* Uppsala: Scandinavian Institute of African Studies.

Pachai, Bridglal, ed. (1979). *South Africa's Indians: The Evolution of a Minority.* Washington, DC: Univ. Press of America.

Padayachee, Vishnu (1987). "South Africa and the International Monetary Fund," *Transformation,* No. 3, 31–57.

Pangeti, Evelyn (1986). "Agribusiness in Colonial Zimbabwe: The Case of the Lowveld," in A. Teichova et al., eds., *Multinational Enterprise in Historical Perspective.* Cambridge: Cambridge Univ. Press.

Parson, Jack (1981). "Cattle, Class and the State in Rural Botswana," *Journal of Southern African Studies,* VII, No. 2, April, 236–55.

Phimister, Ian (1988). *An Economic and Social History of Zimbabwe, 1890–1948.* London: Longmans.

Pickles, John (1988). "Recent Changes in Regional Policy in South Africa," *Geography,* LXXIII, No. 73, June, 233–39.

Pickles, John, & Jeff Woods (1988). "Reorienting South Africa's International Links" *Capital and Class,* No. 35, Summer, 49–55.

Pickles, John, & Jeff Woods (1989). "Taiwanese Investment in South Africa," *African Affairs,* LXXXVIII, October, 507–28.

Pityana, Sipho (1988). "The Black Middle Class at the Crossroads," *Sechaba,* Jan., 7–10.

Preece, Howard (1989). "South Africa's narrowing economic scope," *The Southern African Economist,* February/March.

Queiroz, Artur (1978). *Angola do 25 de Abril ao 11 de Novembro: a via agreste da liberdade.* Lisboa: Ulmeiro.

Raftapoulos, Brian (1986). "Human Resources Development and the Problem of Labour Utilization," in I. Mandaza, ed., *Zimbabwe: The Political Economy of Transition, 1980–86.* Dakar: Codesria, 275–317.

Ranger, T.O. (1970). *The African Voice in Southern Rhodesia, 1898–1930.* London: Heinemann.

Reis, João & Armando Pedro Muiuane (1976). *Datas e documentos da história da FRELIMO.* Lourenço Marques: Imprensa Nacional.

Rhodesia. Central Statistical Office (CSO) (1978). *Rhodesia Monthly Digest of Statistics* (Supplement). Salisbury: Government Printers, July.

Roberts, Alun (1980). *The Rossing File: the Inside Story of Britain's Secret Contract for Namibian Uranium.* London: Campaign Against the Namibian Uranium Contract.

Robson, Peter (1985). "Regional Integration and the Crisis in Sub-Saharan Africa," *Journal of Modern African Studies,* XXIII, No. 4, December, 603–22.

Roesch, Otto (1988). "Rural Mozambique since the Frelimo Party Fourth Congress: The Situation in the Baixo Limpopo," *Review of African Political Economy,* No. 4, September, 73–91.

Rogerson, Chris (1987). "The State and the Informal Sector: A Case of Separate Development," in *South African Review, 4.* Johannesburg: Ravan Press, 412–22.

Salamon, H. (1975). "Modernising Gold Mining: A Challenge to Research," *Mining Survey,* LXXVII, No. 2, 26–27.

Santos, Amirico Ramos de (1984). "Problemas de desenvolvimento dos recursos dos homens em Africa," *Economia e socialismo* (Lisbon), 60.

Saul, John & Stephen Gelb (1981, 1986). *The Crisis in South Africa,* original and rev.ed. New York: Monthly Review Press.

Savage, Michael (1985). "Imposition of Pass Laws on the African Population in South Africa 1916–1984" *African Affairs,* LXXXV, No. 339, April, 181–205.

Schaedel, Martin (1984). *Eingeborenen Arbeit. Formen der Ausbeutung unter der Portugiesischen Kolonialherrschaft in Mosambik.* Köln: Pahl Rugenstein Verlag, Series Hochschulschriften 165.

Schaefer, Emmett (1988). "Zimbabwe: A Country Profile." Manuscript.

Schmidt, Elizabeth (1988). "Farmers, Hunters and Gold-Washers: A Reevaluation of Women's Role in Precolonial and Colonial Zimbabwe," *African Economic History,* XVII, 45–80.

Schneier, Steffen & Iraj Abedian (1987). *An Analysis of Formal Sector Employment in South Africa: Its Implications for Poverty and Future Economic Strategies.* SALDRU Working Paper No. 70. Cape Town: SALDRU.

Seidman, Ann (1974). "The Distorted Growth of Import-Substitution: The Zambian Case," *Journal of Modern African Studies,* XII, No. 4, December, 601–31.

Shaul, J.R.H. (1960). "Demographic Features of Central Africa," in K. M. Barbour & R. M. Prothero, eds., *Essays in African Population.*

Westport, CT: Greenwood Press, 31–48.

Shopo, Tom (1985). "The Agrarian Question in Zimbabwe: A Review Article," *Zimbabwe Journal of Economics,* I, No. 2, January, 39–44.

Simkins, Charles (1981a). "Agricultural Production in the African Reserves of South Africa, 1918–1969," *Journal of Southern African Studies,* VII, No. 2, April, 256–83.

Simkins, Charles (1981b). *The Economic Implications of African Resettlement,* SALDRU Working Paper No. 43. Cape Town: SALDRU.

Simkins, Charles (1981c). *The Demographic Demand for Labour and Institutional Context of African Unemployment in South Africa: 1960–1980,* SALDRU Working Paper No. 39. Cape Town: SALDRU.

South Africa (1982). *South African Statistics 1982.* Pretoria: Government Printer.

South Africa (1988). *South African Statistics 1988.* Pretoria: Government Printer.

South Africa (1989). *Bulletin of Statistics.* Pretoria: Government Printer, March.

South Africa. Central Statistical Services (1986). *South African Labour Statistics 1986.* Pretoria: Government Printer.

South Africa. Central Statistical Services (1989). *South African Labour Statistics 1989.* Pretoria: Government Printer.

South Africa. Commissioner for Customs and Excise (1973 et seq.) *Foreign Trade Statistics. Vol. 1.* Pretoria: Government Printer.

South Africa. Department of Foreign Affairs and Information (1973–1986). *Official Yearbook of the Republic of South Africa.* Johannesburg: Chris van Rensburg.

South Africa. Ministry of Defence (1986). *White Paper on Defence and Armaments Supply (1986).* Pretoria: Ministry of Defence.

South Africa. National Manpower Commission (1984). *Report on an Investigation into the Levels of Collective Bargaining and Works Councils, the Registration of Trade Unions and Employers' Organisations and Related Matters, and the Industrial Court.* Pretoria: Department of Manpower.

South Africa. National Manpower Commission (1986). *Certain Aspects of Strikes in RSA.* Pretoria: Government Printer.

(n.a.) *South Africa: The Sanctions Report.* (1989). Prepared for the Commonwealth Committee of Foreign Ministers on Southern Africa.

London: Penguin in association with James Currey.

South African Institute of Race Relations (SAIRR) (1965–89). *Race Relations Survey.* Johannesburg: SAIRR.

Southall, Roger (1982). *South Africa's Transkei: The Political Economy of an 'Independent' Bantustan.* London: Heinemann.

Southall, Roger (1986). "Migrants and Trade Unions in South Africa Today," *Canadian Journal of African Studies,* XX, No. 2, 161–85.

Southern African Development Coordination Conference (SADCC) (1980). "Southern Africa: Toward Economic Liberation. A Declaration by Governments of Independent Africa Made at Lusaka on 1st April, 1980," *Record of the Southern Africa Development Coordination Summit Conference.* Lusaka: manuscript.

Southern African Development Coordination Conference (SADCC) (1983). *SADCC Maseru.* Harare: Mambo Press.

Southern African Development Coordination Conference (SADCC) (1986a). *SADCC Macro-Economic Survey 1986.* Gaborone: SADCC.

Southern African Development Coordination Conference (SADCC) (1986b). *SADCC Intra-Regional Trade Study.* Bergen: Chr. Michelsen Institute.

Southern African Development Coordination Conference (SADCC) (1986c). "The Costs of Destabilization of Member States of SADCC," reprinted as *Annex B, Overview* (to Harare annual conference), Gaborone.

Southern African Development Coordination Conference (SADCC) (1988). *SADCC Regional Economic Survey.* Gaborone: SADCC.

Southern African Development Coordination Conference (SADCC) (1989). *Annual Progress Report 1988–89.* Gaborone: SADCC.

Southern African Development Coordination Conference (SADCC) (1990). *Annual Progress Report 1989–90.* Gaborone: SADCC.

Southern Africa Dossier (1986). "Current South African Pressure on Lesotho," No. 31.80, July.

Southern Africa Dossier (1988). "The Cuito Cuanavale Syndrome, Some Notes on Pretoria's Tactical and Strategic Options after the Angolan Debacle," No. 40.200, October.

Southern Africa Dossier (1989a). "The 1989/90 South African Budget and the Continuing Crisis of the Apartheid Economy," No. 47, April.

Southern Africa Dossier (1989b). "Changes in South African Domestic and

Regional Policy since F.W. De Klerk Became State President", No. 58.175, December.

Southern Africa Dossier (1989c). "Some notes on the Potential Significance of F.W. de Klerk's accession to the National Party Leaderhship," No. 45.200, March.

Southern Africa Dossier (1990). "South Africa: Perspectives After F.W. De Klerk's February 2 Speech", No. 61.175, February.

Southern African Economist (1988). "The Great Trek of the Multinationals," I, No. 1, February-March, 14–15.

Southern African Labour & Development Research Unit (SALDRU) (1986). *Handbook of Labour and Social Statistics.* Cape Town: SALDRU.

Southern African Research and Documentation Centre (SARDC) (1986). *South Africa Imposes Sanctions against Neighbours.* Pamphlet prepared for Eighth Summit of the Non-Aligned Movement, Harare.

Spinola, Antonio de (1976). *Ao serviço de Portugal.* Lisboa: Atica.

Spinola, Antonio de (1978). *Pais sem rumo. Contributo para a história de um revolução.* Lisboa: Ed. SRIRE.

Stahl, C.W. (1981). "Migrant Labour Supplies, Past, Present and Future; with Special Reference to the Gold-Mining Industry," in W. R. Böhning, ed., *Black Migration to South Africa.* Geneva: ILO, 7–44.

Standish, Barry (1987). *Some Statistics on Public Sector Employment in South Africa 1920–1985,* SALDRU Working Paper No. 69. Cape Town: SALDRU.

Stephens, Jeanne (1986). "A Baixa de preços e a preservação da dependência: a resposta sul-Africana às initiatives do sector de transportes em Moçambique e na SADCC," *Estudos Moçambicanos,* Nos. 5/6, 129–71.

Stockwell, John (1978). *In Search of Enemies: A CIA story.* New York: W. W. Norton.

Stoneman, Colin (1978). "Foreign Capital and the Reconstruction of Zimbabwe," *Review of African Political Economy,* XI, January-April, 62–83.

Stoneman, Colin, ed. (1981). *Zimbabwe's Inheritance.* London: Macmillan.

Stoneman, Colin (1989). "The World Bank and the IMF in Zimbabwe," in B. Campbell & J. Loxley, eds., *Structural Adjustment in Africa.* London: Macmillan, 37–66.

Taiwan (1988). *Statistical Yearbook of the Republic of China (1988)*. Taipei: Republic of China.

Taju, Gulamu (1988). "RENAMO: os factos que conheçemos," *Cadernos de História*, 7, Novembro, 5–44.

Tandon, Yash (1985). "SADCC and the Preferential Trade Area (PTA): Points of Convergence and Divergence," in T. Shaw and Y. Tandon, eds., *Regional Development at the International Level*. New York: Lanham, II, 113–33.

Thompson, C. (1987). "Cooperation for Survival: Western Interest vs. SADCC," *Issue: A Journal of Opinion*, XVI, No. 1, 30–36.

Torp, Jens Erik (1989). "Mozambique," in J. E. Torp, L.M. Denny, & D. I. Ray, eds. *Mozambique, São Tomé and Principe: Economics, Politics and Society*. London: Pinter, 1–117.

United Nations (1983). *Handbook of International Trade and Development Statistics*. New York: United Nations.

United Nations (1985). *Reference Book on Major Transnational Corporations in Namibia*. New York: United Nations.

United Nations (1986). *Statistical Yearbook, 1983/84*. New York: United Nations.

UNICEF (1989). *Children on the Frontline. The Impact of Apartheid Destabilization and Warfare on Children in Southern and South Africa*, 3rd ed. New York: UNICEF.

United Nations Development Programme (UNDP) & World Bank (1989). *African Economic and Financial Data*. Washington, DC: World Bank.

United Nations Economic and Social Council, Commission of Transnational Corporations (1985). *Role of Transnational Corporation in the Military and Nuclear Sectors of South Africa and Namibia—Report of the Secretary-General*, E/C.10/AC.4/1985/4. New York: United Nations.

United Nations Center on Transnational Corporations (1984). *Policies and Practices of Transnational Corporations Regarding their Activities in South Africa and Namibia*, E/C.10/1983/Rev.1. New York: United Nations.

UNESCO (1959) *Economic Survey of Africa since 1950*. New York: United Nations.

UNESCO (1977) *Statistical Yearbook*. New York: United Nations.

UNESCO (1989) *Statistical Yearbook*. New York: United Nations.

United Nations Industrial Development Organization (UNIDO) (1990). *Industry and Development. Global Report 1989/90.* Vienna: UNIDO.

United States Agency for International Development (USAID) (1989). *USAID Highlights,* VI, No. 2, Spring.

United States Department of Commerce (1988). *Japanese Capital Exports: Trends and Implications for the LDCs.* Washington, DC: Committee for Economic Development.

Valigy, Ismael (1988/89). *O Papel da política externa da RPM face a estratégia de desestabilização sul-Africana a 1978/88.* Instituto Superior de Relacões Internacionais (ISRI), Maputo.

Vambe, Lawrence (1972). *An Ill-Fated People: Zimbabwe Before and After Rhodes.* London: Heinemann.

Vambe, Lawrence (1976). *From Rhodesia to Zimbabwe.* London: Heinemann.

van Zyl, J. C. (1984). "South Africa in World Trade," *South African Journal of Economics,* LII, No. 1, March, 42–62.

Vieira, Sergio (1990a). "Vectores da política externa da Frente de Libertação de Moçambique (1962–1975)," *Estudos Moçambicanos,* No. 7, 29–56.

Vieira, Sergio (1990b). "África austral: conflitos, percepções e perspectivas na arena internacional," *Estudos Moçambicanos,* No. 8, 63–96.

Volkskas Bank (1988). *Economic Spotlight,* No. 3, July.

Volkskas Bank (1990). "Challenges for a New Decade," *Economic Spotlight,* February.

Wallerstein, Immanuel (1987). "The Construction of Peoplehood: Racism, Nationalism, Ethnicity," *Sociological Forum,* II, No. 2, Spring, 373–88.

Weinrich, A.K.H. (1975). *African Farmers in Rhodesia: Old and New Peasant Communities in Karangaland.* London: Oxford Univ. Press.

Weissman, Robert (1991). "The Real Purpose of GATT: Prelude to a New Colonialism," *The Nation,* March 18, 336.

Wellington, John (1967). *South West Africa and Its Human Issues.* Oxford: Clarendon Press.

Wheeler, Douglas & Rene Pelissier (1971). *Angola.* New York: Praeger.

Wilson, Francis (1972). *Labour in the South African Gold Mines: 1911–1969.* London: Cambridge Univ. Press.

Wilson, Francis (1976). "International Migration in Southern Africa," *International Migration Review,* X, No. 4, Winter, 451–88.

Witwatersrand Native Labour Association (various). *Annual Report.* Johannesburg: Chamber of Mines.

Wolpe, Harold (1972). "Capitalism and Cheap Labour Power in South Africa: from Segregation to Apartheid," *Economy and Society,* I, No. 4, 425–56.

Wolpe, Harold (1988). *Race, Class, and the Apartheid State.* London: James Curry.

Wood, Brian (1989). "Trade Union Organization and the Working Class," in C. Stoneman, ed. *Zimbabwe's Prospects: Issues of Race, Class, State, and Capital in Southern Africa.* London: MacMillan, 284–308.

World Bank (1976). *World Tables.* 1ed. Baltimore: Johns Hopkins Univ. Press.

World Bank (1980). *World Tables.* 2ed. Baltimore: Johns Hopkins Univ. Press.

World Bank (1984). *World Tables.* 3d ed. (Volume I: *Economic Data;* Volume 2: *Social Data).* Baltimore: Johns Hopkins Univ. Press.

World Bank (1989a). *World Tables.* 1988–89 ed. Baltimore: Johns Hopkins Univ. Press.

World Bank (1989b). *Sub-Saharan Africa: From Crisis to Sustainable Growth.* Washington, DC: World Bank.

World Bank (1980, 1981, 1982, 1983, 1984b, 1985, 1986, 1987, 1988, 1989c, 1990a). *World Development Report.* New York: Oxford Univ. Press.

World Bank (1990b). *World Debt Tables.* Washington, DC: World Bank.

World Bank (1990c). *Angola: A Country Memorandum.* Washington, DC: World Bank.

Zimbabwe. Central Statistical Office (CSO) (1985a). *Statistical Yearbook 1985.* Harare: Central Statistical Office.

Zimbabwe. Central Statistical Office (CSO) (1985b). *Main Demographic Features of the Population of Zimbabwe: An Advance Report Based on a Ten-Percent Sample.* Harare: Government Printers.

Zimbabwe. Ministry of Finance, Economic Planning and Development (1986a). *Zimbabwe Socio-Economic Review, 1980–1985.* Harare: Government Printers.

Zimbabwe. Central Statistical Office (1986b). *Annual Economic Review of Zimbabwe (1986).* Harare: Government Printers.

Zimbabwe. Central Statistical Office (CSO) (1987). *Zimbabwe Statistical*

Yearbook, 1987. Harare: Government Printers.
Zimbabwe. Central Statistical Office (CSO) (1989a). *Main Results of the Labour Force Survey, 1986–1987.* Harare: Government Printers.
Zimbabwe. Central Statistical Office (CSO) (1989b). *Quarterly Digest of Statistics*, March. Harare: Government Printers.
Zimbabwe Rhodesia (1979). *Secret Supplement to the Monthly Digest of Statistics.* Salisbury: Government Printer, June.
Zinyama, Lovemore & Richard Whitlow (1986). "Changing Patterns of Population Distribution in Zimbabwe," *GeoJournal*, XIII, No. 4, 365–84.

Serials

Africa South of the Sahara. (London)
Africa Economic Digest. (London)
Beira Corridor Group Bulletin. (Harare)
Business Day. (Johannesburg)
Cape Times. (Cape Town)
Diario do Governo. (Maputo)
Domingo. (Maputo)
The Economist. (London)
Financial Mail. (Johannesburg)
Financial Times. (London)
Herald. (Harare)
International Herald Tribune. (Paris)
International Labour Reports. (Barnsley, Yorkshire)
Mining Survey. (Johannesburg)
Mozambiquefile. (Maputo)
The Nation. (New York)
The New Nation. (Johannesburg)
Noticias. (Maputo)
Race Relations Survey. (Johannesburg)
Rand Daily Mail. (Johannesburg)
South African Barometer. (Johannesburg)
Southern African Dossier. (Maputo)
The Star. (Johannesburg)
Star International Airmail Weekly. (Johannesburg)

Sunday Times. (Johannesburg)
Wall Street Journal. (New York)
Weekly Mail. (Johannesburg)